“If you are looking (as I was) for the
Catholic perspective on the environmen
all-encompassing, accessible, practical, and well-edited. Well-versed in the data of our ecological crisis, they [contributors] offer us their instructive strategies buttressed with the resources of the scriptures and the traditions and animated by a realistic yet hopeful vision. It’s an empowering project. By the way, if you weren’t thinking of teaching such a course, buy this book anyway. You’ll be developing a syllabus on the topic before you get to Winright’s convincing conclusion.”

—James F. Keenan, Boston College

“*Green Discipleship* will be a wonderful textbook for teachers and students. Faculty will find that the twenty-one essays cover a wide range of topics for a course on theology and the environment. Undergraduate students will find the essays written in a style that is accessible and with content that is informative. Helpful features that include review and reflection questions, an extensive glossary of terms, a bibliography, and an essay on library research make this volume a first-rate educational resource.”

—Kenneth R. Himes, OFM, department
of theology, Boston College

“Look no further . . . a powerful ensemble of articles that is on the cutting edge of religious environmental ethics . . . the place to start for scholars and ministers who on their own want to bring themselves abreast of the best of the literature. This book will be a centerpiece in the conversation on religious ethics and the environment for some time.”

—Todd Whitmore, University of Notre Dame

GREEN DISCIPLESHIP

Catholic Theological Ethics and the Environment

TOBIAS WINRIGHT, editor

ACKNOWLEDGMENTS

Interconnectedness will prove to be an important idea in the pages that follow. It seems an apt word for acknowledging my debt to the many people who helped this volume come to fruition. Of course, I wish to thank, first of all, the twenty-one contributors who diligently produced the book's chapters, many of which underwent three or four drafts for fine tuning. Although many of us have been accustomed to writing academic dissertations and articles for scholarly journals, it became apparent that it's no easy task to compose chapters that are accessible, informative, and engaging for readers, especially undergraduates. Here is where the contributors' experiences as gifted classroom teachers proved beneficial, though. I am grateful for their efforts, their patience, and their commitment to making this volume happen. My graduate research assistant, Blake Hartung, also deserves mention for his work on the book's glossary of terms and select bibliography.

In addition, I am thankful to the Sisters of the Humility of Mary, who in 2004 awarded me a grant to create a new course on theology and the environment when I taught at Walsh University, which is affiliated with the Brothers of Christian Instruction and located in North Canton, Ohio. Since moving to Saint Louis University in 2005, I have continued to teach *Green Discipleship: Theology and the Environment* to undergraduates, and I appreciate the insights I have gained and the inspiration I have received from many wonderful students. The College of Arts and Sciences at Saint Louis University has also helped to make this volume possible with a summer Mellon Research Grant. During June 2009, I read first drafts of these chapters while sitting outside along the verdant banks of the Adige River, with its swift currents sweeping along the valley nestled in the mountains surrounding Trent, Italy. As a visiting scholar at the Fondazione Bruno Kessler, I was able to devote a lot of time to this project, and I am grateful to Antonio Autiero, who is the director of the religious sciences area in the Humanities there, and to James Keenan, SJ, who holds the Founders Professorship in Theology at Boston College, for making that time in Trent possible.

To be sure, I owe a lot to Jerry Ruff, who is the editorial and acquisitions director at Anselm Academic. His upbeat humor, wise advice, and keen eye have all been invaluable. Bradley Harmon, the sales and marketing director, has also offered encouragement and assistance along the way. The working dinners for many of the contributors gathered at various academic conferences these past few years are much appreciated! Also, I appreciate the four reviewers, who carefully read an earlier draft of this volume, for their constructive criticisms that, I think, helped to produce a better book.

Finally, I give heartfelt thanks for my wife, Liz, and daughters, Clare and Lydia, who have allowed me the time and space to work on this project.

PUBLISHER ACKNOWLEDGMENTS

Thank you to the following individuals who reviewed this work in progress:

Mark Graham
Villanova University, Villanova, Pennsylvania

Kevin J. O'Brien
Pacific Lutheran University, Tacoma, Washington

Monserrate Ocampo
Saint John's University, Jamaica, New York

Kathleen O'Gorman
Loyola Institute for Ministry, New Orleans, Louisiana

Created by the publishing team of Anselm Academic.

Cover images royalty free from iStock

Printed in the United States of America

7027

ISBN 978-1-59982-024-8

Dedicated to my daughters, Clare Niamh and Lydia Maeve Winright.

The God of gods inspire you,
And fill your heart with song;
Trill greetings in the morning,
And praises all day long.

"A Prayer for Song Birds," in *A Child's Book of Celtic Prayers*, written and compiled by Joyce Denham, illustrated by Helen Cann (Chicago: Loyola Press, 1998), 8–9.

CONTENTS

PART III
Christian Tradition

PART IV
Fundamental Moral Theology

PART V
Social Ethics

PART VI

Insights from Other Religions

PART VII

Issues and Applications

INTRODUCTION

FROM SAVING THE WHALES TO PROTECTING THE PLANET AS A "DUTY INCUMBENT ON EACH AND ALL"

Tobias Winright

Karl Barth, who is considered one of the most significant Protestant theologians of the twentieth century, reportedly advised young theologians, clergy, and Christians in general to "take your Bible and take your newspaper, and read both."[1] Although doing so would have required some discipline several decades ago, today reading Scripture and keeping up with the daily news is an even more daunting task, given how we are inundated with information provided by twenty-four-hour news networks, Internet newspapers, electronic magazines, and links to stories shared by friends on online social networks, as well as the traditional print sources of journalism. Nevertheless, a scan of the headlines scrolling across the computer screen or the news ticker at the bottom of the television screen is revealing.

Though there are always the usual stories about politics, the economy, and conflicts at home and abroad, in recent years the attention given to environmental issues has increased dramatically. A quick sampling of headlines includes: "More than an oil spill" (*Los Angeles Times*, May 11, 2010); "Hong Kong issues warning as air pollution sets record" (*New York Times*, March 22, 2010); "Cuyahoga River's fire is marked around the world" (*Plain Dealer*, June 21, 2009); "Fretting about the last of the world's big cats" (*New York Times*, March 7,

1."Theologians: Barth in Retirement," *Time*, May 31, 1963, available at *http://www.time.com/time/magazine/article/0,9171,896838,00.html*, accessed February 2, 2011.

2010); "Wanted: A New Home for My Country" (*New York Times Magazine*, May 10, 2009); and "India's Holy Ganges to get a cleanup" (*the Wall Street Journal*, February 13, 2010).

To be sure, bad news abounds about environmental problems. Biologists estimate that at least 1,000 plant and animal species become extinct annually (that's three species per day). Indeed, some scientists say that this is a human-caused mass extinction on a scale approaching the disappearance of the dinosaurs 65 million years ago.[2] Rising sea levels threaten to inundate populated areas such as the Maldives, a string of islands in the Indian Ocean, where 300,000 citizens, their president has suggested, might need to evacuate to another country. The Gulf of Mexico is still reeling from the effects of BP's *Deepwater Horizon* oil spill, which lasted for three months in 2010 and is the largest in the history of the industry. Of course, the list could go on.

At the same time, there is some good news. In northeast Ohio, the Cuyahoga River, once one of the most polluted rivers in the United States and famous for being "the river that caught fire" in 1969, is now a scenic home to fish and other wildlife thanks to efforts by environmentalists to clean it up. Similar work is currently under way on the Ganges River in India. Moreover, some animal species once on the verge of extinction, such as the American bald eagle, which a few decades ago needed to be protected by the Endangered Species Act, are now thriving. Indeed, once in a while I even see some of these magnificent birds flying along the Mississippi River near and around Saint Louis. So the news is mixed, though it certainly seems the headlines pointing to negative things happening to nature outnumber those highlighting the positive.

However, have you seen headlines like the following? "Leaders of pro-environment Christian group say oil spill shows clean energy is a moral issue" (*Baltimore Sun*, June 17, 2010); "Zen and the art of protecting the planet" (*Guardian*, August 26, 2010); "Conservative Evangelicals embrace God and green" (*Christian Science Monitor*,

2. My daughter Clare, who at the time of my writing this is six years old and has claimed to be a paleontologist for more than three years now, expected me to make note of this. For more on this loss of biodiversity, see Steven Bouma-Prediger, *For the Beauty of the Earth: A Christian Vision for Creation Care*, 2nd ed. (Grand Rapids, MI: Baker Academic, 2010), 29–32.

March 25, 2010); "Orthodox head brings 'green' views to D.C." (*Washington Times*, November 2, 2009); and "The Pope vs. climate change deniers" (*Washington Post*, February 19, 2010). In fact, in an article about "15 Green Religious Leaders," published on July 24, 2007, by the online magazine *Grist*, Pope Benedict XVI was included, along with Orthodox Patriarch Bartholomew I, the Dalai Lama, Anglican Archbishop of Canterbury Rowan Williams, and others across the religious spectrum.[3]

Thus, in addition to the environmental efforts of secular organizations that may be familiar to us, such as Greenpeace and the Sierra Club, we can now add the world's religions. Jewish philosopher Roger Gottlieb observes, "Religions have become part of the all too scarce good news on the environmental front—one more element in a worldwide environmental movement."[4] Nor are major religious leaders the only ones speaking out on the importance of caring for the earth. As Mark I. Wallace notes, "Today, many North American churches, synagogues, mosques, and other places of worship are transforming themselves into forward-based earth-care centers committed to protecting God's creation, sustainable lifestyles, and safeguarding the public health."[5] A groundswell of people in communities of faith is striving to care for creation. For example, Saint Clare Catholic Church in O'Fallon, Illinois, where I am regularly invited to speak, is putting up a wind turbine to serve as the parish's new source for electrical power, as well as implementing a number of other environmentally friendly practices in the parish.

That this is news to many of us isn't surprising. As the chapters that follow will acknowledge, until recently, religions—including Christianity—have either ignored the environment or been implicated in its degradation. Ecology is a relatively recent concern for people of faith, including theologians, especially when compared with other moral issues—such as war, sexual behavior, and economic justice—that have occupied their attention over the centuries.

---

3. Kate Sheppard, "15 Green Religious Leaders," *Grist*, July 24, 2007, available at *http://www.grist.org/article/religious/*, accessed June 2, 2011.

4. Roger S. Gottlieb, *A Greener Faith: Religious Environmentalism and Our Planet's Future* (Oxford: Oxford University Press, 2006), 7.

5. Mark I. Wallace, *Green Christianity: Five Ways to a Sustainable Future* (Minneapolis: Fortress, 2010), 16.

A scientific consensus seems to have clearly emerged. Many, though not all, environmental problems are indisputably caused by humans (in technical jargon referred to as *anthropogenic effects*). These include oil spills, deforestation, pollution of rivers, toxic dumps, acid rain, and more. Of course, debate continues concerning climate change, or global warming; however, the Intergovernmental Panel on Climate Change (IPCC), which is viewed as the most reliable source of scientific information on this question, issued a report in 2007 that states, "Most of the observed increase in globally averaged temperatures since the mid-20th century is *very likely* due to the observed increase in anthropogenic greenhouse gas concentrations."[6] *Very likely* here indicates a likelihood greater than 90 percent, notes Stephen Bouma-Prediger, a Reformed Christian scholar of religion and the author of one of the best available books on the Bible and creation care.[7] Major religious leaders appear to regard these findings as persuasive, as well. Pope Benedict XVI, for example, warns that "it would be irresponsible not to take seriously" these "signs of a growing crisis," including the "problems associated with such realities as climate change, desertification, the deterioration and loss of productivity in vast agricultural areas, the pollution of rivers and aquifers, the loss of biodiversity, the increase of natural catastrophes and the deforestation of equatorial and tropical regions."[8]

Many scientists, worried over these alarming environmental trends, are calling for major changes in how we live as individuals and societies. However, science, strictly speaking, cannot answer the question: Why should endangered species or polluted oceans or disappearing rain forests matter morally at all? Normative questions like

---

6. "IPCC, 2007: Summary for Policymakers," in *Climate Change 2007: The Physical Science Basis* (contribution of Working Group I to the Fourth Assessment Report of the Intergovernmental Panel on Climate Change; Cambridge: Cambridge University Press, 2007), 10 (italics in the original).

7. Bouma-Prediger, *For the Beauty of the Earth*, 52 and 192, endnote 99.

8. Pope Benedict XVI, "If You Want to Cultivate Peace, Protect Creation: Message for the 2010 World Day of Peace," which is reprinted in this text in chapter 3 with the Vatican's permission, par. 4. For more on climate change, see Celia Deane-Drummond, *Eco-Theology* (Winona, MN: Anselm Academic, 2008), 4–9; Michael S. Northcott, *A Moral Climate: The Ethics of Global Warming* (Maryknoll, NY: Orbis, 2007); and Robert Traer, *Doing Environmental Ethics* (Boulder, CO: Westview, 2009), 257–274.

this fall within the purview of ethics.[9] In other words, by addressing human behavior and how one ought to live, a transition has been made from the descriptive to the prescriptive, which is the domain of ethics. Ethics is systematic reflection devoted to *ought* or *should* questions. It is the study of human morality, which has to do with questions such as, What sort of persons ought we be or become? How should we live and what ought we to do?

Indeed, there is a connection between *who* we *are* (our identity, our character, our values, etc.) and *how* we *behave* (our actions, our deeds, our policies, etc.). These are big questions that have occupied great thinkers through much of history and continue to be addressed by philosophers, theologians, and others today. From Plato to Kant and from Aristotle to Peter Singer, philosophers have wrestled with how to think about and respond to these kinds of questions. In recent years, environmental problems have also caught the attention of philosophical ethicists.[10] If environmental degradation or restoration are human activities at all, involving choices that reflect deeply held views of ourselves, our place, and our role in the world, then there is the need for environmental ethics—just as there is an ethics of war and peace, an ethics of business and economics, an ethics of medicine and healthcare, and so on.

Environmental questions, however, are not restricted to philosophical or professional ethics. As Gottlieb notes in connection with the environmental crisis we face today, "As well as political, economic, and technological, our plight is *spiritual:* it involves our deepest concerns about what is of truly lasting importance in our lives."[11] Religions, therefore, also have much to teach about the meaning of life, about our purpose on this planet, about how to view humankind vis-à-vis the rest of nature, and about how we ought to live and act. In short, religious ethics are involved. In Christianity today, the subdiscipline within theology that is charged

9. Christine E. Gudorf and James E. Huchingson, *Boundaries: A Casebook in Environmental Ethics*, 2nd ed. (Washington, DC: Georgetown University Press, 2010), 4.

10. The philosophical literature on environmental ethics is vast and growing. For a recent example, see Dale Jamieson, *Ethics and the Environment: An Introduction* (Cambridge: Cambridge University Press, 2008).

11. Gottlieb, *A Greener Faith*, 11; emphasis his. See also Deane-Drummond, xi.

with addressing environmental concerns is variously referred to as Christian ethics, moral theology, or theological ethics.

As a Catholic theological ethicist, I did not think, teach, or write about the environment at the outset of my career in the late 1990s. This is not to say, though, that nature wasn't ever on my mind. Growing up on a small farm in the rural Midwest, I loved spending time outside and, in particular, exploring the woods. While attending St. Joseph's Catholic School in Blakeslee, Ohio, as a young boy, I learned about Saint Francis of Assisi, and I would attempt (in vain) to communicate, as the stories claimed he did, with the birds and squirrels I encountered. During those years (the 1970s), my teachers not only tried to teach us to be pro-life in connection with the issue of abortion, but they also introduced us to the "save the whales" campaign under way at the time. Etched into my memory, moreover, are some television commercials—including one with a tear trickling down the cheek of a Native American at the sight of trash and pollution, as well as another with Woodsy Owl and his motto for the U.S. Forest Service, "Give a hoot, don't pollute!"—that had begun to raise public awareness of environmental problems.

However, years later during my training to become a theological ethicist, though I studied moral questions pertaining to medicine, war, and sex, I never had a course devoted to environmental problems (aside from an undergraduate science course on the subject). Nevertheless, in 1995 as a graduate student at the University of Notre Dame, I was invited to help my professors, Maura A. Ryan and Todd David Whitmore, with a conference on "The Challenge of Global Stewardship," which initially exposed me to theological thinking under way about population, consumption, sustainable development, and other related issues.[12] In addition, I was fortunate to get to know Stephen Bede Scharper, who was teaching at Notre Dame at the time and who is the author of a book on this subject, as well as (with his wife Hilary Cunningham) *The Green Bible*.[13] Also, my close friend

---

12. See the book that resulted from this conference: Maura A. Ryan and Todd David Whitmore, eds., *The Challenge of Global Stewardship: Roman Catholic Responses* (Notre Dame, IN: University of Notre Dame Press, 1997).

13. Stephen Bede Scharper and Hilary Cunningham, *The Green Bible* (Brooklyn, NY: Lantern, 2002); also see Stephen Bede Scharper, *Redeeming the Time: A Political Theology of the Environment* (New York: Continuum, 1997).

and fellow student at the time, David Weiss, was especially interested in theology and ecology, and he later taught a popular course on the subject at Luther College in Decorah, Iowa, which planted in me the resolve to go and do likewise at some point.

That opportunity arose in 2004 when I was teaching theological ethics at Walsh University, which was founded by the Brothers of Christian Instruction in North Canton, Ohio. The Sisters of the Humility of Mary, who operate Villa Maria,[14] a retreat and educational center just across the border in western Pennsylvania, generously gave me a grant to read on the subject and to construct a new course on theology and the environment to teach at Walsh, a course I now continue to offer regularly at Saint Louis University. Indeed, I suspect "Green Discipleship: Theology and the Environment" will be a permanent course of my repertoire of teaching responsibilities, especially because Christian concern about ecology has gone from giving isolated attention to saving the whales, to making it a vital component of Christian discipleship, as reflected in Benedict XVI's sweeping imperative statement: "Protecting the natural environment in order to build a world of peace is thus a duty incumbent upon each and all."[15]

In teaching this course over the years, I have used many different books.[16] However, I have longed for a text that provides a solid

---

14. For more information about their conference center and educational programs, including ecospirituality, organic farming, and more, see *http://www.humilityofmary.org/index.html* (accessed March 3, 2011).

15. Benedict XVI, "If You Want to Cultivate Peace, Protect Creation," par. 14.

16. A sampling of recent books on religion or Christianity and ecology that I have used in undergraduate (and one MA-level) courses includes, Deane-Drummond, *Eco-Theology;* Gottlieb, *A Greener Faith;* John Hart, *What Are They Saying about Environmental Theology?* (New York and Mahwah, NJ: Paulist Press, 2004); Brennan R. Hill, *Christian Faith and the Environment: Making Vital Connections* (Maryknoll, NY: Orbis, 1998); Pamela Smith, *What Are They Saying about Environmental Ethics?* (New York and Mahwah, NJ: Paulist Press, 1997); Traer, *Doing Environmental Ethics;* and Wallace, *Green Christianity.* I have also supplemented an anchor text by using case studies for class discussions from books such as, Gudorf and Huchingson, *Boundaries,* and James B. Martin-Schramm and Robert L. Stivers, *Christian Environmental Ethics: A Case Method Approach* (Maryknoll, NY: Orbis, 2003). For a textbook that includes selections from a wide range of religions and worldviews, see Richard C. Foltz, ed., *Worldviews, Religion, and the Environment: A Global Anthology* (Belmont, CA: Wadsworth, 2003).

baseline for students, who may have had little to no prior theology at the university level. I sought a text that would survey the current state of the environmental question in theology while pointing toward directions for creative exploration in the future. I envision this present volume as that text.

My intent for *Green Discipleship: Catholic Theological Ethics and the Environment* is that it might serve as an anchor text that is accessible, engaging, and challenging to students—one that instructors find easy to use in the classroom and that they can supplement when they deem fit with more in-depth materials from elsewhere. In this way, I see this book as similar to Mark J. Allman's *Who Would Jesus Kill?: War, Peace, and the Christian Tradition*, which covers the major historical and contemporary moral perspectives on war and peace in Christian theological ethics (with some attention to Judaism and Islam), with some consideration of new thinking currently under development.[17] It's a wonderful anchor text in my course on "War and Peace in the Christian Tradition" that I can easily supplement with articles and books about the areas that Allman highlights. *Green Discipleship*, in my view, ought to serve a similar purpose.

Celia Deane-Drummond defines ecology as "contemporary concern for the environment."[18] This book, like hers, focuses on Christian theological ethics, with some attention to other religious perspectives, so it might be considered to be a contribution to what she calls "eco-theology," which strives to "uncover the theological basis for a proper relationship between God, humanity and the cosmos."[19] Christian theological ethicists reason about issues by drawing on a range of sources of moral wisdom, including the Bible, the tradition of the church, and the human sciences.[20] The same approach applies to thinking ethically about the environment. Most of the contributors, though not all, to this volume are Catholic theological

17. Mark J. Allman, *Who Would Jesus Kill?: War, Peace, and the Christian Tradition* (Winona, MN: Anselm Academic, 2008).

18. Deane-Drummond, ix.

19. Ibid., x, xii.

20. For a handy introduction to how Christian theological ethicists do what they do (method), see Allman's initial chapter, "A Crash Course in Christian Ethics," in *Who Would Jesus Kill?*, 19–60.

ethicists. Some contributors instead are experts in other areas of theology or religious studies. A few contributors are actually specialists in other fields, including ecology, sociology, and biology (though these authors also possess advanced degrees in theology).

In his book *A Greener Faith*, Gottlieb identifies three basic approaches evident among theologians and religion scholars who are dealing with environmental questions: reinterpretation, criticism, and vital new contributions. I think there are traces of each of these in the chapters that follow. Some chapters reinterpret traditional texts—such as the Bible, the writings of past theologians such as Aquinas, and the rubrics of worship—and find that these "in fact contain powerful ecological messages, or at least provide some important resources to help improve our relation to nature."[21] Even if these teachings were ignored or marginalized previously, they can be explored and tapped to help people of faith to respond to the environmental problems facing us today. Indeed, a similar process of reinterpretation is under way in other religions, including Judaism, Buddhism, and Islam that also are being "mined for [their] environmental resources."[22]

Second, many of the chapters, in addition to retrieval, "offer direct and unflinching criticism."[23] At times, the Bible has been interpreted in ways that are dualistic, emphasizing the spiritual over against the material, or anthropocentric, focusing on humans at the expense of the rest of creation. The same goes for the teachings of many theologians in the history of the church. For example, feminist and liberation theologians have critiqued in the tradition, respectively, patriarchy and the failure to consider things from the perspective of the oppressed poor—both of which are, they argue, connected with attitudes and practices that result in environmental degradation.

The third mode that Gottlieb identifies involves "vital new contributions to religion's ongoing evolution," because the "environmental crisis calls for critical theological creativity."[24] This approach does not plow up new earth that was submerged, ignored, or wrongly

21. Gottlieb, *A Greener Faith*, 20.

22. Ibid., 29.

23. Ibid., 31.

24. Ibid., 36.

used; rather, it pioneers new territory. For example, Mark I. Wallace, in his *Green Christianity*, calls for a "Christian animism" that holds that "all things are bearers of divinity" and that "all of Earth's vital fluids that make planetary existence possible—blood, mucus, tears, milk, semen, sweat, urine—are infused with sacred energy."[25] Though his book includes pages devoted to both retrieval and criticism, it undoubtedly explores theological ideas that are new to many undergraduate readers. Likewise, some of the chapters that follow consider the work of theologians who push the theological envelope in ways similar to Wallace, such as Sallie McFague and Thomas Berry, and a few chapters break new ground.

This volume consists of seven parts, with twenty chapters. In part I, attention is given to the "signs of the times." At the close of the Second Vatican Council (1962–1965) in *Gaudium et spes* (Pastoral Constitution on the Church in the Modern World), the Catholic bishops called for the Church to scrutinize the "signs of the times" (in other words, to consider what is actually going on in the world, especially the major problems people are facing) and then to interpret them "in the light of the gospel."[26] Thus, in chapter 1, ecologist Cathy Mabry McMullen examines current trends in her field and the varying degrees with which ecologists are receptive to working with—and learning from—religions in order to address environmental problems. Chapter 2, by sociologist Michael Agliardo, SJ, focuses on the rise of religious environmentalism in recent decades and highlights how the 2001 pastoral letter from the Catholic bishops of the Northwest on the Columbia River Watershed demonstrates the constructive role religion can play in the public sphere. Chapter 3 provides further evidence of the prominent place that care for the environment occupies today in Catholicism by reprinting, with the Vatican's permission, Pope Benedict XVI's "If You Want to Cultivate Peace, Protect Creation: Message for the 2010 World Day of Peace."

Part II, includes two chapters on the scriptures and care for creation. The Second Vatican Council suggested that the discipline of

---

25. Wallace, xiv, 40.

26. *Gaudium et spes* (Pastoral Constitution on the Church in the Modern World), in *Documents of Vatican II*, ed. Walter M. Abbot, SJ (Piscataway, NJ: New Century, 1966), 201–202, no. 4.

moral theology "should be more thoroughly nourished by scriptural teaching."[27] Therefore, chapter 4, by Randall Smith, meditates on the Hebrew Scriptures (the Old Testament)—especially the Genesis creation accounts—and humankind's vocation as stewards within creation. Thomas Bushlack, in turn, studies key passages in the New Testament that point toward the renewal, not only of humankind, but of all creation. Part III consists of two chapters that similarly retrieve wisdom from the Christian tradition. In chapter 6, ecologist and Franciscan friar Keith Douglass Warner, OFM, explores Saint Francis of Assisi's life of ecological consciousness and its legacy among Franciscans for innovative insights about our ecological vocation of radical discipleship. Chapter 7, by Daniel P. Scheid, considers Saint Thomas Aquinas, the Thomistic tradition, and the ways that the cosmic common good should shape our thinking and our lives as "cocreators" with God.

Part IV comprises four chapters that deal with fundamental or basic considerations in theological ethics. In chapter 8, biologist and theologian Nicanor Pier Giorgio Austriaco, OP, investigates the natural moral law, which has played a prominent role in Catholic ethics over the centuries, and how it should guide humans to discern their authentic good, the common good, and the ecological good. Chapter 9, by Nancy M. Rourke, offers a Christian environmental virtue ethics that strives for the formation of people of character who are good neighbors to everyone and everything. Liturgical scholar Stephen B. Wilson, in chapter 10, explores how worship—especially the Eucharist—should inform and transform how Christians understand and engage creation. Chapter 11, by Marcus Mescher, analyzes fresh ways of understanding Jesus' parable of the Good Samaritan and tackles head-on the question of whether it is possible for Christians to be loving neighbors to nature rather than only to other people.

Part V has chapters that theologically examine wider institutional, structural, and social dimensions—including the political and economic—to environmental problems. In chapter 12, Christopher P. Vogt explicates Catholic social teaching and highlights the

---

27. "Decree on Priestly Formation," in *Documents of Vatican II*, ed. Walter M. Abbot, SJ (Piscataway, NJ: New Century, 1966), 452, no. 16.

concept of authentic human development as a promising personal and social framework for economic decision making that serves both humankind and the rest of creation. This is followed by chapter 13 by Kari-Shane Davis Zimmerman, detailing the work of three prominent feminist theologians and the ways that the domination of nature has been related to Christian beliefs about God, humankind, and creation. Chapter 14, by Kathy Lilla Cox, then describes how the ecological crisis especially affects the world's poor and considers what liberation theologians have to say about how we should care for creation and address the problem of poverty.

In part VI, three chapters consider the "greening of faith" in some other religions. *Nostra Aetate* (Declaration on the Relationship of the Church to Non-Christian Religions), from the Second Vatican Council, taught that the Catholic Church "rejects nothing which is true and holy" in other world religions, and it exhorted Catholics to "prudently and lovingly, through dialogue and collaboration with followers of other religions and in witness of Christian faith and life, acknowledge, preserve, and promote the spiritual and moral goods found among these [people], as well as the values in their society and culture."[28] Accordingly, in chapter 15 historian and Jewish studies professor Hava Tirosh-Samuelson canvasses, in addition to the Hebrew Bible, a wide range of literary sources in the history of Judaism that articulate deep ecological concerns that could inspire conservation policies and a distinctive Jewish ecotheology. In chapter 16 June-Ann Greeley introduces us to the ecological conversation under way in Islam, especially centering on the *Qur'an*. David Clairmont, in chapter 17, examines early teachings that have been central to Buddhist approaches to moral problems, how these teachings relate to Buddhist interpretations of the natural world, and how Buddhist critiques about ideas of God and creation relate to Buddhist ecological teachings today.

In part VII, three chapters deal with what is known as applied or special ethics. That is, they draw on insights, lessons, principles, and themes of the sort that surfaced in previous sections

---

28. *Nostra Aetate* (Declaration on the Relationship of the Church to Non-Christian Religions), in *The Documents of Vatican II*, ed. Walter M. Abbott, SJ (Piscataway, NJ: New Century, 1966), 662–663, no. 2.

and chapters, and then they attempt to apply them in addressing concrete environmental issues. Chapter 18, by Julie Hanlon Rubio, uses family ethics as a portal for tackling environmental ethics and argues that care for creation and its most vulnerable creatures requires Christian households to break out of conventional food systems to eat more justly. In chapter 19, Mark J. Allman argues that Christians possess a distinctive moral obligation to address the world's water crisis because of the prominent role water plays in the Bible and in Christian worship. Finally, chapter 20, by Matthew A. Shadle, focuses on the ways the issues of war and environmental destruction intersect, as well as the problems these intersections pose for ethical reasoning and then identifies promising resources from both Christian tradition and contemporary thinkers for developing solutions to these problems.

Unfortunately, not every possible perspective or topic related to theology, ethics, and the environment can be covered in one volume. Obviously, in the section on the Christian tradition, more chapters could have been included on, for example, Patristic theologians in the earlier history of Christianity or on Orthodox, United Methodist, and Lutheran perspectives. Where possible, contributors tried to be as ecumenical as possible, referring to Protestant and Orthodox theologians, beliefs, and practices. Also, the section on social ethics could have included a chapter on African American contributions to ecotheology and perhaps explored "environmental racism" in the United States.[29] The section on insights from other religions likewise could have included chapters on Taoism, Native American spirituality, and traditional African religions. Alas, this volume cannot cover everything. However, I certainly encourage instructors to supplement this text with such materials.

Before concluding this Introduction, I want to say a word about some of the terminology in this volume. First, throughout the book's chapters, the words *nature*, *earth*, *environment*, and *creation* appear,

---

29. On this topic, I highly recommend Bryan Massingale, "An Ethical Reflection upon 'Environmental Racism' in the Light of Catholic Social Teaching," in *The Challenge of Global Stewardship: Roman Catholic Responses*, eds. Maura A. Ryan and Todd David Whitmore (Notre Dame, IN: University of Notre Dame Press, 1997), 234–250.

and they are used interchangeably. The default word most of the time will be *creation*, because it is more of a theological term. In his book, Bouma-Prediger uses the word *earth* rather than these other words, including *creation*, because for him the term *earth* is "concrete, denoting both the planet on which we live and the very stuff of which we are made."[30] Although I agree about that, and I concur with him and Gottlieb[31] that whatever it is we're talking about includes us humans too, I also believe that we (and everything around us) are made up of stardust. Plus, there is a lot of space junk orbiting the planet today, and it is possible that we humans will leave more footprints (hopefully not carbon ones) on the moon and perhaps elsewhere in the future. Therefore, in this volume, though all of these terms will be used, *creation* will be seen most often because it is a theological term that encompasses the earth, humankind, and whatever other parts of the cosmos we affect.

In addition, a word about *discipleship* is in order. Although earlier I highlighted a number of serious environmental problems we face today, I believe that what the following chapters have to offer is important even if there were no ecological crisis. Discipleship has received more emphasis in moral theology in recent decades, especially since the Second Vatican Council. Irish Catholic Enda McDonagh, for instance, has written that by "adopting discipleship as one dominant theme of their reflections and explorations, theologians . . . are compelled to address the Scriptures in text and context more directly and seriously than some doctrinal and moral traditions of the immediate past."[32] Theological ethicists will also take into account the community of faith, gleaning insights from saints and fellow disciples past and present, as well as give attention to the liturgy, which is an "expression or source for Christian morality and the life of discipleship."[33] Moreover, theological ethicists will focus on praxis, life as it is lived, as well as attend to the

30. Bouma-Prediger, xv. He also notes that *creation* includes angels.

31. Gottlieb writes, "Our relations with nature are not just about penguins and brooks, but about ourselves" (30).

32. Enda McDonagh, *The Making of Disciples: Tasks of Moral Theology* (Wilmington, DE: Glazier, 1982), 4.

33. Ibid., 5.

"various subcategories" within "the traditional range of theological disciplines."[34] In my view, the chapters collected in this volume accomplish much of what McDonagh has in mind. In short, these chapters offer thoughtful guidance for a way of life—let's call it green discipleship—that Christians ought to be pursuing anyway.

---

34. Ibid. For more evidence of how discipleship has become a prominent theme in Catholic moral theology, see Bernard Häring, CSSR, *Toward a Christian Moral Theology* (Notre Dame, IN: University of Notre Dame Press, 1966), 18–19; and more recently, Patricia Lamoureux and Paul J. Wadell, *The Christian Moral Life: Faithful Discipleship for a Global Society* (Maryknoll, NY: Orbis, 2010), 9–11,18–20; and M. Therese Lysaught, "Love and Liturgy," in *Gathered for the Journey: Moral Theology in Catholic Perspective*, eds. David Matzko McCarthy and M. Therese Lysaught (Grand Rapids, MI: Eerdmans, 2007), 24–42.

READING THE SIGNS OF THE TIMES

CHAPTER 1

THE SIGNS OF THE TIMES:
The State of the Question among Ecologists

Cathy Mabry McMullen

KEY TERMS

environmental degradation
human impacts
conservation
ecologist
sustainability
signs of the times
plant dispersal
virtue

INTRODUCTION

The ecological community largely agrees about the severity of the negative impact that humans are having on Earth, an agreement that spans diverse arenas of study. Global climate change, soil and water depletion and degradation, deforestation, loss of species, and genetic diversity are just a few examples of such human impacts.[1] Ecologists, scientists who study the relationships between organisms and their environment, widely agree that these changes are endangering global life-support systems that sustain human life, particularly such fundamental requirements as clean water and healthy topsoil. At

1. Peter Vitousek, et al., "Human Domination of Earth's Ecosystems," *Science* 277 (1997): 494–499; Paul Ehrlich, "Human Natures, Nature Conservation, and Environmental Ethics," *BioScience* 52 (2002), no 1:31–43.

the same time, there is growing and widespread agreement among the world's religions about the severity of the environmental crisis.[2] Ecology and religion widely concur on the severity of global ecological problems; however, efforts to collaborate on their solution are not widespread. Although there is an eager and increasing willingness on the part of the faith community to develop a partnership with scientists to address environmental problems, scientists share no such consensus for collaboration with the religious community, particularly with respect to Christianity. Although in the past, scientists might have been justified in not considering religion as conversation partner—given religion's lack of interest in, and at times outright hostility toward, environmental concerns—today many religious movements are at the forefront of raising ecological concerns, providing a new opportunity for collaboration.

This chapter touches briefly on the relationship between the Catholic Church and the modern world envisioned in the Second Vatican Council. A more extensive discussion follows of four components of the scientific response to global ecological problems: (1) the consensus within the scientific community on the scope of the problems; (2) barriers within science that make it difficult for scientists to propose and act on solutions; (3) the relationship among scientists, ethics, and religion; and (4) perspectives from the scientific community on how to become a more effective social movement, including through engagement with religion.

A GOSPEL CALL

Gaudium et spes (The Church in the Modern World), or "joys and hopes," from the initial words of the statement, was the final document issued by the Second Vatican Council of the Roman Catholic Church in December 1965. The first half of this lengthy text addressed basic doctrinal topics—in particular, the Church's relationship with the twentieth-century world—while the second half

---

2. Roger S. Gottlieb, "The Beginnings of a Beautiful Friendship: Religion and Environmentalism," *Reflections* 94, no. 1 (2007): 10–13. This entire issue of *Reflections* is an excellent compendium on the role of religion in addressing environmental problems, with a focus on Christianity.

offered pastoral treatments of especially urgent contemporary issues, including marriage, family, culture, economics, political community, and peace and war. In this document, the Church addressed both the Christian faithful and the rest of the world, and in doing so, moved Catholic social teaching from a more abstract basis to one that takes into account human experience.

This methodological shift is evident in the document's call for the Church to scrutinize the "signs of the times" and then to interpret them "in the light of the gospel."[3] As David J. O'Brien and Thomas A. Shannon note, *Gaudium et spes* "offered a systematic and synthetic ethical framework for dealing with world problems" so that the Church could be "in service to real people in the concrete circumstances of human history. . . ."[4] According to M. C. Vanhengel, OP, and J. Peters, OCD, for the expression "signs of the times" to be truly significant and not theologically trivialized, two elements are necessary: an accumulation of facts that all point in the same direction, and this direction must be generally acknowledged by the public.[5]

GOSPEL ROOTS

The phrase *signs of the times* was first officially used in Catholic social teaching in 1963 by Pope John XXIII in his encyclical *Pacem in terris* ("Peace on Earth"), in which each chapter of the document ends with a brief section on the characteristics of the present day, or the signs of the times. The phrase originally surfaced in the Gospel according to Matthew: "You know how to interpret the appearance of the sky, but you cannot interpret the signs of the times" (Matthew 16:3b).

3. *Gaudium et spes*, in *Documents of Vatican II*, ed. Walter M. Abbot, SJ (Piscataway, NJ: New Century, 1966), 201–202, no. 4.

4. David J. O'Brien and Thomas A. Shannon, "Introduction," in *Catholic Social Thought: The Documentary Heritage* (Maryknoll, NY: Orbis, 1992), 165.

5. M. C. Vanhengel, OP, and J. Peters, OCD, "Signs of the Times," *Concilium* 25 (Mahwah, NJ: Paulist Press, 1967): 145.

SIGNS OF THE TIMES

The Scientific Consensus on the Existence of a Crisis

The current scientific consensus on the declining state of the environment satisfies the criteria spelled out at Vatican II concerning what constitutes a sign of the times. It is hard to overstate how completely the science of ecology has embraced human impact as the global "environmental crisis." This consensus is reflected in how thoroughly the academic study of ecology is shaped by the paradigm of studying the underlying mechanisms of the crisis and the desire to provide a scientific basis for mitigating negative human impacts on Earth's systems.

Major ecological professional societies devote many resources to applied ecology, most prominently in the form of diverse publications. For example, two of the four journals published by the Ecological Society of America (ESA), a flagship professional society for ecologists, focus on applying ecological research to problems created by human actions. *Ecological Applications* is a journal "open to research and discussion papers that integrate ecological science and concepts with their application and implications. Of special interest are papers that develop the basic scientific principles on which environmental decision-making should rest, and those that discuss the application of ecological concepts to environmental problem solving, policy, and management."[6] Recent *Ecological Applications* articles have included, for example, "Effectiveness of engineered in-stream structure mitigation measures to increase salmonid abundance: A systematic review," "Changes in vegetation in northern Alaska under scenarios of climate change, 2003–2100: Implications for climate feedbacks," and "Legacies of historical land use on regional forest composition and structure in Wisconsin, USA (mid-1800s–1930s–2000s)."

Another ESA journal, *Frontiers in Ecology and the Environment*, "focuses on current ecological issues and environmental challenges"[7] and is intended to be an interdisciplinary journal that appeals to

---

6. Ecological Society of America, *http://esapubs.org/esapubs/journals/applications.htm*, accessed July 7, 2009.

7. Ecological Society of America, *http://www.frontiersinecology.org/generalinformation.php*, accessed July 7, 2009.

scientists, teachers, policymakers, and managers. As its mission suggests, the journal attempts to integrate big topics. For example, the February 2009 issue of *Frontiers* was devoted entirely to the concept of "ecosystem services," or the things nature provides to people,[8] with articles on such topics as including ecosystem services in decision making and implementing projects that include these services. Other common topics addressed in the journal include wildfires, nutrient pollution, agriculture and ecology, protection of marine and coastal systems, stream ecology, forest management, and exotic species invasion and control.

Many more specialized societies are also devoted to addressing the ecological problems caused by humans. Two of the more prominent include the Society for Ecological Restoration International (SER) and the Society for Conservation Biology (SCB). The SER mission is "to promote ecological restoration as a means of sustaining the diversity of life on Earth and reestablishing an ecologically healthy relationship between nature and culture." SCB is a "professional organization dedicated to promoting the scientific study of the phenomena that affect the maintenance, loss, and restoration of biological diversity."[9] Both societies sponsor journals that publish original research, as well as other materials, such as newsletters and list servers, designed to influence audiences beyond their immediate membership, including land managers and policymakers.

The consensus on environmental problems is also reflected in the plethora of texts offered by university and academic publishers. In recent years, for example, a Wiley-Blackwell flyer advertised more than ten titles related to climate change and global warming. Island Press is a publishing house with a "core mission" of publishing books that seek solutions to environmental issues. A recent 68-page catalog included books that spanned a comprehensive list of environmental topics, including climate and energy, biodiversity and wildlife, ecological restoration, food and agriculture, and human health and the environment, with another eight hundred titles in press.

8. Susan Ruffo and Peter Kaveiva, "Using Science to Assign Value to Nature," *Frontiers in Ecology and the Environment* 7, no. 1 (2009): 3.

9. Society for Ecological Restoration, *http://www.ser.org/about.asp;* Society for Conservation Biology, *http://www.conbio.org/AboutUs/*, accessed July 7, 2009.

Scientific Barriers to Taking Action

Despite this consensus on the human impacts on the environment, often no corresponding consensus exists on actions that might address these impacts (at least not when resources are limited, and tradeoffs between conservation and human needs must be taken into account). At least two strains subsist within ecological science that make it difficult for scientists to act in unison and effectively, both pertaining to the nature of modern ecological research.

First, how to apply the results of research to real-world problems is often not clear or straightforward. Research results are frequently inconsistent and, therefore, lead to ambiguous conclusions. A classic example of this inconsistency relates to plant dispersal. Humans have been altering plant communities throughout history, particularly by harvesting forests for wood products and to clear land for agriculture. One of the most-studied phenomena in ecology is the ability of different plant species to disperse. A large body of research in both Europe and North America has focused on the dispersal of forest plant species after land converted to agriculture was abandoned and allowed to revert to forest. The goal of these studies is to evaluate whether humans have had a permanent impact on forests, as not all plant species are able to return as a result of their limited dispersal capacity. This research is important, not only for current conservation but also because the ability of plants to disperse and migrate will have a large influence on how different species respond to changing climate. This extensive body of research, however, has not led to consistent conclusions that would allow researchers to target dispersal-challenged species for conservation.[10] One reason is that ecological science is rarely practiced as a coordinated effort to understand and solve specific problems. Thus, research programs are tailored to individual interests and preferences and the length of grant cycles; and even slightly different research questions, methods, and periods of study influence the results of such programs, preventing them from being

10. Kathryn M. Flinn and Mark Vellend, "Recovery of Forest Plant Communities in Post-Agricultural Landscapes," *Frontiers in Ecology and the Environment* 3, no 5 (2005): 243–250.

comparable.[11] Without the ability to compare, consistent patterns that can be applied to address an issue are difficult to find.

Moreover, scientists and managers increasingly recognize the existence of an "implementation gap" between research scientists on one hand and on-the-ground managers on the other. The gap describes a situation in which much of what is published in the academic literature about conservation is not actually applied to successful conservation practices.[12] The problem often arises because academic scientists and the people who manage land have distinctly different work cultures and different reward systems, particularly in the types of achievement they recognize. Under the academic-reward system, the highest status is given to innovative and cutting-edge research that can be published in high-impact international journals, which appeal to a broad international community of scientists who are working in primarily academic settings. This system tends to under reward research that is applied or directed at problem solving.[13] In addition, research results are published in specialized peer-reviewed journals with a largely academic circulation, while many on-the-ground managers lack access to university research libraries and tend to base their decisions on case studies, long-term experience, and trial and error.[14]

---

11. Catherine M. Mabry and Jennifer M. Fraterrigo, "Species Traits as Generalized Predictors of Forest Community Response to Human Disturbance," *Forest Ecology and Management* 257 (2009): 723–730; L. Roy Taylor, "Objective and Experiment in Long-Term Research," in *Long-Term Studies in Ecology*, ed. Gene E. Likens (New York: Springer-Verlag, 1989), 20–70.

12. David Ehrenfeld, "War and Peace and Conservation Biology," *Conservation Biology* 14, no. 1 (2000): 105–112; Tony Whitten, Derek Holmes, and Kathy MacKinnon, "Conservation Biology: A Displacement Behavior for Academia?" *Conservation Biology* 15, no. 1 (2001): 1–3; Robert J. Cabin, "Science-Driven Restoration: A Square Grid on a Round Earth," *Restoration Ecology* 15, no. 1 (2007): 1–7.

13. Peter A. Lawrence, "The Mismeasurement of Science," *Current Biology* 17, no.15: R583–R585; Stuart E. G. Findlay and Clive G. Jones, "How Can We Improve the Reception of Long-Term Studies in Ecology?" in *Long-Term Studies in Ecology*, ed. Gene E. Likens (New York: Springer-Verlag, 1989), 201–202; Reed F. Noss, "The Failure of Universities to Produce Conservation Biologists," *Conservation Biology* 11, no. 6 (1997): 1267–1269.

14. See Wendell Berry, "*Life Is a Miracle*" (Washington DC Counterpoint, 2000) for a thorough exploration of the contrast between these two worldviews.

Practical constraints also often work against fully integrating research science and natural-resource management. Managers often need to act immediately, before a research-based understanding of a system has been developed.[15] Good examples of the need for immediate management action are the need to control new exotic pests, plants, and insects before they become established and displace native species, and the need to act quickly to protect rare or endangered species. Moreover, many management actions are difficult to carry out in a research-based format. For example, publishable research requires that a study have replicated treatment areas and untreated

NEW EXOTIC PESTS

Reed canary grass (*Phalaris arundinacea*) is well known for its ability to aggressively invade native wetlands and riparian areas, displacing native species and converting these formerly species areas to stands of vegetation that is nearly all reed canary grass. The precise reason the plant is so invasive is not clear to scientists, but invasion has been associated with sediment-rich waters from stormwater and agricultural runoff.

Although reed canary grass may be native to North America, the invading plants are believed to be a more aggressive ecotype introduced from Europe or a hybrid between the native and European ecotype. Reed canary grass spreads both through high seed production that then enters the seed bank and vegetatively through the roots. There is extensive research and management literature on reed canary grass control, but so far, there is no highly successful management prescription for extensive invasions, and control measures must be continued indefinitely.

15. Jay B. McAninch and David L. Strayer, "What Are the Tradeoffs between the Immediacy of Management Needs and the Longer Process of Scientific Discovery?" in *Long-Term Studies in Ecology*, ed. Gene E. Likens (New York: Springer-Verlag, 1989), 203–205; Connie L. Dettman and Catherine M. Mabry, "Lessons Learned about Research and Management: A Case Study from a Midwest Lowland Savanna, U.S.A.," *Restoration Ecology* 16, no. 4 (2008): 532–541.

control areas. Data often need to be collected at specific times and with high precision. However, these are often difficult for managers to achieve due to lack of time and resources. Lack of institutional structures to bring scientists and managers together contributes to these limitations.[16]

ECOLOGICAL SCIENCE, PROBLEM SOLVING, ETHICS, AND RELIGION

Aldo Leopold (1887–1948), widely regarded as one of the founders of the modern conservation movement and restoration ecology, wrote compellingly about extending the sphere of ethical concerns beyond humans to include the natural world. His best-known work, *A Sand County Almanac*, combines his astute observation of land, animals, and humans and culminates in his view that humans must have an ethical relationship to land and animals. He is beloved by ecologists and conservationists as an accomplished scientist who could also write passages such as, "It is inconceivable to me that an ethical relation to land can exist without love, respect, and admiration for land, and a high regard for its value. By value, I of course mean something far broader than mere economic value; I mean value in the philosophical sense."[17] It is hard to overemphasize the impact that Leopold has had on many ecologists, not only for the continued freshness of his ideas, but also for the compelling language he provides from within science to speak of ethics and moral obligations.

Yet as a social movement, conservation is widely perceived as having failed to make meaningful improvements in creating more sustainable human societies and in limiting degradation of ecosystems. Conservation is failing to conserve—and remarkably, given the disparate sources, there is something of a consensus on this point. As stated starkly in a recent column in the journal *Conservation Biology*,

---

16. Cabin, "Science-Driven Restoration"; Dettman and Mabry, "Lessons Learned"; Bernard T. Bormann, Richard W. Haynes, and Jon R. Martin, "Adaptive Management of Forest Ecosystems: Did Some Rubber Hit the Road?" *BioScience* 57, no. 2 (2007): 186–191.

17. Aldo Leopold, A *Sand County Almanac* (New York and Oxford: Oxford University Press, 1968), 223.

"There can be little question that conservation as a cultural reform movement is in sad shape today."[18] The processes within science described previously are one area of concern. In addition, many scientists recognize that an untapped ethical dimension to conservation science and natural resource management is needed to transform these efforts from science into an effective social movement.

Thus, many calls for increasing the effectiveness of conservation acknowledge that conservation scientists must engage the fields of social science, spirituality, morality, and ethics. These calls recognize that achieving conservation goals will require fundamental changes in how we live. Moreover, many scientists admit that conservation goals are unlikely to be achieved without confronting destructive human actions—war, greed, poverty, and consumer culture—and replacing them with more ethically based motivators.

Unfortunately, the scientific community lacks a unifying foundation for ethical practice that would provide a cohesive basis for moral reflection and action and that functions similarly to the normative texts and traditions of specific religions. This lack of cohesion is reflected in the multiple philosophies that appear in the scientific literature attempting to motivate widespread action. Ecologist David Egan notes this rather starkly, "Leaders in the environmental movement have failed to build robust political coalitions, articulate a coherent morality, and figure out who we are and who we need to be."[19]

ECOLOGY AND CONSERVATION AS A MORE EFFECTIVE SOCIAL MOVEMENT

The need to increase effectiveness is reflected in a wide range of papers appearing in ecological journals calling for ecology and conservation science to be more effective in public policy, in decision making, and as a social movement. These papers generally emphasize one of three approaches: (1) the need for more and better science and better communication of the science to the public and policymakers;

18. Eric T. Freyfogle, "Conservation and the Culture War," *Conservation Biology* 17, no. 2 (2003): 354.

19. David Egan, "People Are Wearing Out the Planet," *Ecological Restoration* 23, no. 4 (2005): 229.

(2) the need to include ethical language and spirituality as part of our approach to solving environmental problems but without relying on specific traditions; and (3) the need to engage Christians and other faith traditions, because they provide a specific context and moral language that can motivate the kinds of action and changes in behavior that are needed.

Three prominent ecological scientists, William Schlesinger, Paul Ehrlich, and Jane Lubchenco, exemplify the first perspective, emphasizing a need for greater knowledge and better education to increase conservation effectiveness. Schlesinger asks what must be done "to transform human behaviors to enable the persistence of life on Earth under human stewardship." He sets aside ethics and aesthetics as rationales for preserving biodiversity and looks to the "wonderful new tools with which to do our science better," including molecular techniques, mass spectrometry to analyze Earth's chemistry, eddy covariance methods to measure net carbon exchange, and remote sensing. "Mercifully," he writes, "each day we see increases in our computational abilities to synthesize all the data." Although at the end of his article, Schlesinger recognizes that poverty and hunger leave some people unable to act sustainably while many wealthier individuals simply choose not to act sustainably, he doesn't attempt to reconcile these observations with his hopeful message about the power of new and better data.[20]

Ehrlich acknowledges the need to include social scientists "in seeking solutions to the menacing dilemma of the destruction of humanity's life-support system."[21] Reaching these goals, he argues, requires a change in norms and ethics in both the biophysical and social sciences by borrowing successful marketing strategies from business. "We need to help steer cultural evolution by 'marketing' a set of environmental ethics: doing the necessary psychological and market research, selecting appropriate goals, and carefully monitoring the performance of the 'product' in a free marketplace of ideas."[22] Although Ehrlich doesn't address the role of religion directly in this

---

20. William H. Schlesinger, "Global Change Ecology," *Trends in Ecology and Evolution* 21, no. 6 (2006): 348–351.

21. Paul Ehrlich, "Human Natures," 32.

22. Ibid., 39.

transformation of behavior, one can infer that he doesn't envision a direct engagement with religion as he wonders why religion persists among some scientists while "most leading scientists consider it of no interest in explaining how the world works."[23]

For her part, Lubchenco writes, "We can no longer afford to have the environment be accorded marginal status on our agendas"[24] and proposes a new social contract for science that includes three elements: addressing the most urgent environmental problems first, widely communicating the knowledge gained to inform the decisions of individuals and institutions, and exercising "good judgment, wisdom and humility." Although she recognizes social justice as a component of a sustainable biosphere, her contract does not include social scientists but emphasizes continuation of fundamental research, new research and management approaches, training interdisciplinary scientists, communication, and "educating citizens about the issues."[25] She concludes that credible scientists delivering science-based assessments are "powerful tools in communicating knowledge to inform policy and management decisions."[26]

Other ecologists envision spiritual, social, and ethical dimensions to increasing conservation effectiveness and motivating change—while not engaging the Christian faith community directly—either by pointing to other religious traditions as a source of inspiration and ethics, or more commonly, by general calls to include spirituality and ethics as part of the conservation movement. Barbara Patterson, an ecologist who focuses on wildlife conservation, writes, "The challenge for environmental ethics is to find a solid rational justification for why nature should be protected from human actions."[27] She discusses ethics based on instrumental value, intrinsic value, and biocentric approaches and advocates a Buddhist approach centered upon oneness in hopes of overcoming the dualism between

23. Ibid., 38.

24. Jane Lubchenco, "Entering the Century of the Environment: A New Social Contract for Science," *Science* 279 (1998): 496.

25. Ibid., 495.

26. Ibid., 496.

27. Barbara Patterson, "Ethics for Wildlife Conservation: Overcoming the Human-Nature Dualism," *BioScience* 56, no. 2 (2006): 149.

humans and nature in much of Western society. Patterson writes, "Whereas the Western approach to nature has been a violent one focused on conquering nature, the Eastern approach has been characterized by respect for the rhythms, processes and phenomena of the natural world."[28]

British scientists Paul Jepson and Susan Canney recognize that values give the conservation movement relevance. People take action to protect nature, say Jepson and Canney, when arguments are framed in terms that resonate with the combination of imagination, feelings, and rationality that guide decision-making in our everyday lives.[29] *Biodiversity*, they argue, has become the label attached to conservation action. Although this term resonates with scientists, it does not "integrate with culture and does not represent the feelings, meanings and practices of everyday life." These authors call for using arguments based on aesthetics and ethics for their power. For example, the English Lake District, Yosemite, and Serengeti parks would never have been preserved had the arguments been based on abstract scientific concepts such as carbon sequestration and bioprospecting, rather than on the successful appeal to beauty, spirituality, and preservation of a sense of place.[30]

David Orr, a philosopher who has a regular column in the journal *Conservation Biology*, has written several provocative articles that address spirituality, values, and conservation. "God is dead, as Nietzsche would have it, but this belief has not resulted in any flowering of the human condition," he writes.[31] Because literature has been a primary means to develop greater moral imagination, conservation needs to develop a "literature of redemption" analogous to that of the southern writers who wrote about slavery and racism, argues Orr. "A literature of redemption made it possible for others to feel what it was like to be a slave or to be abused because of color." In much the same way, conservation biologists are engaged in a struggle to save

---

28. Ibid., 147.

29. Paul Jepson and Susan Canney, "Values-led Conservation, Global Ecology and Biogeography," *Global Ecology and Biogeography* 12, no. 4 (July 2003): 271.

30. Ibid., 273.

31. David Orr, "A Literature of Redemption," *Conservation Biology* 15, no. 2 (2001): 305.

diversity that "implicitly questions human domination of nature and the extent of our moral responsibilities."[32] He notes, however, that conservation lacks the "foundational documents" such as the Bible and the U.S. Constitution that were available to the Southern writers, but stops short of suggesting that specific foundational texts could be used to challenge power, as the Bible was used to address racism.

While Orr recognizes that "spiritual acumen" is required to solve our environmental and sustainability problems, this spiritual acumen "cannot be achieved with a return to some simplistic religious faith of an earlier time. It must be founded on a higher order of awareness that honors mystery, science, life and death." He continues, "A robust spiritual sense may not mean that we are created in the image of God, but it must offer hope that we may grow into something more than a planetary plague."[33]

Philosopher Kyle Van Houten, also drawing a parallel between success in overcoming racism and the ethical direction in which conservation and ecology need to move, suggests that abstract moral prescriptions are not enough. "To succeed as a social cause, conservation needs a hope that academic science itself cannot provide. Conservation needs a cultural legitimacy that inspires enthusiasm, allegiance, and personal sacrifice—in other words, actual changes in human behavior."[34] The practice of "the biblical tradition, in particular, named racism a problem and fanned the movement into a flame."[35] Enthusiasm and solidarity were legitimized, in other words, through the language and practices of Christianity. In contrast, he argues that the use of "socially generic recommendations" in conservation ethics helps to explain the "remarkable unpopularity" of conservation with the public. Conservation ethics instead must be expressed "in the language of social traditions if they are to be authentic and realized." Despite the contrast he draws between the success in addressing racism through its grounding in the

---

32. Ibid., 305–306.

33. David Orr, "Four Challenges of Sustainability," *Conservation Biology* 16, no 6 (2002): 1459.

34. Kyle S. Van Houten, "Conservation as Virtue: A Scientific and Social Process for Conservation," *Conservation Biology* 20, no. 5 (2006): 1371.

35. Ibid., 1370.

particularity of the Bible and Christianity and the abstract moral proscriptions of the much less successful conservation movement, he stops short of suggesting conservation engage specifically with Christianity. However, he does acknowledge that the challenge facing conservation is "to identify the dialect within particular traditions that names nature conservation a virtue."[36]

Though these examples illustrate the willingness and even eagerness of many ecologists to include spirituality as part of ecological ethics and to motivate change, they stop short of suggesting that ecologists engage religious communities directly. The question is whether these worthy and principled prescriptions are sufficient to motivate change and to be a political force for change, or are they, as Van Houten suggests, abstract moral prescriptions that do not inspire the hope and passion needed for change. In addition, there remains a "deep and somewhat virulent hostility" among some scientists to introducing spiritual and religious perspectives to the debate about sustainability, which impedes the wider acceptance of sustainable ways, writes Jonathan Porritt. The "critical inheritance" of religion, he says, "is deemed illegitimate by those who continue, quite forlornly, to exhort people to 'respect Nature' and 'consume responsibly' from the stony ground of stripped down secular materialism."[37]

Thus, it was striking when the prominent international science journal *Nature* published an editorial in 2006 that stated, "Scientists should welcome the recent move by leading Evangelicals to call for action on climate change." Because Americans are as a nation deeply devout, the editorial continues, "their [Evangelical] statement provides unprecedented opportunity for science to make a real impact on a broad segment of U.S. society." The editorial does not advocate a top-down, educate-the-public approach. Rather, it states, "The [climate-change] scientists should engage them [society] at every possible level, starting at their local church."[38]

Forest ecologist Nalani Nadkarni has put this suggestion into practice. Although acknowledging she is not particularly religious

---

36. Ibid., 1371.

37. Jonathon Porritt, "Sustainability without Spirituality: A Contradiction in Terms?" *Conservation Biology* 16, no. 6 (2002): 1465.

38. "A Warm Welcome," *Nature* 440 (2006): 128.

herself, she took a "church-by-synagogue-by-temple approach" to communicate about ecology and to engage people and help them learn how to be better stewards of the forest. She writes, "Although some scientists consider religion to fall outside of the way they understand the world, I thought that if I could communicate how people of different faiths describe trees in their own holy texts and in their own places of worship, I might inspire followers to learn about how to be better stewards of forest ecosystems." Thus, she visited a wide range of places of worship and delivered talks that she developed using the sacred texts particular to each religious tradition. Her approach also emphasizes two-way learning, as she learned about trees from each of these different faith perspectives as well. "By placing discussions

ALDO LEOPOLD

ALDO LEOPOLD (IMAGE © CORBIS)

Aldo Leopold is best known for his book *A Sand County Almanac*, published in 1949. He writes about the connection between people and nature and the application of ethics to land, combining a scientist's astute observation of the natural world with the ability to write about it lyrically and with feeling. *A Sand County Almanac* has become a classic in conservation—with his essay "The Land Ethic" one of the most widely quoted. Leopold was born in Iowa and educated at the Yale School of Forestry. He worked for the U.S. Forest Service from 1909 to 1933, when he joined the faculty at the University of Wisconsin. In addition to *A Sand County Almanac*, he wrote a classic textbook, *Game Management*, and dozens of articles.

about how crucial nature is to human well-being in settings outside the university, both the scientist and the non-scientist may be more open to exchanging ideas," she concludes.[39]

CONCLUSION

Effective action requires the involvement of faith communities because they are, as Bill McKibbon writes, the one remaining institution subversive enough to "make people doubt, even for a minute, the inevitability of their course in life."[40] This view does not ask that ecologists accept the faith position of Christianity or any religious faith, but it does suggest that for conservation to be an effective social movement, it needs to include all the cultural resources available, including religion. In 1949, Leopold wrote, "No important change in ethics was ever accomplished without an internal change in our intellectual emphasis, loyalties, affections, and convictions. The proof that conservation has not yet touched these foundations of conduct lies in the fact that philosophy and religion have not yet heard of it."[41] Religion, as will be amply explored in what follows, has now heard the message about conservation. The unanswered question is the extent to which the science of ecology will embrace this discovery.

QUESTIONS FOR REVIEW

1. In what ways is the scientific consensus on environmental problems reflected?
2. Explain two reasons scientists find it difficult to act jointly and effectively when attempting to address negative human impacts on the environment.
3. What point is illustrated by the plant dispersal example?

---

39. Nalani M. Nadkarni, "Ecological Outreach to Faith-Based Communities," *Frontiers in Ecology and the Environment* 6, no. 5 (2007): 332–333.

40. Bill McKibbon, "Creation Unplugged," *Region and Values in Public Life, The Center for the Study of Values in Public Life at Harvard Divinity School* 4, no. 2/3 (1996):19.

41. Leopold, *A Sand County Almanac*, 209–210.

4. What is needed, in addition to good science, to create and sustain an effective social movement in ecology?
5. What does David Orr mean by "literature of redemption," and why does he think the conservation movement needs to develop it?

IN-DEPTH QUESTIONS

1. Which, if any, environmental problems today satisfy M. C. Vanhengel and J. Peters's two conditions for something to be considered "signs of the times"? Why?
2. Describe an effort you are familiar with to solve an environmental problem. Was it effective? Why or why not?
3. What do you think are the possible strengths of recent calls by some scientists for scientists to engage specific faith traditions, such as Evangelical Protestants, Buddhists, and others, in seeking to address environmental problems? What are some weaknesses or concerns someone might raise about this effort?

CHAPTER 2

RESTORING CREATION AND REDRESSING THE PUBLIC SQUARE:

Religious Environmentalism and the Columbia River Pastoral

Michael Agliardo, SJ

KEY TERMS

conservationism
preservationism
protectionism
religious environmentalism
stewardship
Thomas Berry
framing
public sphere
National Religious Partnership for the Environment (NRPE)
Columbia River Pastoral Letter

INTRODUCTION

In the United States in the 1960s and 1970s, the involvement of religious communities in environmental issues was not something one could take for granted. This chapter reviews the recent history of the mainstream U.S. environmental movement, and in particular, the rise of religious environmentalism, noting the obstacles that had to be overcome so religious leaders could bring their various traditions to bear on contemporary environmental concerns. The chapter then examines one exemplary success of these efforts, the publication by the Catholic bishops of the Northwest of a pastoral letter on the care for the Columbia River Watershed. It concludes with some general reflections on the constructive role that religion can play in public life.

PROLOGUE

In 1984, Lutheran pastor and public intellectual Richard John Neuhaus wrote *The Naked Public Square*.[1] The book has since become a classic reference text in the ongoing debate concerning the place of religion in U.S. public life. Neuhaus warned against the proposition, advanced by some at the time, that religion be regarded as a purely private set of beliefs. By labeling religion "private," the idea was that talk to and about God be relegated to home and church, but when it came to public life, religion had to be silenced. Neuhaus, who later became a Catholic priest, warned that gagging religion in this way would be farcical, because religion is supremely relevant to the ethical and political decisions that people do in fact make in the United States. Beyond that, such gagging would be bad for democracy. Why? Because our finest insights regarding social justice and ethics have consistently come from our religious traditions. Neuhaus feared that if we stripped U.S. public life of the transcendent orientation and robust insights of biblical faith, public life would degenerate into little more than moral opportunism and ethical minimalism. While various constituencies grasped for their own rights, the meaning of freedom would devolve into the notion of allowing one to do anything so long as it did not interfere with the like prerogatives of others. Any sense of common vision or larger purpose would evaporate.

That Neuhaus would even have to make an argument in defense of the public role of religion speaks to the profound cultural transformation that has overtaken the United States since the 1960s. Prior to that period, religious leaders and religious rhetoric had been a part of every major social movement in U.S. history, from abolition to the temperance movement, from Depression-era relief policy to the civil rights movement. Although some religious interventions were noble and others regrettable, the fundamental importance of religious participation in public life was taken for granted. Since the 1960s, however, Americans have been rethinking the place of religion in culture and in public life. Though excluding religion from public life is a position as extreme as it is undemocratic, the facile assumption that

1. Richard John Neuhaus, *The Naked Public Square: Religion and Democracy in America* (Grand Rapids, MI: Eerdmans, 1984).

a particular tradition or set of religious ideas represents the moral consensus of society at large is no longer taken for granted, either. Just what role religion should play in public life remains a practical question to which Americans continue to hammer out the answer.

At the time when Neuhaus wrote *The Naked Public Square*, one public issue, environmentalism, attracted only peripheral attention from religious leaders. During the preceding decade and more, many church groups focused on social justice issues but failed to connect environmental concerns with them. Meanwhile, leaders of the U.S. environmental movement pursued a largely secular course, ignoring or even sidelining the potential involvement of religious groups. However, once religious leaders did take proenvironmental positions, they not only proved important allies for other environmentalists, but also added a dynamic to the public debate that was otherwise lacking. The history leading to religious involvement in environmental issues in the United States will be looked at in the following pages. One instance of such involvement, the Columbia River Pastoral Letter Project, will be cited as an example of the kind of contribution religious leaders can make to environmental debates. Overall, this history then illustrates some of the ways in which religion can contribute to public life in this post-sixties era.

ENVIRONMENTALISM AND MAINSTREAM RELIGION: DIFFERENT CAMPS?

Fundamentally speaking, environmental issues are perennial, and religious leaders have long brought the insights of faith to bear on them. Other contributors to this volume discuss the ecological implications of Scripture and Christian tradition. Yet, when first articulated, these insights were not viewed as forms of "environmentalism," and even now, the inherent environmental dimension of these insights is often overlooked. Likewise, many Native American religious traditions have important ecological dimensions, but these also were rarely viewed as forms of environmentalism per se. Because of the way ideas and actions are framed, we do not always recognize what becomes obvious when viewed from a different perspective. For example, a number of Christian groups in America have long promoted respect for the land and a simple way of life that has rich ecological implications we now readily recognize. One such group is the Catholic Rural Life Conference. Founded in 1923, this organization integrates respect for the land and a spirituality with profound ecological sentiment. Yet its story and impact are rarely included in standard accounts of American environmentalism.

In an earlier era, the main reason Native Americans and groups such as the Catholic Rural Life Conference were not classed as environmentalist had to do with how environmentalism was framed. Framing is an important notion in the social sciences, one associated with a number of different schools of thought. In brief, it derives from the insight that humans do not make sense of events and institutions in isolation. Rather, humans place such things in some framework or context within which they interpret their significance, and that framework has to be built. Framing is the construction and application of an interpretive framework, and it takes place in the midst of particular historical circumstances. How such a framework is built will vary according to time, place, and culture.

Accordingly, in the United States in the mid-twentieth century, environmentalism was framed in a certain way. At that time, when people referred to environmentalism, they had in mind activities associated with two broad, sometimes interrelated approaches, commonly labeled *conservationism* and *preservationism*. Conservationists were people who emphasized the careful management of natural resources with a view to long-term sustainability. Gifford Pinchot (1865–1946), a famed pioneer of the scientific management of natural resources, and the U.S. system of national forests that he helped to found exemplify the conservationist approach. Meanwhile, preservationists viewed nature not so much as a source of raw materials to be carefully managed for human consumption but rather as something to be appreciated in its own right and integrity. John Muir (1838–1914), the U.S. system of national parks, and the beautiful landscapes featured in Sierra Club calendars exemplify the preservationist ideal. Since the activities of Native Americans, of the Catholic Rural Life Conference, and of many other groups were not readily classed as conservationism or preservationism, they were not seen as environmentalism, even though from the broader perspectives people endeavor to employ today, the environmentalist dimension of these activities would be more readily apparent.

In the 1960s, a new frame emerged in the United States that soon came to dominate popular thinking regarding environmentalism: protectionism. Protectionism here refers not merely to protecting the environment "out there" but also more broadly to the idea of safeguarding the overall ecological health of a region, a circumstance upon which both human welfare and the welfare of the other denizens of the environment depend. The protectionist frame arose in response to the fear that we humans were destroying the very planet on which we live. Early in the 1960s, two developments in particular helped to galvanize U.S. citizens around this frame: the fear provoked by above-ground nuclear weapons testing, which released radioactive isotopes into the atmosphere, and the publication of Rachel Carson's *Silent Spring*, which analyzed the effect on nature and humans of the rampant use of insecticides (especially DDT).[2] As the decade continued to unfold, a number of environmental leaders waxed ominous—even apocalyptic—about the threat humans posed to nature and to themselves. The theme of self-destruction due to pollution, nuclear annihilation, overpopulation, resource depletion, and other social trends dominated the news and the popular imagination.

At the same time, as the sixties unfolded, some leaders of the mainstream environmental movement, which had never been deeply rooted in traditional religion to begin with, framed their agenda in increasingly secular or even anti-Christian terms. This eventually provoked various reactions, including some vocal religious leaders' returning the favor and dismissing environmentalism as a whole.

For one, as new organizations in the environmental movement took shape during this decade, they increasingly relied on science, organizational sophistication, and legal expertise. They looked to science, social science, and law as their *de facto* sources of authority and legitimation and not to religious leaders or religious tradition. Indeed, the environmentalism of the sixties shared a similar ethos with other social movements of the day, especially such movements as emerged on college campuses. Like these, they drew on the intellectual resources of the academy, which frequently inculcated a critical stance vis-à-vis tradition and established institutions. Hence, whereas many earlier U.S. social movements courted religious participation or

2. Rachel Carson, *Silent Spring* (Boston: Houghton Mifflin, 1962).

even were born in religious communities, those emerging in the sixties often took on a more secular cast.

Of course, secularity wears different stripes. For example, it may simply represent the neutral ground on which committed believers from a range of different traditions are able to stand together. Or it may reflect the view that the issues at stake are not religious in a decidedly relevant sense. It may indeed reflect a deliberate hostility toward religion as such. During the sixties, U.S. environmentalism was not always hostile to mainstream religion, but by the next decade, a certain estrangement had set in that went beyond the general anti-institutional ethos of the decade. Indeed, what happened to environmentalism in the sixties serves as a particular case study of how key sectors of society and mainstream religion can become estranged from one another.

It must be noted at the outset that even before the 1960s, when mainstream environmentalism did draw on religious themes, it did not always draw on mainstream institutional religion. John Muir, who was inspired by the transcendentalism of Ralph Waldo Emerson, is a case in point: throughout his extensive writings, Muir professed his dedication to "the Book of Nature"—and not the Bible—as a primary source of revelation about God. Similar spiritualities marked the environmentalism of the sixties and beyond. The groups associated with *deep ecology*, a term coined by the Norwegian philosopher Arne Naess in 1973, exemplify this tendency.[3] The perspective Naess crystallized became the inspiration for various forms of "earth-based spirituality," spirituality that revolves around finding the sacred in nature.

At the same time, other developments in the sixties made the divide between mainstream environmentalism and mainstream religion increasingly overt. In 1967, UCLA historian Lynn White Jr. published a pivotal essay in the widely read journal *Science* that heightened this divide.[4] White argued that "The Historical Roots of Our Ecologic Crisis" (to quote the title of his essay) derive from the

---

3. Arne Naess, "The Shallow and the Deep, Long-Range Ecology Movement: A Summary," *Inquiry* 16 (1973): 95–100.

4. Lynn White Jr., "The Historical Roots of Our Ecologic Crisis," *Science* 155, no. 3767 (1967): 1203–1207.

worldview of Judaism and Christianity. According to White, by viewing God as transcendent and humans as God's representatives with dominion over Earth, the Bible "demystified" nature (stripped it of religious significance) and reduced it to an object for human exploitation. Other authors in the environmental camp (such as Paul Ehrlich and Garrett Hardin) vigorously advanced views on population control, and some of the extreme solutions they proposed alarmed religious and civic leaders alike. Meanwhile, in 1968, Pope Paul VI published the encyclical *Humanae vitae* (*On Human Life*), which not only spoke out in defense of the dignity of human life but also went so far as to condemn artificial birth control. Given these developments, environmentalists and prominent Catholic spokespersons, in particular, found themselves locked in an increasingly acrimonious debate, especially over population issues. Meanwhile, some groups that drew on deep ecology, such as Earth First! (the exclamation mark is part of the group's name) eventually officially adopted non-Christian religious symbols in their publications to emphasize their break with conventional religion.[5] In response, some Christian fundamentalists eventually denounced environmentalism as nature worship and idolatry, even going so far in their rejection of "tree hugging" as to explicitly read Genesis in precisely the terms denounced by Lynn White Jr.

In the United States during the sixties and seventies, not only religious traditionalists held environmental causes at a distance. Many who considered themselves to be on the liberal end of mainstream religion also were reluctant to take up environmentalism because of their heavy investment in social justice causes. They noted that in the United States, environmental advocacy often advanced with little regard for the poor, rural peoples, indigenous peoples, or people in developing nations. For these religious advocates of social justice, human advancement was the priority, and environmentalism seemed a luxury for backpackers and stargazers. They could not embrace an environmentalism they felt disregarded or even pitted itself against human welfare.

---

5. For a discussion of this development, as well as this general trend in ecospirituality, see Bron Taylor, "Earth and Nature-Based Spirituality, Part I: From Deep Ecology to Radical Environmentalism," *Religion* 31, no. 2 (2001): 175–193, and "Earth and Nature-Based Spirituality, Part II: From Earth First! and Bioregionalism to Scientific Paganism and the New Age," *Religion* 31, no. 3 (2001): 225–245.

Again, this is an issue of social construction. In the United States as the terms were framed at the time, social justice and environmentalism were often seen as adversaries. By contrast, in many other societies, especially those that lacked the abundant resources and expansive frontier of the United States, social competition often involved competing claims over natural resources, and as a result, social justice issues often had a concomitant environmental dimension. Such is still the case in northern India, where industry competes with local farmers over access to water; in Brazil, where ranchers clear forest on which local and indigenous communities depend; and in the Philippines, where commercial fish farming leads to the destruction of coastal mangrove estuaries and the ecosystem that supports traditional fishermen. In these and other societies, environmental advocates habitually take up such issues as the commodification of land, deforestation, water pollution, erosion, and other environmental problems, with an eye toward how these problems affect the most disadvantaged people in society.

In sum, as the seventies unfolded, key voices in the mainstream religious and environmental communities in the United States had become increasingly estranged. Some environmentalists portrayed religion as justifying exploitation of Earth and irresponsible population growth. Meanwhile, some religious advocates criticized environmentalists as antihuman, antisocial, antireligious neo-pagans. The way these groups framed one another made it difficult for religious environmentalism to emerge in the United States. Indeed, to many observers, *religious environmentalism* seemed an oxymoron.

BUILDING BRIDGES: THE EMERGENCE OF THE NATIONAL RELIGIOUS PARTNERSHIP FOR THE ENVIRONMENT

Ultimately, the estrangement between mainstream religion and mainstream environmentalism in the United States hindered environmental progress. In fact, a number of groups attempted to capitalize on this estrangement to advance their own agendas—agendas that, in their view, environmentalists blocked. Such movements as the Sagebrush Rebellion (which emerged in 1980) and the Wise Use Agenda (1988) portrayed environmentalism and big government as foes allied in a struggle to undermine private property and the free market. As the Cold War wound down, some protagonists attempted to paint environmentalism as the new hiding place of erstwhile communists—the new threat to economic advancement and human freedom (which they argued were intrinsically intertwined). Some fundamentalist ministers echoed these themes, using them to attack those who in their view represented a threat to religion. In the process, they whipped up antienvironmentalism to rally religious conservatives who supported a free-market, anti-regulatory position. More recently, opposition to the Earth Charter,[6] a statement of broad principles in support of environmental sustainability and social justice, has attracted similar ire among religious traditionalists because they believe it promotes a worldview based on relativism and secular humanism. Again, free market proponents have stoked and exploited this ire to counter support for environmental causes.

Although some conservative religious voices bought into this counterpoising of religion and environmentalism, most major U.S. groups eventually rejected dichotomizing the two. Some critically reviewed the premises that pitted religion and environmentalism against each other in the first place. For example, a series of evangelical Protestants responded to White's essay in *Science* by arguing that rather than arbitrary "domination," the passage in Genesis that he cited gives humans "stewardship" over creation, a stewardship for which they are accountable to God. Properly understood, this passage grounds, rather than undermines, an authentic environmental ethic. In 1970, Francis Schaeffer's *Pollution and the Death of Man: The Christian View of Ecology* provided an early, comprehensive statement of the Evangelical position.[7] In addition, during the 1970s, the National Council of Churches and several of its member denominations developed national-level committees for promoting awareness of

---

6. The idea of an Earth Charter first surfaced in 1992 in connection with the Rio Earth Summit. However, drafting the version currently in circulation did not formally commence until 1994, when proposals in the United Nations bogged down. Then certain international elites such as Maurice Strong (former director of the United Nations Environmental Programme) and Mikhail Gorbachev (former president of the USSR) decided to pursue the charter as an initiative of civil society instead.

7. Francis A. Schaeffer, *Pollution and the Death of Man: The Christian View of Ecology* (Weaton, IL: Tyndale, 1970).

and action on environmental issues. The latter included the United Methodist Church, the Episcopal Church, the Presbyterian Church (PC USA), and the United Church of Christ. Notably, these committees integrated standing social justice perspectives into their ecological concerns. One important exemplar of this integration was a study sponsored by the United Church of Christ showing that toxic waste sites were disproportionately located near minority communities,[8] a finding that led to the development of the frame of *environmental racism*.

Since early in his pontificate, John Paul II also signaled his support for an environmental ethic. In 1979, he underscored the importance of ecological concerns by designating Saint Francis the patron of ecology (echoing, as it turns out, a call put forward in the closing line of White's 1967 essay). In several subsequent statements throughout the 1980s, John Paul II continued to address environmental issues.

U.S. Catholics were slow to mobilize around environmental issues, however. Rather, the statements of the National Conference of Catholic Bishops on war and peace (*The Challenge of Peace*, 1983) and the economy (*Economic Justice for All*, 1986) were representative of the concerns of the U.S. Catholic Church at the time. These were major position papers on issues confronting contemporary society, framed in terms of social justice concerns, but with little overt attention to the ecological dimensions of these issues. One notable exception to this trend in Catholic circles was Thomas Berry, a priest who founded the Riverdale Center of Religious Research in 1970. That center served as the institutional base for Berry's work of rethinking the place of humans amid life on Earth and in the cosmos in general. Berry's work eventually attracted a substantial following, especially among U.S. Catholic religious sisters.

By the late 1980s, environmentalism increasingly gained a place on the agenda of the U.S. Catholic Church. Catholic religious leaders and academics more and more turned their attention to environmental issues. In 1986, Catholic representatives, including Berry and members of the National Catholic Rural Life Committee,

---

8. Benjamin F. Chavis Jr. and Charles Lee, "Toxic Wastes and Race in the United States" (United Church of Christ Commission for Racial Justice, 1987).

collaborated with evangelicals and representatives of the National Council of Churches to form the North American Conference on Christianity and Ecology (NACCE). Catholics began to publish on environmental themes, among them Monsignor Charles Murphy of the Boston archdiocese, who wrote *At Home on Earth* in 1989.[9] Among the U.S. bishops, Los Angeles archbishop Roger Mahony was an important promoter of environmental concerns when he chaired the bishops' Domestic Policy Committee in the late eighties.[10] These people stressed not only the importance of religion for environmentalism but also of environmentalism for religion. Environmental concerns were not issues on which the Church could afford to remain silent. Thus, the ground was laid for a Catholic framework for religious environmentalism.

One leader working hard to overcome some of the past divides and mobilize the religious community around environmentalism was Paul Gorman. Gorman, a staff member of the Episcopal Cathedral of Saint John the Divine in New York City, together with the Cathedral's dean, James Parks Morton, conceived a bold plan to dramatize the need to bring religious leaders on board with the environmental movement. They enlisted Carl Sagan, the well-known astronomer and popularizer of science, to issue an appeal to the religious community to collaborate with science in addressing the ecological woes of our day. This "Appeal for Joint Commitment in Science and Religion," eventually signed by thirty-three prominent scientists and Nobel laureates, was issued in Moscow in January 1990.[11] A committee of five representatives of various faiths then solicited co-signatures from major religious leaders around the world.

---

9. Charles M. Murphy, *At Home on Earth: Foundations for a Catholic Ethic of the Environment* (New York: Crossroad, 1989).

10. This detail and many that follow concerning the work of the U.S. bishops, the formation of the National Religious Partnership for the Environment, and the Columbia River Pastoral Letter Project emerged in the course of research and interviews conducted by this author. See Michael Agliardo, "Public Catholicism and Religious Pluralism in America: The Adaptation of a Religious Culture to the Circumstance of Diversity, and its Implications" (doctoral dissertation in sociology, University of California–San Diego, 2008).

11. This appeal was issued at the Moscow meeting of the New York-based Global Forum of Spiritual and Parliamentary Leaders on Human Survival. It was hosted by no less a Global Forum member than Mikhail Gorbachev.

In the United States, the Moscow statement served as a precedent for the formation of the National Religious Partnership for the Environment (NRPE). After Gorman returned to the United States, he became the director of the Joint Appeal of Religion and Science for the Environment. Over the next two years, with the support of then-senator Al Gore, among others, Gorman organized a series of conferences in Washington that brought together religious figures, congressional leaders, scientists, and the heads of major U.S. environmental organizations. Religious leaders affirmed their commitment to addressing the ecological woes of the age. Environmental leaders such as Carl Pope, executive director of the Sierra Club, admitted that their earlier failure to reach out to religion had been counterproductive.[12] Not only had they failed to garner support from the religious community, they also had made it easy for their opponents to frame environmentalism as the foe of religion. In the wake of these meetings, Gorman secured a series of grants to fund the NRPE, which was initially set up for three years as a resource center in support of the major U.S. faiths as they grappled with the environmental issues of the day. The NRPE was launched in September 1993.

By this time, the path had been paved for U.S. Catholic participation in the NRPE. As noted above, then-archbishop Mahony had already urged the U.S. bishops to initiate consultations on the Church and the environment. Even before the Moscow statement, John Paul II had made ecology the theme of his 1990 World Day of Peace message. In 1991, the National Conference of Catholic Bishops issued its response to the pope's concerns with the pastoral letter "Renewing the Earth."[13] In the talks that Gorman helped to foster among religious, political, and environmental leaders, James Malone, bishop of Youngstown, represented the Catholic bishops. Once the NRPE took shape, the bishops established their Environmental Justice Program as a partner institution and as their standing mechanism for addressing environmental concerns.

---

12. Carl Pope, "Religion and the Environment" (talk given at the Symposium on Religion, Science and the Environment, Santa Barbara, California, November 8, 1997) at *http://www.christianecology.org/CarlPope.html*, accessed June 4, 2008.

13. National Conference of Catholic Bishops, "Renewing the Earth: An Invitation to Reflection and Action on the Environment in Light of Catholic Social Teaching" (Washington, DC: United States Catholic Conference, 1991).

In addition to the Environmental Justice Program of the Catholic bishops, the NRPE had three other partners: the National Council of Churches, the Consultation on the Environment and Jewish Life, and the Evangelical Environmental Network. From the start, the NRPE was meant to be a support for member organizations in their work for the environment. It was a place for religious leaders to come together, learn about the issues, learn from one another, secure funding, and then develop educational materials and programs suited to their respective constituencies and religious traditions. Each partner pursued only such joint activities as seemed advisable to its members. The NRPE rarely sponsored joint statements or programs in its own right.

This loose, collaborative structure allowed the NRPE to avoid the kinds of controversies that had fractured the earlier NACCE. The NACCE had foundered almost from the outset. The stumbling block was its attempt to craft a consensus statement regarding religion and environmental issues. Though more traditional Christians sought to root their efforts in the Bible, others such as Thomas Berry envisioned a broader collaboration among all religious groups in support of an expansive religious-ecological vision. The NACCE was not able to advance a consensus that could include both camps; neither could it develop a flexible enough structure to accommodate their diversity. By contrast, because it supported members' efforts to root their activism in their own traditions, the NRPE succeeded when the NACCE had foundered.

RELIGIOUS LEADERS WADE INTO THE COLUMBIA RIVER DEBATES

According to the terms of the NRPE, each member constituency received an equal amount of funding, and each was free to design its own activities. The activities sponsored by the Environmental Justice Program (EJP)of the Catholic bishops fell into four broad categories: (1) public policy, (2) education, (3) leadership development, and (4) grants for local projects. Under public policy, staff pursued research so that the Domestic Policy Committee could be properly informed regarding select issues (such as climate change). When advisable, staff and committee members could then represent the bishops' views before Congress and appropriate government agencies. Under education, the EJP produced materials to be distributed to Catholic parishes throughout the United States. These materials made the crucial link between environmental issues and the Church's social justice teaching. Under leadership development, the EJP sponsored a number of initiatives, including conferences for scholars whose work touched on things Catholic; these scholars were encouraged to integrate environmentalism into their areas of research. The EJP also sponsored regional retreats for diocesan staff to learn about and pray over the call to Christian environmental responsibility. It also sponsored an advisory meeting on environmental issues at the national-level conference for Catholic diocesan social action directors held each year. Finally, the office provided grants to support environmental efforts sponsored by local dioceses.

One of the regional meetings sponsored by the EJP took place in 1995 at Mount Angel Abbey, a religious community and seminary complex about 30 miles south of Portland. That meeting brought together staff of the Oregon and Washington State Catholic Conferences (the public policy arms for the bishops of their respective states), representatives of the local dioceses, professors from Catholic universities in the region, and people from the EJP office in Washington, D.C. Papers were given and participants reflected on the contribution the Church could make to the ecological well-being of the region. In the end, the meeting proved to be the seedbed for a five-year project in which Catholic leaders of the region wrestled with its environmental issues. In doing so, they made a distinctive contribution to the public life of the region.

According to one meeting participant, Russ Butkus, a theologian at the University of Portland, the impetus for undertaking an environmental project arose not from a particular issue that begged addressing, so much as from the search for a way to bring Catholic faith and social teaching to bear on environmental concerns generally. Participants thought that wrestling with concrete issues would serve to deepen the Church's environmental theology at this early stage in its development. They also sought to encourage local Catholics to appreciate the ways in which environmental issues were also religious issues. At the same time, they did not want to pursue this activity simply as an in-house Catholic exercise. Instead, they envisioned an exercise in communal reflection that would contribute to the public life of the region. In other words, they were convinced that Catholic theology could also be a resource for the wider public.

In the end, the staff of the Oregon and Washington State Catholic Conferences settled on the Columbia River as the apt focus for their efforts. The reasons for their choice were both symbolic and practical. On a symbolic level, they noted that in the Bible, water represents life, birth, and renewal. On a practical level, the Columbia River knit together the region ecologically; it was also at the heart of a nexus of problems that bedeviled the region. These issues included the fate of the dams that interrupted the natural flow of the river and the migration of the region's salmon, nuclear contamination from the aging plant at Hanford, mining and use of pesticides in the region, struggles over access to water resources, and the significance of the Columbia as the center of the cultural life of Native Americans of the area. The fate of the Columbia thus had significant ecological, economic, cultural, and religious implications. Disputes over the relevant issues had set different constituencies in the region at odds with one another. Under the leadership of William Skylstad, the bishop of Spokane, the bishops of the Northwest set course to wade into these issues.

A steering committee for what came to be known as the Columbia River Pastoral Letter Project was eventually formed, and in 1997, it began applying for funding. One of its first contributions was an EJP regional grant. The project then unfolded in four phases. The first phase was designated "Reading the 'Signs of the Times'/ Reading the River." During this phase, the project's steering committee endeavored to acquaint itself with the concrete history and circumstances of the ecoregion: its geological and human history, its economic life, local environmental-management policies, the region's cultural life, and so forth. In pursuing this course, committee members followed the proposal in *Gaudium et spes* (The Church in the Modern World, one of the key documents that emerged from the Second Vatican Council), which, as discussed in chapter 1, urged the Church in its pastoral work to take into account the concrete circumstances of contemporary humans ("the signs of the times"). Much of the activity during this phase took place in the form of "readings" (conferences) held in different cities throughout the region. Each of the readings was organized around a particular issue, and people on all sides of each issue were invited to "testify," that is, bear witness and provide input.

During the second phase of the project, the steering committee reflected on the information gathered during the first phase, bringing to bear not only Catholic social teaching but also Catholic spirituality, Native American spirituality, and relevant theological and spiritual resources of the region. Out of these reflections came "The Columbia River Watershed: Realities and Possibilities," a transitional document summing up the process thus far.[14] This document was released to the public, bringing a wider range of people into the process. The third phase then involved listening sessions in which the larger public offered feedback to the transitional document. After two subsequent internal drafts, the final draft, entitled "The Columbia River Watershed: Caring for Creation," was released on February 22, 2001.[15] A fourth phase, involving implementation of the document among the seven dioceses that sponsored it, was to take off from there.

This process was in many ways similar to that which the entire U.S. episcopate pursued when it published the aforementioned pastoral letters on war and peace (1983) and on the economy (1986). In both cases, rather than practicing theology in the abstract, the bishops embarked on a process involving reflection on the concrete issues of the day. They scheduled extensive meetings in which they gathered information and opinions from a wide range of relevant experts. They released drafts of their reflections for public commentary. They also explored the relationship between broader religious and ethical commitments on the one hand and practical problems on the other. By making this connection, the bishops challenged the supposition

---

14. Columbia River Pastoral Letter Project, "The Columbia River Watershed: Realities and Possibilities: A Reflection in Preparation for a Pastoral Letter" (Seattle: Columbia River Pastoral Letter Project, 1999). This author obtained a copy from Sr. Sharon Park, OP, of the Washington State Catholic Conference.

15. Columbia River Watershed Catholic Bishops, "The Columbia River Watershed: Caring for Creation and the Common Good—An International Pastoral Letter by the Bishops of the Region" (Seattle: Columbia River Pastoral Letter Project, 2001), at *http://www.columbiariver.org/files/pastoral-english.pdf*, accessed May 24, 2008.

that theology was an abstract set of principles relevant only to private prayer and personal morality. Moreover, by inviting such widespread participation, they also countered the perception that it involved some obscure process in which truth was handed down from on high. The process they pursued was very open and very public.

In the end, the U.S. bishops' pastoral letters on nuclear weapons and on the economy provoked both approbation and objection from many quarters. So did the Columbia River pastoral letter. There were those who feared from the outset that the bishops would not understand the realities of economic life in the Pacific Northwest and instead favor every other environmental and moralistic cause that pleaded for a hearing. Others objected that the bishops were not experts on environmental science and that they should stick to their own area of competence. In response, the bishops made it clear that they were not attempting to adjudicate the fundamental questions facing society but rather to contribute to the public debate surrounding those questions. They also acknowledged that many issues they were reflecting on fell outside their areas of expertise and authority. At the same time, they pointed out that as pastors in the region, they had a legitimate concern for its well-being. Indeed, whereas people who were tied to this or that economic interest often suffered a corresponding bias, the bishops were pastors to people on all sides of the debate, from miners and nuclear scientists to members of the environmental community and Native Americans. Moreover, there were moral and religious dimensions to all the issues upon which they were reflecting. Those dimensions were what they were trying to address. Hence, they had not only a right and competence to speak out but also a positive responsibility.

The main outcome of this project, the Columbia River pastoral letter, was a remarkable document—one that is still cited as an example of the kind of contribution that religion can make to ecological reflection and to public life more generally. Several points about the document should be noted: First, the bishops did take to heart that they were contributing to a larger process, not trying to resolve it or run society. The letter has a deliberate, reflective, dialogical tone. Second, the bishops also took to heart that their competence was limited to being moral and religious authorities, not environmental scientists or economists. Third, they did not want to produce a document with a limited shelf life. Instead, they sought to outline principles that would outlive this or that particular concrete issue. For this reason, although they reflected on a range of concrete issues, in the end, the document they published was a broader reflection on community and ecological responsibility rather than a detailed analysis of those concrete issues. Fourth, the bishops took it upon themselves to inject into the issues several dimensions that had been lacking. Not only did they place these issues in a larger theological framework but also their pastoral letter stressed how all the different constituencies in the region—stakeholders who often saw themselves at odds with one another—were also members of a larger community, people with a shared history and a shared stake in the ecological health of the region. This last insight addressed a key goal of the letter: bringing people together so they could constructively resolve the contentious issues polarizing the region. Overall, insofar as the project was meant to explore how religion can contribute to public life, it did not exhaust all the possibilities, but it provided one model worthy of study.

Press coverage of the stages of the Columbia River Pastoral Letter Project underscored the public significance of the effort. Newspapers in the region reliably covered various developments relating to the project, and others farther afield picked up its major contours. When the transitional document came out, *The Salt Lake Tribune* published two articles that delved into religious questions raised by the pastoral, as well as the significance of pastoral letters as vehicles for social teaching. *The Los Angeles Times* observed that the pastoral "reflects a growing determination by the church to inject issues of ethics, social justice and spiritual stewardship into what has historically been a debate about economics and the environment." Mark O'Keefe, writing for the Portland *Oregonian*, held out this hope for the pastoral:

> Because new theology leads to new behavior and new alliances, this greening of Christianity eventually could influence such issues as salmon recovery, dam management, cattle grazing and nuclear waste. It could provide a spiritual language to describe the epiphany many experience hiking in the Columbia River Gorge or fly-fishing in an Oregon

A family hikes along the Columbia River in northwestern United States.

> stream, no matter what their religion. And it could give fresh energy to an environmental movement that often suggests what we should do about the Earth without communicating why.[16]

When the final letter came out, it also received coverage throughout the West. Some coverage took a community-interest angle: One group in the community (which happens to be a religious group) has come out to stress humans' role as stewards of the environment. In other coverage, reporters delved into the stewardship ethic itself and its religious undergirding. In doing so, they underscored the relevance of that theme for the reading public. While the secular press was not as finely attuned to the theological nuances of the transitional and final documents as the Catholic press, overall the secular press took the documents as seriously as it did their potential effect on the life of the region. In addition, the Columbia River pastoral letter was for a time regularly cited in national coverage when reporters

16. Mark O'Keefe, "On God's Greener Earth," *The Oregonian*, May 16, 1999, B02.

were reviewing the ways in which religion was "advocating for the environment" or "going green."

Projects such as that which produced the Columbia River pastoral letter brought religious environmentalism into being and showed concretely what form it can take. They forged links where there had been division. Not only do such efforts bring together religion and environmental issues; they also can bring together stakeholders who have previously been at odds. Joel Sisolak, director of the Seattle-based organization "Friends of the Cedar River Watershed," provides an example of the importance of these linkages. Sisolak confided that at one time, when he appeared before Catholic parishes to ask that they support the restoration work of his organization, he had to argue that this was relevant to their life as a religious community. After the Columbia River pastoral letter had been published, he no longer had to do so. The case had been made.

RELIGION IN PUBLIC LIFE: A VITAL CONTRIBUTION

The practical difference that religious participation in environmental causes makes remains to be measured. Will the "ascetic" dimension of religion inspire citizens to make greater sacrifices for the environment than they otherwise would? Will the transcendent framework of religion enable people to more meaningfully integrate environmentalism into their individual lives and philosophies? Will religious groups provide crucial support for legislation and public initiatives? These remain open questions. However, it is clear that a qualitative shift has been accomplished. A divide has been healed. Once an oxymoron to some, "religious environmentalism" is now more or less taken for granted.

By articulating what religious environmentalism is all about, religious groups have shown how ecology is a religious issue in its own right. They have brought out the religious significance of what had often been seen as "merely" economic, environmental, or managerial issues. In doing so, they have also underscored the public significance of "private" religious perspectives.

In addition, the Columbia River Pastoral Letter Project demonstrated that religion has a unique capacity to bring people together. In commenting on the efforts of the bishops, John Harrison of the Northwest Power Planning Council noted how important it was to have them stake their moral authority on attempting an unbiased perspective amid debates that seemed to admit no center ground.[17] It often turns out that because religion is a cross-cutting, long-term involvement, people on all sides of a given local issue belong to the same religious community. Not only does that enable religion to serve as a common, overarching frame upon which all can draw, but also it empowers pastors to better serve as honest brokers in public debate.

The Columbia River Pastoral Letter Project exemplified another important role of religion in public life. Social theorists such as Jürgen Habermas argue that modern democracies suffer when issues before the community are transformed into technical problems to be handed over to "experts" for resolution. Then issues become dissociated from the "life world" (ordinary concerns) of people. As a result, it is more likely the issues will be adjudicated by power and money rather than by open debate and rational reflection.[18] Religion, on the other hand, draws on concerns that are closer to home. As a result, the efforts of religious leaders and the language of religion can reconnect ordinary people to the issues that are at stake in complex debates. The bishops of the Northwest took the time to sort through the issues and do just that.

In the modern era, religion has had to adapt to a different place in society than it held previously in the West. In an earlier era, "traditional" society had its official religion, and with it came an official ethical and moral framework for that society. The United States was the first nation in history to officially disestablish religion from the state, setting what became the pattern for the contemporary West. However, that did not mean religion was banished from public life. The United States also

17. "This is so often a debate between biologists and economists who have an economic interest in the river, and you simply don't know who to believe. What has been lacking for the most part is this sense of morality religious leaders can bring," said Harrison, who was speaking for himself, not the council. Mark O'Keefe, "Bishops Raise Morality Issue for Columbia: A Draft Pastoral Letter Views the Watershed as a 'Sacramental Commons' in Need of Guidance," *The Oregonian*, May 12, 1999, A01.

18. Habermas developed these ideas in *The Theory of Communicative Action*, 2 vols. (Boston: Beacon Press, 1984, 1987).

created a limited state, thereby opening that space for public debate and public life known as "civil society." U.S. citizens are free to form civic, cultural, and religious associations of all stripes, and those groups have a freedom to influence policy and to debate the common good in a way that was previously unknown. The Columbia River Pastoral Letter Project exemplified one way in which religion was able to make a positive contribution to a vital concern in society today.

In the present day, the divide between mainstream religion and the environmental community has been rethought. Religious leaders have affirmed their right and their duty to speak out on environmental issues. They have laid the foundation for an authentic religious environmentalism. Building on this foundation is the work of the present generation.

QUESTIONS FOR REVIEW

1. Theorists who emphasize social constructivism point out that issues in society are not just "given." We come at them with particular assumptions from a particular angle. How issues are viewed emerges from a given social history. How was environmentalism constructed in the United States in the mid-twentieth century? How did the U.S. understanding of environmentalism grow and change during the 1960s and 1970s?
2. The case of environmentalism during the 1960s and 1970s is one instance of the secularization of public life in the United States. What were some of the factors that originally alienated the environmental movement and many mainstream religious communities from one another?
3. Certain opponents of the environmental movement in the United States tried to recruit religious groups, especially conservative Christians, to their cause. What position did they espouse? What made them assume they could find allies among certain religious conservatives?
4. What important dimension of environmental issues did religious groups emphasize? How had this been neglected or underplayed by traditional mainstream environmental groups for much of the history of the U.S. environmental movement?

5. What is the National Religious Partnership for the Environment, and when was it founded?
6. What contribution did the Columbia River Pastoral Letter make to the environmental debates of the Pacific Northwest? What does this demonstrate about the positive role that religion can play in public life?

IN-DEPTH QUESTIONS

1. Environmental issues can be socially constructed in purely biological and ecological terms, and they can be constructed as social justice issues as well. Likewise, environmental issues can be constructed in secular terms, and they can be constructed with an explicit religious dimension. The Columbia River Pastoral Letter Project was an effort to do just that—to reconstruct environmentalism as a religious issue. What are some of the ways you might reframe environmental issues to bring out their religious dimension?
2. If environmental issues, which were once viewed by Christians in the United States as alien territory, turn out to have an important Christian dimension, what might that say about other issues that are viewed as the provenance of purely secular considerations?
3. Must religious groups resolve all their theological differences before they can collaborate on issues of common concern such as environmental issues? What does the history of the National Religious Partnership for the Environment teach us in that regard?
4. The Columbia River pastoral letter was not written to address a particular environmental issue or realize a particular political outcome. It "merely" aimed to stimulate the "religious imagination" of the citizenry of the Pacific Northwest, Catholic and non-Catholic alike, so they could better grasp the religious dimension of the range of environmental issues the region faced. Does that mean for religion to participate in public life, it should only offer general moral and religious considerations but never specific policy recommendations?
5. Is the political arena the only place religious groups can or must operate to make a difference in regard to environmental issues?

CHAPTER 3

IF YOU WANT TO CULTIVATE PEACE, PROTECT CREATION:

Message for the 2010 World Day of Peace

Pope Benedict XVI

KEY TERMS

Rerum novarum
integral human development
environmental refugees
solidarity
prudence
principle of subsidiarity
human ecology
ecocentrism

EDITOR'S NOTE

On July 24, 2007, the online magazine *Grist* posted an article featuring "15 Green Religious Leaders," among them, Pope Benedict XVI. Indeed, from the beginning of his papacy in 2005, the pope has frequently spoken on the topic of care for creation—especially in his addresses to young people. In his social encyclical *Caritas in veritate* (Charity in Truth), which was issued on June 29, 2009, and addressed the world's economic crisis, Benedict devoted five paragraphs to environmental problems and humanity's responsibility for them. He followed this on January 1, 2010, with his Message for the Celebration of the World Day of Peace, "If You Want to Cultivate Peace, Protect Creation." In that message, reprinted here with the Vatican's permission, Benedict identified care for the environment as a significant moral issue for Catholics and the world. The pope's thinking is already affecting Catholic thinking about ecology, as evidenced in several chapters in this volume. In addition, under Benedict's watch, the Vatican recently installed 2,700 solar panels on the roof of the 10,000-seat Pope Paul VI Auditorium and is considering similar installations for other buildings. Even the pope's home near Regensburg, Germany, has had solar panels installed. The Vatican, moreover, is exploring ways to offset its carbon dioxide emissions, and through these efforts, it is expected to become the world's first sovereign state that can claim to be carbon neutral.

■ ■ ■

1. At the beginning of this New Year, I wish to offer heartfelt greetings of peace to all Christian communities, international leaders, and people of good will throughout the world. For this XLIII World Day of Peace I have chosen the theme: *If You Want to Cultivate Peace, Protect Creation*. Respect for creation is of immense consequence, not least because "creation is the beginning and the foundation of all God's works,"[1] and its preservation has now become essential for the pacific coexistence of mankind. Man's inhumanity to man has given rise to numerous threats to peace and to authentic and integral human development—wars, international and regional conflicts, acts of terrorism, and violations of human rights. Yet no less troubling are the threats arising from the neglect—if not downright misuse—of the earth and the natural goods that God has given us. For this reason, it is imperative that mankind renew and strengthen "that covenant between human beings and the environment, which should mirror the creative love of God, from whom we come and towards whom we are journeying."[2]

2. In my Encyclical *Caritas in veritate*, I noted that integral human development is closely linked to the obligations which flow from *man's relationship with the natural environment*. The environment must be seen as God's gift to all people, and the use we make of it entails a shared responsibility for all humanity, especially the poor and future generations. I also observed that whenever nature, and human beings

1. *Catechism of the Catholic Church*, 198.

2. Benedict XVI, Message for the 2008 World Day of Peace, 7.

in particular, are seen merely as products of chance or an evolutionary determinism, our overall sense of responsibility wanes.[3] On the other hand, seeing creation as God's gift to humanity helps us understand our vocation and worth as human beings. With the Psalmist, we can exclaim with wonder: "When I look at your heavens, the work of your hands, the moon and the stars which you have established; what is man that you are mindful of him, and the son of man that you care for him?" (Ps 8:4–5). Contemplating the beauty of creation inspires us to recognize the love of the Creator, that Love which "moves the sun and the other stars."[4]

3. Twenty years ago, Pope John Paul II devoted his Message for the World Day of Peace to the theme: *Peace with God the Creator, Peace with All of Creation*. He emphasized our relationship, as God's creatures, with the universe all around us. "In our day," he wrote, "there is a growing awareness that world peace is threatened . . . also by a lack of *due respect for nature*." He added that "*ecological awareness,* rather than being downplayed, needs to be helped to develop and mature, and find fitting expression in concrete programs and initiatives."[5] Previous popes had spoken of the relationship between human beings and the environment. In 1971, for example, on the eightieth anniversary of Leo XIII's Encyclical *Rerum novarum* [Rights and Duties of Capital and Labor], Paul VI pointed out that "by an ill-considered exploitation of nature (man) risks destroying it and becoming in his turn the victim of this degradation." He added that "not only is the material environment becoming a permanent menace—pollution and refuse, new illnesses and absolute destructive capacity—but the human framework is no longer under man's control, thus creating an environment for tomorrow which may well be intolerable. This is a wide-ranging social problem which concerns the entire human family."[6]

4. Without entering into the merit of specific technical solutions, the Church is nonetheless concerned, as an "expert in humanity," to call

3. Cf. Benedict XVI, *Caritas in veritate* (Charity in Truth), no. 48.

4. Dante Alighieri, *The Divine Comedy, Paradiso*, XXXIII, 145.

5. John Paul II, Message for the 1990 World Day of Peace, 1.

6. Paul VI, *Octogesima Adveniens* (Apostolic Letter of Pope Paul VI), 21.

attention to the relationship between the Creator, human beings and the created order. In 1990, John Paul II had spoken of an "ecological crisis" and, in highlighting its primarily ethical character, pointed to the "urgent moral need for a new solidarity."[7] His appeal is all the more pressing today, in the face of signs of a growing crisis, which it would be irresponsible not to take seriously. Can we remain indifferent before the problems associated with such realities as climate change, desertification, the deterioration and loss of productivity in vast agricultural areas, the pollution of rivers and aquifers, the loss of biodiversity, the increase of natural catastrophes and the deforestation of equatorial and tropical regions? Can we disregard the growing phenomenon of "environmental refugees," people who are forced by the degradation of their natural habitat to forsake it—and often their possessions as well—in order to face the dangers and uncertainties of forced displacement? Can we remain impassive in the face of actual and potential conflicts involving access to natural resources? All these are issues with a profound impact on the exercise of human rights, such as the right to life, food, health, and development.

5. It should be evident that the ecological crisis cannot be viewed in isolation from other related questions, since it is closely linked to the notion of development itself and our understanding of man in his relationship to others and to the rest of creation. Prudence would thus dictate a *profound, long-term review of our model of development*, one which would take into consideration the meaning of the economy and its goals with an eye to correcting its malfunctions and misapplications. The ecological health of the planet calls for this, but it is also demanded by the cultural and moral crisis of humanity whose symptoms have for some time been evident in every part of the world.[8] Humanity needs a *profound cultural renewal;* it needs to *rediscover those values which can serve as the solid basis* for building a brighter future for all. Our present crises—be they economic, food-related, environmental or social—are ultimately also moral crises, and all of them are interrelated. They require us to rethink the path which we are traveling together. Specifically, they call for a lifestyle marked

---

7. John Paul II, Message for the 1990 World Day of Peace, 10.

8. Cf. Benedict XVI, *Caritas in veritate*, 32.

by sobriety and solidarity, with new rules and forms of engagement, one which focuses confidently and courageously on strategies that actually work, while decisively rejecting those that have failed. Only in this way can the current crisis become an *opportunity for discernment and new strategic planning.*

6. Is it not true that what we call "nature" in a cosmic sense has its origin in "a plan of love and truth"? The world "is not the product of any necessity whatsoever, nor of blind fate or chance. . . . The world proceeds from the free will of God; he wanted to make his creatures share in his being, in his intelligence, and in his goodness."[9] The Book of Genesis, in its very first pages, points to the wise design of the cosmos: it comes forth from God's mind and finds its culmination in man and woman, made in the image and likeness of the Creator to "fill the earth" and to "have dominion over" it as "stewards" of God himself (cf. Gen 1:28). The harmony between the Creator, mankind and the created world, as described by Sacred Scripture, was disrupted by the sin of Adam and Eve, by man and woman, who wanted to take the place of God and refused to acknowledge that they were his creatures. As a result, the work of "exercising dominion" over the earth, "tilling it and keeping it," was also disrupted, and conflict arose within and between mankind and the rest of creation (cf. Gen 3:17–19). Human beings let themselves be mastered by selfishness; they misunderstood the meaning of God's command and exploited creation out of a desire to exercise absolute domination over it. But the true meaning of God's original command, as the *Book of Genesis* clearly shows, was not a simple conferral of authority, but rather a summons to responsibility. The wisdom of the ancients had recognized that nature is not at our disposal as "a heap of scattered refuse."[10] Biblical Revelation made us see that nature is a gift of the Creator, who gave it an inbuilt order and enabled man to draw from it the principles needed to "till it and keep it" (cf. Gen 2:15).[11] Everything that exists belongs to God, who has entrusted it to man,

9. *Catechism of the Catholic Church*, 295.

10. Heraclitus of Ephesus (c. 535–c. 475 B.C.), Fragment 22B124, in H. Diels-W. Kranz, Die Fragmente der Vorsokratiker, Weidmann, Berlin, 1952, 6th ed.

11. Cf. Benedict XVI, *Caritas in veritate*, 48.

albeit not for his arbitrary use. Once man, instead of acting as God's co-worker, sets himself up in place of God, he ends up provoking a rebellion on the part of nature, "which is more tyrannized than governed by him."[12] Man thus has a duty to exercise responsible stewardship over creation, to care for it and to cultivate it.[13]

7. Sad to say, it is all too evident that large numbers of people in different countries and areas of our planet are experiencing increased hardship because of the negligence or refusal of many others to exercise responsible stewardship over the environment. The Second Vatican Council reminded us that "God has destined the earth and everything it contains for all peoples and nations."[14] The goods of creation belong to humanity as a whole. Yet the current pace of environmental exploitation is seriously endangering the supply of certain natural resources not only for the present generation, but above all for generations yet to come.[15] It is not hard to see that environmental degradation is often due to the lack of far-sighted official policies or to the pursuit of myopic economic interests, which then, tragically, become a serious threat to creation. To combat this phenomenon, economic activity needs to consider the fact that "every economic decision has a moral consequence"[16] and thus show increased respect for the environment. When making use of natural resources, we should be concerned for their protection and consider the cost entailed—environmentally and socially—as an essential part of the overall expenses incurred. The international community and national governments are responsible for sending the right signals in order to combat effectively the misuse of the environment. To protect the environment, and to safeguard natural resources and the climate, there is a need to act in accordance with clearly-defined rules, also from the juridical and economic standpoint, while at the same time taking into due

12. John Paul II, *Centesimus annus* [Evangelical Letter on the Hundredth Anniversary of *Rerum novarum*], 37.

13. Cf. Benedict XVI, *Caritas in veritate*, 50.

14. Pastoral Letter *Gaudium et spes*, 69.

15. Cf. John Paul II, *Sollicitudo rei socialis* (The Concern [of the Church] for the Social Order), 34.

16. Benedict XVI, *Caritas in veritate*, 37.

account the solidarity we owe to those living in the poorer areas of our world and to future generations.

8. *A greater sense of intergenerational solidarity* is urgently needed. Future generations cannot be saddled with the cost of our use of common environmental resources. "We have inherited from past generations, and we have benefited from the work of our contemporaries; for this reason we have obligations towards all, and we cannot refuse to interest ourselves in those who will come after us, to enlarge the human family. Universal solidarity represents a benefit as well as a duty. *This is a responsibility that present generations have towards those of the future*, a responsibility that also concerns individual States and the international community."[17] Natural resources should be used in such a way that immediate benefits do not have a negative impact on living creatures, human and not, present and future; that the protection of private property does not conflict with the universal destination of goods;[18] that human activity does not compromise the fruitfulness of the earth, for the benefit of people now and in the future. In addition to a fairer sense of intergenerational solidarity there is also an urgent moral need for a renewed sense of *intragenerational solidarity*, especially in relationships between developing countries and highly industrialized countries: "the international community has an urgent duty to find institutional means of regulating the exploitation of non-renewable resources, involving poor countries in the process, in order to plan together for the future."[19] *The ecological crisis shows the urgency of a solidarity which embraces time and space*. It is important to acknowledge that among the causes of the present ecological crisis is the historical responsibility of the industrialized countries. Yet the less developed countries, and emerging countries in particular, are not exempt from their own responsibilities with regard to creation, for the duty of gradually adopting effective environmental measures and policies is incumbent upon all. This would be accomplished more easily if self-interest played a lesser role in the granting of aid and the sharing of knowledge and cleaner technologies.

17. Pontifical Council for Justice and Peace, *Compendium of the Social Doctrine of the Church*, 467; cf. Paul VI, *Populorum progressio* [On the Development of Peoples], 17.

18. Cf. John Paul II, *Centesimus annus*, 30–31, 43.

19. Benedict XVI, *Caritas in veritate*, 49.

9. To be sure, among the basic problems which the international community has to address is that of energy resources and the development of joint and sustainable strategies to satisfy the energy needs of the present and future generations. This means that technologically advanced societies must be prepared to encourage more sober lifestyles, while reducing their energy consumption and improving its efficiency. At the same time there is a need to encourage research into, and utilization of, forms of energy with lower impact on the environment and "a world-wide redistribution of energy resources, so that countries lacking those resources can have access to them."[20] The ecological crisis offers an historic opportunity to develop a common plan of action aimed at orienting the model of global development towards greater respect for creation and for an integral human development inspired by the values proper to charity in truth. I would advocate the adoption of a model of development based on the centrality of the human person, on the promotion and sharing of the common good, on responsibility, on a realization of our need for a changed life-style, and on prudence, the virtue which tells us what needs to be done today in view of what might happen tomorrow.[21]

10. A sustainable comprehensive management of the environment and the resources of the planet demands that human intelligence be directed to technological and scientific research and its practical applications. The "new solidarity" for which John Paul II called in his Message for the 1990 World Day of Peace[22] and the "global solidarity" for which I myself appealed in my Message for the 2009 World Day of Peace[23] are essential attitudes in shaping our efforts to protect creation through a better internationally-coordinated management of the earth's resources, particularly today, when there is an increasingly clear link between combating environmental degradation and promoting an integral human development. These two realities are inseparable, since "the integral development of individuals necessarily entails a joint effort for the development of

---

20. Ibid.

21. Cf. Saint Thomas Aquinas, *Summa Theologica*, II–II, q. 49, 5.

22. Cf. No. 9.

23. Cf. No. 8.

humanity as a whole."[24] At present there are a number of scientific developments and innovative approaches which promise to provide satisfactory and balanced solutions to the problem of our relationship to the environment. Encouragement needs to be given, for example, to research into effective ways of exploiting the immense potential of solar energy. Similar attention also needs to be paid to the world-wide problem of water and to the global water cycle system, which is of prime importance for life on earth and whose stability could be seriously jeopardized by climate change. Suitable strategies for rural development centered on small farmers and their families should be explored, as well as the implementation of appropriate policies for the management of forests, for waste disposal and for strengthening the linkage between combating climate change and overcoming poverty. Ambitious national policies are required, together with a necessary international commitment which will offer important benefits especially in the medium and long term. There is a need, in effect, to move beyond a purely consumerist mentality in order to promote forms of agricultural and industrial production capable of respecting creation and satisfying the primary needs of all. The ecological problem must be dealt with not only because of the chilling prospects of environmental degradation on the horizon; the real motivation must be the quest for authentic world-wide solidarity inspired by the values of charity, justice and the common good. For that matter, as I have stated elsewhere, "technology is never merely technology. It reveals man and his aspirations towards development; it expresses the inner tension that impels him gradually to overcome material limitations. *Technology in this sense is a response to God's command to till and keep the land* (cf. Gen 2:15) that he has entrusted to humanity, and it must serve to reinforce the covenant between human beings and the environment, a covenant that should mirror God's creative love."[25]

11. It is becoming more and more evident that the issue of environmental degradation challenges us to examine our life-style and the prevailing models of consumption and production, which are often unsustainable from a social, environmental and even economic

24. Paul VI, *Populorum progressio*, 43.

25. Benedict XVI, *Caritas in veritate*, 69.

point of view. We can no longer do without a real change of outlook which will result in *new life-styles*, "in which the quest for truth, beauty, goodness and communion with others for the sake of common growth are the factors which determine consumer choices, savings and investments."[26] Education for peace must increasingly begin with far-reaching decisions on the part of individuals, families, communities and states. We are all responsible for the protection and care of the environment. This responsibility knows no boundaries. In accordance with the *principle of subsidiarity* it is important for everyone to be committed at his or her proper level, working to overcome the prevalence of particular interests. A special role in raising awareness and information belongs to the different groups present in civil society and to the non-governmental organizations which work with determination and generosity for the spread of ecological responsibility, responsibility which should be ever more deeply anchored in respect for "human ecology." The media also have a responsibility in this regard to offer positive and inspiring models. In a word, concern for the environment calls for a broad global vision of the world; a responsible common effort to move beyond approaches based on selfish nationalistic interests towards a vision constantly open to the needs of all peoples. We cannot remain indifferent to what is happening around us, for the deterioration of any one part of the planet affects us all. Relationships between individuals, social groups and states, like those between human beings and the environment, must be marked by respect and "charity in truth." In this broader context one can only encourage the efforts of the international community to ensure progressive disarmament and a world free of nuclear weapons, whose presence alone threatens the life of the planet and the ongoing integral development of the present generation and of generations yet to come.

12. *The Church has a responsibility towards creation*, and she considers it her duty to exercise that responsibility in public life, in order to protect earth, water and air as gifts of God the Creator meant for everyone, and above all to save mankind from the danger of self-destruction. The degradation of nature is closely linked to the

26. John Paul II, *Centesimus annus*, 36.

cultural models shaping human coexistence: consequently, "when 'human ecology' is respected within society, environmental ecology also benefits."[27] Young people cannot be asked to respect the environment if they are not helped, within families and society as a whole, to respect themselves. The book of nature is one and indivisible; it includes not only the environment but also individual, family and social ethics.[28] Our duties towards the environment flow from our duties towards the person, considered both individually and in relation to others.

Hence I readily encourage efforts to promote a greater sense of ecological responsibility which, as I indicated in my Encyclical *Caritas in veritate*, would safeguard an authentic "human ecology" and thus forcefully reaffirm the inviolability of human life at every stage and in every condition, the dignity of the person and the unique mission of the family, where one is trained in love of neighbor and respect for nature.[29] There is a need to safeguard the human patrimony of society. This patrimony of values originates in and is part of the natural moral law, which is the foundation of respect for the human person and creation.

13. Nor must we forget the very significant fact that many people experience peace and tranquility, renewal and reinvigoration, when they come into close contact with the beauty and harmony of nature. There exists a certain reciprocity: as we care for creation, we realize that God, through creation, cares for us. On the other hand, a correct understanding of the relationship between man and the environment will not end by absolutizing nature or by considering it more important than the human person. If the Church's magisterium expresses grave misgivings about notions of the environment inspired by ecocentrism and biocentrism, it is because such notions eliminate the difference of identity and worth between the human person and other living things. In the name of a supposedly egalitarian vision of the "dignity" of all living creatures, such notions end up abolishing the distinctiveness and superior role of human beings. They also

---

27. Benedict XVI, *Caritas in veritate*, 51.

28. Cf. ibid., 15, 51.

29. Cf. ibid., 28, 51, 61; John Paul II, *Centesimus annus*, 38, 39.

open the way to a new pantheism tinged with neo-paganism, which would see the source of man's salvation in nature alone, understood in purely naturalistic terms. The Church, for her part, is concerned that the question be approached in a balanced way, with respect for the "grammar" which the Creator has inscribed in his handiwork by giving man the role of a steward and administrator with responsibility over creation, a role which man must certainly not abuse, but also one which he may not abdicate. In the same way, the opposite position, which would absolutize technology and human power, results in a grave assault not only on nature, but also on human dignity itself.[30]

14. *If you want to cultivate peace, protect creation.* The quest for peace by people of good will surely would become easier if all acknowledge the indivisible relationship between God, human beings and the whole of creation. In the light of divine Revelation and in fidelity to the Church's Tradition, Christians have their own contribution to make. They contemplate the cosmos and its marvels in light of the creative work of the Father and the redemptive work of Christ, who by his death and resurrection has reconciled with God "all things, whether on earth or in heaven" (Col 1:20). Christ, crucified and risen, has bestowed his Spirit of holiness upon mankind, to guide the course of history in anticipation of that day when, with the glorious return of the Savior, there will be "new heavens and a new earth" (2 Pet 3:13), in which justice and peace will dwell for ever. Protecting the natural environment in order to build a world of peace is thus a duty incumbent upon each and all. It is an urgent challenge, one to be faced with renewed and concerted commitment; it is also a providential opportunity to hand down to coming generations the prospect of a better future for all. May this be clear to world leaders and to those at every level who are concerned for the future of humanity: the protection of creation and peacemaking are profoundly linked! For this reason, I invite all believers to raise a fervent prayer to God, the all-powerful Creator and the Father of mercies, so that all men and women may take to heart the urgent appeal: *If you want to cultivate peace, protect creation.*

30. Cf. Benedict XVI, *Caritas in veritate*, 70.

QUESTIONS FOR REVIEW

1. What does Benedict XVI mean when he refers to "environmental refugees"? What are some possible causes of this phenomenon, and how might environmental refugees contribute to tension and conflict in the world?
2. What is problematic, in Benedict XVI's mind, with the view of nature and of humans as attributable to chance or random atoms coming together?
3. When Benedict XVI calls for a rediscovery of values that will contribute to a brighter future, which values does he have in mind and what do these values mean to you?
4. What does Benedict XVI mean by *intergenerational solidarity* and *intragenerational solidarity?*
5. In what ways are the protection of creation and peacemaking profoundly linked?

IN-DEPTH QUESTIONS

1. What does Benedict XVI mean by *ecocentrism* and *pantheism*, and why does he regard these as problematic?
2. What does Benedict XVI say about the Church's role in protection of creation and peacemaking? What are some things or practices that you think the Church could do to carry out the pope's call?
3. Compare the understanding of the salvific or redemptive implications of Christ's work that you had before reading Benedict's letter with how he seems to describe it in connection with the protection of creation and peacemaking.
4. What do you think Benedict XVI has in mind when he refers to the absolutizing of technology and human power, and why does he believe this exacerbates environmental degradation and contributes to conflict among people?
5. What does Benedict XVI mean by the principle of subsidiarity, and what are the implications of this for determining who is responsible for protecting creation?

THE SCRIPTURES

CHAPTER 4

Creation and the Environment in the Hebrew Scriptures:
A Transvaluation of Values

Randall Smith

CHAPTER 5

A New Heaven and a New Earth:
Creation in the New Testament

Thomas Bushlack

CHAPTER 4

CREATION AND THE ENVIRONMENT IN THE HEBREW SCRIPTURES:

A Transvaluation of Values

Randall Smith

KEY TERMS

Babylonian Exile
covenant
creation
Mosaic Law

INTRODUCTION

The creation story in Genesis 1 is often said to have had deleterious effects on people's attitudes toward the environment. It is viewed as making possible a more instrumental view of nature, bidding humankind to "have dominion" over all creation. This chapter suggests, to the contrary, that by looking at the covenantal context within which Genesis 1 was written, we come to understand that Scripture was written precisely to correct these misapprehensions and give humankind a new appreciation for nature. Properly understood, Genesis 1 bids us to leave behind our natural human tendencies to want to use God (or the gods) to dominate and control the world and exhorts us to see the world as a place prepared for human life and human flourishing, where humans can enjoy communion with God and other creatures, as long as humans follow God's laws—that is, the laws of justice, righteousness, dignity, and respect that have been built into the very fabric of creation—acting "in the image of" the Creator-God revealed to us as one who is "with and for the world."

THE TWOFOLD INDICTMENT OF GENESIS 1

One frequently hears the criticism that the creation story in Genesis 1 has had deleterious effects on people's attitudes toward the environment. Often this criticism will be related to one of two indictments of the story. The first of these is that by demythologizing nature, Genesis 1 made possible a more instrumentalist view of creation. Whereas the sun, moon, and stars had earlier been considered gods or the abode of the gods, Genesis 1 told people these were merely "luminaries" that mark the days and seasons for the benefit of humans. So too the mountains, lakes, and rivers were no longer personified as gods or considered the abodes of gods. Rather, they too were said to be created for the benefit of humans. This made possible a view of nature as something before which humans no longer stand in awe, but as something humans *use*—as something made to serve *their* benefit and purposes.

The second indictment involves outrage over the passage in Genesis 1:28 in which God apparently commands the newly created humans to "have dominion over" all living things. "What could be more arrogant?" critics argue. "Isn't this the sort of mindset that has encouraged abuse of the environment?" Even those who find the charge of demythologization not entirely convincing sometimes find this passage troubling.

These two indictments were made famous by a 1967 article, "The Historical Roots of Our Ecologic Crisis," in *Science* by Lynn White, a professor of medieval history at UCLA. The charges have been repeated so often since, however, that they have become part of the folklore of the ecological movement.

What makes this reading of the creation account in Genesis 1 especially ironic is that it ends up ascribing to it precisely the sort of worldview this Scripture was written to correct. The creation story in Genesis 1, in fact, was meant to reorient people's way of thinking about their relationship to God and to the world.

THE REAL AGENDA BEHIND GENESIS

Genesis 1 bids us to leave behind our human tendencies to want to use God (or the gods) to attempt to dominate and control the world—a human tendency that found a powerful expression in much of ancient pagan idolatry. Thus, precisely by demythologizing nature and by counteracting the human predisposition toward control of the world associated with pagan idolatry, Genesis 1 opened a new horizon in understanding the environment. No longer was the world thought to be a threatening place subject to fate, to chance, and to the whim of various gods; no longer, a place where safety was bought at a steep price through sacrifices, sometimes in blood, to appease the gods. Under the influence of the book of Genesis, the world increasingly came to be seen as a place prepared for human life—as a "garden," in which humans could flourish along with all the other plants and animals. There, humans could enjoy a profound communion with God and other creatures as long as humans walk *with* God, following God's laws—that is, the laws of justice, righteousness, dignity, and respect that have been built into the very fabric of creation—acting in ways that imitate the Creator-God who reveals himself as (to use Karl Barth's felicitous expression) one who is "with and for the world."[1]

Indeed, precisely by correcting and clarifying what it means to be "in God's image and likeness," Genesis 1 helps humans to realize that their natural tendencies to want to dominate and control others and nature would lead ultimately to their ruin and the devastation of the world, whereas true human flourishing involves a righteous life of service and stewardship in the image and likeness of the God who is both just and loving and who has freely given existence to humans and the world. The real tragedy of misreading Genesis 1 in the way White and others do is precisely that it causes one to miss the original message of the text about human care and responsibility for others and the world, a message desperately needed today.

READING INTO THE TEXT VS. READING IN CONTEXT

The Protestant Old Testament scholar Walter Brueggemann shows how to avoid these two methods of misconstruing the Bible by

1. See Karl Barth, *Church Dogmatics*, vol. 4, part 3 (London: T&T Clark, 1961, 2004), 414.

suggesting that one try to read it "like insiders."[2] One does that by putting oneself as much as possible into the mindset of the authors and by appreciating the faith convictions that animated their writing. The best place to begin is with what Brueggemann calls "the primal narrative" of the Old Testament, namely, the "simple, elemental, and non-negotiable story line which lies at the heart of biblical faith." This story, he says, "is presented with the passion of fresh believers and with the simplicity of a community which had screened out uncertainties and felt no reason to explain. It is an affirmation in story form which asserts, 'This is the most important story we know, and we have come to believe it is decisively about us.'"[3] It is the story the community tells itself as a reminder of who it is and from where it has come. All other stories either point forward in anticipation of this watershed event or look backward to it as the decisive center of history. It is the story the community tells when hard times befall it or disaster threatens.

Most scholars agree that the primal narrative was the Exodus, an event that includes the following: (a) God's liberation of the people from slavery in Egypt, (b) God's protection of the people during the 40-year period of wandering in the wilderness, (c) God's establishment of a covenant with them and giving them the Law, and (d) God's bringing them into the Promised Land.

Because of the way the Bible is currently arranged, with Genesis coming before Exodus, many assume that the creation story in Genesis 1 must have been written long before the Exodus, and thus independently of it. Modern biblical scholarship suggests otherwise, however. It seems clear now that the creation story in Genesis 1 was written by an author who was part of a faith community that had already experienced the miracle of the Exodus. Indeed, many contemporary biblical scholars believe that the creation story now in Genesis 1 was written centuries after the Exodus, by a highly educated Jewish author, sometime during the Babylonian Exile (597–538 BCE).

In such dire circumstances, in the shadow of a shameful defeat, all sorts of questions likely arose for the author and his community:

---

2. Walter Brueggemann, *The Bible Makes Sense* (Winona, MN: Saint Mary's Press, 1977), 45. See also Gerhard Von Rad, "The Theological Problem of the Old Testament Doctrine of Creation," in *Creation in the Old Testament,* ed. Bernhard Anderson, (Philadelphia: Fortress, 1984), 53–64.

3. Ibid, 46.

Is God against us? Is God aware of our suffering? Hearing our cries? Is our faith in vain? Is our suffering meaningless? Will the forces of human tyranny have the final word? In the face of defeat and despair, the author of Genesis 1 turned to his faith for answers that opened new horizons of understanding regarding God's true nature. In his commentary on the creation stories in Genesis, Pope Benedict XVI describes the situation thus:

> And so, being driven out of their own land and being erased from the map was for Israel a terrible trial: Has our God been vanquished, and is our faith void? At this moment the prophets opened a new page and taught Israel that it was only then that the true face of God appeared and that he was not restricted to that particular piece of land. He had never been: He had promised this piece of land to Abraham before he settled there, and he had been able to bring his people out of Egypt. He could do both things because he was not the God of one place but had power over heaven and earth. Therefore he could drive his faithless people into another land in order to make himself known there. And so it came to be understood that this God of Israel was not a God like the other gods, but that he was the God who held sway over every land and people. He could do this, however, because he himself had created everything in heaven and on earth.[4]

CREATION AND THE COVENANT

Reading Genesis 1 in the light of the Exodus event and God's covenant with the Hebrew people at Sinai can help to correct many common misunderstandings of this text. What might it mean to view God's act of creation in light of the rescue of the Jewish people from their slavery in Egypt? In both instances, God acts freely and is not subject to or limited by any greater force or constraint, whether it be a pharaoh's army or the forces of chaos and pure nothingness. God's creative act is

4. Pope Benedict XVI, *"In the Beginning . . . ": A Catholic Understanding of the Story of Creation and the Fall*, tr. Boniface Ramsey (Grand Rapids, MI: Eerdmans, 1995), 11–12.

not due to any prior debt or deserving on the part of the people. Thus God's is an act of divine love, not merely of divine power. God does not act, as does the pharaoh, as a powerful tyrant whose actions are the result of fear of the people and whose laws enslave. God acts, rather, as a gracious giver of life, whose commandments are meant to preserve his people's freedom and flourishing in a land God has prepared for them. It is this God of the covenant in whose image humans are made, not the God of power one may have imagined.

Without this prior faith in the God of the covenant, it would be difficult to have faith in the goodness of creation. When one considers the raw, untamed forces of nature—earthquakes, hurricanes, floods, and volcanoes—it is easy to imagine that the world must have been made by an angry or capricious god or gods or that perhaps its fundamental constitution has been determined by cruel fate or blind chance. Either way, the welfare of humankind would be neither essential to the cosmos nor particularly important. It is entirely possible, given this view, to believe that one's lot in life is to offer gifts and sacrifices to placate angry, capricious deities as much as possible in order to curry their favor. This was an altogether common view of the gods in the ancient world.

One may well recognize that this view is closer to one's own than one would care to admit. People sometimes act as though they need only obey and worship God to receive God's favor and gifts, or at least to keep the forces of death and destruction at bay a while longer.

If, however, like the Jewish author of Genesis 1, one thought that the God who redeemed the chosen people from slavery with great signs and wonders, led them dry-shod through the sea, made a covenant with them, gave them laws, and brought them into the Promised Land was the same God who created the entire universe, then one might view creation quite differently. Seeing the God of creation in light of the story about the God of the covenant would reveal that the Creator is not flighty, whimsical, angry, jealous, or domineering, but rather loving, just, and self-sacrificing, who made the universe, not for himself, but for humans. In answer to the question, "Why did God create the universe?" one can say, with Pope Benedict, that "God created the universe in order to enter into a history of love with humankind."[5]

---

5. Ibid., 30.

CREATION AND THE LAW

And yet, Scripture also teaches that a relationship of love must go both ways. Humans are responsible for acting in ways appropriate to the gifts they have been given. The God who created the world is the same God who not only rescued the Jews from their slavery in Egypt but also confirmed them in their freedom by making a covenant with them and giving them the Law.

Whereas humans in the modern world often tend to think of God's law as a burden, as the willful obligations laid upon them by a God who seems to be, as C. S. Lewis reports an English schoolboy once put it, "the sort of person who is always snooping around to see if anyone is enjoying himself and then trying to stop it,"[6] the biblical authors understood the Law to be an expression of God's love and concern for his people. So, for example, in Deuteronomy 4:7–8, Moses asks the people: "For what great nation is there that has gods so close to it as the Lord, our God, is to us whenever we call upon him? Or what great nation has statutes and decrees that are as just as this whole law which I am setting before you today?" By following this law, they come to understand, they will attain wisdom and flourishing. "Observe [these commandments] carefully," says Moses in Deuteronomy 4:6, "for thus will you give evidence of your wisdom and intelligence to the nations, who will hear of all these statutes and say, 'This great nation is truly a wise and intelligent people.'" Humans' problem, however, is that they more often think of the covenant as an elevation to a position of privilege rather than as a call to moral responsibility. Given the Jewish view of the Law, it would be more accurate to say that the call to moral responsibility is the privilege, just as the Law is the gift.

That is why it is so important to understand the relationship in the Old Testament between the God of the covenant and the God of creation. Reflecting on creation in the light of the covenant, the Jewish people came to understand the true meaning of creation: that it was an undeserved gift from God. And having been tutored over the generations by the Law, the Jewish people were also prepared for the necessary concomitant of receiving creation as a gift:

---

6. C. S. Lewis, *Mere Christianity* (San Francisco: HarperSanFransico, 2001), 69.

that is, accepting the moral responsibilities and obligations that come along with that gift.

CREATION IN THE PSALMS

That an explicit thematic connection between creation and God's law must have preexisted among the Jewish people before the writing of Genesis 1 can be shown by means of a short survey of earlier Old Testament texts that deal with creation. Two of the most important Psalms that deal with creation are Psalms 33 and 104. In the Roman Catholic lectionary, either of these two psalms is designated for use in the Easter Vigil liturgy to accompany the reading of the seven-day creation account in Genesis 1. (Note that whenever either of these psalms is read in this context, the congregation will always hear them along with the account of the Exodus given in Exodus 14, because that is the one reading that can never be omitted.) Psalms 33 and 104 talk about God as Creator and contain descriptions of God's creative acts, but neither makes use of the seven-day structure of creation in Genesis 1. All three creation accounts, however, enunciate a similar theology of creation.

Let us begin with Psalm 33:6–7, which contain the following short description of God's creative act: "By the LORD's word the heavens were made; by the breath of his mouth all their host. / The waters of the sea were gathered as in a bowl; / in cellars the deep was confined." That text is prefaced by another in which the psalmist sings the praises of the Creator because of God's justice: "Rejoice, you just, in the LORD; / praise from the upright is fitting. / Give thanks to the LORD on the harp; / on the ten-stringed lyre offer praise. / Sing to God a new song; / skillfully play with joyful chant. / For the LORD's word is true; / all his works are trustworthy. / The LORD loves justice and right / and fills the earth with goodness" (Psalm 33:1–5). Note the connections among creation, praise, and justice. The psalmist is clear that praise and worship are not due because humans fear God's great power but because they have become aware that "The LORD loves justice and right and fills the earth with goodness," and so have resolved to love justice and right and fill the earth with goodness themselves.

Psalm 104:2–5 contains another description of God's creative work—one that, like Psalm 33, adopts a different set of images than those used in Genesis 1. It begins:

You spread out the heavens like a tent;
you raised your palace upon the waters.
You make the clouds your chariot;
you travel on the wings of the wind. . . .
You fixed the earth on its foundation,
never to be moved.
The ocean covered it like a garment;
above the mountains stood the waters.
At your roar they took flight;
at the sound of your thunder they fled.
They rushed up the mountains, down the valleys
to the place you had fixed for them.
You set a limit they cannot pass;
never again will they cover the earth.

(Psalm 104:2–3,5)

Psalm 104 goes on in subsequent verses to recount how God "made springs flow into channels / that wind among the mountains" to give water "to every beast of the field" (Psalm 104:10–11). Moreover, God raises "grass for the cattle / and plants for our beasts of burden." He brings forth "bread from the earth, / and wine to gladden our hearts, / Oil to make our faces gleam, food to build our strength" (Psalm 104:14–15).

Note, however, that it is not just humans for whom God has provided, but for all of God's creatures—plants and animals as well: "The trees of the Lord drink their fill, the cedars of Lebanon, which you planted. / There the birds build their nests; / junipers are the home of the stork" (Psalm 104:16–17). It is not only the great and magnificent creatures for which God cares, but also those whose lives are mostly hidden from human eyes. In a delightful bit of poetic particularity, the psalmist specifies: "The high mountains are for wild goats; / the rocky cliffs, a refuge for badgers" (Psalm 104:18). Even the badgers weren't forgotten! Again, several lines later, the psalmist writes about God's care for the creatures of the sea: "Look at the sea, great and wide! / It teems with countless beings, living things both large and small . . . / here Leviathan [the whale], your creature, plays. / All of these look to you / to give them food in due time. /

When you give to them, they gather; / when you open your hand, they are well filled" (Psalm 104:25–28).

At the dramatic climax of his description, the psalmist, in a kind of marvelous summary, declares: "How varied are your works, LORD! / In wisdom you have wrought them all" (Psalm 104:24). The use of the word *wisdom* in the context of creation is noteworthy because wisdom is something one usually finds associated in the Psalms with the Law, as for example in Psalm 19:8–9: "The law of the LORD is perfect, / refreshing the soul. / The decree of the LORD is trustworthy, / giving wisdom to the simple. / The precepts of the LORD are right, / rejoicing the heart. / The command of the LORD is clear, / enlightening the eye." Indeed, if one were to look more closely at precisely this passage in Psalm 19, one would find that its praise of the Law's wisdom occurs within the context of an especially beautiful praise of the glory of God's creation, which begins: "The heavens declare the glory of God; / the sky proclaims its builder's craft" (Psalm 19:2). When several verses later the psalmist turns to his encomium of the Law, the transition can seem textually a bit startling. In verse 7, a lovely description of the work of the sun appears: "From one end of the heavens it comes forth; / its course runs through to the other; nothing escapes its heat"; and then the psalmist is off and running in praise of the Law:

> The law of the LORD is perfect,
>   refreshing the soul.
> The decree of the LORD is trustworthy,
>   giving wisdom to the simple.
> The precepts of the LORD are right,
>   rejoicing the heart.
> The command of the LORD is clear,
>   enlightening the eye.
> The fear of the LORD is pure,
>   enduring forever.
> The statutes of the LORD are true,
>   all of them just;
> More desirable than gold,
>   than a hoard of purest gold,

> Sweeter also than honey
>   or drippings from the comb.
> By them your servant is instructed;
>   obeying them brings much reward.
>
> (Psalm 19:8–12)

What explains this odd transition or, perhaps, this odd lack of transition?

One needs to understand that for the psalmist, just as the heavens "declare the glory of God" by obeying the decrees of the Lord, so too do humans when they obey God's decrees. God, who "in wisdom has wrought all things," reveals some of that wisdom to humans in the Law. By following the Law, humans learn to be wise; that is, they learn to exist in and for the world in the manner intended by its Creator. The Law is, as it were, the instruction manual God the Creator provides along with his creation, saying in effect: "If you want to know how to flourish in the world I have made, you might want to consider starting with these basic principles: Don't kill. Don't steal. Don't commit adultery. Love your neighbor as yourself." Such commandments are, as Pope Benedict XVI has described them, "an echo of creation," signs that "point to the spirit, the language, and the meaning of creation; they are a translation of the language of the universe, a translation of God's logic, which constructed the universe."[7] Put more simply, one might describe God's law as a translation of the language of love by which God has created the universe.

BACK TO CREATION IN GENESIS 1

Because Genesis 1 was likely written after the other creation texts reviewed thus far—written, indeed, precisely with a view to reaffirming Israel's traditional faith in the covenant and the Law in the face of their defeat and exile by the Babylonian Empire—one can take what was learned about the ancient Hebrew notion of creation and apply it to the reading of that reputedly "dangerous" text in Genesis 1. One could find evidence there of the themes that have been discussed thus far: the connection between creation and God's wisdom, and

---

7. Benedict XVI, 26.

humankind's response in praise and righteousness. To see it clearly, one needs to take a step back from the text—as one steps back from a great painting to see it whole—and notice the overall structure of the creation narrative in Genesis 1.

Listing the things created on each of the six days—remembering that God rests on the seventh day—one finds the following items:

1. On the first day, God says, "Let there be light." Light is separated from darkness; the light is called "day," the darkness, "night."
2. On the second day, God creates a "dome" and places it in the midst of "the waters," separating the "water above the dome" from the "water below it."
3. On the third day God separates the dry land from the water and creates vegetation, more specifically "every kind of plant that bears seed and every kind of fruit tree on earth that bears fruit with its seed in it."
4. On the fourth day, God creates the greater light to rule the day (the sun) and the lesser lights to rule the night (the moon and the stars), putting them in the heavens to "mark the fixed times, the days and the years."
5. On the fifth day, God creates only two types of living creature: birds and fish.
6. Finally, on the sixth day, God creates all the land animals—that is, all kinds of "creeping things"—including, of course, that animal created in God's image, namely humans. (Genesis 1:3-27)

There are some rather odd features of this list, including how, for example, four "days" pass before the sun is created, and what is causing those "seed-bearing plants and trees" to grow if no sun provides them light. However, those problems arise only if one insists on taking the list literally as a historical account—as though those things were being listed like items in a newspaper article titled, "What I Saw at Creation."

Reexamine the list. Note that the first three days systematically prepare an environment for the inhabitants created on each of the final three days. The creation of day and night makes way for inhabitants. The creation of the sky and the oceans prepares an environment for the birds that fly in the sky and the fish that swim in the sea. Finally, the preparation of the dry land and the creation of vegetation prepares the appropriate environment for the land animals and for the ones who can praise God with their actions, the humans "made in the image and likeness of God." This fairly simple message might be summarized by Psalm 104:24: "How varied are your works, LORD! / In wisdom you have wrought them all." From the bounty of God's wisdom and love, everything is created, and creation invites one into a covenant; it calls forth from humans a commitment to and responsibility for creation similar to God's own.

ARE DEMYTHOLOGIZING AND INSTRUMENTALIZING NATURE THE SAME?

Recall that the first indictment against the Old Testament accounts of creation was that by demythologizing nature, these passages had thereby instrumentalized it. That is, by making the sun, moon, and stars, lakes and oceans, plants and animals no longer "gods" deserving of "worship," the Old Testament authors present nature as something made solely for human use. By reading the Genesis creation account in context, however, one finds this charge without merit. By affirming their faith in a God who creates in wisdom and righteousness, the Old Testament authors did away with older views that suggested the universe was made by capricious, warring deities and that humans had to make their way in life jockeying for power and position, trying to placate one god or another. Instead, theirs is a theology of creation that envisions the universe as the gift of a righteous and loving Creator. In this view, humans' lot in life is not a constant battle against powerful and impersonal forces that care nothing about them. Rather, humans are called to praise God by living righteously and caring for God's creatures.

In sum, humans call out to the universe to ask: Why are we here? What is life for? The answers the universe gives depend on the story one thinks it tells. If humans think the universe is essentially a battlefield, then it will tell them to "kill or be killed." If they imagine the universe to be the gift of a loving and just God in whose image they have been made, then it will tell them to imitate God by engaging in acts of justice and love.

TWO VIEWS OF WHAT IT MEANS TO HAVE DOMINION

The second indictment against the Genesis 1 account of creation relates to the notion that humans were to "have dominion" over all creatures. In response to this criticism, one should begin by noting the stipulation that humans were to "have dominion" comes right after the creation of humans "in the image and likeness of God." One could read and interpret what it means to "have dominion" in terms of what it means to be "in the image and likeness of God." The word *dominion* derives from the Latin root *dominus*, meaning, "lord." If one considers the Lord as the one, true, living God who has entered into a covenant with God's people—if that is one's concept of lordship rather than of someone "lording over" a people—then one might conceive of God's command for humans to "have dominion" over Earth differently: as a duty to care for it rather than to command and control it.

There is a tendency to read the word *dominion* in terms of a human appetite for power and wealth rather than in terms of the providential care God displays in salvation history. This tendency has been exacerbated by contemporary technological culture. It is noteworthy that many readers of Genesis 1 fail to notice that the dominion with which humans are entrusted refers only to the plants and animals and not to all of creation, as is often mistakenly supposed. This makes the image of the human person much more like that of a farmer or a shepherd than that of a contemporary technician. Indeed, a farmer would be more likely to understand what dominion over the animals in his or her care entails than would be those who are inclined to think of dominion in either political or technological terms, and usually in the sense of domination.

Anyone who has spent time around farm animals knows that a farmer's dominion has almost nothing to do with control. There is simply no controlling horses, cows, chickens, and hogs—those novices who try end up frustrated and worn out. An experienced farmer understands that one either learns the ways of animals—how and when to feed them, what and when not to feed them, how large a pen they need, how much exercise they must have, how they give birth to their young, how long they must stay with their mother—or farmer and animals alike will not survive.

CULTIVATING THE GARDEN AND KEEPING THE LAW

Another important corrective to misinterpretations of human dominion surfaces in the parallel creation account in Genesis 2—3. The editor who put together the two creation stories in Genesis 1 and Genesis 2—3 did so for a reason, which may well be that, although written centuries apart, these two narratives manifest the same basic theology of creation, even as the account in Genesis 2 extends the story to include the specifically moral dimensions of such a theology. In Genesis 2, rather than using the image of the six days to communicate the idea that God has prepared an environment propitious for human flourishing, the author uses the image of a garden, in which God causes to grow "various trees . . . that were delightful to look at and good for food" (Genesis 2:9). In creating the world, God has prepared for humans a verdant place in which to flourish—if, that is, they care for that garden appropriately. Notice God's instruction in Genesis 2:15: "The Lord God then took the man and put him in the garden of Eden, to cultivate and care for it." Interestingly, the first word in this series, *cultivate*, comes from a root (*abad*) that means, "to serve." The second, *keep*, which is also translated as "to take care of," comes from a root (*shamar*) that means "to keep, watch, preserve" and even "to exercise great care over." It would not be much of a stretch, then, to say that another possible translation of this verse would be to say that God had commanded humans to serve and preserve the world entrusted to their care.

There is in Genesis 2—3, as in the other creation texts, a moral dimension as well. The worm in the apple that results in the loss of this garden has to do with humans' disobedience of God's law. In the context of the time in which it was written (probably as early as the tenth century BCE), it may well be that the garden to which the author is referring is the Promised Land, and the temptation that the serpent represents is the temptation to idolatry. Recall that at the end of Genesis 1 (verse 26), God says, "Let us make man in our image." The implication is that humans are supposed to cut and form themselves in God's image. The human tendency, however, is to cut and form God to their image: to turn God into the lord one would wish God to be—powerful, controlling, and fearsome—rather than recognizing God as the kind of Lord he has revealed himself to be: loving, righteous, and self-sacrificing. Thus, the temptation to idolatry involves not merely the making of statues and giving them human characteristics, but also that one makes gods over in one's own image.

In the ancient world, when one was a farmer, one's "god" was usually the god of the harvest. When one was a soldier, one's god was usually the god of war, and so on for blacksmiths, merchants, hunters, fathers, mothers, and young women who desired beauty: each of them had their specific god. However, biblical revelation shows the "worshipper" in these instances has merely created a god in his or her own image, a god to satisfy his or her own desires and designs. Thus, the real danger is not simply the making of statues. The real danger is that humans will forsake the covenant and the gift God has given to them in the Law in order to pursue the worship of gods who promise control over history and nature but ask no moral conversion of heart and life.

Instead of attempting to control nature by bribing the gods to force nature into conformity with human desires, the creation stories in the Old Testament bid them to cultivate the garden God has given them. To *cultivate the garden*, in this view, is synonymous with to *keep the law*. That is to say, to cultivate the garden, humans must first cultivate the virtues united under the overarching virtue of love. There will be no order in the garden if there is no order in the human soul. Ultimately, to care for the garden, one's heart must be made over into the image and likeness of the God who loves and cares for all.

CONCLUSION

The Jewish people came to believe that the source of their existence as a people was the source of the existence of all the world; that the same God who had rescued them from slavery, entered into a covenant with them, and given them his law—who had in this way revealed himself to be a God who is "with them and for them"[8]—was also the God who had made all the world. He had done so, moreover, with the same will for the salvation and flourishing of all. The Jewish people began to see, in other words, that their primal narrative was not merely their narrative as a people; rather it was the key to the primal narrative of the whole cosmos. If that is true, then all humans are a covenant people now, living in a covenantal world, with covenant responsibilities: to exist, as God does, "with the world and for the world," and to rejoice in God's creation by living righteously with all of God's creatures.

Scripture reveals a God who creates out of wisdom and love. God's creation involves a commitment of wisdom and righteousness and calls forth a similar commitment. Humans are called into a covenant with God, which is also a covenant with neighbor and nature.

Scripture presents a distinctly moral dimension to creation. Humans are made in the image of God and called to show that likeness to others: through allowing creation to show forth the glory of God; through causing nature to "rejoice"; by singing "joyfully to the Lord"; by being "righteous"; by realizing, as Psalm 33:5 says, that "the Lord loves justice and right." The antithesis of this attitude of thankfulness and rejoicing is to attempt to become the "lord" of creation and thereby the cause of its enslavement. Acting without righteousness, as Saint Paul suggests in Romans 8:20 (and chapter 5 will explore further), humans make creation "subject to futility."

That humanity has fallen short is hard to deny when one surveys the damage done. However, Genesis would argue, the problem did not begin in 1967 or at the outset of the Industrial Revolution, when the spirit of the instrumentalization of nature began in earnest. The problem began at the beginning, when men and women first chose to see themselves as gods, rather than acknowledging their Creator as the one, true, living God. It began when men and women chose their own will-to-power over the moral law of all creation. Indeed, if the book of Genesis is to be believed, then the problem can only be solved by getting at the heart of men and women and calling them to fidelity to God, to one another, and to the world they are meant to steward.

---

8. Karl Barth, *Church Dogmatics*, 414.

REVIEW QUESTIONS

1. What are the two major modern indictments of the creation story in Genesis 1? Why, according to the author, is the interpretation of Genesis 1 that supports these two indictments especially ironic?
2. What, according to Old Testament scholar Walter Brueggemann, is the "primal narrative" of the Old Testament? Of what relevance is the story of the Exodus to one's understanding of the story of creation recounted in Genesis 1?
3. When do many scholars think the creation story in Genesis 1 was written? What new understanding about the nature of God did the Jewish people discover during this time, according to Pope Benedict XVI?
4. How, according to the author, should we understand the order of the six "days" of creation in Genesis 1?
5. What, according to the author, are the two different ways of understanding what it means for humans to "have dominion" over the plants and animals?

IN-DEPTH QUESTIONS

1. What difference does it make to one's understanding of the creation story in Genesis 1 to read it in the light of the Exodus event?
2. Consider for a moment the following possible alternative understandings of creation:

   (a) Creation is the by-product of a cosmic battle between the gods.

   (b) Creation happens by "fate"; the gods are more powerful than humans but are as much subject to fate as humans are.

   (c) Creation is the result of God's desire to have creatures to bow down in homage.

   (d) Creation happens by chance. Existence is essentially meaningless.

3. What would be the implications for human life and for human attitudes toward the environment given each scenario? Now compare these with the understanding of creation that suggests creation is the product of a just and loving God who creates to invite humans into a fellowship of love.
4. What difference would it make to one's understanding of what it means to "have dominion" over the plants and animals if one thought about it from the point of view of farmers or shepherds (as many of the original audience were) rather than from the current industrial-technological point of view?
5. What, according to the author, is the real problem with idolatry? Why is idolatry a problem with respect to one's treatment of the environment? Would it make any difference if, instead of cutting and forming God to human image, the believer felt the need to be made over into God's image?
6. What difference would it make to the way you live your life and treat those around you if you thought of Earth's stewardship as a gift? Would it make any difference to you if you thought of such stewardship as an expression of God's wisdom—as a key, in other words, to humans flourishing in this world?

CHAPTER 5

A NEW HEAVEN AND A NEW EARTH:

Creation in the New Testament

Thomas Bushlack

KEY TERMS

divine providence
Dei verbum
hermeneutics
fusion of horizons
eschatology
Hellenistic
Logos
incarnation
kenosis
exegesis

> Then I saw a new heaven and a new earth; for the first heaven and the first earth had passed away. (Revelation 21:1)

INTRODUCTION AND METHODOLOGY

In comparison with the Hebrew Scriptures, surprisingly little work has been completed by scholars focusing on the New Testament as a source for environmental theology and ethics. Perhaps this is because the Hebrew Scriptures provide more immediate stimulation for the imagination in relation to the ecological concerns that define current times. Yet, one should not be deterred from looking to the New Testament as a source for better understanding a Christian scriptural view of the role of creation (both human and nonhuman) within God's plan of salvation history. When read in conjunction and in continuity with the

Hebrew Scriptures, the New Testament adds important insights into the Christian belief that God's providential wisdom and plan of salvation, ultimately revealed and fulfilled in Christ, encompass creation itself.

As noted by Cathy Mabry McMullen in the first chapter, from 1962 to 1965 the Catholic bishops of the world gathered in Rome for the Second Vatican Council and discussed the role of the Church in the modern era. Toward the end of this council, the bishops published an important document in which they upheld the sacred nature of Scripture as divine revelation and in which they encouraged Catholic scholars to incorporate modern methods of historical research and textual interpretation into their study of it. Since the publication of *Dei verbum* (Dogmatic Constitution on Divine Revelation), Catholic biblical scholarship has tended to focus on the mandate to discover the original intention of the author. *Dei verbum* states:

> Seeing that, in sacred scripture, God speaks through human beings in human fashion, it follows that the interpreters of sacred scripture, if they are to ascertain what God has wished to communicate to us, should carefully search out the meaning which the sacred writers really had in mind, that meaning which God had thought well to manifest through the medium of their words.[1]

This is an important development in Catholic biblical scholarship, because until the Second Vatican Council, there was disagreement about whether these modern developments of textual interpretation (more specifically, the belief that God's word is mediated through human words in a "human fashion") could be fruitfully applied to Scripture without destroying its sense as the sacred Word of God.

However, once one begins to look to the New Testament to address some of the contemporary moral questions that present themselves vis-à-vis humans' relationship with the environment, one quickly encounters the limits of such an approach. The importance and potential limitations of this approach are noted by scholars who recognize that the authors of the New Testament did not foresee

---

1. "Dogmatic Constitution on Divine Revelation" (*Dei verbum*), no. 12, in *The Sixteen Documents of Vatican II: Constitutions, Decrees, and Declarations*, ed. Austin Flannery, OP (Northport, NY: Costello, 1996), 97–116.

the possibility of wide-scale environmental destruction, at least not a destruction caused by human activity.[2] Thus, to find an appropriate method to incorporate the theological insights regarding creation in the New Testament into a contemporary environmental theology, a further mediating step is needed.

The field of hermeneutics, that is, the science and art of textual interpretation, offers a helpful manner forward in this situation and has had a profound influence upon biblical scholarship. Norman Gottwald, a biblical scholar who has made significant contributions to the early development of modern biblical research, describes how certain concepts of interpretation and application can be helpful for those seeking guidance to contemporary problems in the ancient texts of the Bible. He writes,

> Ancient and modern texts come together in a fashion which has been called a "fusion of horizons" and in a process which is called "hermeneutical circulation." We are always moving in dialectical fashion from our complex present into a complex past and back again. Our basic placement is present, but we come to a fuller grasp of the present by "distancing" ourselves from a locked-in situation through critical engagement with biblical texts and societies.[3]

What Gottwald describes is a process whereby one begins by formulating a question that arises from one's experience in the contemporary world; this is the modern "horizon." By bringing this question to bear on one's reading and understanding of an ancient text (Scripture) addressed to an ancient world, one begins to move into the ancient horizon and the world of the text. Doing this distances one from the contemporary world, making the familiar strange by presenting it through the world of Scripture. Finally, by bringing this new perspective from the ancient

2. Anne Clifford, CSJ, "Foundations for a Catholic Ecological Theology of God," in *"And God Saw That It Was Good": Catholic Theology and the Environment*, eds. Drew Christiansen and Walter Grazer (Washington, DC: United States Catholic Conference, 1996), 23; and Brennan Hill, *Christian Faith and the Environment: Making Vital Connections* (Maryknoll, NY: Orbis, 1998), 7.

3. Norman Gottwald, "The Biblical Mandate for Eco-Justice Action" in *For Creation's Sake: Preaching, Ecology, and Justice*, ed. Dieter T. Hessel (Philadelphia: Geneva, 1985), 32.

text back into one's contemporary perspective, one creates a "fusion of horizons" in a "circle" formed between the ancient text and world and contemporary experience. These connections spark the biblical imagination, such that one can view contemporary problems through the lens of a biblically inspired worldview.

The aim in this chapter is to develop a theological-ecological imagination rooted in the Word of God as a foundation for Christian ethical reflection and action. The basic question it brings to the texts of the New Testament is the following: what is the role of creation within God's plan of salvation in and through Christ as it is presented in the New Testament? When the pertinent texts regarding creation in the New Testament are considered, it becomes evident that the fullness of redemption in Christ entails some form of physical, embodied existence, albeit one that is transformed from the manner in which one currently experiences it. This, in turn, implies that the whole of created reality—not just human reality or the human soul separated from the body—has a role to play in the eschatological hope of salvation found in Christian faith. Such a hope refers to the hope one has for the *eschaton*, or the end of time.

For those accustomed to understanding Christian salvation as the existence of an eternal soul disconnected from one's body and from physical reality, this approach may seem rather surprising. Creation has integrity in the New Testament that is not only derivative of, or grounded in, the promise of salvation offered to humankind. This biblical vision of the integrity of creation has important implications for a Christian theology of the environment, for the manner in which one reads Scripture, for one's ethical decisions regarding creation, and for the kind of future existence for which one hopes when trusting in the salvation God offers through Jesus Christ.

Now consider in detail some of the relevant texts from the New Testament that can be fruitful in developing this environmental theology. This list, or treatment, of the relevant texts does not purport to be exhaustive. Rather, texts have been chosen that seem to offer the most helpful or challenging insights into the question at hand. It would also be helpful to read this chapter with a Bible nearby to examine the actual scriptural text before reading the commentary provided here.

LUKE 4:16–23: JESUS' PROCLAMATION OF THE KINGDOM OF GOD

There are a multitude of examples of Jesus' interactions with, and care for, creation in the New Testament: He tells his disciples that God cares for and feeds the birds of the air (cf. Luke 12:24). In miracles, Jesus shows his oneness with and power over nature as in the multiplication of the loaves and fishes (cf. Matthew 14:13–21, Mark 6:30–44, Luke 9:10–17, John 6:1–15), in walking on water (cf. Matthew 14:22–33, Mark 6:45–52, John 6:19–21), and in his healing of physical ailments or raising others from the dead (cf. Lazarus: John 11:1–44; Jairus' daughter: cf. Matthew 9:18–25, Mark 5:22–42, Luke 8:41–56); and many of Jesus' parables draw directly upon examples from nature (e.g., the parable of the seed: cf. Matthew 13:1–9, Luke 8:4–8). Yet, perhaps no passage from the gospels portrays more succinctly the message of the kingdom of God than in Jesus' reading from the scroll of Isaiah in the synagogue, when he announces the fulfillment of God's promises to the Hebrew people in their midst (cf. Luke 4:16–23).

Several layers of meaning are attached to the three verses that Jesus quotes from Isaiah, layers his hearers in the synagogue would have understood. Having just returned from 40 days and nights of fasting in the desert, Jesus begins his ministry in the Gospel of Luke with these words from Isaiah:

> The Spirit of the Lord is upon me,
> because he has anointed me to bring good news to the poor.
> He has sent me to proclaim release to the captives,
> and recovery of sight to the blind [Isaiah 61:1], to let the oppressed go free [Isaiah 58:6], to proclaim a year of the Lord's favor [Isaiah 61:2]. . . .
> Today this scripture has been fulfilled in your hearing.
>
> (Luke 4:18–19,21)

To those present, this would have been an audacious claim. First, Jesus' Jewish contemporaries would have known that he was quoting from the section of the book of Isaiah (cf. chapters 40–66) in which an earthly vision of God's redemption is proclaimed. To the Hebrew people, this was an enduring and compelling vision of hope for a land to call their own in which to experience peace, security, and fecundity. Second, by proclaiming a "year of the Lord's favor" (verse 19) Jesus' hearers would have known that he was referring to the concept of a Jubilee year, established in the Law of Moses in the book of Leviticus. In chapter 25 of Leviticus, an important element of the covenant of justice among God, the Hebrew people, and the land is established by God's command that they allow the land to rest every seventh year, and that every 49 years they are to forgive any outstanding debts. God's people are to be faithful to the covenant by following this example of God's justice; a justice in which care for the oppressed and the land are inseparable. Jesus is picking up the central themes of the covenant established between God and God's people and using them as the foundations of his earthly ministry. In the covenant, which Jesus does not eradicate but rather fulfills, care for the oppressed, the widow, and the orphan leads to a blessing of abundance and prosperity in the land that God had given to his people. In Jesus' vision of the kingdom of God, he announces the inauguration of a social, as well as ecological, rejuvenation in which "social justice and ecological health are bound together."[4] This passage from Luke is just one of many examples of the ways in which Jesus shows care and concern for all of creation throughout the Gospels.

JOHN 1:1–14: LOGOS CHRISTOLOGY—WHAT IF GOD WERE ONE OF US?

In this text, Jesus Christ is identified as the Word, or Logos, of God, the one through whom "all things came into being" (John 1:3), thereby linking Christ with the work of creation in Genesis 1–2. Calling Jesus the Word, or Logos (which is Greek for *word*), would have connected him with concepts familiar to many in both the Jewish and Hellenistic ancient world. Those familiar with the Hebrew Scriptures would recognize the reference to the personification of wisdom as it is found, for example, in the books of Proverbs and the Wisdom of Solomon. In Greek philosophy (especially in Stoic thought), the Logos referred to the divine reason, wisdom, and order

4. Steven Bouma-Prediger, *For the Beauty of the Earth: A Christian Vision for Creation Care* (Grand Rapids, MI: Baker Academic, 2001), 157.

that exist throughout the universe. Thus, the author of the Gospel of John is indicating that in the person of Jesus, there exists a continuity between the Hebrew Scriptures, the New Testament, and ancient Greek philosophy: Jesus is the embodiment of the wisdom of the creator and sustainer of the entire universe.

Moreover, the Gospel's author introduces the phrase "all things" (Greek: *ta panta*), which will become an important phrase in many of the key passages to be considered. This phrase also indicates that Jesus is the creator and sustainer of all forms of life and all of creation, not just the human creation. Finally, the Gospel of John indicates that "the Word became flesh and dwelt among us" (John 1:14). The word used here in the Greek, *eskenosen*, literally means "to take up residence or to tabernacle,"[5] and its root refers to a tent as a dwelling place. Hence, it could also be translated as God "pitched his tent among us." This "image refers to the people of Israel wandering in the wilderness. Wherever they went they would pitch a big tent—a tabernacle—and God would reside with them. In Jesus, God tented among us."[6] The theme of the Incarnation, given its most classic expression by John, indicates that the movement in salvation history that brings humankind into closer communion with God is the act of God's choice to dwell in the flesh, to pitch his tent, among us.

EPHESIANS 1:10; COLOSSIANS 1:15–20: CHRIST, THE ULTIMATE TRANSFORMER, THE COSMIC CENTER OF ALL THINGS

If the Prologue to the Gospel of John presents an earthly and fleshly vision of God's creation and Incarnation in Jesus Christ, then in these two passages, Paul presents a cosmic vision of Christ vis-à-vis the universe. In Ephesians 1:10, Paul declares that Christ will "gather up all things in him, things in heaven and things on earth." Notice again the repetition of the theme that Christ, the Logos, is the creator and

5. Frederick William Danker, ed., *A Greek-English Lexicon of the New Testament and Other Early Christian Literature,* 3rd ed. (Chicago: University of Chicago Press, 2000), 929.

6. Bouma-Prediger, *For the Beauty*, 31.

sustainer of "all things"; he is the one who holds all things together. This phrase, "all things," is also repeated four times in one of the most beautiful hymns in the New Testament: Colossians 1:15–20. Paul repeats what John has established, that all "things visible and invisible" (verse 16) have been created through Christ; he then adds that "in him all things hold together" (verse 17), and that "through him God was pleased to reconcile to himself all things" (verse 20). This is a compelling vision put forth by Paul in which Christ, the firstborn and head of all creation and of the Church, becomes the lens through which Christians see the entirety of reality, encompassing all of creation and all that is not visible to the human eye or comprehensible to the human mind. In this cosmic vision, all things are held together, sustained, and redeemed in Christ. For Paul and for the New Testament writers as a whole, creation (and indeed, all of reality) is understood only in and through the person and actions of Jesus Christ.

Moreover, as the Logos, the center of creation in which all things cohere and hold together, Christ is vested with great power. Yet, this is not the kind of power that he uses to dominate or "lord it over them" (Matthew 20:25). Christ "did not regard equality with God as something to be exploited, / but emptied himself, / taking the form of a slave, being born in human likeness" (Philippians 2:6–7). This is what is referred to as Christ's *kenosis*, which in Greek means "self-emptying." Thus, despite being one with and equal to God, Jesus did not seek to dominate creation; his model was one of service, self-sacrificing love, and gentle care and concern for all of humanity and creation.

1 CORINTHIANS 15: THE RESURRECTION OF THE BODY

Although Paul is able to present his readers with potent cosmic images of Christ, he also refers to the human experience of embodiment to draw analogies and comparisons to what existence will be like when the fullness of redemption has been accomplished. It may be helpful to place this particular chapter of 1 Corinthians into the larger context of the Judeo-Christian world that Paul is addressing.

PHARISEES AND SADDUCEES

The Sadducees were the priestly aristocracy, the ruling class who presided over sacrifices in the Jerusalem Temple. They traced their roots back to Zadok, the high priest during the kingships of David and Solomon, who were among the first kings of the ancient Israelite dynasty (beginning in approximately 1000 BCE). The Pharisees challenged the primacy of the rule of the Sadducees and taught that all were called to faithfully practice the Law of Moses (found in the Pentateuch or Torah, the first five books of the Hebrew Scripture: Genesis, Exodus, Leviticus, Numbers, and Deuteronomy) through careful study and reflection. They began the study of the Law in the synagogues, which were gathering places for worship and Torah study in villages throughout the region.[7]

During the period of Christ's life and immediately following, there was an ongoing debate among Jewish scholars about whether God would bring about a resurrection of the body. There were two competing schools of thought on this point: one represented by the Pharisees and the other by the Sadducees.

The Pharisees claimed that the body would be resurrected, while the Sadducees did not. In the first letter to the Corinthians, Paul, who was a Pharisee before his conversion to Christ (cf. Acts 23:6), takes the Resurrection of Christ as further and more definitive proof of what he had already held to be true as a Pharisee. For Paul, Christ's Resurrection from the dead is definitive proof of a general resurrection of the dead (cf. 1 Corinthians 15:12).

Yet, this belief in resurrection encourages the question of what kind of body those resurrected from the dead will inhabit. In answering this question, Paul ties together two words commonly used to designate embodied existence. In verse 38, he uses the word *body*

7. Cyrus Adler, et al., eds., *The Jewish Encyclopedia* (New York: Ktav Publishing House, 1964), vol. 9, "Pharisees," 661–666; vol. 10, "Sadducees," 630–633.

(Greek: *soma*), and in verse 39, he uses the term *flesh* (Greek: *sarx*). Thus, "Paul links the human body [*soma*] with the same kind of physical reality that animals, birds, and fishes share in [*sarx*], albeit in different ways."[8] In drawing together these two manners of expressing our embodied existence, Paul is demonstrating that one's body, whether as it is now or as it will be in the resurrection, cannot be imagined in the absence of the material existence of the rest of creation; that is, "all things." However, Paul's belief should not be used to claim that the resurrected body would be exactly as it is now. For Paul writes that one's current body is but a "bare seed" (verse 37) of the spiritual, resurrected body that is to come (verses 42–44). When the fullness of redemption has arrived, our perishable bodies shall put on an imperishable body, capable of immortality (verse 54), in the same way that Christ's resurrected body became imperishable, yet remained in a physical body (cf. Luke 24:39).

First Corinthians 15 is strong evidence for the Christian belief that the future redemption promised in Christ will entail some kind of embodied existence, albeit one that is radically transformed. The implication is that for those redeemed in Christ to assume some altered form of embodied existence, the entirety of creation must also be altered to sustain and foster an imperishable and immortal body. The idea of altering the entirety of creation "suggests that the world of nature is by no means absent from the eschatological program set out in the New Testament . . . The world of nature is an integral component of God's new creation work."[9] The Christian tradition has tended to favor a vision of redemption focused narrowly on the redemption of the soul divorced from its physical, embodied existence. If one is to take the resurrection of the body seriously, following here the scriptural witness, then one must seriously consider that redemption will affect not only one's soul, but also one's body, as well as the entirety of creation.

---

8. George H. Kehm, "The New Story: Redemption as Fulfillment of Creation," in *After Nature's Revolt: Eco-Justice and Theology*, ed. Dieter T. Hessel (Minneapolis: Fortress, 1992), 101. See also Holmes Rolston, "Does Nature Need to Be Redeemed?" *Horizons in Biblical Theology* 14, no. 2 (1992): 143–172.

9. Douglas J. Moo, "Nature in the New Creation: New Testament Eschatology and the Environment," *Journal of the Evangelical Theology Society* 49, no. 3 (2006): 482.

ROMANS 8:18–23: THE COSMIC REDEMPTION OF CREATION

Paul deals directly with the redemption of creation in the eighth chapter of the letter to the Romans. Speaking about the hope that inspires and sustains the Christian on the journey to God, Paul indicates that even the creation itself participates in this hope and longing: "For the creation waits with eager longing for the revealing of the children of God" (verse 19). Why would the creation itself wait with eager longing for redemption? One answer to this question suggests that perhaps the creation itself has been affected by human sinfulness. This reading is supported by Paul's words when he writes that "creation was subjected to futility" (verse 20), and that "creation itself will be set free from its bondage to decay and will obtain the freedom of the glory of the children of God" (verse 21). In this section, Paul is referring to the curse placed upon Adam and Eve as a result of their sin in Genesis 3:17 when God proclaims, "cursed is the ground because of you," which indicates a curse has been placed upon creation as well.

In other words, not only humans, and not only the disembodied soul of humans, are in need of redemption. The entirety of creation is in need of, and participates in, the redemption of Christ. This may strike many as somewhat shocking, especially if they have been formed in a religious upbringing that places a greater emphasis on the redemption of the human soul apart from the body or creation. In Romans 8, Paul makes a direct connection between the redemption of creation and the redemption of the body (note that Paul does not use the word *soul* [*psuche*] here, but rather *body* [*soma*]). It is important to keep this element of Paul's thought in mind, especially when encountering passages in which he seems to indicate a strong opposition between "the desires of the flesh" and those of the spirit (Galatians 5:16–18). Despite these examples in which Paul's rhetoric can seem overly hostile to "the flesh" (see also Romans 7:23–24), in Paul's thought, there is no radical separation of the body from the soul, neither of the body and the flesh from the rest of created existence; all of these elements will participate in the redemption offered through Christ.

2 PETER 3:10: THE PASSING AWAY OF THE PRESENT REALITY: WHAT IS TRULY LEFT BEHIND?

This text presents the greatest challenge to the interpretation of the role of creation in the New Testament that is being offered in this chapter. The text has been broken down into sections (a–c) to facilitate analysis:

> [a]But the day of the Lord will come like a thief, and then the heavens will pass away with a loud noise, [b]and the elements will be dissolved with fire, [c]and the earth and everything that is done on it will be disclosed. (2 Peter 3:10)

This passage is commonly used by those Christians who argue against the idea that Christian faith demands protection of the environment.[10] If God is simply planning to destroy Earth and everything on it to prepare the way for the salvation of disembodied human souls, then what is the point of protecting Earth and the environment from harm? Such an argument might be made from this text. Careful analysis of this passage is necessary to arrive at an interpretation of the text that is faithful to the meaning of the Scripture and that can still account for thc continued existence of creation and the resurrected body.

The key to this passage revolves around understanding what is meant by two terms: *dissolved by fire* (verse 10[b]) and *disclosed* (verse 10[c]). The first phrase is rendered from the Greek, *kausoumena luthesetai*, which literally states that, the elements "while burning will be destroyed." The second section (10[c]) is translated from the Greek word *heurethesetai*, which means, "to be found out, discovered, or disclosed."[11] There is no escaping that verse 10[b] indicates that the elements will be destroyed. In dealing with this difficult text, it is problematic that many translations have taken the meaning of destruction from 10[b] and carried its meaning into 10[c]. Doing so leads to what one

---

10. David Horrell, et al., "Appeals to the Bible in Ecotheology and Environmental Ethics: A Typology of Hermeneutical Stances," *Studies in Christian Ethics* 21 (2008): 219–238.

11. Danker, *Greek-English Lexicon*, 411–412.

scholar considers "perhaps the most egregious mistranslation of the entire New Testament,"[12] and it lends credibility to reading this text as if the natural elements of creation will be completely destroyed at Christ's return. For example, both the King James Version and the Revised Standard Version translate verse 10^c as "the earth . . . shall be burned up." The difficulty in ascertaining the meaning of the whole of verse 10 lies in the tension between these sections, with the first seeming to indicate destruction by fire and the second referring to what will be found out, laid bare, or discovered.

If we are able to avoid the pitfall of transposing the meaning of verse 10^b into verse 10^c, then a possible translation presents itself that preserves previous scriptural insights about the continued existence of a transformed creation in the final stages of God's divine plan. Verse 10^b likely refers back to verse 7 in which Paul writes "the present heavens and earth have been reserved for fire, being kept until the day of judgment" (2 Peter 3:7). If verses 7 and 10 were linked, it would provide evidence for seeing the fire in 10^b as a reference to a fire of purification in preparation for judgment rather than for destruction. Moreover, there is a connection between a destructive fire and the act of purification and judgment before God in some important texts of the Hebrew Scriptures (e.g., Isaiah 30:30, Nahum 1:6, Micah 1:3–4). If one thinks of the destruction by fire noted in this verse as referring to a purification and judgment, and if one keeps the meaning of parts 10^b and 10^c of this verse separate, then this text can be defended against those who interpret it to refer to the complete destruction of the natural world. One might argue that this will be the end of the world, as one knows it, not necessarily the end of the *entire* world. While it still seems appropriate to maintain the reference to a consuming fire in 10^b, it can also be reconciled with the later verb in 10^c, *heurethesetai*, which as noted previously means "will be found out/disclosed." In this sense, the purifying fire of God's judgment (10^b) leads to a disclosure of all that is done on Earth (10^c) as a necessary element of the judgment that precedes the redemption promised in Christ. This interpretation would still leave room for the possibility of a creation that has been transformed and purified by God's judgment but not one that has been destroyed. In

12. Bouma-Prediger, *For the Beauty*, 77.

fact, the fire of destruction could be a reference to removing and purifying all that has become accursed in the creation due to the Fall and human sin (Genesis 3), thereby, disclosing the true nature of the entire Earth as God originally intended it to be before sin and the Fall. Interpreted in this manner, 2 Peter 3:10 can be reconciled with the vision of the transformed reality that Paul references in 1 Corinthians 15. If this interpretation of 2 Peter 3:10 is correct, then a feasible translation of the text might read, "the elements will be purified by fire, and the earth and everything that is done on it will be disclosed" (author's translation).

REVELATION 21–22: A NEW HEAVEN AND A NEW EARTH

Shortly after the passage discussed previously in 2 Peter, the author writes that "we wait for new heavens and a new earth" (2 Peter 3:13), and this theme arises again in the Revelation of John at the end of the book. Written around 100 CE and the latest biblical example of the genre of apocalyptic literature, the Revelation is notoriously difficult to interpret. Apocalyptic literature refers to works that reveal (apocalypse literally means "unveiling") what is happening during a time of intense persecution and how God will act to bring about the end of evil or suffering and usher in a new age in which peace and justice reign. As a genre of the Hebrew Bible, it began to be developed after the period of the Jewish exile (587–538 BCE) and can be witnessed, for example, in the book of Daniel.

In this poetic dream sequence, the author of Revelation is given a vision of the heavenly city, the new Jerusalem, that will come down from heaven and establish God's kingdom on Earth. The end of Revelation has a close parallel with the beginning of the Gospel of John, in which reference is made to God's dwelling (literally, tabernacling/pitching his tent) among mortals (cf. Revelation 21:3). The entire movement of these two chapters is one of God's presence dwelling among creation, rather than the human soul transcending the natural world and rising to spend eternity in a disembodied heavenly existence. Passages like this one demonstrate that the New Testament, "contrary to popular Christian parlance, does not usually claim that we will spend eternity in heaven, but in a new heaven and a new earth."[13] Once again, a close reading of the New Testament reveals that the promise of Christian salvation is not identified as the disembodied existence of an eternal soul but as the radical transformation of the human current embodied existence, in which the perfection that can only be brought forth by God's grace is given as a gift to dwell "among mortals" (Revelation 21:3). Finally, drawing attention back to the cosmic redemption proclaimed in Romans 8 and the undoing of the curse upon creation in Genesis 3, Revelation states that "nothing accursed will be found there anymore" (22:3). In this vision, the creation has been freed from its curse and has returned to the original intention of the Creator, in which "death will be no more" (21:4). The author ends his description of the revelation given to him by leaving his readers with a compelling image of a redeemed world in which the natural elements of creation (light, earth, water) all maintain a significant role within the new and heavenly Jerusalem established by God. This image is beautifully portrayed in the tree of life, whose leaves "are for the healing of the nations" (Revelation 22:2).

CONCLUSION: ENDING WHERE WE BEGAN

It has been suggested that Genesis 1–3 and Revelation 20–22 should be read as one grand *inclusio*, "clearly pointing to the unity of the testaments."[14] An *inclusio* is a literary tool sometimes used by the authors of Scripture, in which an important theme occurs at the introduction and then again at the end of a text and highlights the theme as an important element in interpreting everything that falls between. Interpreted this way, the story of creation, sin, and the Fall in Genesis 1–3 and the cosmic, embodied redemption in Revelation 20–22, present convincing evidence for the Christian expectation that the redemption offered in Christ will entail a transformation, but not destruction, of the physical and material existence of the universe.

13. Moo, "Nature in the New Creation," 464.

14. Ronald Manahan, "Christ as Second Adam," in *The Environment and the Christian: What Does the New Testament Say About the Environment?* ed. Calvin Dewitt (Grand Rapids, MI: Baker House, 1991), 46.

Such an understanding has important implications both for biblical exegesis and for the way such exegesis contributes to the development of environmental theology and ethics. In the first instance, the hermeneutical experiment contributes to efforts to challenge assumptions operative in biblical interpretation until fairly recently. The first of these assumptions is that salvation is directed primarily toward a disembodied existence of contemplation of God. In fact, one could speculate that to perceive such a vision of God, humans will need precisely the kind of transformed and immortal eyes that are promised in the vision of 1 Corinthians 15. Another aspect of biblical exegesis that is shifting—thanks to the growing awareness of the importance of human responsibility for creation—is the manner in which modern biblical interpretation (especially in the nineteenth and early twentieth centuries) has focused almost exclusively on God's saving actions as occurring within history. A major assumption of modern biblical scholarship is that "biblical religion is concerned about history, not about nature."[15] In this dichotomy, pagan religion(s) find god(s) in the miraculous powers of nature, while the Judeo-Christian God is revealed in history. Modern Christians' explication of the role of creation and nature in the New Testament challenges such a narrow assumption. The New Testament clearly shows God's plan *for creation in history*. The two cannot be separated without doing damage to the integrity of the scriptural witness.

This newer understanding also has important implications for the continuing development of an environmental theology and ethic. Creation has an intrinsic value to God that is not merely instrumental. Moreover, it is not just that humankind has one unique role to play in God's plan of salvation, while creation has another. Rather, the two cannot be separated: the human cannot be imagined, either before or after the ultimate fulfillment of God's plan, apart from the created world. Neither can God's justice be conceived of without incorporating a healing care for, and transformation of, creation along with the transformation and redemption of God's people. Therefore, because of the interdependence between creation and the human

15. Theodore Hiebert, "Rethinking Traditional Approaches to Nature in the Bible," in *Theology for Earth Community: A Field Guide*, ed. Dieter T. Hessel (Maryknoll, NY: Orbis, 1996), 23.

body, the harm inflicted upon any element of creation is ultimately harm inflicted upon humans, as well as an affront to the plan for all of creation that God has revealed in Christ.

Moreover, as Saint Paul reminds Christians, they are called to "put on the Lord Jesus Christ" (Romans 13:14) and to "have the mind of Christ" (1 Corinthians 2:16) within them. Another way of thinking about this is to recognize that all are created in the image of God (cf. Genesis 1:27), and part of the Christian vocation is to live as fully as possible in the dignity of that image. In the hymn from Colossians, Paul writes that Jesus "is the image of the invisible God" (1:15). Hence, Jesus is the model for what it means to be made in the image of God. What this implies for an environmental theology is that one is to look closely at the way Christ treated the natural world around him in his own ministry, because as the divine Logos and image of God, he is the model for Christian life. Jesus practiced his ministry and healing through the use of the natural world in miracles, and his vision of the kingdom of God includes justice, care, and love for creation, for one's neighbors, and for the oppressed. Additionally, in his kenotic self-emptying (cf. Philippians 2:6), Jesus demonstrated that even the Son of God chooses to exercise his power in the form of care for creation and the powerless, for healing and service. Hence, in exercising dominion as humans (cf. Genesis 1:28), humans too are called to practice gentle care and service toward all that God has created. This is an essential element of what it means to develop a biblically informed, theological-ecological imagination.

If one looks at all of created reality through the lens of the Church's experience of the risen Christ, as all of the authors of the New Testament do, it becomes apparent that creation has its own unique role to play in God's divine providence and plan of salvation. Although one can never be certain how existence will be for those who are called to eternal life with God, the texts of the New Testament indicate that in the resurrected body, there will be some form of embodied existence that is analogically related to our current experience of human life in the natural world. The Scriptures do not tell that the world will be destroyed in order for the souls of the saved to pass over into a new, disembodied existence, but rather that the world will be judged, purified, and transformed to make way for a new way of living that is beyond one's current comprehension.

Yet this is not simply a future hope that has no bearing for how one lives today. Christian care and concern for the natural world is important *now* precisely because of what one hopes for in the *future*. One does not hope to be saved *from* the world but rather to be saved *in* the world; one awaits a new heaven and a new Earth. This is the hope of the Christian faith and the vision presented by the New Testament, and it entails the renewed and continuing existence of the created universe for all of eternity. Meanwhile, as humans "wait with eager longing" (Romans 8:19) for God's final consummation of history and nature, they are called to continue to develop an environmental theology and an ethic based on it that recognize and respect the inherent integrity of creation for its own sake and for the sake of the special role it plays in God's plan of salvation.

QUESTIONS FOR REVIEW

1. Describe what is meant by "hermeneutic circle" and "fusion of horizons" with regard to interpreting the Bible for questions we confront today.
2. In what New Testament passage does the Greek word *kenosis* appear, and what does it mean?
3. Why does Paul say in Romans 8:19 that "the creation waits with eager longing for the revealing of the children of God," and what does he mean by this?
4. In what New Testament passages does the idea of tabernacling or pitching a tent (Gr. *eskenosen*) surface, and what is its significance?
5. Explain why we might interpret the "new heaven and new Earth" of Revelation 21–22 as describing an end to the world as we know it?

IN-DEPTH QUESTIONS

1. Before reading this chapter, what were your notions about "the afterlife"? Why did you have this view, and from where did you receive it? In what ways does it differ from the understanding presented in this chapter?

2. In what ways does this chapter support the claim that the Incarnation demonstrates that for God, matter matters?
3. Explain what is meant by the point about how the New Testament clearly shows God's plan *for creation in history*.
4. What are some themes or insights about humankind, God, and creation that the New Testament shares with the Hebrew Scriptures?
5. In which New Testament passages are "all things" (Greek: *ta panta*) considered? Do you think this means that God loves humans less than or the same as the rest of creation? Explain your response.
6. What are some New Testament themes from this chapter that Pope Benedict XVI highlighted in his 2010 World Day of Peace Message, "If You Want to Cultivate Peace, Protect Creation," from chapter 3? What are some New Testament themes from this chapter that Benedict did not address?

CHRISTIAN TRADITION

CHAPTER 6

RETRIEVING SAINT FRANCIS:

Tradition and Innovation for Our Ecological Vocation

Keith Douglass Warner, OFM

KEY TERMS

discipleship
religious ecological consciousness
patron saint
religious retrieval
environmentalist
ecologist
tradition
vocation

The Canticle of the Creatures, by Saint Francis of Assisi (1182–1226)

Most High, all-powerful, good Lord
Yours are the praises, the glory, and the honor and the blessing.
To You alone, Most High, do they belong,
And no human is worthy to mention Your name.
Praised be You, my Lord, with all Your creatures,
Especially Sir Brother Sun,
Who is the day and through whom You give us light.
And he is beautiful and radiant with great splendor;
And bears a likeness of You, Most High One.
Praised be You, my Lord, through Sister Moon and the stars,
In heaven You formed them clear and precious and beautiful.
Praised be You, my Lord, through Brother Wind,

And through the air, cloudy and serene, and every kind of weather,
Through whom You give sustenance to Your creatures.
Praised be You, my Lord, through Sister Water,
Who is very useful and humble and precious and chaste.
Praised be You, my Lord, through Brother Fire,
Through whom You light the night,
And he is beautiful and playful and robust and strong.
Praised be You my Lord, through our Sister Mother Earth,
Who sustains and governs us,
And who produces various fruit with colored flowers and herbs.
Praised be You, my Lord, through those who give pardon for
 Your love,
And bear infirmity and tribulation.
Blessed are those who endure in peace
For by You, Most High, shall they be crowned.
Praised be You, my Lord, through our Sister Bodily Death,
from whom no one living can escape.
Woe to those who die in mortal sin.
Blessed are those whom death will find in Your most holy will,
for the second death shall do them no harm.
Praised be You my Lord and give him thanks
And serve him with great humility.[1]

INTRODUCTION

Saint Francis of Assisi is widely acclaimed as the preeminent example of Christian care for creation. British royalty, scientists, leaders of other faiths, diverse scholars, and ordinary believers have claimed him as their inspiration in this age of ecological crisis. Why does he have such a broad appeal? First, Francis recognized God's work in creation and loved it. *The Canticle of the Creatures* celebrates his passionate and sensory love of creation. He celebrated the beauty of God in creation and loved God all the more for this gift. Second, Francis experienced God in creation, and this is a most helpful

1. All texts of the writings by and about Saint Francis are taken from Regis Armstrong, OFM Capuchin, Wayne Hellman, OFM Conventual, and William Short OFM, eds., *Francis of Assisi: Early Documents,* vol. I: *The Saint* (New York: New City Press, 1999). Subsequently referred to as FA: ED. *The Canticle* is on pages 113–114.

starting point for contemporary Christian theology. Many Christians have overemphasized the "stain of original sin" and forgotten the more fundamental reality of creation as the good gift of God. Third, Francis provides an example of reflective action. His encounter with the pain of the world inspired him to pray with passion but also to act with compassion and proclaim the Good News of Jesus Christ.

Francis' radical Christian discipleship—his dedication to living the gospel of Jesus Christ—and passionate love of creation represent an important example of religious ecological consciousness, which means an awareness of humans' inescapable ecological interdependent relationship with Earth, its elements and living organisms.[2] Francis' ecological consciousness influenced his religious imagination, his vision for moral living, his prayer, and his preaching. His life gives witness to an ecological wisdom, to how human beings can live a good life in relationship to the Earth. His witness can inspire in us a vocational response, devoting one's whole life to God's love and the needs of the world. Francis is among the most beloved Catholic saints, and his example speaks to men and women of all traditions and to those who do not profess any religious faith. By exploring his ecological witness, we can learn how faith traditions more generally can participate in broader efforts to create a more sustainable society.

Yet, Francis lived in the Middle Ages on the Italian peninsula without any notion of science or what modern people would call environmental problems. How can he be a patron saint of ecologists, given that he died more than six centuries before the invention of ecological science? Similarly, many who today tout him as a religious environmental hero ignore the problem of selectively plucking his admirable features out of his historical context. Lynn White Jr., for instance, describes Francis as "clearly heretical," ignoring the inconvenient truth that Pope Gregory IX canonized Francis a saint in 1228, two years after his death, in the Catholic Church. Many find Francis inspiring, but few acknowledge the tricky issues of selectively retrieving features from a medieval saint's biography.

These problems are aggravated by the complex and often contradictory character of the writings by and about Francis. He was a medieval man in a society quite different from ours today, and one cannot

2. Christopher Uhl, *Developing Ecological Consciousness: Paths to a Sustainable World* (Lanham, MD: Rowman & Littlefield, 2004).

SAINT FRANCIS OF ASSISI

IMAGE © THE GALLERY COLLECTION/CORBIS

"St. Francis of Assisi Preaching to the Birds," a predella painting from "The Stigmatization of St. Francis," ca. 1295–1300. Francis is widely loved and respected for his radical Christian discipleship and passionate love of creation, which many today regard as a model for religious ecological consciousness.

Francis' care for creation is but one expression of his vocation, which was rooted in his passionate love of Jesus Christ. Francis was foremost a follower of Jesus, but in him, there was no tension between loving God and loving all creatures of God. His life was marked by a succession of intense religious experiences—what might be called conversion events—that drew him deeper into the mystery of God. Francis was the most popular saint of the Middle Ages because of the dramatic and public expressions of his conversion events and because he made the message of God's love accessible to ordinary people. His life inspires faith in Jesus Christ and care for creation. In 1967, Lynn White Jr. proposed Francis as "the patron saint of ecologists"[3] and twelve years later, Pope John Paul II enacted this suggestion.

slavishly mimic him. To do so would require pretending modern people were also medieval. Looking to Francis for inspiration requires attention to the fundamental differences between his world and today's. Present-day people have to interpret his example, to translate the significance of his witness in his times into terms that are meaningful in the context of

3. Lynn White Jr. "The Historical Roots of Our Ecologic Crisis," *Science* 155, no. 3767 (1967): 1203–1207.

PATRON SAINTS

What is a patron saint, and why does the Catholic Church have them? The lives of patron saints are presented as examples of Christian faith and virtue. Through the centuries, the Church has informally and formally recognized distinguished Christian and held them up as examples for the inspiration of all. They are selected years or centuries after their death to speak to the spiritual aspirations of a contemporary society. Pope John Paul II took Lynn White Jr.'s initial, almost casual suggestion that Francis be named a patron saint, but named Francis an example for a wide range of people working on a broader agenda of social transformation, a much bigger vision than the science of ecology alone offers.

contemporary culture. This requires deciding on appropriate expressions of his wisdom, insight, and consciousness to guide life choices today. To do so entails exercising wisdom in interpreting Francis.

To make Francis' witness meaningful in contemporary culture, one must undertake a retrieval process. Religious retrieval is a broad set of activities taking place across all faiths to select the most appropriate beliefs, human values, and ritual practices to represent their religious identity to the modern world. The selective retrieval of traditions is a fundamental task in the "greening of religions," because this is the chief feature that distinguishes religious environmentalism from other expressions of environmental concern.[4]

This chapter addresses the problem of interpreting the witness of Francis by explaining how and why he and his ecological wisdom have been retrieved. It will draw from the broader reappropriation of Franciscan spirituality and illustrate general issues in the retrieval and reinterpretation of tradition in the greening of religions. This chapter begins by describing how Pope John Paul II represented Francis as a model of environmental care. It examines the key features of

4. See Roger S. Gottlieb, *A Greener Faith: Religious Environmentalism and Our Planet's Future* (Oxford: Oxford University Press, 2006).

Francis' ecological wisdom and then pivots perspective to examine how Franciscans are reinterpreting this wisdom today as part of a broader retrieval process. It concludes by proposing that tradition and innovation are both necessary in the greening of discipleship.

THE "PATRON SAINT OF ECOLOGISTS"

In 1979, Pope John Paul II named Saint Francis of Assisi "heavenly patron of those who promote ecology," referring to Francis' *Canticle of the Creatures*.[5] Ten years later, the pope launched Catholic concern for the environment with his World Day of Peace Message, "The Ecological Crisis: A Common Responsibility."[6] So great was the impact of "The Ecological Crisis" that it ended the debate about *whether* Catholics should be concerned about the environment, and the discussion shifted to *how* Catholics should express their care for creation.[7] John Paul II articulated new ethical duties for Catholics, indeed for the whole human family. He diagnosed the environmental crisis as rooted in a moral crisis for humanity: sin, selfishness, and a lack of respect for life. He proposed several remedies, religious and ethical. He said humanity should explore, examine, and "safeguard" the integrity of creation. He described duties of individuals and institutions of all kinds: for the nations of the world to cooperate at an international level in the management of Earth's goods, for individual nations to care for their citizens, and for individuals to undertake an education in ecological responsibility, for oneself, for others, and for Earth. In the final section of "The Ecological Crisis," John Paul II addressed "my brothers and sisters in the Catholic Church, in order to remind them of their serious obligation to care for all creation." He expressed "hope that the inspiration of Saint Francis will help

5. Pope John Paul II, "*S. Franciscus Assisiensis caelestis Patronus oecologicae cultorum eligitur*," *Acta Apostolica Sedis* 71 (1979): 1509–1510.

6. Pope John Paul II, "The Ecological Crisis: A Common Responsibility," World Day of Peace Message 1990, in *And God Saw That It Was Good: Catholic Theology and the Environment*, eds. Drew Christiansen, SJ, and W. Grazer (Washington, DC: United States Catholic Conference, 1996).

7. Keith Douglass Warner, OFM, "The Greening of American Catholicism: Identity, Conversion and Continuity," *Religion and American Culture: A Journal of Interpretation* 18, no. 1 (2008): 113–142.

us to keep ever alive a sense of 'fraternity' with all those good and beautiful things which Almighty God has created."

The difference in language between White's proposal and the official English translation of John Paul II's announcement is subtle but important; it merits close analysis because it indicates how concern for Catholic identity shapes this retrieval process. White proposed Francis as the patron saint of ecologists, but the original Latin in the 1979 Vatican document named Francis patron of *oecologicae cultorum*, officially translated as "those who cultivate or promote ecology." What did the pope have in mind with this term? In the United States, one distinguishes environmentalist (a public advocate for environmental protection) from ecologist (a scientist who practices a subfield of biology). In Italian and the Romance languages, however, many people use the terms *ecology* and *environmental concern* interchangeably. In Europe, those who "promote ecology" are environmental advocates and not necessarily ecological scientists. Thus, in the North American context, the meaning of the original Latin could readily be translated as *environmentalists*, *environmental educators*, or *environmental advocates*. Latin, the language of official Catholic documents, has no word for *environmentalist*, so the pope had to select a different term. Yet, modern American terms were not chosen for the official English translation, perhaps because most Catholic leaders—even those highly concerned about the environment—have warily avoided these labels and their associated controversies.

Still, it is important to note that John Paul II was quite open to conducting dialogue with the sciences. He repeated the term *ecology* and its derivatives throughout his pontificate, expressing concern about the direction of human society and reminding his audiences of their moral duties. Taken as a whole, his environmental teachings support stewardship but reframe the rationale and approach within a broad Catholic worldview shaped by Catholic social teaching principles.[8] In the last years of his life, he emphasized human duties to future generations.

---

8. Marjorie Keenan, RSHM, *From Stockholm to Johannesburg: An Historical Overview of the Concern of the Holy See for the Environment 1972–2002* (Vatican City: Pontifical Council for Justice and Peace, 2002).

> It is necessary, therefore, to stimulate and sustain the "ecological conversion," which over these last decades has made humanity more sensitive when facing the catastrophe toward which it was moving. . . . Therefore, not only is a "physical" ecology at stake, attentive to safeguarding the habitat of different living beings, but also a "human" ecology that will render the life of creatures more dignified, protecting the radical good of life in all its manifestations and preparing an environment for future generations that is closer to the plan of the Creator.[9]

The pope affirmed that the biological and physical world of creation is important but that human flourishing is important as well. He also said humankind's "ecological vocation" is more urgent than ever, given the grave threats to the environment.[10] These examples illustrate how John Paul II advocated a profound, critical analysis of the root causes of the environmental crisis. Most conventional environmentalists address the problems of heedless industrial growth and flawed public policy. Pope John Paul II challenged everyone to recognize that the ecological crises are rooted in a much more profound problem, a disordered understanding of what it means to be human in relationship to God and to fellow humans. His critique went further than conventional U.S. environmentalism and called for deeper reflection on making better choices, wiser choices that can uphold gospel values. His concerns reflect his continued insistence on a strong and clear Catholic identity and his vision of bringing this tradition to bear on the problems of modernity. Throughout his pontificate, John Paul II affirmed the importance of solidarity and awareness of our inescapable interdependence. In light of the breadth of his environmental teaching, *oecologicae cultorum* can reasonably be translated as *ecological consciousness*, and Francis is the patron saint of those who promote it.

---

9. Pope John Paul II, General Audience Address, January 17, 2001; available at *http://conservation.catholic.org/john_paul_ii.htm,* accessed December 18, 2008.

10. Pope John Paul II, "God Made Man the Steward of Creation," *L'Osservatore Romano*, January 24, 2001, 11.

CHRIST, FRANCIS, AND CREATION

Francis' relationship with creation should be understood within the broader context of his religious journey: its essential themes of passionate love for Jesus Christ, the desire to follow him, contemplative prayer, ongoing conversion of life, and a spirituality of brotherhood with everyone and everything. Francis' historical record has an astonishing diversity of material. Until recently, most of the popular books about of his life have been based on medieval legends written decades or centuries after his life, by people who did not personally know him. These include many later additions of questionable historical accuracy. Since the Second Vatican Council, scholars have emphasized Francis' own writings because they convey his voice. This new scholarship emphasizes his dedication to following Jesus Christ, his love of the Gospels and the Eucharist, his practice of contemplative prayer, and his public proclamation of God's love and peace. Some surprising insights have emerged. For example, Francis was not a priest; he split his time between wilderness hermitages and urban preaching; and he had no intention of starting a religious order. He set out to foster lay vocations among all people.

Some of the new scholarship has addressed his relationship with Earth, highlighting his love of animals and the elements.[11] The medieval stories about Francis describe spiritual encounters with rabbits, fish, worms, bees, crickets, and lambs. The most famous story is that of him preaching to the birds, but contemporary popularization in the form of Francis as a garden statue completely fails to recognize the radical significance of this encounter.[12] His first biographer explains:

> After the birds had listened so reverently to the word of God, he began to accuse himself of negligence because he had not preached to them before. From that day on, he

11. Dawn M. Nothwehr, OSF, ed., *Franciscan Theology of the Environment: An Introductory Reader* (Quincy, IL: Franciscan Press, 2003); Roger D. Sorrell, *St. Francis of Assisi and Nature* (New York: Oxford University Press, 1988).

12. Keith Douglass Warner, OFM, "Get Him Out of the Birdbath!" in *Franciscan Theology of the Environment*, ed. Dawn M. Nothwehr (Quincy, IL: Franciscan Press, 2002), 361–376.

> carefully exhorted all birds, all animals, all reptiles, and also insensible creatures, to love the Creator, because daily, invoking the name of the Savior, he observed their obedience in his own experience.[13]

The true significance of this story is that Francis awoke to the communion of life he shared with the birds, not that he preached to them. This encounter prompted Francis to further integrate his love of creation with his religious identity and responsibilities. Just as his storied encounter with a leper furthered his religious conversion, so did that with the birds. In ethical terms, nonhuman creatures facilitated an expansion of Francis' moral imagination, because they indicated to him the next set of tasks in his religious journey.

The Canticle of the Creatures best conveys Francis' voice about his experience of creation. Francis reveled in the sun, gazed upon the stars, danced with the air, was drawn to the fire, marveled at water, and caressed the earth. The *Canticle's* vivid images emerged from Francis' sustained contact with the elements and his prayer with the Psalms and gospels. The *Canticle* echoes Psalm 148 and Daniel 3:57–88 and suggests a courtly song of praise to the Creator of the cosmos. Francis, like most vowed religious, would have prayed these regularly, and their imagery would have captured and conveyed his own experience. Francis spent up to one half of each year praying with a few brothers in the wilderness.[14] The early friars practiced contemplative prayer: the practice of responding to love by opening one's heart and by deepening one's awareness of God's love. Contemplation is not liturgical or intercessory prayer. It is not public prayer and does not ask for anything, but rather deepens one's understanding of the depth and breadth and all-encompassing character of God's love.[15]

---

13. Thomas of Celano, "The Life of Saint Francis" in FA:ED, page 234 ff. Technically this is a hagiography, not a biography.

14. W. J. Short, OFM, "Recovering Lost Traditions in Spirituality: Franciscans, Camaldolese and the Hermitage," *Spiritus* 3 (2003): 209–218.

15. I. Delio, OSF, K. D. Warner, OFM, and P. Wood, *Care for Creation: A Contemporary Franciscan Spirituality of the Earth* (Cincinnati, OH: St. Anthony Messenger Press, 2008).

The *Canticle* is a fruit of sustained contemplative spiritual practice, celebrating God's love for all creation and reflected back by creation's praise. It cannot be properly understood apart from Francis' love for Jesus Christ, as expressed through his devotion to the Incarnation and Passion, as experienced through his senses when praying in the wilderness. The *Canticle* discloses Francis' recognition of creation as an expression of God's generous love, that creation has inherent value because God creates it, not because of its material or instrumental value to humans.[16] This is true ecological wisdom.

The renewal of scholarship about Francis began with careful attention to the specifics of his writings and the careful reading of stories about him. The focus of Franciscan scholarship is now shifting to investigate how his religious intuition has shaped the Franciscan tradition: in prayer, preaching, thinking, and acting for the past eight centuries. This work by scholars—women and men, lay and vowed religious—is done to understand the breadth of the Franciscan tradition in history and to open fresh perspectives on how to live out the Franciscan vocation today.[17] Most Franciscans are women, and thus, a great deal of scholarly effort has been devoted to understanding Francis' counterpart Saint Clare, and more recently, Franciscan laywomen. Clare is a powerful witness to contemplative living.[18] The rediscovery of diverse expressions of Franciscan spirituality lived out by laywomen points to the recurrent themes in feminine Franciscan spirituality.[19] In parallel, scholars are now articulating Francis' intuitive spirituality with the philosophical, theological, and cosmological vision of his followers. Saint Bonaventure and Blessed John Duns Scotus are the two most prominent figures in this phase of retrieval.

---

16. Keith Douglass Warner, OFM, "The Moral Significance of Creation in the Franciscan Theological Tradition: Implications for Contemporary Catholics and Public Policy," *University of Saint Thomas Law Journal* 5, no. 1 (2008): 37–52.

17. J. Chinnici, OFM, "Institutional Amnesia and the Challenge of Mobilizing our Resources for Franciscan Theology," in *The Franciscan Intellectual Tradition*, ed. E. Saggau, OSF (Bonaventure, NY: Franciscan Institute Publications, 2002), 105–150.

18. Regis Armstrong, OFM, Capuchin, *Clare of Assisi—The Lady: Early Documents* (NY: New City Press, 2006); Ilia Delio, OSF, *Clare of Assisi: A Heart Full of Love* (Cincinnati, OH: Saint Anthony Messenger Press, 2007).

19. Darlene Pryds, *Women of the Streets: Early Franciscan Women and Their Mendicant Vocation* (Saint Bonaventure, NY: Franciscan Institute and the Secretariat for the Franciscan Intellectual Tradition, 2009).

Bonaventure proposed numerous theological metaphors for understanding creation, and these open fresh avenues for dialogue between science and religion. Scotus articulated a profound and provocative relationship between the Incarnation and creation that provides an alternative approach to Catholic environmental ethics. The Franciscan movement today is actively retrieving the wisdom of these historical figures to inspire and guide humanity into the future.

TRADITION AND INNOVATION FOR ECOLOGICAL VOCATION

This entire book implicitly bears two important questions facing all religious groups seeking to articulate an environmental ethos: which elements (scriptures, rituals, saints, prayer styles, understandings of God) from a tradition can be used to foster a greener discipleship? How should these be integrated with contemporary environmental concerns? It is important to recall that all the environmental teachings in all the world's religions took shape before humans had the capacity to cause the contemporary environmental problems, in other words, before modern environmental ethics were needed. All religions have some ethical resources in their traditions, but they also carry problematic teachings from an environmental perspective, such as the belief in human total superiority to other creatures or the need to reject the world as somehow inferior to communion with the divine.

Reclaiming the importance of tradition is a key feature distinguishing religious from other forms of environmentalism. The word *tradition* comes from the Latin *tradere*, meaning, "to transmit or deliver." This indicates that traditions are not static treasures to be defended but rather living memories and values and ways of being that are shared from one generation to the next. Transmitting tradition becomes more challenging when confronting new problems. Reclaiming tradition for religious environmental ethics requires multiple steps.

- Of all the elements in a religious tradition spanning millennia, which should be selected for *retrieval*? This requires discretion, for some elements of a tradition should be left in the past, and others could be helpful for inspiring action today.

- In light of the current ecological crises, how should humans *reinterpret* these elements, in other words, explain their meaning in an age of ecological crisis? Francis loved creation, but he was not an environmentalist. Pope John Paul II reinterpreted Francis' life as a medieval person to be a model to help us foster greater ecological consciousness today.
- How can these processes *renew* religious identity more generally? This requires thinking critically about what values humans want to animate them today and identifying examples from the past to help in their journey into the future. However, it also requires engagement with new ideas, such as science. Ecological knowledge is an essential component of any environmental ethic today. Thus, renewal is necessarily innovative, because it entails synthesizing the past with present knowledge to create new solutions to problems.

Weaving together the responses to these questions takes the form of a vocation, for they direct attention to the needs of the world. These problems will not be addressed only by individuals or by individual actions but rather by a collective revisioning of humanity. Francis witnesses to what the Catholic and Christian tradition can contribute to this vision of humanity in relationship with nature, but every religious tradition is actively undertaking retrieval efforts to address modern environmental crises. The authentic answer to these questions consists not merely in data nor only in good intentions but also the practice of living one's spiritual life with ecological consciousness.

CONCLUSION

Pope John Paul II urged humanity to fulfill its "ecological vocation" to care for Earth. He fused this classic term from Catholic spirituality with something "new"—*ecology*. This new term draws attention to the wisdom resources from Catholic history but integrates them with contemporary conceptual scientific tools for understanding the ecological consequences of humans' foolish and irresponsible treatment of Earth. Thus, the term *ecological vocation* captures and conveys the wisdom of Catholicism in just two words, fusing tradition and innovation.

THE SAINT FRANCIS PLEDGE

The Catholic Coalition for Climate Change has a Web site with more information for Catholic individuals, families, and parishes about care for the environment. It includes a Saint Francis Pledge that people can make as a way of covenanting their vocation as caretakers of Earth: *http://catholicclimatecovenant.org/the-st-francis-pledge/.*

The example of Francis can inspire people to respond to the cry of Earth with love, compassion, and generosity. People cannot simply mimic him but can look to his example as they formulate their own vocational responses to a world of environmental crises. A contemporary vocational response can draw from Francis' example of ecological consciousness but will have to synthesize something new by combining inspiration, a contemporary moral vision, and the best scientific information. This is how people can best transmit their tradition in an age of ecological crisis.

QUESTIONS FOR REVIEW

1. What is meant by *ecological consciousness*, and how does Saint Francis exemplify it?
2. What is meant by *vocation*, and what does Pope John Paul II say about humanity's ecological vocation?
3. What is meant by *oecologicae cultorum?*
4. Why does the Catholic Church have patron saints? What is their significance?
5. What is the true ecological wisdom that is derived from Saint Francis' *Canticle of the Creatures* and his recognition of creation as an expression of God's love?

IN-DEPTH QUESTIONS

1. Identify ways in which Saint Francis' *Canticle* emphasizes humankind's kinship with creation. How might this view of our relationship with creation affect how we live and how we treat nature?
2. Why is the contemporary popularization of Saint Francis as a garden statue or a birdbath problematic? How might placing such a statue in one's garden instead be a positive practice? What kinds of spiritual practices might contemporary Catholics, as well as those of other religious traditions, undertake to respond to the environmental witness of Francis?
3. What are two teachings in the Christian tradition that are problematic from an environmental perspective? Why? What are some other possibly problematic teachings in the history of Christianity from an environmental perspective?
4. What was your understanding of the word *tradition* before this reading? Why is it important to remember that tradition is not static? How can tradition develop and innovatively address new questions, such as those regarding the environment, while remaining faithful to its past and its origins?
5. What does it mean to be inspired by a saint's example without necessarily imitating him or her?

CHAPTER 7

SAINT THOMAS AQUINAS, THE THOMISTIC TRADITION, AND THE COSMIC COMMON GOOD

Daniel P. Scheid

KEY TERMS

Summa Theologiae
intrinsic goodness
participation in God
"two books" of revelation
eternal law
natural appetites
diversity of creatures
sustainability
common good
cocreation

INTRODUCTION

This chapter focuses on the work of Thomas Aquinas and identifies five aspects of his theology that may contribute to ecological ethics: (1) the intrinsic goodness of creation, (2) the importance of ecological diversity, (3) the order of creation as the greatest good, which aligns with the modern understanding of sustainability, (4) a common good that applies to the entire cosmos, and (5) humanity's vocation to become "cocreators" with God and bring creation to a greater flourishing.

AQUINAS AND ECOLOGICAL ETHICS

Thomas Aquinas (ca. 1225–1274) is regarded as one of the greatest theologians in the Christian tradition. A priest and member of the

SAINT THOMAS AQUINAS

Saint Thomas Aquinas (1225?–1274), an Italian scholastic philosopher. The detail is from a fresco by Fra Angelico. (Florence S. Marco Museum)

Born ca. 1225 in what is now Italy, Thomas Aquinas joined the recently founded Dominican order and quickly became renowned for the breadth and clarity of his thought. Under the tutelage of Saint Albert Magnus, Aquinas absorbed the newly discovered teachings of Aristotle and developed not only a great appreciation for the wondrous variety of creatures and how they operate but also a theological, and even mystical, awareness of the mystery that things exist at all. He is best known for his two major works, *Summa Theologiae* and *Summa Contra Gentiles*, which are still looked to as outstanding syntheses of Christian faith and reason. In 1879, Pope Leo XIII exhorted the study of Aquinas as a model for Christian philosophy "for the good of society, and for the advantage of all the sciences" (Pope Leo XIII, *Aeterni Patris* [On The Restoration of Christian Philosophy]). Aquinas is the patron saint of universities and theology students.

Dominican order, Aquinas wrote an astounding number of works of theology, philosophy, commentaries on scripture, sermons, and political theory. His most famous work, *Summa Theologiae* (hereafter *ST*), sets out to present a comprehensive understanding of Christian faith by integrating Aristotelian philosophy into a Christian worldview.[1]

1. Thomas Aquinas, *Summa Theologica*, tr. Fathers of the English Dominican Province (Chicago: Benziger Brothers, 1948).

Scores of modern thinkers continually return to his writings and discover remarkably relevant ideas for contemporary questions.

Yet when considering strands of Christian theology that are helpful for developing ecological ethics, Aquinas may not be an obvious choice. There is no narrative tradition of his kindness to animals or examples of a poetic nature-loving mysticism as there is with some of the early Christian saints or as shown in chapter 6 regarding his near contemporary, Saint Francis of Assisi. Indeed, some of his thought sounds directly opposed to a contemporary appreciation of Earth. Aquinas assumed that God had given dominion of Earth to humans and that all other creatures exist to serve humans. He believed that humans are permitted to kill plants and animals as they need, because God intends humans to use the goods of Earth to live, and as long as they did not steal from one another, they could do no injustice to nonhuman animals.

That does not justify, however, any use whatsoever of Earth. Aquinas would almost certainly criticize the kind of unbridled consumption that is fomenting contemporary environmental concerns—as various leaders from many religious traditions have also emphasized. Instead, any treatment or use of animals, plants, and so on must be marked by the virtue of temperance. Humans are meant to use only what is necessary to sustain the body and enable them to pursue their deeper and more important desires—primarily loving God and their neighbor. Exhibiting inordinate concern for material goods or coveting and consuming things to find happiness in them draws attention away from God and from what leads to true human happiness. Aquinas thus insists that humans not use earthly creatures immoderately or extravagantly but instead "only for as much as the need of this life requires" (*ST* II–II: q. 141, a. 6).

Beyond a healthy suspicion of rampant consumerism, however, it is unclear how Aquinas, or someone thinking in the Thomistic tradition, should respond to problems such as global warming, widespread species extinction, and increasing levels of pollution. Because his thought predates evolutionary theory, Aquinas presupposed that God created all the species as they currently are, and he could not have understood the dynamism and fluctuation that modern science now describes in nature. Aquinas could not provide a detailed explanation of how ecosystems function together, and his theological ethics do not offer specific guidelines for how humanity should deal with particular problems like climate change.

What Aquinas does offer, however, is a comprehensive and metaphysically nuanced worldview that unites God, the universe, and humanity into a holistic paradigm. Aquinas thought deeply about creation, and his understanding of the human person and God is closely linked to his conception of the universe. His writing reflects the ancient Christian idea of the "two books" of revelation, or God's self-disclosure, that can teach us about God: Scripture and creation. Aquinas reminds us of the importance of understanding the natural world: reflecting on creation and its relationship to God enables humans to admire God's wisdom, God's goodness, and God's power, so that "it is evident that the consideration of creatures helps to build up the Christian faith" (*Summa Contra Gentiles* [hereafter *SCG*] II: 2, n. 6).[2] Willis Jenkins extrapolates on this theme by positing that creatures are the primary means by which humans name God and thus come to know and praise God. Jenkins argues that destroying a species eliminates a way in which humans can have access to God: "Technological ecocide appears to us as a mode of deicide: the extinction of species is the impoverishment of God's self-giving for us . . . it reduces the fullness of God's availability to us through the world."[3] The loss of various creatures and ecosystems results in a loss of various ways of knowing and relating to God. Aquinas thus encourages a contemplative ecological ethic: humans come to know God through creation and the various creatures they encounter, both on Earth and in the heavens.

Because the natural world has such an important role in helping humans come to understand and to love God, the reverse is also true: misunderstandings about creation, and about humanity's place in the universe, can lead to a false understanding of God: "For errors about creatures sometimes lead one astray from the truth of faith, in so far as they disagree with true knowledge of God" (*SCG* II: 3, n. 1). When one holds false ideas about Earth or the universe or one

2. Thomas Aquinas, *Summa Contra Gentiles*, tr. Fathers of the English Dominican Province (Chicago: Benziger Brothers, 1924).

3. Willis Jenkins, "Biodiversity and Salvation: Thomistic Roots for Environmental Ethics," *Journal of Religion* 83 (2003), 412.

fails to appreciate the value of various creatures and the goodness that God has imparted to them, one implicitly insults God's wisdom and power: "To detract from the creature's perfection is to detract from the perfection of the divine power" (*SCG* III: 69, n.15). Aquinas persuades his readers that a proper theology of creation is beneficial not just to address ecological concerns but also is in fact an important facet in knowing God and attaining human happiness. A right view of creation can lead humans into a closer and better relationship to God, while a false one can lead them away from God—a strong impetus for making sure they get it right. Aquinas depicts the human as inextricably linked to the rest of creation, and he helps to describe why humans should care about what happens to nonhuman animals, plants, and Earth itself. Aquinas, and those inspired by his work, can, therefore, provide a number of important insights about humanity's place in creation that can contribute to constructing a valid ecological ethic for the twenty-first century.

AQUINAS' INTEGRATED VIEW OF CREATION: THE GOODNESS OF CREATION AND THE COSMIC COMMON GOOD

Aquinas provides the theological foundation for five key principles in ecological ethics: first, all creatures are intrinsically good and valuable; second, third, and fourth, the critical importance of ecological diversity, sustainability, and the common good; and fifth, humanity's role in contributing to, and not detracting from, the goodness of creation.

Intrinsic Goodness

Aquinas outlines a theological justification for attributing an intrinsic value to every creature in the universe. There has been a recent debate among ecological ethicists whether nonhuman creatures, such as trees and animals, have their own value or whether they are valuable because of the services they provide to humans. As mentioned earlier, Aquinas affirmed humanity's dominion over Earth, and he believed that all creatures "lower" than humans exist to serve them. Nonetheless, Aquinas also saw as a shared feature among all creatures that they depend on God and are primarily oriented to serve God's purposes. Though there are myriad differences among creatures—Aquinas would assuredly not attribute equal value to both a rock and a dog or to a mosquito and a human—there is a commonality shared by all beings in the way they depend on God and are meant to return to God.

This commonality merits further explanation. First, God is the source of all creatures, the reason that all beings—or that anything at all—exists. The doctrine of creation does not speak primarily about the universe's temporal origins (i.e., whether the universe began ten thousand years ago or roughly fourteen billion years ago) but about its contingency and total dependence on God. God is "extrinsic" to the universe, meaning that God does not exist as a finite creature like humans but transcends them all. Still, God is not somewhere else far removed from the universe, or a big person "somewhere out there" watching creation from a distance. On the contrary, God is present to all through the act of creation. Here the term *creation* signifies a kind of relationship between God, who exists necessarily by dint of who God is, and creatures, whose existence flows forth from God. Aquinas uses the language of "participation" to express this relationship. Every creature "participates" in God's being and exists because of this participation. As a result, every creature is "good" insofar as it exists; whatever other goods or deficiencies it may have, it is good because God is present in it as the principle of its being, its innermost cause. Rather than avowing a deistic God who sets the universe in motion and then departs, as many of the founders of the United States held, Aquinas argues for a Creator pervasively involved in every creature, at every moment of its existence. God remains present in each creature, whether it is a rock, a fly, or Beethoven, throughout its existence. In this way, God is not really "outside" of the universe at all. God is most intimately present in every creature as the source of its very being.

Second, God is the end, the goal, of all creatures and of the universe as a whole. God has arranged the universe according to an immutable law, the Eternal Law. Just as every creature participates in God, so too does each creature participate in the Eternal Law, which provides for a variety of inclinations and desires. This is a kind of inner blueprint for each creature, and every member of every species fulfills its purpose when it properly attains those ends instilled in it by

God. Though every creature has its own inclination, those proclivities, or "appetites," differ according to its species. Aquinas uses a broad understanding of inclination—it applies not only to humans, who can recognize their inmost desires, and not only to animals, who have inclinations whether they can recognize them or not, but also to any species of creature whatsoever. Hence, Aquinas can speak of a kind of appetite or love that everything has for God. A rock falls to the earth according to a law of gravity; a plant takes in nutrients to grow and further its life; a lion tracks down prey and seeks to mate and produce offspring: all of these follow a particular tendency instilled in them by God, and they glorify God by realizing the potentials given to them by God. When a tree bends its limbs to take in sunlight or an asteroid falls to Earth or a mosquito bites one's skin, it is acting on inclinations instilled in it by God. In doing so, it fulfills its purpose, and in this way, Aquinas says it "returns" to God and serves God's will.

AQUINAS ON HUMAN DOMINION AND EACH CREATURE'S INTRINSIC GOODNESS

In the following passage, Aquinas balances human dominion over other creatures with every creature's intrinsic goodness and value to God:

> So, therefore, in the parts of the universe also every creature exists for its own proper act and perfection, and the less noble for the nobler, as those creatures that are less noble than man exist for the sake of man, whilst each and every creature exists for the perfection of the entire universe. Furthermore, the entire universe, with all its parts, is ordained towards God as its end, inasmuch as it imitates, as it were, and shows forth the Divine goodness, to the glory of God. Reasonable creatures, however, have in some special and higher manner God as their end, since they can attain to Him by their own operations, by knowing and loving Him. Thus it is plain that the Divine goodness is the end of all corporeal things. (*ST* I: 65, a. 2)

Thus, Aquinas gives good reason for saying animals, trees, and so on are intrinsically valuable apart from human use: all creatures are intrinsically good because they have been created and preserved by God; and they have a particular set of aptitudes by which they may return to God, and fulfilling those inclinations or "appetites" glorifies God.

Ecological Diversity

Aquinas also offers a defense of ecological diversity, rooting it not in a contemporary concern for endangered species but in a theological interpretation of God's purposes for creation. Aquinas argues that a diversity of creatures with varying inclinations is not only part of God's Eternal Law but also is necessary for the universe to fulfill its purpose of imitating the divine goodness. Though humans certainly occupy a privileged rung in the hierarchy of creatures, there must still be many different kinds of creatures to show the goodness and wisdom of God. Aquinas often uses the language of "part-whole" to express this relationship: The universe constitutes a whole, and each creature is a part. Humans, however lofty in their abilities and vocation, remain only one part of the whole. When a part is harmed or destroyed, the well-being of the whole suffers as well. Hence, the totality of creatures—the universe as a whole—surpasses in greatness any individual creature. One might imagine that because humans are the greatest of bodily creatures that a universe predominantly filled with humans would be superior to one with fewer humans. Yet for Aquinas, the perfection of the universe consists in a multitude of creatures: "For goodness, which in God is simple and uniform, in creatures is manifold and divided; and hence the whole universe together participates [in] the divine goodness more perfectly, and represents it better than any single creature whatever" (*ST* I: q. 47, a. 1). No one creature, in its finitude, could adequately represent the simplicity and goodness of God—not even a human.

Of course, not all creatures are equal. Aquinas affirms a diversity of inclinations, some more important and more inclusive than others. A rock may have a natural inclination to obey the law of gravity, but the animal's inclination to reproduce and raise offspring makes the animal superior to the rock, because the animal has the rock's inclination and adds to it more complex drives. Likewise, the human's inclination to know and love God and to love one's neighbor surpasses the innate inclinations of other animals. Nevertheless, God intends for a variety of creatures, with differing "nobilities," to make up the entire universe. In the following quotation, Aquinas provocatively considers the most opposite comparison: angels, who surpass humans in intelligence, and rocks, which are lifeless. Even though angels are clearly superior, rocks are still an essential part of the universe:

> Although an angel taken absolutely may be better than a rock, still both natures taken together (*utraque natura*) are better than either one alone: and hence a universe in which there are angels and other things is better than where there would be angels only, because the perfection of the universe is seen essentially according to the diversity of natures, by which diverse degrees of goodness are filled, and not according to the multiplicity of individuals in one nature.[4]

Though one creature may be superior to another, no creature is superior to the universe as a whole. Aquinas testifies to the importance of ecological diversity: God does not will a mere multiplicity of individuals in one species, even the human species. Instead, only a variety of creatures can adequately represent God's simple goodness, and it is the universe as a whole that is the best in God's creation. Aquinas counsels looking at the big picture, just as he regularly privileges the whole over the part, the universe over particular species, and species over individual creatures. Humans cannot justify a wholesale destruction of a species simply because it enables a growth in human population. Moreover, a loss of diversity has negative effects on humans' capacity to know God. As shown previously, humans come to know God through the creatures they encounter. If they live in a world devoid of a variety of species, they lose access to aspects of God.

---

4. In *I Sentences*, 44.1.2 ad 6, quoted in Oliva Blanchette, *The Perfection of the Universe According to Aquinas: A Teleological Cosmology* (University Park, PA: Pennsylvania State University Press, 1992), 125–126.

Sustainability

Although Aquinas offers a clear argument for ecological diversity, he intensifies his argument by claiming that the greatest aspect of creation is the order and interconnections among the diverse creatures that God has created. That is, not only does God will a multitude of species, but also the best part of creation is the way these myriad creatures are ordered to one another and depend on one another for their existence. Just as only the universe composed of distinct species of creatures can best imitate the divine goodness, the order of these creatures in the universe is the highest created good for all creatures. (God remains the greatest good of all.) A diversity of creatures best manifests God's goodness, while the harmonious order among these various parts best glorifies God. Aquinas continually underscores the supreme value of the whole of the universe over any of its individual parts: "Now the best among all things caused is the order of the universe, wherein the good of the universe consists, even as in human affairs 'the good of the nation is more God-like than the good of the individual'" (*SCG* II: 42, n. 3). The "end," or goal, of the universe, therefore, is not merely the flourishing of the human person (though Aquinas does include them) but also the "mutual order of the parts" of the universe as God has instituted them. Just as the good of the nation exceeds the good of any one citizen, so the order of the universe surpasses, or is "more God-like," than the good of any one species.

In this way, Aquinas signals the importance of sustainability, or the ordered interconnections among species and the various ecosystems that sustain them. *Sustainability* is a modern word with many different and even conflicting definitions. It is not a term Aquinas ever used, and neither would he have recognized the need for humans to protect the interrelationships he discerned among creatures. Yet, his teaching on the priority of the ordered interconnections among creatures aligns with a contemporary scientific understanding of the intricate and reciprocal relationships among creatures within ecosystems, and among ecosystems on Earth. It is not enough to have a diversity of creatures, if those creatures are not able to fulfill their innate inclinations in relationship to other creatures. Hence, Aquinas encourages humans to promote not just biological diversity but also ecological sustainability. If the order among creatures is the greatest good of the universe, then humans must make every effort to ensure that this pattern can continue in the future. The ecological contexts in which water, bugs, plants, animals, and humans coexist and co-flourish are the greatest aspect of creation, and together, they best show God's goodness and offer God the greatest praise and gratitude. In the following quotation, Aquinas depicts God as a master craftsman who envisions a beautiful home, and its beauty comes not from any one spectacular feature but from the order of the whole:

> Since the good of the whole is better than the good of each part, it does not befit the best maker to lessen the good of the whole in order to increase the good of some of the parts: thus a builder does not give to the foundation the goodness which he gives to the roof, lest he should make a crazy house. Therefore God the maker of all would not make the whole universe the best of its kind, if He made all the parts equal, because many degrees of goodness would be wanting to the universe, and thus it would be imperfect. (*SCG* II: 44, n. 17)

Not all parts of a house are equal, nor are all creatures on Earth equal, but Earth would indeed be a "crazy house" if it consisted solely of humans and a few other species sustained through human intervention. Only when all the parts of Earth operate in harmony with the others, fulfilling their own particular purposes, does the beauty of Earth shine forth.

Cosmic Common Good

When Aquinas discusses the superiority of the whole over the part, he uses the term *common good* to express this relationship. The common good refers to the set of conditions under which a community and every member of that community may flourish. In modern Western societies, citizens tend to think of themselves primarily as individuals and tend to neglect the notion of a common good. Aquinas believed that humans are naturally social and meant to live in societies with others and that there is a good to human life that cannot be found in isolation from others. At the same time, Aquinas clearly does not mean to valorize a totalitarian state in which the individual is involuntarily sacrificed for the perceived good of others. Instead, the common good signifies that God seeks the well-being of the whole, and each individual part flourishes when it fulfills its proper role.

Aquinas took the term *common good* from Aristotle, and he likewise limited the common good to the good of the city-state or the nation-state: each citizen was meant to contribute to the state's overall well-being. By appealing to the common good, Aquinas acknowledges the interdependence of people. Citizens cannot fare well when the state crumbles around them.

In recent years, however, many have expanded the concept of the common good and, thus, widened the circle of concern. For example, Pope John XXIII contended in his 1961 encyclical *Mater et Magistra* (Christianity and Social Progress) that the common good must no longer be limited to nation-states, because he recognized that "one of the principal characteristics of our time is the multiplication of social relationships, that is, a daily more complex interdependence of citizens" (no. 59). Given Aquinas's understanding of the importance of biological diversity and ecological sustainability and the insights of contemporary science that highlight the interdependence among all earthly creatures, it seems reasonable to extend the meaning of the common good to include all creatures. From God's perspective, the universe constitutes a single unified whole, unified due to its common participation in God and to the order that God has instituted in it. Humans are interdependent not only on other humans but also on a host of creatures for their survival (for food, clothing, etc,) and for their happiness (the beauty of oceans and mountains to lift the human soul). The "cosmic common good" includes human well-being and incorporates the flourishing of all the diverse creatures God has created. A common good pervades the entire universe, which includes human happiness but also transcends it, because the good of all creatures ends in God.

Humanity's Role

When one rightly understands the importance of diversity and sustainability within creation and judges human actions according to a cosmic common good, one is led to a new conception of humanity's dominion over nature. Clearly the concept cannot mean a position of total control, whereby humans may do whatever they wish with impunity. As ecological scientists point out, that has never been the case—humans have always depended on Earth for their well-being. Aquinas defends this theologically: humans are one part of a larger whole, whose greatest feature is the ordered interconnections among creatures.

As the only creatures on Earth gifted with such a degree of intelligence and free will, humans have a privileged role in promoting the cosmic common good through their wise governing of other creatures. *Dominion* does not mean "to dominate" but to have a thoughtful and judicious participation in God's governing of the entire universe.

For Aquinas, government seeks two ends, "the preservation of things in their goodness and the moving of things to good" (*ST* I: q. 103, a. 4). One can detect two aspects of humanity's role in the cosmic common good. First, humans are meant to preserve things "in their goodness." Aquinas believes that each part flourishes when it contributes to the good of the whole, and not when it seeks to benefit itself at the cost of the whole. Because the common good transcends individual goods, "each part naturally loves the common good of the whole more than its own particular good" (*ST* II–II: q. 26, a. 3). The good of the whole surpasses the good of the individual, and the part strives not to accommodate the good of the whole for itself, but seeks to give itself to the good of the whole. "The part does indeed love the good of the whole, as it becomes a part, not however so as to refer the good of the whole to itself, but rather itself to the good of the whole" (*ST* II–II: q. 26, a. 3, ad 2). Humans must be sure not to pervert or destroy the ordered interconnections they discover in nature for their own private good. Diverse ecosystems and the creatures they sustain should be perceived as for the good of the whole Earth and not merely as "resources" waiting to be exploited for the good of a few select individuals.

Aquinas makes an analogy between a hand and an individual citizen as both parts of a larger whole: just as the hand naturally exposes itself to danger to protect the body, so will a virtuous citizen risk wealth and life on behalf of the safety of the community. He reasons this way because humans are naturally part of a community and do not belong outside of it. When one takes this principle in light of Aquinas's rich and integrated theology of creation, one is made aware that humans are a natural part of Earth and the cosmos, as well. So too should virtuous humans limit themselves and their interests on behalf of the cosmic common good to preserve the goodness of various creatures and the mutual order of the various parts of Earth. It is, therefore, inconceivable that humans should use their reason and will to contravene God's providential ordering that prefers a multitude of species and a harmonious relationship among them.

In this light, the rapid rate of species extinction, even if it is brought about to sustain the also rapidly increasing human population, violates the order and unity of the universe and defies the cosmic common good. First, taking some responsibility for God's providential ordering means not diminishing the goodness of other creatures. Because God has ordered all creatures to attain God as an end in accordance with their natural inclinations and aptitudes, a creature may be good insofar as it exists but lacking in the good that God desires for it. The goal is not merely to keep nonhuman creatures alive or in existence, though this is clearly a key priority. Rather, Aquinas argues, they ought to be allowed and enabled to pursue the activities and inclinations instilled in them by God as a part of their contribution to the cosmic common good. Humans ought to preserve the goodness of Earth that enables such a rich diversity of creatures and ecosystems.

Second, Aquinas suggests a more engaged approach whereby humans move other creatures to goodness. For Aquinas, every finite creature participates in God and seeks to become as like God as it can. Thus, rocks are like God insofar as they exist; animals, as they are alive; and humans, as they use their reason and free will to know and love God. Humans are considered "higher" or more gifted creatures not merely because lower creatures are ordered to serve them, but also because they have the opportunity to participate more fully in God's governing of creation. It is good to exist and to protect and enhance one's life, but it is much better to be a cause of goodness in others and to bring other creatures into existence: "The creature approaches more perfectly to God's likeness if it is not only good, but can also act for the good of other things." (*SCG* II: 45, n. 4). God, who is supremely good, is the model for goodness. In the act of creation, God shares his goodness with a vast universe of creatures, allowing them to participate in his being and life. Humans obviously cannot create as God does, but through the capacities of reason and free will, humans can become cocreators with God, bringing all of creation into greater flourishing. Although all creatures desire to become closer to God, humans "seek a likeness to God by being a cause of others. Wherefore Dionysius says (Coel. Hier. iii.) that it is of 'all things most godlike to be God's co-operator'" (*SCG* III: 21, n. 8).

Humans are called to promote the cosmic common good not only by preserving the order among creatures but also by furthering the conditions that support ecological diversity and sustainability. The greatness of being human is not in the ability to control and exploit Earth but in promoting the good of others, both human and nonhuman alike. Humans become more like God when they enable other creatures to attain their innate ends and when they further the order and harmony that God wills for creation. For ecological ethics, then, this means that humans must work to preserve those ecosystems and creatures that add to the diversity and sustainability of life on Earth. Moreover, humans must seek to enhance the flourishing of these creatures and enable the many complex interconnections among them to grow and thrive.

The U.S. Catholic bishops have suggested a similar approach in their 1992 *Renewing the Earth,* in which they argue that "the human family is charged with preserving the beauty, diversity, and integrity of nature as well as fostering its productivity."[5] As the only self-provident creatures, humans are called to contribute to the ordered interconnections among creatures (nature's "beauty, diversity, and integrity") and to move other creatures to goodness ("fostering its productivity"). Aquinas would caution against interpreting nature's "productivity" in terms of economic growth; instead, because the order of the universe is its greatest attribute, humans must foster nature's ability to create new life and harmonious interconnections, rather than merely what it is able to yield for human consumption.

Though Aquinas encourages humans to bring about greater life, they ought to approach this task cautiously. Being a cocreator does not justify any action whatsoever. On the contrary, humans should

5. United States Catholic Bishops, *Renewing the Earth* (Washington, DC: United States Catholic Conference, 1992).

not presume to know for certain what will bring about greater flourishing. At times, people have attempted to "improve" nature only to find that they could not have anticipated the repercussions, (e.g., bringing nonnative plants such as kudzu to America, only to have the kudzu dominate much of the countryside in the southern United States). The order among creatures in nature is fantastically complex, and though humans are called to promote the flourishing of nature and enhance its fecundity, they must undertake this task with humility.

AQUINAS IN THE TWENTY-FIRST CENTURY

Many thinkers and theologians have been inspired by Aquinas's thought and have taken up aspects of his work or expanded into new directions to address ecological concerns. For example, Aquinas teaches us to learn about creation to gain a better understanding of God. One of the leading figures of environmental theology and a self-proclaimed "geologian," Passionist priest Thomas Berry, CP (1914–2009) follows in this Thomistic tradition by incorporating the story of the universe as science tells it to better understand God and to reveal a new vision of humanity's place in the universe: "This new story of the universe is our personal story as well as our community story. . . . Our single greatest need is to accept this story of the universe as we now know this as our sacred story."[6]

Like Aquinas, Berry has a mystical sense of the mystery and sacredness of creatures, and so he argues that we can come to know and love God through our encounter with creation. Berry emphasizes the sacramental nature of the universe: that every creature, and especially the universe as a whole, reveals something about God, the source from whom all things come and to whom all return. Berry learned from Aquinas that God intended interconnections among creatures in the universe and that only a diversity of creatures best approximates God's goodness. Thus, Berry calls everyone to "perceive the natural world as the primary revelation of the divine, as primary scripture, as the primary mode of numinous presence."[7] Valuing the natural inclinations of all creatures and their participation in God, as

---

6. Thomas Berry, *The Great Work* (New York: Bell Tower, 2000), 83.

7. Thomas Berry, *Dream of the Earth* (San Francisco: Sierra Club Books, 1988), 105.

Aquinas teaches, Berry declares that "we must say that the universe is a communion of subjects rather than a collection of objects."

A good example of the Thomistic vision as interpreted by Thomas Berry at work today can be found at Genesis Farm, a 226-acre farm in northwest New Jersey founded in 1980 by the Dominican Sisters of Caldwell, New Jersey. Genesis Farm conducts a certificate program in "Earth literacy" designed to awaken students' ability to "read" the book of nature through "the story of an evolutionary universe and our embeddedness in Earth's web of life."[8] In addition, the farm operates as a community garden, supporting small local farms, growing healthy food, and encouraging a spiritual connection between residents and the land. The mission of the farm is grounded in a vision of the earth as a revelation of God, and the many educational programs at Genesis Farm focus "on connections between the health of Earth and of human communities within particular bioregions." Like Aquinas, these Dominican sisters appreciate the importance of diversity and sustainability and the interconnections among creatures. Moreover, they contend that what Earth needs is a transformation in humans' perceptions so they learn to see humanity as part of a greater whole and to understand that humans cannot flourish while the rest of Earth deteriorates. Most importantly the Dominican sisters recognize the value of all creatures, because the entire universe is pervaded by the power and presence of the mystery of God.

Genesis Farm, inspired by the writings of Thomas Berry, is an excellent example of Aquinas's theological legacy, calling people to become responsible cocreators with God by protecting the goodness of Earth and promoting its greater flourishing. Such efforts are not just important for addressing ecological concerns but also are intrinsic to realizing our human vocation and to growing in love of God and neighbor.

CONCLUSION

Aquinas provides a stirring vision of humanity's place and role within creation, and he offers a theological basis for a rigorous ecological

8. All excerpts come from "Genesis Farm," Sisters of Saint Dominic, *http://www.genesisfarm.org*, accessed January 28, 2011.

ethic. Of course, Aquinas lived before evolutionary theory or the discovery that Earth is just one of billions of planets in a vast universe. Humans can no longer presume that they are the center of the universe or that the world as it presently appears has existed this way since the beginning of creation. The complexity of Earth's many ecosystems and the rich diversity of animals have developed over time, and even occasional extinctions and setbacks are part of the process of life. Nevertheless, Aquinas reminds us of the importance of a proper understanding of creation, and he provides a helpful language for talking about the intrinsic goodness of nonhuman creatures, of the importance of biological diversity, of ecological complexity and sustainability, and of orienting our behavior toward the cosmic common good. A Thomistic perspective on creation can be a worthy contributor to a robust and sustainable ecological ethic.

QUESTIONS FOR REVIEW

1. What is meant by the "two books" of revelation idea? What do you think of it and why? Do you think God can speak to us through creation? What have you heard?
2. How does Aquinas define the common good? Have you seen evidence of this understanding of the common good in North American society today? Do you believe that contributing to the well-being of others helps you flourish or brings you closer to happiness? Do you think that can be true of nonhumans as well? Why or why not?
3. When Aquinas claims that every creature possesses intrinsic value, what does he mean?
4. What does Aquinas mean when he says every creature "participates" in God's being?
5. What is the Eternal Law, and how does each creature participate in it?
6. How does Aquinas signal to us the importance of sustainability, and how is sustainability understood?

IN-DEPTH QUESTIONS

1. How do we understand a common good of the planet but still recognize that some death will be inevitable? Is it reasonable to speak of a "common good" in which some creatures inevitably kill others to live?
2. How does the idea of a "cosmic common good" fit with our social understanding of humans' relationship with other creatures? How does it relate to contemporary TV shows like *Man vs. Wild* that encourage a hostile or confrontational attitude?
3. Given the reality of human sinfulness and selfishness, does the notion of a "cosmic common good" seem too simplistic? What will give humans the incentive to self-sacrifice not only for other humans but also for other species?
4. Aquinas argues that the universe requires not only a diversity of creatures but also that the mutual order of these parts is the greatest aspect to creation. What bearing do you think this has on the ethical validity of zoos? If a zoo keeps an animal in captivity because it is the only way to preserve its existence but is denying the animal what it needs to fulfill its natural inclinations, is that acceptable?
5. What perceptions and beliefs do you think most need to be transformed for people to work for greater sustainability?

FUNDAMENTAL MORAL THEOLOGY

CHAPTER 8

Living the Natural Moral Law and Respecting the Ecological Good

Nicanor Pier Giorgio Austriaco, OP

CHAPTER 9

The Environment Within: Virtue Ethics

Nancy M. Rourke

CHAPTER 10

Toward a Eucharistic Ecology

Stephen B. Wilson

CHAPTER 11

Neighbor to Nature

Marcus Mescher

CHAPTER 8

LIVING THE NATURAL MORAL LAW AND RESPECTING THE ECOLOGICAL GOOD

Nicanor Pier Giorgio Austriaco, OP

KEY TERMS

natural law
personal good
common good
ecological good
ultimate end
subordinate ends

INTRODUCTION

By changing the global climate, expanding urban land use, polluting the water and air, and overharvesting biological resources, human activity has precipitated and accelerated the deterioration of the environment. For example, today, many freshwater sources are threatened by defective disposal of human and animal waste, indiscriminate release of industrial pollutants, uncontrolled runoff of agriculture-use fertilizer, and coastal influxes of saltwater into aquifers as groundwater is depleted. If present trends continue, scientific experts project that by midcentury, as much as three quarters of the planet's population could face scarcities of freshwater.[1] How should citizens of faith and of right conscience respond to this ecological crisis?

---

1. For details and discussion, see Peter Rogers, "Facing the Freshwater Crisis," *Scientific American* 299 (2008): 46–53.

In an answer to a question from a priest during a meeting with the clergy of several dioceses in northern Italy, Pope Benedict XVI urged young people to respond to the global ecological crisis by listening to Earth and obeying its voice. "We must learn the inner laws of creation, of this earth," the pope explained, "we must learn these laws and obey these laws if we wish to survive."[2] To fully grasp the meaning of the pope's words, this chapter will reflect a natural-law ethic that is grounded in the claim that humans are called to listen to and to live according to the natural moral law that is inscribed within the very heart of creation.

The chapter will begin by exploring the relationship between the natural moral law and divine providence as understood by Catholic moral theology: essentially, that the natural moral law manifests God's guidance of humans. Next, the chapter will focus on how a natural law ethic can guide humans to properly discern their authentic human good. To live according to the natural moral law, one must act so that every act—from choosing what to eat for breakfast to buying a light bulb—is ordered toward this good of realizing authentic friendships with God and with neighbor. Finally, the links between the personal good, the common good, and the ecological good will be explored. Humans must act in a manner that protects and preserves the environment. They must learn to be authentic friends of creation.

THE NATURAL MORAL LAW AS A MANIFESTATION OF DIVINE PROVIDENCE

A natural law ethic is grounded in the affirmation that to live a good life, one must live in accordance with nature generally and with human nature more specifically. It emerges from a vision of the cosmos that sees humanity as a constituent part of a creation that is moving toward its own goodness and proper perfection under God's governance.

---

2. Benedict XVI, "Meeting of the Holy Father Benedict XVI with the Clergy of the Dioceses of Belluno-Feltre and Treviso, Church of St. Justin Martyr, Auronzo di Cadore, Tuesday, 24 July 2007," *http://www.vatican.va/holy_father /benedict_xvi/ speeches/2007/july/documents/hf_ben-xvi_spe_20070724_clero-cadore_en.html*, accessed December 28, 2010.

As chapter 4 details in connection with the Hebrew Scriptures, God created the cosmos for his own glory, which is realized in the manifestation and communication of the divine goodness. Thus, from the beginning of time, God has continued to guide the universe toward its end. As the *Catechism of the Catholic Church* (CCC) explains, "We call 'divine providence' the dispositions by which God guides his creation toward this perfection: By his providence God protects and governs all things which he has made, 'reaching mightily from one end of the earth to the other, and ordering all things well'."[3] Providence signifies not only God's care and solicitude for his creatures but also his absolute sovereignty over the course of both natural and human history: "Many are the plans in a man's heart, / but it is the decision of the LORD that endures" (Proverbs 19:21, NAB).

To guide creation, this theological teaching asserts, God imprinted a directedness into things that inclines them to their ultimate end, or goal, which is the divine goodness itself. As such, all creatures, by nature, are disposed toward the good things they need for their perfection: squirrels are inclined to eat the nuts that are good for them as rodents, while hawks are inclined to eat the squirrels that are good for them as raptors. In eating what they eat, these animals fulfill those purposes they have by virtue of the fact that they are animals they are. They are obeying the laws inscribed into their very natures and perfecting themselves as the creatures that they were meant to be by their providential Creator.

Squirrels and hawks blindly obey the laws inscribed in their nature. As nonrational creatures, they are directed by divine providence toward the single end that is their survival as individuals and as a species. In pursuing this end, they manifest the glory of God. Humans are also inclined toward their perfection. The CCC asserts, however, that the Creator has given humans the power to freely share in divine providence by giving them the dignity of being true causes in the accomplishment of the divine plan.[4] To put it another way, God has given humans rational intellect and free will first to understand and then to follow the interior inclinations that direct them toward

---

3. Vatican Council I, *Dei Filius* 1: DS 3003; cf. *Wis* 8:1; *Heb* 4:13. In *Catechism of the Catholic Church*, no. 302.

4. Cf. *Catechism of the Catholic Church*, no. 306.

those goods they need for their perfection and happiness. In doing this, they live in accordance with the integrity and design of creation, an approach to the moral life that has traditionally been described as a natural law ethic. Thus, the natural moral law is not a list of rules but a species-specific set of movements within all humans that not only allows them to understand their perfections but also directs them toward their fulfillment. In the end, this law manifests God's providential guidance of them.

RECOVERING A NATURAL LAW ETHIC AND RESPECTING PERSONAL GOOD

At the heart of a natural law ethic is the claim that human acts are good if they help one to be the person one was created to be, by fulfilling those inclinations that perfect one. To illustrate and to justify this moral principle, consider a doctor. What is a good physician? To answer this question, one first has to determine what a doctor is for. A doctor is an individual who is called to heal. Thus, a good doctor is a physician who, through repeated acts of healing, becomes a person who can heal well. In light of this, an act of healing is good for a doctor. It makes her realize her purpose. In contrast, an act of harming, an act that detracts a doctor from her purpose, is a bad act. In an analogous way, good human acts are those freely chosen acts that perfect humans and realize their personal good. These acts correspond with those inclinations that humans have by virtue of the fact that humans are humans. Therefore, according to a natural law ethic, to discern what is good for humans, one needs to discover the purposes, what classically have been called the ends, of the human person.

Reflecting on the inclinations imprinted in human nature, the renowned medieval theologian Saint Thomas Aquinas (see also chapter 7) proposed that humans were created for friendship. At one level, humans are called to be friends with their neighbors in truth and in charity. Attaining this end would contribute to an earthly but imperfect happiness. However, this natural ultimate end is distinct from, inferior to, and ordered toward, humans' supernatural ultimate end, that of friendship with the Triune God—Father, Son, and Holy Spirit—in the beatific vision. As the CCC explains in its first paragraph, humans were created for God who calls them to himself: "God, infinitely perfect and blessed in himself, in a plan of sheer goodness freely created man to make him share in his own blessed life."[5]

Furthermore, according to Aquinas, reason discovers four subordinate ends—life, procreation, community, and truth, either from immediate experience or from reflection and inference—that are required for each person to become authentic and exemplary friends of God and of neighbor. These perfective ends are interrelated and mutually support other. First, people are inclined toward life so they can strive for their goals and perfection. They need to be alive and healthy to become good friends. This is the most basic end necessary to achieve all other natural human ends. Next, humans are inclined toward marriage and the friendships they can share with their spouses and their children. Third, humans are inclined toward social life, because as social creatures, they can attain their perfection only in communion with others. Or to put it another way, people, by nature, are called to develop friendships within the commonweal to help them attain their human fulfillment. Finally, humans are inclined toward the truth, because it is truth that gives their lives meaning and purpose. Ultimately, they need to know the truth about God, who is the cause of all that exists, to attain, with the help of grace, the happiness that is friendship with the Trinity. Together, these two ultimate and four subordinate ends, defined by fundamental human inclinations, constitute the essential ingredients for a good human life. They constitute the grammar of human excellence.

According to a natural law ethic, to act according to human nature and the integrity of creation, humans need to act in a way that realizes these subordinate and universal ends so they can attain their personal good that is friendship with God and with neighbor. As Pope Benedict XVI explained, "Each person finds his good by adherence to God's plan for him, in order to realize it fully: in this plan, he finds his truth, and through adherence to this truth he becomes free (cf. John 8:22)."[6] One needs to act so that every act is ordered

5. *Catechism of the Catholic Church*, no. 1.

6. Benedict XVI, *Caritas in veritate*, no. 1. For a summary of Pope Benedict XVI's teaching on creation and environmental responsibility, see Woodeene Koenig-Bricker, *Ten Commandments for the Environment: Pope Benedict XVI Speaks Out for Creation and Justice* (Notre Dame, IN: Ave Maria Press, 2009).

toward the good. One must judge each act according to whether it promotes life and authentic friendships with God and with neighbor. Thus, in light of the natural moral law, drinking water to keep alive and healthy is an act of charity (i.e., the virtue of love). In drinking water, the acting person realizes a personal good. That person also fulfills the commandments to love oneself and to love neighbors for love of God.

In contrast, there are acts that "by their very nature [are] 'incapable of being ordered' to God, because they radically contradict the good of the person made in his image."[7] In other words, these acts are evil because they do not promote the perfection of the individual human. They prevent humans from developing authentic friendships with God and with their neighbors by attacking their perfective ends. For example, in light of the natural moral law, drinking excessive alcohol is a bad act. It damages one's health, and in some cases, even endangers one's life and the lives of one's neighbors. It also undermines one's ability to develop authentic friendships with one's neighbor and with God, who cannot truly be known and loved in the drunken state.

RECOVERING A NATURAL LAW ETHIC AND RESPECTING THE COMMON GOOD

To recapitulate, a natural law ethic calls humans to seek the good in all of their actions. As explained previously, they do this by acting to realize their personal good that is friendship with God and with neighbor, the good that perfects the individual, which is constituted by the ultimate and subordinate ends that define the good life. However, humans are also social creatures who necessarily live in communities, so their personal good is inherently linked to the good of human society. Thus, in addition to living out personal good, they must also act to realize the good of the community, the good classically called the common good.

A common good is that state of affairs in which many people can share at the same time without in any way lessening or splitting

---

7. John Paul II, *Veritatis splendor* (The Splendor of Truth), no. 80.

the good. For instance, the peace of the state is a common good provided it is a genuine peace of the whole from which no one is excluded. When one shares peace, one does not lessen the peace that can be experienced by others. The common good is the sum total of all the common goods necessary for individuals to attain their ultimate end. The CCC defines it as "the sum total of social conditions which allow people, either as groups or as individuals, to reach their fulfillment more fully and more easily."[8] Today, these social conditions—these common goods—include, among others, the availability of freshwater, transportation, health care, justice and law enforcement systems, a healthy economy, and an educational system that forms morally upright and virtuous citizens. All of these are societal goods that are necessary for the perfection of the human person. Thus, in one's actions, one needs to seek and to respect the common good. In fact, there are times—for example, when one is called to serve on a trial jury even when it is inconvenient or when one abstains from taking long showers during a drought—when one is called to sacrifice one's personal good for the preservation of the common good.

RECOVERING A NATURAL LAW ETHIC AND RESPECTING THE ECOLOGICAL GOOD

As a social creature, a human is a member of a community. However, as one creature living within a creation of incredible diversity and beauty, he or she is also an integral part of the environment. Thus, the perfection of each individual cannot be separated from the good of the environment, a good that can be called the ecological good. As Pope Benedict XVI explained in his social encyclical, *Caritas in veritate* (Love in Truth), "The way humanity treats the environment influences the way it treats itself, and vice versa."[9] This ecological good is composed of those conditions necessary for the integrity and well-being of the environment. It includes the sustainable use of

8. *Gaudium et spes* (Pastoral Constitution on the Church in the Modern World), no. 26. The citation is from *Vatican Council II: The Conciliar and Post Concilliar Documents*, 927. Quoted in *Catechism of the Catholic Church*, no. 1906.

9. Benedict XVI, *Caritas in veritate*, no. 51.

our natural resources, the preservation of our diverse ecosystem, and the conservation of the environment, among other goods. Therefore, to live out a natural law ethic, humans have to ask if each action promotes not only personal good and the common good but also the ecological good. They have to act in a manner that protects and preserves the environment not only for themselves and their children but also for all people, as well as for the sake of the environment itself, both now and in future generations. As Pope Benedict XVI declared, "In nature, the believer recognizes the wonderful result of God's creative activity, which we may use responsibly to satisfy our legitimate needs, material or otherwise, while respecting the intrinsic balance of creation."[10] To put it simply, humans have to learn to be authentic friends of creation.

In recent times, humans' ignorance of the ecological good has brought about the global environmental crisis. For instance, their blindness to the truth and integrity of creation has wounded their relationship with the animals and plants with which they share the world. Instead of living in mutual harmony with these other living things, humans have chosen to dominate and to exploit them without concern for their integrity and well-being. Animals, too, are God's creatures, and humans need to respect them as companions and integral components of creation who are all called to glorify the Creator. As Pope Benedict XVI once bemoaned, the industrial use of animals in such a way that their identity as creatures is degraded and their well-being is compromised—and here he was specifically referring to practices in which geese are fed in such a way to produce as large a liver as possible and hens are packed together in unhealthy conditions—contradicts the relationship of mutuality that comes across in the Bible.[11]

How then do individuals respect the ecological good? Many people today assume that the solution to the global ecological crisis lies in a worldwide and sustained effort to reduce each individual's carbon footprint, a measure of the effect human activities have on the environment that relates to the amount of greenhouse gases

10. Ibid, no. 48.

11. Joseph Ratzinger (Pope Benedict XVI), *God and the World* (San Francisco: Ignatius Press, 2002), 78–79.

produced in day-to-day living. Although doing so undeniably would be helpful, simply reducing humans' carbon footprints will not be enough, because the ecological crisis calls for much personal and communal sacrifice, demands that will not easily be embraced in a self-indulgent society.

Each person will be required to pay more for less for the sake of the environment. Friendship, including one's friendship with creation, demands sacrifice. One informal study by Cambridge Econometrics has projected that the effect of proposed climate change policies on consumers in the United Kingdom would increase air travel costs by 140 percent, electricity costs by 15 percent, and household goods costs by 2 percent.[12] Another study, this one by the Belfer Center for Science and International Affairs at Harvard University, predicts that reducing oil consumption and carbon emissions in conformity to proposed climate change policies in the United States will double the price of gasoline such that it will cost $7.00 per gallon by 2020.[13] Clearly, humans are being called to sacrifice their personal good for the protection and preservation of the ecological good.

Communally, humans will also be challenged to live more austere lives. Societies too will need to adopt ecofriendly practices. Taxes may have to be levied to advance the ecological good by changing personal and communal behaviors, cutting waste, and promoting cleaner technologies. These ecotaxes could then be used to improve public transport systems or to promote environmentally friendly farming practices. For instance, farm irrigation consumes large quantities of water. A 10-percent drop in irrigation, facilitated by plugging leaks in the irrigation water-delivery system, applying drip-irrigation methods, and modifying crops to require less water would free more water than is used by all other consumers. This transformation, however, will also be difficult. This became especially clear during the 2009 UN Climate Change Conference in Copenhagen, Denmark,

12. For details and discussion, see Jim Giles, "We Can Afford to Go Green," *New Scientist* 204 (2009): 8–10.

13. W. Ross Morrow et al., "Analysis of Policies to Reduce Oil Consumption and Greenhouse Gas Emissions from the U.S. Transportation Sector," *Energy Policy* 38 (2010): 1305–1320.

when both rich and poor countries haggled over the cost of embracing climate-friendly industrial policies.[14] No nation was willing to make the necessary fiscal sacrifices for the sake of the common and the ecological good.

Therefore, as Pope Benedict XVI explained, it will be important for societies to undergo a moral conversion if they are truly going to restore the integrity of creation. There are two dimensions of this moral conversion. First, individuals and communities must acquire virtue and self-mastery—they will need to curb indulging their desires in a consumer-driven culture—so they can adopt new lifestyles that are truly ecofriendly:

> The way humanity treats the environment influences the way it treats itself, and vice versa. This invites contemporary society to a serious review of its lifestyle, which, in many parts of the world, is prone to hedonism and consumerism, regardless of their harmful consequences. What is needed is an effective shift in mentality which can lead to the adoption of new lifestyles 'in which the quest for truth, beauty, goodness, and communion with others for the sake of common growth are the factors which determine consumer choices, savings, and investments'.[15]

In the same way that people are called to sacrifice for the common good, they are called to sacrifice their personal interests for the ecological good. They should be willing to pay more for food and water and to live with fewer consumer choices and fewer conveniences if these sacrifices are to encourage sustainable development and the preservation of Earth.

Next, individuals and communities must recover a profound respect for human dignity. As Pope Benedict XVI has said, a society that respects the sanctity of human life will have the requisite moral resources to demand the sacrifices of its citizens necessary for the healing and the consecration of the environment:

---

14. John M. Broder, "Many Goals Remain Unmet in 5 Nations' Climate Deal," *The New York Times*, December 18, 2009, *http://www.nytimes.com/2009/12/19/science/earth/19climate.html*, accessed December 28, 2010.

15. Benedict XVI, *Caritas in veritate*, no. 51.

> In order to protect nature, it is not enough to intervene with economic incentives or deterrents; not even an apposite education is sufficient. These are important steps, but *the decisive issue is the overall moral tenor of society.* If there is a lack of respect for the right to life and to a natural death, if human conception, gestation, and birth are made artificial, if human embryos are sacrificed to research, the conscience of society ends up losing the concept of human ecology and, along with it, that of environmental ecology. . . . Our duties toward the environment are linked to our duties toward the human person, considered in himself and in relation to others.[16]

In other words, according to the pope, recovering a true relationship with creation necessarily involves recovering an authentic understanding of how humans relate to one another, especially people who are marginalized and most vulnerable, including the unborn, the handicapped, and the dying. To be authentically pro-environment, one has to be authentically pro-life, and vice versa. More concretely, the moral commitments that should make humans speak out against resource depletion and industrial pollution must also provoke them to stand up against abortion and euthanasia. Only a society that selflessly defends the dignity of the poor, the weak, the dying, and the marginalized will be virtuous enough to embrace and to advance the sacrifices needed to care for and to preserve the integrity of the environment. Only a true friend of neighbor can authentically become a true friend of creation, and vice versa. This is what it means to live out a natural law ethic in its fullness. This is what is required to heal creation.

CONCLUSION

How should college students of good conscience respond to the global environmental crisis? They should live according to nature by respecting the natural law. This will challenge them to evaluate each of their actions in light of their personal good, the common good,

16. Ibid.

and the ecological good. They should adopt practices at home and in the dormitory that are ecofriendly, bearing the three R's of environmentalism in mind: reduce, reuse, and recycle. Small changes adopted by everyone—for instance replacing bottled water with home filtered water—can make a large effect on the environment: it takes 1.5 million barrels of oil, enough to fuel 100,000 cars for a year, to make the plastic bottles for water used every year in the United States, and only one in five is recycled.

As explained previously, however, these personal and individual changes will not be enough. The ecological crisis calls for a social transformation. As they have done in the past with regard to other significant moral issues facing society, college students can be the cultural catalysts for this moral transformation. They can begin by educating themselves so they learn the inner laws of creation. This education should be grounded in prayer, prayer that can reveal the mind of the Creator. Next, by embracing virtue and self-mastery, college students could begin to live their lives according to the natural moral law. In doing this, they would model the simpler lives that will be needed to sustain the personal and social ecological conversions needed to heal the environment. As proenvironmental pro-life advocates, they could live countercultural lives that challenge both liberal and conservative ideologies, as well as partisan politics. In doing so, they will witness to the truth that all humans are called to be stewards of Earth.

QUESTIONS FOR REVIEW

1. How are humans and other creatures naturally inclined toward perfection? How are humans different, though, from other creatures with regard to this natural inclination?
2. According to Saint Thomas Aquinas, what are the ends of the human person?
3. How is the common good defined, and how is it understood today as including the rest of creation?
4. Define and distinguish between ultimate end and subordinate end.
5. What is meant by divine providence? Why is this significant for how humans view creation? Does this perspective on divine

providence differ at all from how it is commonly viewed today, or is it pretty much the same? How?

IN-DEPTH QUESTIONS

1. Have you ever made the connection that Pope Benedict XVI makes between being pro-life and being a caretaker of Earth? What do you think the pope means when he says, "The way humanity treats the environment influences the way it treats itself, and vice versa"? Elaborate on this point with your own examples.
2. What do you think it means to try to "live according to nature"? Does such a lifestyle rule out the use of technology and other modern conveniences altogether? Why or why not?
3. Do you think that persons who are not Catholic Christians—perhaps they belong to another religion or culture, or perhaps they are agnostic or atheist—would find a natural law ethic to be a reasonable and persuasive approach to understanding human morality and how we should live vis-à-vis the environment? Why or why not?
4. Do you think Aquinas's claim that reason discovers four subordinate ends (life, procreation, community, and truth) required for humans to become authentic persons and friends with God and neighbor makes sense? Why or why not? Do these four subordinate ends encompass everything, or is anything left out? Explain.
5. Does the claim that there are acts that "by their very nature [are] 'incapable of being ordered' to God" seem persuasive to you? Why or why not? If so, what are some examples, and how are they incapable of being ordered to God? If not, use some examples to explain why. Assuming the author is correct, provide an example of an environmental act that he might say is incapable of being ordered to God.

CHAPTER 9

THE ENVIRONMENT WITHIN: Virtue Ethics

Nancy M. Rourke

KEY TERMS

end
agent
prudence
temperance
fortitude
cardinal virtue
theological virtues
infused virtue
acquired virtues
subsidiary virtue

INTRODUCTION

This chapter will introduce Christian environmental virtue ethics, first by explaining how virtue ethics works, then defining *virtue*, then demonstrating the significance of role models. Finally, the chapter will describe environmental virtues. Virtue ethics of all varieties focus on humans' moral character. Environmental virtue ethics does this with the belief that good people are also good participants within creation.

AIM OF ENVIRONMENTAL VIRTUE ETHICS

Consider two customers in a grocery store. The first asks the cashier to double-bag his groceries because he has several blocks to walk home from the store. The second also asks for double bags, but only because she wants the same number of bags that the previous customer received. She knows that plastic bags cause problems for the environment, and she knows she doesn't need them, but she thinks it is only reasonable that she receive as much as anyone else. Fair is fair!

If indeed it is morally good to limit the use of plastic bags because of their effect on the environment, one might evaluate these two people's practices when it comes to shopping. Both request double bagging at the grocery store. The consequences of their acts are the same. Are their requests then morally equivalent?

Though the acts are the same, the reasons for the requests differ, and this difference seems important in considering the requests' moral significance. The intention (or end) of an act is a central focus in theological ethics. Of course, most everybody wants to make life better, to make the world a better place. However, is that the only way to think about morality? An act may turn out to have positive consequences, but does that suffice to show that the act is morally good? Rather it seems that the morality of an act has more to do with what the person doing the act (or agent) intends. Because the intention, the end, of the second customer seems somewhat petty, one might evaluate her act as less morally good than the first customer's.

Christian virtue ethics focus on the end of an act instead of on the consequences because the end says more about the agent. If one agrees that it is better to focus on good people rather than on good actions, then one might appreciate a virtue ethics approach to the environment. The goal of virtue ethics is not better decisions but better deciders. How does this moral approach work and how does it fit with environmental ethics?

Consider another example. A "wealthy eccentric" homeowner decides to kill his yard's grass, plants, and trees and to cover the ground with asphalt.[1] This hypothetical neighbor argues that he owns the land and has the right to do with it whatever he wants. He does not enjoy the plants, and they require work to keep up. Therefore, he reasons, there is no reason to keep them.

Now, one can argue that those plants have other purposes than the pleasure of this homeowner. However, does one need to make that argument to find something wrong with his decision? Suppose instead that one did agree that the purpose of his yard's grass, plants, and trees is just to please him, and that there is no reason to tend to these things

1. Ronald Sandler, "Introduction," in *Environmental Virtue Ethics*, eds. Ronald Sandler and Philip Cafaro (Lanham, MD: Rowman & Littlefied, 2005), 1.

if they fail to meet that purpose. Would there be any other reason to argue that his actions are morally problematic? Perhaps the problem is that there is something morally questionable about the kind of person who would do this. Virtue ethics believes that doing and being are connected.[2] This is not to say that the outcome or the nature of someone's actions is irrelevant to virtue ethics; both are significant. Rather than focusing primarily on what people *do*, however, environmental virtue ethics pays attention to how people *are*.

Environmental virtue ethics aims for the formation of good people, because good people are good ecological participants or good neighbors to all that is (human, plant, animal, water, stone, and earth). Clearly, human participation in ecological systems can be harmful. The approach considered in this chapter holds that more environmentally virtuous humans could make creation's ecological systems healthier. Furthermore, virtue ethics theorizes that a person whose character leads to acting with care toward the environment is also a person whose character is good in other ways. That individual will be attentive and attuned to the world he or she lives in and will act in ways that enhance the strength, health, and enjoyment of those lives with which he or she interacts. Such a person will be and feel good, and the goodness and flourishing reflected will have a positive effect on surrounding lives.

Goodness and flourishing go hand in hand. Flourishing includes being strong, happy, and well balanced. The idea is found in Christian virtue ethics and in Aristotle (who calls it *eudaimonia*); it refers to both moral goodness and health and happiness. In Christian virtue ethics, flourishing's connection with goodness emerges from the belief that everything God made is good and that God intends it all to flourish. To be virtuous is to live in pursuit of God's loving hopes for humans. An ecological system made of such flourishing beings is itself a flourishing environment, and a flourishing environment facilitates the health, enjoyment, and happiness of all who live in it. For an environmental virtue ethic, this means that goodness and wellness grow together.[3]

---

2. "The environmentally virtuous person—precisely because of his or her virtue—will be disposed both to recognize the right thing and to do it for the right reasons" (Ronald Sandler, "Introduction," p. 6).

3. Laura Westra, "Virtue Ethics as Foundational for a Global Ethic," in *Environmental Virtue Ethics*, eds. Ronald Sandler and Philip Cafaro (Lanham, MD: Rowman & Littlefield, 2005), 83.

FLOURISHING COMMUNITY: THE CORAL REEF

Rachel Carson describes the lives of a coral reef in a way that shows ecosystems' interconnectedness.

> The world of the reef is inhabited by echinoderms of every sort: starfishes, brittle stars, sea urchins, sand dollars, and holothurians all are at home on the coral rock. . . . All are important in the economy of the marine world—as links in the living chains by which materials are taken from the sea, passed from one to another, returned to the sea, borrowed again. Some are important in the geologic processes of earth building and earth destruction—the processes by which rock is worn away and ground to sand, by which the sediments that carpet the sea floor are accumulated, shifted, sorted and distributed. And at death their hard skeletons contribute calcium for the needs of other animals or for the building of the reefs.[4]

The flourishing of each participant of an ecosystem plays a role in keeping the whole ecosystem healthy. Healthy parts, in balance with each other, make a healthy whole. Changes in the numbers or habits of one form of life will lead to changes elsewhere in the ecosystem. Goodness, health, sickness, or weakness in a part (such as humans or pine trees or sea urchins or honeybees) contributes to goodness, health, sickness, and weakness in the whole. Similarly, the parts of one person flourish when that person flourishes, and, generally speaking, that person will not flourish with weak, sick, tired, or unbalanced organs, chemistry, habits, or other such essential characteristics.[5] It is possible to look at virtues in the same way. Virtues

4. Rachel Carson, *The Edge of the Sea* (Boston, : Houghton Mifflin, 1955), 221–222.

5. Remember, though, that humans can flourish when certain elements are weaker than average or even absent (such as arms, legs, eyesight, hearing ability, tonsils, fertility, to name only a few examples).

(and vices) "live" within a person, and not one of them can function or develop without having an effect on the others. Virtues and vices are shaped by a person's choices and actions, and they grow and strengthen together.

THE VIRTUES

A virtue is the right amount of a good characteristic, usually formed by actions that, through repetition, have become habits. These habits are "acquired by the frequent practice of intended courses of action that make us more inclined toward one way of acting than another."[6] Habits can be good or bad. Too much or not enough of a good characteristic is not virtue but a vice. For example, repeated acts of courage make a person stronger in courage, but acting out of courage for no reason other than to prove one's bravery might be foolhardy or reckless. Courage is a virtue, but excessive courage is recklessness (a vice), and insufficient courage is cowardice (also a vice). A virtue has the right balance.

According to virtue ethics, one special kind of virtue, an infused virtue, becomes a part of an individual through God's grace and can be recognized by the actions that person performs, both externally and internally. These virtues are gifts from God. A person doesn't earn them. Acquired virtues, on the other hand, do require human effort. These virtues are strengthened when one chooses actions that "exercise" them. Imagine virtues as muscles that strengthen with use. In this way, one can visualize how actions influence character. "Morality does not take root in people except through physical, concrete actions. We do not become virtuous by merely wishing or intending to be virtuous. We acquire a virtue only through repeated and habitual courses of action that eventually affect the way we live and act."[7]

Whether infused or acquired, virtues are not silent character traits. If dormant, they are not really virtues. Notice that it makes no sense to say that a person who has never had to wait for something must have the virtue of patience. (One may never have felt impatient, but that does not necessarily mean that one has the virtue of

6. James Keenan, "How Catholic Are the Virtues?" *America* 176 (June 7, 1997), 16.

7. Ibid., 18.

patience!) Once the opportunity to exercise patience appears, patience will develop and strengthen within a person. As this happens, other virtues will be nurtured as well. Consider this example:

A student may decide to walk to his off-campus job rather than drive because he wants to decrease his carbon footprint. His job is a 20-minute walk away. In choosing to walk, he exercises patience (it will take longer to get there), but he also tests his courage (because his friend may mock him for walking even though he has a car). He practices relying on hope (his decreased carbon footprint is hardly perceptible to him, so he won't be able to experience his reward for reducing it). He is learning to be better organized and more efficient (so that he is ready to leave for work earlier than previously), and he exercises self-restraint (because he enjoys driving) and humility (he knows that there is a chance he will arrive at work looking less crisp and fresh than he would like after a 20-minute walk). As he repeatedly chooses to walk to work, it becomes a practice, and each character trait he calls on to develop this practice becomes habitual, as well. He grows in patience, courage, hope, efficiency, self-restraint, and humility, and in the process, his virtues interact with and bolster each other. As he comes to see this commute as his regular way of getting to work, he exercises these virtues with less and less effort. Patience, courage, hope, etc., become his normal way of being. He now *has* those virtues—they are simply parts of his character. Eventually, he will find that his walks to work are enjoyable. Without meaning to, he will have carved out time during his week to learn a new neighborhood, to watch the seasons change, and to exercise his body. For virtue ethics, the enjoyment aspect of growing in virtue may be unexpected, but it is no coincidence. (More will be said about this later.)

Admittedly, virtue ethics has its critics. Because individual persons are its focus, some doubt whether virtue ethics can look broadly enough to facilitate deeper social criticism. One theologian has warned that virtue ethics alone does not suffice; it needs social justice working with it.[8] This implies that virtue ethics is too narrow to critique social injustices. This insightful criticism reminds virtue ethics thinkers that the social aspects of a person play essential roles

8. Daryl Trimiew, "Presidential Address," presented at the annual meeting of the Society of Christian Ethics, Chicago, IL, January 8–11, 2009.

in that person's character, and vice versa. When virtue ethicists forget this, social ethics could be ignored.

On the other hand, others find virtue ethics too broad. How can such a focus, which boils down to having the right attitude, be enough to assure right action? Attitude is too vague a category, and habits are not everything. What can virtue ethics say about the person who is about to attack someone but who will be very sorry afterward and learn much from the experience? The person attacked might not agree that the thing that matters most, ethically speaking, is that the attacker learned from this experience and is developing in virtue. The

ENVIRONMENTAL ROLE MODELS: RACHEL CARSON

PHOTO COURTESY U.S. FISH AND WILDLIFE SERVICE

Rachel Louise Carson (May 27, 1907 –April 14, 1964) was a Pittsburgh, Pennsylvania-born zoologist and biologist whose landmark book, *Silent Spring,* is often credited with having launched the global environmental movement.

Rachel Carson's loving and systematic observations of the natural world demonstrate virtues of patience, attentiveness, and gratitude. As a person, she also shows us how the practice of such virtues gave her much enjoyment. "In my thoughts of the shore, one place stands apart for its revelation of exquisite beauty. It is a pool hidden within a cave that one can visit only rarely and briefly when the lowest of the year's low tides fall below it, and perhaps from that very fact it acquires some of its special beauty. Choosing such a tide, I hoped for a glimpse of the pool."[9]

9. Carson, 2.

person attacked might be inclined to say that the hurt matters more than the assailant's learning experience. Virtue ethics might overlook the problem of a morally good agent who does one very harmful and destructive action. This problem raises the question of what matters most in moral reasoning: an agent's moral character or the results of her actions? One's answer to this question will determine in large part whether one favors virtue ethics as an approach.

THE WORLDS OF VIRTUES

How acquired virtues develop has been discussed, but which of these are most significant for environmental virtue ethics? One way to answer this question is to consider people who are environmental role models. Try to think about the "content" of a virtue (like courage) without imagining a person who exemplifies it! In fact, virtue ethics expects individuals to learn from the people they admire—in other words, from role models. By practicing the virtues for which they admire role models, moral agents may find that they can gain and strengthen desired virtues. Rachel Carson, whose book *Silent Spring* brought the ecological impact of human chemical use to public consciousness, is often cited as an environmental role model for her loving and detailed attention to the creatures and plants that live on beaches. Aldo Leopold, a twentieth-century conservationist, demonstrates enjoyment, dedication, and attunement to his nonhuman neighbors in a way that speaks of his patience, care, and humor. Other environmental role models include Henry David Thoreau and John Muir. These individuals demonstrate virtues of attentiveness, care, gentleness, patience, dedication, persuasiveness, and knowledge.

Role models present different versions and combinations of environmental virtues, but focusing on cataloging the virtues themselves is also possible. One philosopher lists the "dirty virtues," as she calls them. Calling virtues "dirty" is a way of reminding people of their intrinsic connectedness with dirt and with everything around them. This term also invites one to remember that one's virtues are not only for facilitating social interactions with other humans. People also need virtues that help them to be the best possible participants in their ecologies. Dirty virtues help people to live in good relationship with the animals, plants, water, air, and earth that are our neighbors and without which we would not survive.[10] Louke van Wensveen lists these virtues as respect for nature, friendship, "adaptability, benevolence, care, compassion or solidarity, gratitude, healing, hope, inclusivity, joy, justice, moderation or restraint, openness, passion, perseverance, realism, self-examination, sensuousness, sharing, spontaneity, vulnerability, wisdom, and wonder."[11] Many environmental virtue ethicists identify *attunement* (or an attentiveness and a willingness to adjust to one's environments) in particular as a significant dirty virtue.[12]

Because virtue ethics focuses on an individual's ability to *become* a good person, acquired virtues are a primary concern. Virtues are acquired and continually perfected as one practices being the kind of individual one wants to be. It is Christian belief that God also helps in this process. Look again at the idea of infused virtues.

Christianity recognizes three infused virtues in particular as theological virtues. Faith, hope, and charity are given by God's grace. They are called "theological" because they are directly connected to God. The infused virtues direct the formation and exercise of all other virtues. As one theologian notes, "We do not become virtuous or holy by our efforts alone."[13] The efforts of the Holy Spirit are also necessary, and the gifts of faith, hope, and charity are God's way of contributing to human goodness. Let's consider each of these briefly.

Faith, as the "assurance of things hoped for, the conviction of things not seen," (Hebrews 11:1 NRSV) has to do with trusting. Faith, according to virtue ethics, is an ability, not a list of beliefs one thinks to be correct. It is a leaning toward or a following after something before there is absolute certainty of its existence. It makes sense that faith is seen as an infused rather than an acquired virtue. How

10. Louke van Wensveen, *Dirty Virtues: The Emergence of Ecological Virtue Ethics* (Amherst, NY: Humanity Books, 2000), 3–4.

11. Van Wensveen adds that many of these virtues are overlooked because some people associate them with femininity (Louke van Wensveen, "The Emergence of Ecological Virtue Language," in *Environmental Virtue Ethics*, eds. Ronald Sandler and Philip Cafaro [Lanham, MD: Rowman & Littlefield, 2005], 17, 21).

12. Nancy M. Rourke, "God, Grace and Creation: Shaping a Catholic Environmental Virtue Ethic," in *God, Grace and Creation: College Theology Society Annual Volume* 55 (Maryknoll, NY: Orbis, 2010), 223.

13. John W. Crossin, "Some Developing Aspects of Virtue Ethics," *Josephinum Journal of Theology* 7 (2000): 115.

would a person start building faith without help from God? The gift of faith is God's way of drawing one closer.

Hope is closely connected to faith. It is easy to see how hope is a virtue. As shown previously, virtues are closely linked to action, and hope does not exist in a person without affecting that person's actions. One can choose to rely on hope or not, certainly, but only with God's grace does hope exist within one in the first place. The theological virtue of hope is important to environmental ethics because it enables a person to continue to live lightly in creation even when it is clear that too few others are doing the same. Hope sustains when one knows that one's own efforts are not enough.

Charity is the first of theological virtues. Charity and love are inseparable, and to focus on the theological virtue of charity is to focus on the fact that all one's ways of relating to others (human, plant, animal, and earth) come from one's relationship with God, Creator and mutual lover of all that one loves well. Charity functions ecologically, in a sense: it orders one's connections—to God, and to others in light of one's love for God. In charity, one seeks and nurtures all these connections because one's interconnectedness gives ways to express one's love of God. One is a friend to others *for God's sake* when one has the theological virtue of charity. Because of this, charity is the virtue that makes sure that all one's formations and expressions of virtue are directed to God.

When considering the infused virtues together with the acquired virtues, one sees that moral growth happens in many ways at once: through exercise of virtues, through examples set by role models, through God's grace, and through interactions with all the lives around one. Moral growth is not a strictly intellectual process; it involves one's whole self, and it works with one's environment. Environmental virtue ethics erodes the barriers usually used to separate oneself from one's contexts. Environmental virtues prevent humans from valuing their selves, their independence, and their own importance above all else.

CARDINAL VIRTUES

Moral theology has a long history of naming and defining cardinal virtues. A cardinal virtue is one that is acquired for its own sake and not for the sake of strengthening another virtue. Moral theology traditionally organizes all the acquired, moral virtues under four cardinal virtues: fortitude, temperance, justice, and prudence. This way of organizing the virtues helps one to see how each virtue distinctively contributes to one's character. In this way, people can understand how the virtues interact with one another. For example, patience and perseverance come together as a part of the cardinal virtue of fortitude. Neither can develop in a moral agent without the other, and both are necessary for an agent to develop fortitude.

What exactly is fortitude? Fortitude relates to strength, endurance, perseverance, and patience. It organizes and shapes these virtues (and others), and together they power an agent's ability to maintain effort through difficulty. Fortitude is important for environmental ethics for two reasons: First, it sustains efforts that certainly will not bring immediate results. When one considers that some attempts to live in a more sustainable manner will not bring immediate benefits but will limit the severity of future disasters, one can see the need for fortitude. One needs fortitude to stay motivated and to anticipate the benefits of moral life across a longer term. Second, fortitude gives an agent the strength to let go of the desire to control the environment to an extreme degree. Humans fear losing control, sacrificing comfort, and being at nature's mercy. Now, fear of nature is reasonable for humans (furless, clawless, wingless humans!) but it is still possible to fear nature too much. Fortitude exists when an agent responds to a balance of reasonable but not excessive fear. Turning on air conditioning when heat is intolerable and must be managed is reasonable. Cranking on air conditioning before the temperature rises for fear that soon the heat might become uncomfortable could be an excessive concession to fear.

As a cardinal virtue, fortitude is less directly connected to action decisions than its subsidiary virtues (such as patience and perseverance), but it governs their development. Cardinal virtues like fortitude root subsidiary virtues deeply into one's character, as aspects of one's personality. They also direct the development of subsidiary virtues so that they, in balance, improve one's overall moral character. Temperance, which relates to self-restraint, seems an obvious fit for environmental virtue ethics, though this might be for the wrong reasons. To be sure, temperance opposes consumption as an end in itself,

THE ROLE OF SUBSIDIARY VIRTUES: WHY ONE SHOULD NOT GIVE THE CARDINALS ALL THE ATTENTION

Although cardinal virtues are "cardinal," they are not more important than subsidiary virtues. Subsidiary virtues deserve more attention than they usually receive, because they are more immediately connected to the actual decisions and actions one faces. Ethical deliberation might benefit more from considering the subsidiary virtues than the cardinal virtues, in that case, "because they go closer to providing guidance for particular actions and therefore are truer. . . . "[14]

and that is very important for environmental ethics. However, due to its connection with moderation and the rejection of excessive enjoyment, temperance has developed a negative "sour grapes" image that is undeserved. Temperance does not require obsessive self-restraint and self-denial, a view that reflects a shallow understanding of temperance. Temperance does not encourage one to deny pleasures but to enjoy them in their truest and fullest sense. It is about responses to pleasure in "tranquility and serenity of soul." Having temperance means being "rightly pleased."[15] Temperance brings heightened awareness of one's own internal pleasure environment. An agent with temperance will have a clear sense of the ways in which all the pleasures relate to one another and to the agent's fullest flourishing.[16] This means having a sense of pleasure that comes from an honest, informed understanding of the context within which one enjoys things (like food, drink, and sex). Temperance draws enjoyment and ecological awareness together. Humans *are* to enjoy the pleasures of

14. Lisa Fullam, "Sex in 3-D: A Telos for a Virtue Ethics of Sexuality," *Journal of the Society of Christian Ethics* 27 (Fall-Winter 2007), 157, 161.

15. Diana Fritz Cates, "The Virtue of Temperance," in *The Ethics of Aquinas*, ed. Stephen J. Pope (Washington, DC: Georgetown University Press, 2002), 323–324.

16. Ibid., 322.

creation and to enjoy them in ways and to degrees that are good for them and good for all creation. Temperance is sometimes misunderstood as a habit of limiting or avoiding any interaction with the world. Given the harm that humanity has inflicted on the planet's health, this is an understandable impulse. However, it is not a virtue. One ought not deny one's need to relate with the world. Insensibility, or a state in which nothing appeals to a person, is actually a vice that corresponds to the virtue of temperance. Instead of retreating from the environment, humans should become more aware of the ways in which they interact with all the other participants of Earth's ecological systems. Then, they can enjoy more healthy, balanced, and mutually enjoyable interactions with plants, nonhuman animals, and other humans. Dirty virtues that relate to temperance, then, could include joy and restraint, moderation and spontaneity.

Consider a parallel with Catholic sexual ethics. One theologian considers sexuality from a virtue ethics perspective and concludes that humans' problems begin not when they ask too much of sex, but when they ask too little. When humans use sexual experiences just to satisfy their desire for physical stimulation and try to ignore everything else that sex means, it is because they have tried to make sex mean less and be less.[17] They expect less from it; so they come to experience it less fully. One could say the same about ecological awareness. Humans tend to level entire forests, poison air and water, and endanger life's diversity when they think of their world only as an industrial or agricultural resource and nothing more. If the world is just a resource for human lives and endeavors, then there is nothing wrong with mining it solely for human benefit with little concern for the effect on nonhuman lives. On the other hand, humans could learn to see their environments as teeming with companions, sensations, and a wide diversity of ways of life that surround and teach them more than they can imagine. Greater awareness of all that these ecologies have to offer will help humans to find temperate ways of living within them.

Justice plays a prominent role in Christian social teaching, in biblical ethics, and in systematic theologies. As a cardinal virtue, justice appears in Christian ethics in two versions. In one version, the

17. Fullam, 166.

virtue of justice refers to an agent's habitual practice of taking care that all people get what they deserve (here *deserving* includes, but is not limited to, what people need to survive). This first notion of justice limits justice to the human sphere. Of course, habits of justice among humans would improve the whole world, so humans' understanding of justice as a cardinal virtue would be beneficial. This kind of virtue of justice presumes that the world's most significant purpose is to support human life and that humans have a responsibility to ensure that natural resources are distributed in such a way that all humans share equally.

One theologian demonstrates this first sense of justice in this way: "The virtue of justice inclines humans to relate to one another in ways that are conducive to achieving their temporal common good as they seek their eternal common good with God." When she refers to "common good of the community," she means all the human lives in any given ecosystem. She goes on to emphasize that environmental justice means particular attention to the needs of marginalized people and people who are not able to speak for themselves, such as the poor, the "minority residents," and future generations of people.[18] However, this author recommends more strongly the second sense of justice: "A more expansive and ecologically sensitive role for justice is suggested by Aquinas' teaching that the more comprehensive good envisaged by the human, the more the human will corresponds to the will of God, who wills the good of the entire universe."[19]

The second notion of justice as a cardinal virtue refers to a tendency to treat everything and everyone justly. This second notion assumes that "justness" can and should be enacted toward humans, toward nonhuman animals, toward Earth itself, and for the benefit of all (again, in accordance with deserving). It is a foundational belief of Christian theology that God is creator of all, and so nothing in creation is exempt from deserving one's care and attention. Christian theologians throughout history have seen that God expresses Godself through creation, and that creation, therefore, has intrinsic value.[20]

---

18. Jame Schaefer, *Theological Foundations for Environmental Ethics: Reconstructing Patristic and Medieval Concepts* (Washington, DC: Georgetown University Press, 2009), 234–235,243–244.

19. Ibid., 234.

Aquinas, Bonaventure, Augustine, John Chrysostom, and others have taught this and meditated on its meaning. Catholic scholars today reach back to earlier theology in order to revive these traditions of seeing God's desire for all of creation to flourish. The cardinal virtue of justice grows from one's understanding of God's hopes for creation.

ENVIRONMENTAL AWARENESS MEANS AWARENESS OF INTERCONNECTIVITY

"We cannot interfere in one area of the ecosystem without paying due attention both to the consequences of such interference in other areas and to the well-being of future generations." (John Paul II, "Message for the 1990 World Day of Peace," no. 6)

Prudence is the first of the cardinal virtues. Prudence is reason meeting practice. It translates careful practical reason into excellent action. Put simply, prudence is moral wisdom. Like all wisdom, it develops with life experience. An intellectual virtue that functions as a moral virtue, prudence is responsible for accurately and insightfully perceiving the nature of a situation within which an agent acts. It helps one to honestly appraise a situation and to act appropriately. Imagine trying to decide what to do in a tricky situation without understanding the situation's layers and subtleties. Prudence, then, must include environmental and ecological awareness. There is no sufficient

---

20. One theologian discusses recent Catholic teachings and argues that, though official Catholic magisterial writings have not entirely "embraced an ecocentric approach or deep ecology approach to creation," there is a trend "toward recognition of nature as having intrinsic and not simply extrinsic or utilitarian value." As an example, he notes wide Catholic acceptance of the social teaching principle of the integrity of creation (John E. Carroll, "Catholicism and Deep Ecology," in *Deep Ecology and World Religions: New Essays on Sacred Ground*, eds. David Landis Barnhill and Roger S. Gottlieb [Albany, NY: State University of New York Press, 2001], 188, 190). For an overview of several theologians' thinking on creation's intrinsic value, see Schaefer, *Theological Foundations*, 17–27.

practical reason without a good understanding of where one is and of everything that is happening there. Among the dirty virtues discussed above, attunement is a significant subsidiary virtue of prudence.

Philosopher Peter Wenz discusses prudence by narrating examples of well-intentioned first-world assistance that actually worsened the conditions of the poor globally. He tells the story of high-yield varieties of crops (HYVs) in India, which were introduced to combat food shortage and poverty. HYVs used more water than traditional varieties. Wealthier farmers could afford to dig wells deeper to reach the water needed, while farmers who could not access the needed water lost crops. The water table also dropped, and the poorer farmers lost their livelihood once the water they needed became out of reach.[21]

A well-established attentiveness to the world's ecological systems helps prudence predict how the effects of people's actions will reverberate throughout their environments. Prudence is strengthened when people understand that they are deeply and definitively embedded within the ecosystems. On the other hand, willful ignorance of mutual interdependence with the rest of life on Earth stunts prudence's growth. The importance of being aware of one's interdependence is a recurring theme in environmental virtue ethics, and prudence, above all the other virtues, relies on and contributes to people's awareness—and, therefore, also to their self-understanding. Being attuned to the world helps one see oneself more clearly, and that enhanced self-awareness will remind one of a deep interconnectedness with all life.

WHERE AM I? WHAT AM I?

Sometimes Catholic understandings of humanity give the impression that the context within which humans live is only that: a passive window-dressing within which the important stuff (the drama of human life) takes place. With this perspective, ecologies still seem nice, but they are not necessary or relevant to what it means to be human. With

21. Peter Wenz, "Synergistic Environmental Virtues: Consumerism and Human Flourishing," in *Environmental Virtue Ethics*, eds. Ronald Sandler and Philip Cafaro (Lanham, MD: Rowman & Littlefield, 2005), 200–202.

this kind of a theological anthropology, the ecologies within which humans move seem of such small importance to their actual selves that the ecologies might as well not exist at all. Prudence can cultivate a better self-understanding than this. Instead of seeing themselves as beings distinguished and separate from nature (by virtue of their minds), and instead of believing that, therefore, they are not completely integrated into Earth's ecologies but are somehow above them, a prudential theological anthropology helps people remember that they heal or sicken or fail or flourish always together with their environments. To understand this, people must practice awareness, attentiveness, and attunement to the worlds within which they live. Environmental ethicists agree. "We are finding out who we are by finding out where we are and how we are emplaced there," says Presbyterian minister and environmentalist Holmes Rolston III.[22] Environmental and legal scholar Laura Westra warns against separating oneself from the environments when one defines oneself, arguing that any "specious separation of humans from their natural environment is inappropriate both conceptually and scientifically and therefore practically invalid."[23]

One sees a version of this kind of awareness in Catholic magisterial documents as they point out connections among poverty, injustice, and patterns of environmental exploitation. A recently released papal encyclical notes: "There is need for what might be called a human ecology, correctly understood. The deterioration of nature is in fact closely connected to the culture that shapes human coexistence. . . . Just as human virtues are interrelated, such that the weakening of one places others at risk, so the ecological system is based on respect for a plan that affects both the health of society and its good relationship with nature. . . . "[24] Awareness of one's interconnections is a necessary component of a person's development of prudence. In a sense, knowing *who* one is and *where* one is mean the same.

---

22. Holmes Rolston III, "Environmental Virtue Ethics: Half the Truth but Dangerous as a Whole," in *Environmental Virtue Ethics*, eds. Ronald Sandler and Philip Cafaro (Lanham, MD: Rowman & Littlefield, 2005), 64.

23. Laura Westra, "Virtue Ethics as Foundational for a Global Ethic," in *Environmental Virtue Ethics*, eds. Ronald Sandler and Philip Cafaro (Lanham, MD: Rowman & Littlefield, 2005), 81.

24. Pope Benedict XVI, *Caritas in veritate*, no. 51.

AWARENESS EXPANDS KINSHIP

John Muir, (April 21, 1838–December 24, 1913) American conservationist.

John Muir, a deeply religious environmental writer, demonstrates in his childhood remembrances that observing and interacting with animals changed his understanding of humanity and increased his generosity and his joy at being a part of life on Earth. "Intense experiences . . . bring out the humanity that is in all animals. One touch of nature, even a cat-and-loon touch, makes all the world kin." He reflects on his family's oxen. "We recognized their kinship also by their yawning like ourselves when sleepy and evidently enjoying the same peculiar pleasure at the roots of their jaws; by the way they stretched themselves in the morning after a good rest . . . by their intelligent, alert curiosity, manifested in listening to strange sounds. . . . "[25]

Being aware of one's embeddedness within ecologies is essential to Christian environmental virtue ethics. Prudence is insufficient without this, but equally important, this awareness is a reward in itself. Joy comes with practical recognition of one's embeddedness. One Protestant theologian calls this joy a "satisfying responsiveness."[26] He contrasts this with understandings of the virtues that tend to sever humans from the ecologies. Humans have often linked their ideas about the virtues strictly to independence, which does not reflect

25. John Muir, *Nature Writings* (New York: Penguin Literary Classics, 1997), 78, 48.

26. Willis Jenkins, *Ecologies of Grace: Environmental Ethics and Christian Theology* (Oxford: Oxford University Press, 2008), 134.

the Christian call for vulnerability and relationality, he argues. That humans are not sufficient in themselves is a basic Christian truth. Humans need God. Habitual awareness of the worlds of nature and prudence's attunement to creation remind Christians of that truth.

How exactly does joy grow from attentiveness? Consider a woman who has decided to eliminate meat from her diet because she has learned that high levels of meat consumption hurt the environment in many ways. Though the struggle to form new dietary habits is difficult, her efforts slowly strengthen her virtues. Awareness increases, and she begins to notice the other ways in which her decisions affect the world. She enjoys her newfound awareness of interrelationality with all of life and comes to see her own life as full of possibilities for interaction with other kinds of life. Enhanced awareness of interrelationality brings a new feeling of moving through the world. She begins to understand herself as a part of something greater, and she experiences herself as participating physically, emotionally, mentally, and spiritually in the life of the ecologies within which she lives. One can see how this woman's new awareness of the ways in which she is embedded in her world helps her to grow in joy.

Evidence of this effect of virtue—joy—abounds in the writings of environmental ethicists. Environmentalist Aldo Leopold, a role model mentioned earlier, is an excellent example. Leopold describes his connection with the land during the early hours of the day: "One hundred and twenty acres, according to the County Clerk, is the extent of my worldly domain. But the County Clerk is a sleepy fellow, who never looks at his record books before nine o'clock. What they would show at daybreak is the question here at issue. Books or no books, it is a fact, patent both to my dog and myself, that at daybreak I am the sole owner of all the acres I can walk over. It is not only the boundaries that disappear, but also the thought of being bounded. Expanses unknown to deed or map are known to every dawn, and solitude, supposed no longer to exist in my country, extends on every hand as far as the dew can reach."[27]

The practices and virtues of environmentalists lead to, and are nurtured by, their attunement to the environments in which they live.

---

27. Aldo Leopold, *A Sand County Almanac, and Sketches Here and There* (NY: Oxford University Press, 1949), 41.

When one is attentive to all the life that is around one and to the relationships one has with all that life, one comes to understand oneself better. Accurate self-understanding is essential to virtue ethics. Christian virtue ethics shows one how awareness and practice of the virtues can bring one into greater balance with the world. God meant for the world to flourish, and humans, as participants in that plan, can enjoy the process of growth toward greener discipleship.

QUESTIONS FOR REVIEW

1. Identify and briefly define each of the cardinal virtues. Why are they considered "cardinal"? How is prudence required for the other virtues to be put into practice?
2. What are the three infused theological virtues, and why are they considered "theological"? Which one is considered primary?
3. Why is attentiveness a part of prudence?
4. According to virtue ethics, how does a person's character connect to the actions that person does?
5. Can infused virtues be "worked on"? Can an agent develop infused virtues through his own effort? How?

IN-DEPTH QUESTIONS

1. How are a person's virtues like participants in an ecological system?
2. Do you think accidental or unintended actions affect the formation of one's character? Why or why not?
3. Which definition of *justice* makes the most sense to you? Why?
4. Are infused or acquired virtues more valuable (to human life)? Why?
5. How have you ever felt "kinship" with nonhuman creation? Does kinship imply equality? Why or why not?
6. Given that many criticize virtue ethics for being too narrowly focused, do you agree virtue ethics thought can suffice to actually help the environment?

CHAPTER 10

TOWARD A EUCHARISTIC ECOLOGY

Stephen B. Wilson

KEY TERMS

Gnosticism
orthodox
liturgy
sacraments
pantheism
ecumenical convergence
Eucharist

INTRODUCTION

What does it mean to be a disciple of Jesus Christ, or to put it collectively, what does it mean to be the Church? These questions about identity are important as Christians seek to address the contemporary ecological crisis. Obviously, the environment is not just a Christian concern. As the Second Vatican Council affirmed, the problems and possibilities faced by other humans are also the problems and possibilities faced by those who seek to follow Christ.[1] This point is especially true regarding the environment, because it involves a world shared by all people. Accordingly, efforts to bring about positive ecological change will require responses by people from various nations, cultures and, as shall be shown in Part VI of this volume, religions. As different religions respond, the people of those communities will bring with them resources and perspectives that are uniquely their own.

1. *Gaudium et spes,* (Constitution on the Church in the Modern World), no. 1. Translation from Austin Flannery, ed., *Vatican Council II: The Conciliar and Post Conciliar Documents*, new rev. ed. (Collegeville, MN: Liturgical Press, 1996), 903.

The Catholic Church is no different in this regard, as shown in other chapters in this volume and their examples of specifically Christian sources: Scripture, the spiritualities of various religious orders, Catholic social teaching (CST), and so on. However, one resource might not immediately come to mind—the Church's liturgy, that is, the Church's corporate worship. This chapter explores how the liturgy might *inform* and even *transform* the way people understand and engage the world. It will be developed in a series of steps. First, it will discuss the pivotal role liturgy played in a doctrinal dispute within early Christianity. It will then consider key aspects of contemporary liturgical practice and how they might lead to what could be called a Eucharistic ecology.

LITURGY AND THEOLOGY: A LESSON FROM IRENAEUS OF LYONS

To see why the liturgy may be helpful for thinking through a Christian approach to the environment, a look at the past is useful. One of the early doctrinal difficulties faced by the Church was a series of movements known as Gnosticism (there were several Christian and non-Christian versions of it), which focused on salvation as a kind of "knowledge" (Greek: *gnosis*). Gnostics believed they alone possessed the secret knowledge that brought salvation. For Christian Gnostics, that confidential teaching was thought to have been passed down orally from Jesus to a select few followers, who then passed it along to their heirs. As for the content of this teaching, its basic idea was quite simple. Gnostics believed that the material world was fundamentally evil. The assumption that matter was inherently sinful informed other Gnostic positions. As part of this dualistic view of reality, several Christian Gnostic teachers argued that there were at least two gods. There was the Creator, who created the world and thus evil. Then there was the Supreme God, who brought salvation through Jesus' secret message. Based on what has been said thus far, it is hardly surprising that the Gnostics also rejected the Incarnation. If matter is evil, then why would God assume vile human flesh? Similarly, the Gnostics disputed the Resurrection. If human flesh is itself sinful, then salvation would involve an escape from human bodies rather than their resurrection. According to this dualistic viewpoint, matter does not matter to God.

Although modern Christians may find these ideas amusing as they question basic beliefs of the Christian faith (on the other hand, many Christians today might be surprised to realize that they actually subscribe to dualistic thinking similar to Gnosticism), Gnosticism was regarded by the early Church as a grave threat. Indeed, fundamental doctrines such as the Incarnation and the Resurrection became more fully appreciated because prominent figures in the early Church saw Gnosticism's danger and sought to defend and clarify the importance of these beliefs.

Irenaeus of Lyons was one of the most notable defenders of what was emerging as orthodox Christianity (*orthodox* coming from the Greek *orthodoxos*, meaning, "right opinion or belief"). His most famous work is *Against the Heresies*. The major theme that runs through this book is unity—the unity of divinity and the unity of creation and redemption. In terms of the former, over and against the Gnostic claims that there were at least two gods, Irenaeus strongly asserts that there is but one God, the God revealed in both the Old and New Testaments. In terms of the latter, God brings about both creation and redemption, meaning that both are part of God's "economy," or ordering of reality. Creation is the presupposition of salvation, and salvation brings about the perfection of creation. From Irenaeus's perspective, therefore, creation is essentially good because of its divine origin and destiny.

It is important to note the role that the Eucharist played in Irenaeus's argument. One must keep in mind that the bread and wine used in the Eucharist are produced from wheat and grapes, that is, from creation. Because of this fact, Irenaeus was able to highlight an inconsistency between Gnostic teaching and practice. On the one hand, the Gnostics argued that the material world was evil. On the other hand, they used the material world as part of their "thanksgiving" (Greek: *eucharistia*) to God. As Irenaeus sarcastically put it, "those . . . who maintain that the things around us originated from apostasy, ignorance, and passion, do, while offering unto Him the fruits of ignorance, passion, and apostasy, sin against their Father, rather subjecting Him to insult than giving Him thanks."[2] Irenaeus

2. Irenaeus, *Against the Heresies*, IV.18.4 in *Ante-Nicene Fathers: The Writings of the Fathers Down to A.D. 325*, vol. I: *The Apostolic Fathers with Justin Martyr and Irenaeus*, eds. Alexander Roberts, James Donaldson, and A. Cleveland Coxe (Grand Rapids, MI: Eerdmans, 1981), 486.

completed his argument by noting that in orthodox Christianity, there was perfect conformity between what the Church believed and how it worshipped: " . . . Our opinion is in accordance with the Eucharist, and the Eucharist in turn establishes our opinion."[3]

Irenaeus's argument against the Gnostics is instructive in two ways: The first element is the content of his argument. While the Gnostics considered matter as essentially sinful, he affirmed the goodness of creation. Irenaeus reasoned that God is Creator, and because God is goodness itself, that which God creates must be good. Hence, matter matters to God, and from this perspective, salvation entails overcoming the sin that has corrupted creation.

Not only is creation the object of salvation, but also it is the means. Catholic theology sees examples of this in the Incarnation, whereby God takes on human flesh, as well as in the sacraments in which God uses material elements, such as bread and wine, as the means of sanctifying humanity. This observation brings up the second point: In developing his critique of Gnosticism, Irenaeus used the liturgy as a key source for doing theology. The liturgy, much like the Bible, can provide insights about God and the life of discipleship.

With a nod to Irenaeus, the rest of this chapter will be devoted to examining how the current Catholic liturgy can serve to inform how one might understand the relationship between God, humanity, and the rest of creation. This chapter will do so by looking at three aspects of the liturgy: liturgical texts, the importance of the natural world for worship, and the significance of how the bread and wine are used in the Eucharist.

"LORD, GOD OF ALL CREATION": LITURGICAL TEXTS

The first topic to explore is the textual portions of the Church's liturgy, specifically the Nicene Creed and Eucharistic Prayers. One should keep in mind the purpose of these materials. Their primary purpose is to glorify God. However, they also achieve other ends. As humans praise God, they give thanks for what God has done to elicit their praise. Recalling God's prior actions reminds all of who God is.

3. Ibid., IV.18.5 in *Ante-Nicene Fathers*, 486.

As a result, liturgical texts are theological statements that express the Church's story and basic beliefs.

In addition to being means of praise and theological affirmations, these texts also provide ongoing formation. As people rehearse these statements Sunday after Sunday, they can become ingrained in memory, making them a part of Christian identity—similar to the regular practice of good habits that become character traits, or virtues, as shown in chapter 9. Thus, one of the primary ways a person can learn what it means to be a disciple of Christ is through regular and active participation (not by being "pew potatoes") in the worship.

What do these liturgical texts say about being a disciple in light of environmental concerns? Essentially, they provide insights about the relation between God and creation that can affect how one sees one's role in the world. A good example of this tendency can be found in the Nicene Creed. The creed begins with this profession: "We believe in one God, the Father, the Almighty, maker of heaven and earth, of all that is seen and unseen." Similarly, at the end of the creed, one affirms that the Holy Spirit is "the Lord, the giver of life," which alludes to the Holy Spirit's role in creation. Thus, the creed clearly affirms that God is the maker of all that exists.

In addition to the creed, other aspects of the Eucharistic celebration articulate the importance of God as Creator. For Roman Catholics, this idea is expressed during the prayer that accompanies the Preparation of the Altar, in which God is referred to as "Lord, God of all Creation."[4]

The emphasis on God as Creator can also be found in the opening sections of the Eucharistic Prayers from many Christian traditions. One of the most common formulations of this idea echoes the language of the creed by referring to the Father as the "Creator of heaven and earth."[5] Sometimes, though, the prayers can be more effusive and elegant in their language. For instance, one of the prayers used within Lutheranism states: "O Lord our God, maker of all things. Through

4. *The Sacramentary* (Collegeville, MN: Liturgical Press, 1985), 415.

5. See, for example, *The Book of Common Prayer* (New York: Seabury Press, 1979), 361; *The Book of Common Worship* (Louisville, KY: Westminster/John Knox Press, 1993), 130; *The United Methodist Book of Worship* (Nashville, TN: The United Methodist Publishing House, 1992), 36, 52, 54, 56, 58, 60, 62, 64, 66, 68, 70, 72, 74, 76.

EUCHARISTIC PRAYERS

The prayer that accompanies the Eucharistic rite proper is generally referred to as "the" Eucharistic Prayer, though there are other names for it (for example, the Canon of the Mass, the Great Thanksgiving, and Anaphora) and various forms of it even within a single tradition. In the Roman Catholic Church, four Eucharistic Prayers are used in normal Sunday Masses, though there are additional prayers for specific circumstances such as Masses for children or reconciliation services. For convenience's sake, these four prayers are typically designated by Roman numerals. Thus, the first one is known as Eucharistic Prayer I, the second as Eucharistic Prayer II, and so on.

your goodness you have blessed us with these gifts. With them we offer ourselves to your service and dedicate our lives to the care and redemption of all you have made, for the sake of him who gave himself for us, Jesus Christ our Lord."[6] Not only does this passage affirm God as Creator, but it also highlights the nature of creation as gift, a point that will be developed more fully shortly.

As has already been noted, the creed highlights both the role of the Father and the Holy Spirit in creation. Other liturgical materials, such as Eucharistic Prayer II, highlight the Son's action: "He is the Word through whom you made the universe, the Savior you sent to redeem us."[7] In addition to expressing the Son's part in creation, this prayer also raises a point made by Irenaeus about the unity of creation and redemption. They are linked because they are common actions of God in Christ. Put differently, both creation and redemption serve as expressions of God's love. Eucharistic Prayer IV develops this theme by noting that God brought about creation "to fill your creatures with every blessing and lead all men to the joyful vision of your light."[8] This prayer indicates that one should view all

---

6. *Lutheran Book of Worship* (Minneapolis: Augsburg, 1978), 68.

7. *Sacramentary*, 509.

8. Ibid., 517.

IMAGE © KOKOPHOTO/ISTOCKPHOTO.COM

A priest elevates the chalice as he celebrates the Eucharist.

of creation as a blessing, that is, as a gift from God. As the prayer continues, it shows that the Eucharist is done in thanksgiving for this gift: "Countless hosts of angels stand before you to do your will; they look upon your splendor and praise you, night and day. United with them, and in the name of every creature under heaven, we too praise your glory. . . . "[9] Interestingly, the prayer suggests that when one worships God, one does so as a representative for the rest of creation. This notion can also be found in Eucharistic Prayer III, which states: "Father, you are holy indeed, and all creation rightly gives you praise."[10] The implication of this thought is that the purpose of creation is to offer praise to God. Creation accomplishes this task in part by its God-given beauty. Imagine staring out over an intoxicating vista, possibly the ocean during a glorious sunrise or the mountains as they frame a slowly setting sun. The sheer beauty of such spectacles speaks volumes about God, the source of their existence.

9. Ibid.

10. Ibid., 513.

The sea at dawn.

What can one take away from this brief survey of these key liturgical texts? The Catholic liturgy here offers three interrelated ideas that can inform how one understands and lives in the larger world. First, because God is "the maker of heaven and earth," God has ultimate dominion over creation. There is a human tendency to assume that the natural world belongs to humanity. These materials, however, remind one that, while humans may inhabit Earth, it is ultimately God's. Second, creation, as well as redemption, is graciously offered to humans so that they might receive "every blessing." Humanity receives the world as a gift freely bestowed by God. Creation is an act of grace. Accordingly, humans are to use creation with an appreciation of its status as a gift, not one with which they may do whatever they please, but rather something that has been entrusted to them. Put differently, the dominion that humans have over the rest of creation should take the form of stewardship in which they serve as God's caretakers of the world. Third, the destiny of all creation lies in praising God. Therefore, humans should keep this larger purpose in mind as they serve as stewards of creation.

An example might prove useful to illustrate this last point. In the Mass, the task of the priest is to lead the congregation in its collective worship of God. Really good presiders are like conductors in a symphony. Both lead the musicians or congregants so that each person more effectively contributes to the larger whole. In a similar manner, humans are to nurture other aspects of creation so their beauty can sing forth God's praises. One might keep in mind the insight of the prominent Orthodox theologian Alexander Schmemann, who has argued that humanity's primary vocation is priestly: " . . . In the Bible to bless God is not a 'religious' or a 'cultic' act, but the very way of *life*. God blessed the world, blessed [humans], blessed the seventh day . . . , and this means that he filled all that exists with His love and goodness, made all this 'very good.' So the only *natural* (and not 'supernatural') reaction of [humans] . . . is to bless God in return. . . . "[11] As will be shown in the final section of this chapter, the priestly use of bread and wine in the Eucharist can provide a model for the use of material goods outside the Eucharist. Before discussing this point, though, one first needs to look at the importance of matter from a sacramental perspective.

THE SACRAMENTS AND CREATION: WHY MATTER MATTERS

Of course, worship consists of more than textual components like prayers. It involves vestments, candles, ritualized movement, art, water, bread, wine, and so forth. Accordingly, a wide array of materials from the natural world and human culture make Christian worship possible. Indeed the liturgy is wedded to natural processes in ways that people may fail to appreciate. A good example of one of these processes is time. The natural passage of time provides the framework for liturgical time. Just as the day is marked by the rising and setting of the sun, so too do morning and evening prayer serve as the focal points for the liturgy of the hours.[12] Something similar

11. Alexander Schmemann, *Sacraments and Orthodoxy* (New York: Herder and Herder, 1965), 15, author's emphasis.

12. *Sacrosanctum concilium* (Constitution on the Sacred Liturgy), no. 89. Translation from Austin Flannery, ed., *Vatican Council II: The Conciliar and Post Conciliar Documents*, new rev. ed. (Collegeville, MN: The Liturgical Press, 1996), 25–26.

holds true for the liturgical year. The high point of the liturgical year is Easter, whose date is determined annually by the phases of the moon. In the Northern Hemisphere, Advent and Christmas coincide with winter, the time when days are short and nights are long. This fact enhances the symbolism of these seasons that focus on the birth of Christ, the Light of the World. When the longer period of darkness is juxtaposed with the celebration of Christ's birth, then the gospel reading for Christmas Day (John 1:1–18 or John 1:1–5,9–14) sounds with special resonance: "the light shines in the darkness, and the darkness has not overcome it."[13]

SEX IN THE SACRAMENTS

In Roman Catholicism, human sexuality also finds a legitimate role within sacramental practice. During the Easter Vigil, just before the baptisms, the Easter Candle is plunged into the baptismal water as part of the Blessing of the Water.[14] This action has sexual symbolism. It represents the baptismal water being impregnated by the seed of the Word. That the Church employs this imagery at once shows the goodness of human sexuality, when properly understood, while also showing that worship is rooted in the natural world.

The connection between liturgy and the natural world is especially seen through the materials that are used in various rites such as water in baptism or bread and wine in the Eucharist. Christian theology teaches that God uses these elements from the natural world to confer grace. The key question then becomes: how do they do so? One approach would be to think of them as merely a kind of instrument through which grace is channeled into humans. Perhaps the best analogy for this approach would be a gas pump. If one thinks

13. John 1:5, NA Bible.

14. *The Rites of the Catholic Church*, vol. 1 (Collegeville, MN: Liturgical Press, 1990), 151.

of grace as a kind of fuel for the Christian life, then the sacramental elements would be the "gas pump" through which the "gas" reaches one, the car.

As appealing as it may be to conceptualize the sacraments in this way, it is also problematic. Specifically, it is inconsistent with the prayers used within the rites. In Eucharistic Prayer II, one finds the following statement in the Epiclesis (the invocation of the Holy Spirit): "Let your Spirit come upon these gifts to make them holy, so that they may become for us the body and blood of our Lord, Jesus Christ."[15] Likewise, when the priest consecrates the water for baptism, he likely will utter the following statement: "By the power of the Holy Spirit give to this water the grace of your Son. . . . "[16] What these Eucharistic and baptismal prayers show is that the water, bread, and wine are themselves changed by God's grace, thereby becoming something different from what they were before. The elements are transformed; they have been made holy. After they have been transformed by God's grace, they have the ability to be sacraments by which humans are made holy. This idea carries with it an important implication: creation is capable of holiness, meaning that it is also the object of redemption. This holiness, moreover, is one that elevates and perfects nature, rather than diminishing and destroying it.

If creation can be redeemed, then it follows that creation needs redemption. This twofold claim about creation, that it both needs salvation and can receive it, brings with it a decidedly Christian perspective on the importance of the natural world. Stated differently, the use of creation in the sacraments provides one with a perspective on why matter matters theologically. It does so by steering a middle path between the possible extremes of pantheism, on the one hand, and indifference toward nature, on the other. Pantheism claims that there is a strict identity between *all that exists* (Greek: *pan*) and *God* (Greek: *theos*). Thus, this perspective indicates that the natural world is itself divine. One can observe this belief in the fringes of the modern environmental movement in people who take the phrase "Mother Earth" quite literally. Classical Christian theology opposes pantheism because it fails to adequately differentiate between the Creator and

15. *Sacramentary*, 510, cf. 505, 513, 518.

16. *Rites of the Catholic Church*, 328, 384, 400.

creation. Christian theology distinguishes between a holy God and a sinful world in need of grace. However, the sacramental use of elements from the natural world should also place a check on viewing creation apathetically. Because creation was made by and is being redeemed by God, then it is the object of God's graceful love. This insight carries with it an important ethical implication. Christians should approach the rest of creation with the same kind of love that God does. As will be shown in the next section, one finds such an approach to creation in the Eucharist.

EUCHARISTIC ECOLOGY

Even though material goods such as water, bread, and wine are used in the context of Christian worship, one can make a distinction between them.[17] The baptismal water does not require any human action to be produced, a point that will be revisited in chapter 19 of this volume. For the Eucharist, though, human work becomes vital as wheat and grapes must be grown, harvested, and then manufactured into bread and wine. It is for this reason that at the Presentation of the Gifts, the priest refers to the bread as that which "the earth has given and human hands have made" and the wine as "the fruit of the vine and work of human hands."[18] The bread and wine used in the Eucharist serve to represent the food humans consume on a daily basis. Like other animals, humans need food to survive. However, their use of food differs from that of other animals. Humans have the ability to cultivate and process food. Human food, therefore, can also be an expression of different human cultures as much as it is a basic need to survive. Think of various cuisines—Italian, French, Thai, Mexican, for instance—and how they can differ greatly from one another. The way the food is produced and consumed, moreover, can provide insights into aspects of a specific culture. Consider how fast food epitomizes certain features of American life: hectic

17. Kevin W. Irwin, "The Sacramentality of Creation and the Role of Creation in Liturgy and Sacraments," in *Preserving the Creation: Environmental Theology and Ethics*, eds. Kevin W. Irwin and Judith Lee Kissell (Washington, DC: Georgetown University Press, 1994), 70.

18. *Sacramentary*, 415.

schedules coupled with an emphasis on speed and efficiency (often at the expense of the environment, social interaction, and nutrition).

ECUMENICAL CONVERGENCE

Since the late 1960s, both Roman Catholics and mainline Protestants have made extensive revisions to their liturgical rites, especially the Eucharist. One of the primary factors in this development has been the appropriation of liturgical practices—both prayers and structures—from early Christianity. Because of this trend, the Eucharistic celebrations of contemporary Roman Catholics, Episcopalians, United Methodists, as well as most Lutherans and Presbyterians, tend to share a "family resemblance." Scholars refer to these similarities as "ecumenical convergence." Because of this convergence in ritual structures, the ensuing discussion of the logic of the Eucharist's basic structure is one that holds true for various churches.

If the production and consumption of food gives a window into a given culture, then the way bread and wine are used in the Eucharist can give insights into some of the emphases of Christianity. The starting point for the rite commences before the Eucharist itself. God gives the gift of creation, including grain and grapes, from which humans take their physical sustenance. Before the Eucharist, worshippers take these gifts, transform them into food and drink, and then, during the Eucharist, give them back to God in gratitude for God's prior gifts of creation and Christ. Because food represents life itself, the offering of the bread and wine also represents the giving of worshippers' very lives to God. After they give bread and wine, God transforms these natural elements into the body and blood of his Son and gives them back to worshippers for their spiritual nourishment. The Eucharist "continues" as Christians are sent into the world "to love and serve the Lord."[19] The Eucharistic action, therefore, takes

19. Ibid., 527.

one's life and binds it with Christ as an offering to the world. As can be seen from this description of the dynamic of the Eucharist, the rite is based on a series of exchanges that take place between God and humans. Accordingly, the logic of the rite is one based on self-giving love or charity, the very love that defines what it means to be a disciple of Christ.

Additionally, as each local church celebrates the Eucharist and, thus, embodies self-giving love, that church represents not only the Church as a whole but also the world. Aidan Kavanagh had this idea in mind when he referred to the celebration of the Eucharist as "the church doing world."[20] In its Eucharistic observance, the Church represents the world—but the world as God intended it to be. Creation was not made simply to exist. It was created by God to be in relationship with God. God provides the basis for this relationship through creation and redemption. Creation's role in the relationship is to praise God for those gifts. The Eucharist, then, serves as a "microcosm" of the cosmos transformed by God's grace. In the Eucharist, Christians receive a foretaste of the new creation when all of reality will receive its final redemption.

Because the Eucharist prefigures the new creation, it can also inspire faithful discipleship in the right use of creation through a Eucharistic ecology, which can provide an orientation for the proper use of material resources in the present. In the Eucharist, the Church both praises God and receives sanctifying grace. For Christians, praise of God and an attempt to live sanctified lives should also orient their lives, including how they use creation, in what Eastern Orthodoxy refers to as "the liturgy after the Liturgy."[21] Do they approach creation with an eye toward glorifying God, or do they do so out of selfish reasons such as greed and vanity? As noted previously, because creation is God's gift, humans must engage it in a manner in keeping with its status as a gift, as something to be treasured.

---

20. Aidan Kavanagh, *On Liturgical Theology* (Collegeville, MN: Liturgical Press, 1992), 52–69.

21. See, for instance, Ion Bria, "The Liturgy after the Liturgy," in *Baptism and Eucharist: Ecumenical Convergence in Celebration*, eds. Max Thurian and Geoffrey Wainwright (Grand Rapids, MI: Eerdmans, 1983), 213–218.

GREEN WORSHIP

Christians should also consider the issues highlighted in this section as they relate to the celebration of the liturgy itself. In North America, many Christians attend services at large churches in sprawling suburbs. As a result, getting to and from worship services often involves the significant use of fossil fuels. In addition, many churches use climate control and extensive lighting during services that also deplete natural resources. North American Christians might consider more efficient means of travel such as mass transportation and more fuel-efficient vehicles. There also needs to be a deliberation on how new and existing church buildings, from worship spaces to administrative offices, could be brought into conformity to Leadership in Energy and Environmental Design (LEED) standards on energy use, carbon emissions, water efficiency, and the like. Interestingly, the Vatican has begun to attend to these issues in recent years. The most prominent example of this trend has been the large-scale installation of solar panels throughout Vatican City to the point that it has become the first solar-powered state. This is one area in which local churches, whether Catholic or not, should consider following the Vatican's lead on LEED-like issues.

There is also an anthropological aspect to the issue. As Irenaeus noted, "the glory of God is a living man."[22] By "living man," Irenaeus means a person who is flourishing both physically and spiritually. This insight brings a second question: do humans use material goods in a manner that promotes human life? The phrase *human life* should be understood in the broadest terms possible. It would embrace all people, including people currently living in poverty, as well as future generations.[23] Therefore, the proper use of material goods, including food, should focus on overcoming extreme economic inequality and on sustainability.

22. Irenaeus, *Against the Heresies*, IV.20.7 in *Ante-Nicene Fathers,* 490.

23. Benedict XVI, *Caritas in veritate* (San Francisco: Ignatius Press, 2009), no. 48.

CONCLUSION

This chapter has explored the insights that the liturgy, especially the Eucharist, can provide regarding environmental concerns. In doing so, cues were taken from Irenaeus of Lyons. As part of his broader argument, he highlighted the consistency between the Church's Eucharistic practice and its teaching on the goodness of creation, the Incarnation, and the Resurrection. The environmental challenge humans face today is similar to the threat posed by Gnosticism. Both focus on the status of creation, though they differ in terms of emphasis. Gnosticism raised the question of how creation should be understood, while the environmental crisis centers on how it should be used. As a result of this issue, there is a fundamental question that Christians need to ask themselves, one inspired by Irenaeus. Does human use of creation outside the liturgy conform to its use inside the liturgy? Is human ecology Eucharistic?

QUESTIONS FOR REVIEW

1. According to Irenaeus of Lyons, what is the relationship between the Church's worship and its beliefs?
2. What do the Nicene Creed and the Eucharistic Prayers affirm about the relationship between God and creation? What is humanity's role within this relationship?
3. What does the use of creation in the sacraments indicate about the importance of matter?
4. How might the use of bread and wine in the Eucharist shape how Christians use material goods outside the Eucharist?
5. What was Gnosticism? What might be some modern views that echo key beliefs of Gnosticism?

IN-DEPTH QUESTIONS

1. In what ways does worship shape Christians in a manner similar to the virtues?
2. Will a Christian who attends worship necessarily become Eucharistically ecological? Why not?

3. What are some other examples, similar to the grapes and the wheat for the Eucharist, of ways that humans cooperate with God's grace in working with creation in the "liturgy after the Liturgy" beyond the doors of the church?
4. Explain the difference between a gift that has been entrusted to someone and a gift that has been given to someone that is his or hers to do with as that person chooses. Use an example to illustrate what you mean.
5. Worship in some other Christian denominations shares similarities with the Catholic liturgy of the Mass, while worship in others is quite different. What are some ways that non-Catholic Christian worship practices might and might not nurture and form worshippers to be green disciples of Jesus?

CHAPTER 11

NEIGHBOR TO NATURE

Marcus Mescher

KEY TERMS

parable of the Good Samaritan
neighbor-love
nature-love
anthropocentrism
theocentrism
covenantal right-relationship
accountability
compassion

INTRODUCTION

One challenge to theological approaches to ecological issues is that "care for creation" is missing in the traditional command to love God and love one's neighbor as oneself. How, then, should Christians understand to be in right-relationship with nonhuman creation? Whereas Pope John Paul II and Pope Benedict XVI address the environment in terms of respect and responsibility, ecotheologians such as James Nash and John Hart prefer the language of love. More specifically, Hart argues that the parable of the Good Samaritan—despite its lack of any reference to ecological concerns—provides a springboard for recognizing how "love of nature" flows from love of God and neighbor. This chapter will explore whether and how Christian disciples are called to be loving neighbors to nature.

AN "ESSENTIAL" ASPECT OF DISCIPLESHIP

Pope John Paul II, in his 1990 World Day of Peace statement, declared that "Christians, in particular, realize that their responsibility within creation and their duty toward nature and the Creator are an *essential* part of their faith."[1] In other words, care for creation is not an optional aspect of being Christian. Rather, it should be part and parcel of discipleship, expressed through the everyday actions of Christians. However, given the lack of specific references to this core component of discipleship in the New Testament or subsequent church teaching, it remains unclear *why* and *how* this responsibility is an *essential* part of Christian faith and discipleship.

When Jesus is asked to sum up the heart of his teaching, he imparts the Great Commandment that links love of God and neighbor but says nothing of nature. Yet, Catholic theologian John Hart believes that Luke's version—through the parable of the Good Samaritan—provides a firm basis for understanding right-relationship with God and others in terms of being neighborly to human and nonhuman members of creation.[2] Hart, building on the work of ecotheologians such as Methodist James Nash, argues that Jesus' emphasis on inclusive, merciful love ought to inspire Christians to extend their love beyond human neighbors to include nonhuman creation (NHC).[3] Hart and Nash stand with other ecotheologians who stress the integrity of all creation and human interdependence with NHC; human dependence on countless other species is just one reason why they believe humans should recognize NHC as a neighbor. From this perspective, Christian neighbor-love would also include nature-love.[4]

1. John Paul II, *The Ecological Crisis: A Common Responsibility*, no. 15; emphasis added, *http://www.vatican.va/holy_father/john_paul_ii/messages/peace/documents/hf_jp-ii_mes_19891208_xxiii-world-day-for-peace_en.html*, accessed January 6, 2011.

2. Hart contends that the principles of Christian ecological ethics receive their "foundation" in the Great Commandment specifically outlined in Luke 10:25–37. See John Hart, *Sacramental Commons: Christian Ecological Ethics* (New York: Roman & Littlefield, 2006), 218.

3. James A. Nash, *Loving Nature: Ecological Integrity and Christian Responsibility* (Nashville: Abingdon, 1991), 151–161.

4. Distinctions can and should be made between what terms such as *nature*, *creation*, or *biota* (etc.) include. For the purposes of this essay, *nonhuman creation* will be abbreviated as NHC; and although *nature* includes humankind, to compare *love of neighbor* and *love of nature*, *nature* will connote NHC.

This does not square with current official Catholic teaching, given its anthropocentric tendency to place humanity above the rest of creation.[5] A consequence of viewing all creation as ordered and subject to human life is to relegate NHC to a status that is instrumentally—rather than intrinsically—good. Correspondingly, humans understand their relationship to the environment as "steward," called to provide "care" for the "gift" of NHC. However, some ecotheologians like Hart object to this potentially myopic rhetoric, because a gift is by definition something that is at least gratuitous and possibly even superfluous. Additionally, though it is customary to receive a gift graciously, sometimes gifts are ignored or even rejected. Viewing creation in terms of a gift belies the goodness and integral interdependence of creation as a whole.

Moreover, if the rest of creation is subordinated to human interest, then humans can justify using NHC for what is most efficient, convenient, or profitable for them—as individuals or collectively. Protestant ethicist James Gustafson believes this fails to account for the ways in which humans are constantly participating in "the patterns and processes of interdependence of life in the world."[6] It is more appropriate, Gustafson maintains, to replace this anthropocentrism with a theocentrism that puts faithfulness to God—and God's desire for creation as a whole—first and foremost.

This brings up the question of what it means to be faithful to the Creator and to honor human duty to NHC. Does the traditional triad of love of God, neighbor, and self imply love of nature, or is an alternative ethic to be worked out between humans and nonhumans? For example, Pope Benedict XVI acknowledges that the "book of nature is one and indivisible; it includes not only the environment but also individual, family and social ethics" but suggests the proper

---

5. For example, in his 1995 encyclical *Evangelium vitae* (The Gospel of Life), John Paul II contends that Genesis "places man [*sic*] at the summit of God's creative activity, as its crown, the culmination of a process which leads from indistinct chaos to the most perfect of creation. Everything in creation is ordered to man [*sic*] and everything is made subject to him [*sic*]" (no. 34). *http://www.vatican.va/holy_father/john_paul_ii/encyclicals/documents/hf_jp-ii_enc_25031995_evangelium-vitae_en.html,* accessed January 6, 2011.

6. James Gustafson, *Ethics from a Theocentric Perspective*, vol. 2 (Chicago: University of Chicago Press, 1984), 145.

response is "love of neighbor and respect for nature" rather than respect and love for all creation.[7] As mentioned above, Hart points to the parable of the Good Samaritan to argue that Christian neighbor-love calls disciples to be loving neighbors to nature. This chapter will now consider whether and how this might be possible.

THE GOOD SAMARITAN: NEIGHBOR IN A NEW LIGHT

Hart contends that despite a lack of reference to NHC in the passage, the parable of the Good Samaritan (Luke 10:25–37)[8] provides a basis for how Christian neighbor-love might be extended to nature-love for at least three reasons: First, the passage illuminates how vertical and horizontal right-relationship (between the self and God; the self and others) are inseparable.[9] Part of the parable's aim is to point out that the priest and the Levite are mistaken to think that another task can take precedence over showing love for a neighbor in need. Some commentators go as far as stating that the parable is meant to express that failing to love another in need is a failure to love God.[10]

7. Benedict XVI, "If You Want to Cultivate Peace, Protect Creation," no.12. *http://www.vatican.va/holy_father/benedict_xvi/messages/peace/documents/hf_ben-xvi_mes_20091208_xliii-world-day-peace_en.html*, accessed January 6, 2011.

8. Although some scholars object to calling this narrative the parable of the Good Samaritan (because the phrase is not original to the biblical text), for the sake of familiarity and consistency, this text will refer to both this parable and the third traveler on the road to Jericho as the "Good Samaritan."

9. Though both love of God and neighbor are present in the Hebrew Scriptures, they are separate commands (Deuteronomy 6:5 and Leviticus 19:18). Luke's version resembles similar exchanges in Mark (12:28–34) and Matthew (22:34–40), though in Mark and Matthew, "love of neighbor" is considered secondary to "love of God." Commentators suggest Luke connects these vertical and horizontal commands to highlight that love of God is incomplete without love of neighbor. It is worth noting that in John's Gospel, there is no commandment to love God, only the "new commandment:" "Just as I have loved you, you also should love one another." (John 13:34) Also note the parallel link between love of God and neighbor found in Matthew 25:31–46.

10. Commentators largely agree that Luke's aim is not to be anti-Semitic but to show that the priest and Levite are found wanting in their love of neighbor (and therefore, in their love of God), and that the enemy-Samaritan is more of a neighbor than the victim's own kin or clan. See, for example, Frank Stern, *A Rabbi Looks at Jesus' Parables* (New York: Rowman & Littlefield, 2006).

Vintage color engraving of the Good Samaritan. The parable of the Good Samaritan is told by Jesus in the Gospel of Luke. In the parable, a Jewish traveler is beaten, robbed, and left dead along the road. First a priest and then a Levite come by, but both avoid the man. Finally, a Samaritan comes by, and despite the fact Samaritans and Jews generally despised each other, the Samaritan helps the injured Jew.

Second, this parable breaks through ethnic boundaries that might be used to justify restricting care. Note that the lawyer's question is limit-seeking: "Who is my neighbor?" implies there is a non-neighbor, to whom one is less or not obligated. The lawyer—and Jesus' audience—would have been shocked to hear that a Samaritan, a despised outcast, was to be considered a neighbor, to say nothing of being the one to model neighborliness.[11] This parable teaches that *neighbor* is no longer meant to distinguish insiders from outsiders. As Saint Augustine states, the term *neighbor* is to include every person.[12] Thus, the ethnic tension that is tied into the context of this story would have added a striking challenge to the idea of loving your neighbor as yourself.

11. Some commentators even suggest that if the (presumably Jewish) victim in the ditch had been conscious, he likely would have preferred to be left for dead than be helped by a Samaritan. An illustration of this animosity taken from American history might be imagining a scene in the 1870s, if a Plains Indian were to walk into Dodge City with a scalped cowboy on his horse, checking into a room above a saloon, and staying the night to help the cowboy recover. This is the example Kenneth E. Bailey offers in *Through Peasant Eyes: More Lucan Parables, Their Culture and Style* (Grand Rapids, MI: Eerdmans, 1980), 52.

12. Augustine, *De Doctrina Christiana*, Book I, Chapter 30, no. 31–32.

The third exegetical insight to highlight is the significant turn of phrase Jesus uses to shift the concept of neighbor from object to subject. At the start of the parable, the lawyer asks Jesus, "Who is my neighbor?" (v. 29), but after he tells the parable, Jesus asks the lawyer, "Which of these three, do you think was a neighbor to the man who fell into the hands of the robbers?" (v. 36). The lawyer introduces the neighbor as one's object, but Jesus' question invites his audience to consider what it means to be a neighbor as a subject.

These exegetical insights illustrate how Jesus' closing words, the command to "Go and do likewise," demand more of disciples than a "thin" idea of loving one's neighbors as oneself. Rather, Jesus calls for a boundary-breaking love that is courageous, compassionate, and committed to healing care (recall that the Samaritan provides the funds necessary for the victim to recuperate at the inn). Moreover, it serves as a reminder that disciples cannot turn a blind eye to another in need.[13] This means orienting oneself toward the possibilities of love, rather than to the limits of duty, like the lawyer. This is not to say that Jesus reduces the complexity of what love entails, but instead, that love cannot defer to prejudice, social boundaries, or concerns about recognition, reciprocity, or reward.

All of this may seem ideal in theory but impossible to execute in practice, especially given the reality of human finitude and sin. Nonetheless, the parable of the Good Samaritan reminds Christians that the norm of neighbor-love rests in the practical possibilities of love, inspired by the grace of God.

AN ECOLOGICAL APPLICATION?

With these exegetical remarks in place, we are better positioned to understand how and why Hart believes this portrayal of neighbor-love can and should be considered to include NHC. He writes,

13. "Go and do likewise" (the last line of the parable, v. 37) leaves the audience with a lasting reminder that the emphasis is on the *doing*—not necessarily in exactly the same manner as the Samaritan, but in carrying on the spirit of the Samaritan's merciful action through creative application to one's own context. For more on doing "likewise," see William C. Spohn, *Go and Do Likewise: Jesus and Ethics* (New York: Continuum, 2006).

> Jesus teaches that people should not await someone's cry for help to respond to a call to be a neighbor; they should make themselves neighbors to those who need them. From the parable might be drawn two ideas for ecological ethics: first, assist those who are in need; second, choose to be consistently a neighbor to others. Humans are not the only neighbors who are suffering and need help. Earth and the biotic community are in crisis and in need of assistance. People are called to make themselves neighbors to humankind, *to Earth, and to extended biokind.*[14]

Hart joins other ecotheologians such as Sallie McFague and Wendell Berry who believe that Christian neighbor-love should include the "near neighbor" of NHC.[15] Though such a position is rooted in the recognition of the interdependence of humanity within the integrity of all creation, this seems to collapse an ontological barrier (real or constructed) between humans and NHC. Ecotheologians overcome this limit by stating that, insofar as everything has been created by the same Source, humans share a fundamental "kinship" with the rest of creation, regardless of unique human abilities or responsibilities.[16] Catholic moral theologian Edward Vacek offers a more nuanced position that affirms the ontological and relational value of NHC. Vacek describes human belonging to the rest of creation as "prior to our choice," a bond ignored only "at our peril" due in part because this belonging is tied

---

14. John Hart, *Sacramental Commons,* 218–219; emphasis added.

15. See, for example, Sallie McFague, *Super, Natural Christians: How We Should Love Nature* (Minneapolis: Fortress, 1997), 22. To clarify, McFague uses *near* as synonymous with *proximate* as in closeness, not in semblance. Wendell Berry also discusses this in a number of essays in Norman Wirzba's edited volume, *The Art of the Commonplace: The Agrarian Essays of Wendell Berry* (Washington, DC: Shoemaker & Hoard, 2002).

16. For example, Thomas Berry writes, "Everything in the universe is genetically cousin to everything else. There is literally one family, one bonding, in the universe, because everything is descended from the same source. In this creative process, all things come into being. On the planet earth, all living things are clearly derived from a single origin. We are literally born as a community; the trees, the birds, and all living creatures are bonded together in a single community of life. This again gives us a sense that we belong. Community is not something that we dream up or think would be nice. Literally, we are a single community. The planet earth is a single community of existence, and we exist in this context." In *Befriending the Earth*, ed. Stephen Dunn and Anne Lonergan (Mystic, CT: Twenty-Third Publications, 1991), 14–15.

with our sanctification, since "this realm of nature ultimately is destined to be filled with Christ's life (Ephesians 1:10, 23)."[17]

Pointing out the ontological and relational value of NHC is important because it clarifies that although all of creation is *good*, loving certain members of NHC would be ordered by these relationships. For example, preferential love would be rightly shown to the family pet over an unknown animal hundreds of miles away. Considering relational value also means that humans would love some species differently from others; this makes sense as it would be incompatible with love for self or neighbor to be invested in loving creatures that are indifferent or even a threat to human life.

At this point, two important questions must be addressed. First, are members of NHC to be recognized as neighbors to humans? Second, can humans be loving neighbors to NHC? These questions may be more complex than Hart and other ecotheologians allow.

As the parable of the Good Samaritan indicates, *neighbor* is to be considered as object and subject. It is true that many species are neighborly to humans or at least exist in a way that promotes human life. But as just stated, there are also members and dimensions of creation that are indifferent or even hostile to human life. Thus, quickly it becomes clear that extending the label of *neighbor* to NHC may become too difficult.

This does not mean that humans are necessarily off the hook for being neighborly to NHC. The command in Genesis 1:28 to have "dominion" over the rest of creation led some to justify the subordination of NHC to human interest, which historian Lynn White Jr. cited as a significant reason why Christians bear a "huge burden of guilt" for an underappreciation of NHC and the root causes of ecological distress.[18] However, as shown in chapter 4, this does not

---

17. Edward Vacek, *Love, Human and Divine* (Washington, DC: Georgetown University Press, 1994), 81–82. The question of redemption is an important one to ecofeminist theologian Sallie McFague, who writes, "Within a Christic framework, the body of God encompasses all of creation in a particular salvific direction, toward the liberation, healing, and fulfillment of all bodies. Thus, we can speak of the 'cosmic' Christ, a metaphor for the scope of the body of God within a Christian framework." See *Body of God* (Minneapolis: Fortress, 1993), 160.

18. Lynn White Jr., "The Historical Roots of Our Ecologic Crisis," *Science* 155, no. 3767 (1967), 1203–1207.

grasp *dominion* in its full meaning. What is more, it fails to take into account that in Genesis 9:1–11, God establishes a covenant with Noah that makes humans and other creatures covenant partners.[19]

This is not to suggest that the Noachic covenant establishes a radical equality among all members of creation, human and nonhuman alike. A significant ontological (and moral) asymmetry between humans and NHC follows from the unique abilities humans possess (e.g., to reason and freely choose, to develop technology).[20] This asymmetry may be why official Catholic teaching tends toward anthropocentrism and correspondingly, why love of neighbor is distinguished from respect and responsibility for nature.

Although NHC may not be recognized as *neighbor*, it does not automatically follow that humans cannot be neighborly toward NHC in respect *and* love. Nash argues humans—as covenant partners with God and nonhuman creatures—are called to strive "to be a reflection of the ultimate Lover, to be one who loves *all* that God loves—which covers 'all that participates in being.'" Because "God's love is unbounded, loyal Christian love is similarly inclusive or universal. This love resists confinement of any sort."[21] Nash tries to defend this romantic and rather abstract claim by arguing for and describing love of nature in terms of beneficence, other-esteem or empathy, receptivity, humility, understanding, and communion.[22] However, instead of solving problems, these versions of nature-love raise a greater number of difficulties.

To illustrate, this text will consider a philosophical perspective. Mary Midgley traces a tradition within philosophy that endorses humane and respectful treatment of nonhuman creatures, though the

---

19. See Richard J. Clifford, "Genesis 1–3: Permission to Exploit Nature?" *The Bible Today* 26 (May 1988), 133–137.

20. John Passmore cautions against placing NHC on par with humans, for "if men [*sic*] were ever to decide that they ought to treat plants, animals, landscapes precisely as if they were *persons*, if they were to think of them as forming with man [*sic*] a moral community in a strict sense, that would make it impossible to civilize the world . . . [or] act at all or even to continue living." See *Man's Responsibility for Nature: Ecological Problems and Western Traditions* (New York: Scribner, 1974), 126.

21. James Nash, *Loving Nature*, 141–142.

22. Ibid., 151–161.

tradition typically includes only animals.[23] But kindness to sentient creatures is not tantamount to love; Midgley concludes that a belief that love can and should be shared between humans and animals is simply anthropomorphic. She argues that without rationality, language, communication, or culture, animals cannot be considered to be legitimate partners in love.[24] If love cannot be shared between humans and animals, it would seem impossible for the rest of NHC.

Nash's description of love as beneficence might try to sidestep problems of mutuality, since beneficence is unidirectional. Benevolent love toward NHC seems tenable in theory until one begins to consider what it would require to satisfy Nash's description of beneficence as "uncontainable inclusivity," which in practice may be ultimately ineffectual.[25] For example, what would happen if the good of one species or one creature would conflict with the good of another? And how would beneficent nature-love negotiate a direct conflict with the good of a person or entire community? Does all-inclusive nature-love also require a person to love inert NHC such as a mineral or a sand dune? What about members or aspects of NHC that pose a direct threat to human well-being such as malaria-carrying mosquitoes, killer whales, or natural disasters?

Posing just a few preliminary questions shows that goodwill toward individual members of NHC—much less all the members of NHC with respect to the integrity of all creation—is desirable in theory but would be profoundly complicated, if not practically impossible, to work out any clear ethical norms to guide human action. Furthermore, given that humans struggle to extend goodwill and make sacrifices beyond their kin to neighbors, strangers, and even enemies, one must wonder if it is simply naïve to think that humans could love and make sacrifices for NHC.

---

23. Midgley draws on insights from Augustine, Kant, and Montaigne, specifically. See *Beast and Man: The Roots of Human Nature* (Ithaca, NY: Cornell University Press, 1978), 218–222.

24. Midgley even allows for animals that have been shown to learn how to communicate with humans nonverbally in her argument (*Beast and Man*, 314; on anthropomorphism, see 344).

25. James Nash, *Loving Nature*, 152. Nash adds, "Christian love cannot be reduced to beneficence, but it is decrepit without beneficence."

This last point is more in the spirit of the lawyer's limit-seeking question than in the Samaritan's compassionate and courageous act of love. When Jesus challenges his disciples to "go and do likewise," in practicing vertical and horizontal right-relationship, might this include being neighborly to nature, as Hart contends?

From a philosophical standpoint, it seems terribly difficult to explain how the ontological (and moral) differences between humans and nonhumans could be overcome for any mutual expression of love. However, must love always be mutual? Jesus tells his disciples to love their enemies; surely, this means loving without expecting anything in return.[26] The Gospel of John states that God loves the entire world—not just humans. If *agape* love is to model this Godlike love, might it mean that disciples should also love the world, human and nonhuman?[27] *Agape* love is possible through God's grace and, therefore, is not something that philosophers like Midgley can fully address.[28]

But if *agape* love for NHC is possible, then why do Pope John Paul II and Benedict XVI speak only of respect and responsibility? John Paul II describes human duty to NHC as an "essential" part of Christian faith,[29] and Benedict XVI claims this is a responsibility that "knows no boundaries,"[30] so they do not take human right-relationship with NHC lightly. Perhaps their use of respect rather than *love* is a purposeful piece of rhetoric to avoid the pitfalls of trying to justify the metaphysical possibility or necessity of sharing love between humans and NHC.[31] Although the language of *respect* is at least minimally defensible, Benedict XVI is not only interested in the lowest limit, but also he claims it is imperative that humanity renew and strengthen "that covenant between human beings and

---

26. See Luke 6:27–36.

27. John 3:16 reads, "For God so loved the world that he gave his only Son." Later in John's Gospel, Jesus tells his disciples to love (one another) as he has loved them (13:34–35). In 1 John, one reads that "God is love" and that "We love because [God] first loved us" (4:8, 19).

28. See Aquinas on charity (*caritas*) in the *Summa Theologiae*, II-II q. 23, art. 2.

29. John Paul II, *The Ecological Crisis: A Common Responsibility*, no. 15.

30. Benedict XVI, "If You Want to Cultivate Peace, Protect Creation," no. 11.

31. Note that although these popes distinguish between love of neighbor and respect for nature, they do not consider them competing causes. Rather, they understand respect for nature a derivative of faithfulness to the Creator and ordered to human well-being.

the environment, which *should mirror the creative love of God*, from whom we come and towards whom we are journeying."[32]

Thus, it is possible to love NHC but in a mode different from loving one's human neighbors. We can surmise that to be a loving neighbor to NHC would be shaped by respect and responsibility consonant with the unique ability people have to care for the rest of creation that other species do not share. Making respect and love mutually informing norms could lead toward more of a chastened anthropocentrism that involves a robust responsibility for NHC within the integrity of creation.

If Christian disciples are to reflect God's love in their respectful care for the environment—as both Nash and Benedict XVI explicitly prescribe—they might imagine such care taking on the characteristics of the Samaritan's actions on the road to Jericho: recognizing a need, feeling compassion for the victim (the one in need), having the desire and courage to act, and acting with mercy. As shown, although ecological responsibility is not explicitly addressed in this parable, it still may serve to inspire disciples to "go and do likewise" in a way that honors our responsibility to our NHC covenant partners.

NEIGHBOR TO NATURE

To this point, the text discussion has been of how one reading of the parable of the Good Samaritan invites Christians to be neighborly to nature. Being such a neighbor is one way to honor the "essential part" of the Christian faith that carries out duties to the Creator and all creation in a way that mirrors God's creative love. It replaces an anthropocentric focus on human interest with a theocentric faithfulness to God's desire for all creation; it is a responsible humanism that takes seriously personal and collective accountability as covenant partners.

A chastened anthropocentrism begins with gratitude for the goodness and beauty of creation that demands respect if not

32. Benedict XVI first makes this statement in his 2008 World Day of Peace message, "The Human Family, A Community of Peace" (no. 7). He repeats it in his 2009 encyclical *Caritas in veritate* (no. 50) and in his 2010 World Day of Peace message, "If You Want to Cultivate Peace, Protect Creation" (no. 1); emphasis added.

reverence.[33] It is also marked by humility and concomitant restraint on human activity that may be dangerous or destructive to NHC. Together this builds an ethic of stewardship that does not order all creation solely to human interest or benefit but is oriented toward the participation of all creation to promote integral right-relationship and flourishing. Thus, Christians are to consider what is best for NHC relative to human advantage or well-being with respect to God's love for the entire world, human and nonhuman.

To be neighbor to nature means finding middle ground between arrogant entitlement and paralyzing guilt or fear. Disciples cannot claim free license to treat NHC according to individual whim or collective profit; neither should humans feel overwhelmed by ecological distress nor the weight of responsibility of being neighbor to not just humans but to NHC, as well.[34] Just as with global problems such as poverty, disease, or malnutrition, it is unrealistic to expect each person to effectively create and implement solutions to curb or solve widespread ecological crises on their own.

Being neighborly means prudentially ordering love and respect based on proximity and need. Recall that the Samaritan did not start on the road to Jericho looking for someone to help. However, when he saw another in need, instead of continuing on his way, he walked over to the side of the victim and acted out of respect and mercy. Moreover, the Samaritan got another involved, paying the innkeeper to continue caring for the victim while the Samaritan attended to other matters. In other words, the parable of the Good Samaritan does not demand that persons forsake their own interests or responsibilities; rather, it challenges disciples beyond an ethic of self-interest, to be more aware of and committed to others in need, to do what one can and no less.

---

33. James Gustafson explains that, "from a theocentric perspective, nature evokes in us a sense of the sublime, or more religiously, a sense of the divine, [and] calls for *respect* for nature," in *A Sense of the Divine: The Natural Environment from a Theocentric Perspective* (Cleveland: Pilgrim, 1994), 55.

34. Mary Midgley insists, "The whole point of the story of the Good Samaritan is to get rid of the contract notion when discussing our duty to our neighbor. . . . People have readily become suspicious of suggestions that they could have any duty to animals, because they see this as likely to lay on them an infinite load of obligation, and they rightly think an infinite obligation would be meaningless. *Ought* implies *can*. Indefinite guilt is paralyzing. The position, however, is actually no worse than the one we are already in with regard to people" (*Beast and Man*, 222–223).

Being neighborly to nature will require openness to other members of creation and to develop empathy and compassion for species in distress when possible. It is no secret it is difficult to extend these sympathies to individuals and groups considered alien or enemy, and for many, it will be even more challenging in relation to NHC.

Being neighborly to NHC may not involve mutual love, but it ought to take a cue from Nash's description of nature-love as rooted in humility, which is related to modesty, simplicity, and frugality. If humility finds even the "lowliest human as an equal," Nash believes humility can be extrapolated to embrace all creatures as worthy of moral consideration.[35] Here one might object to Nash's ecological egalitarianism, which does not seem to distinguish between the value of human life in comparison with, say, that of a cockroach. However, an irenic interpretation might connect Nash's description of humility to a sense of ecological solidarity, because his sense of humility recognizes one's place as a creature among other creatures. Given this, one could imagine how a proper sense of humility—vis-à-vis right-relationship with God, others, and NHC—has potential to inspire disciples to make the sacrifices necessary to be good neighbors toward creation, as by adopting ecologically sustainable practices and policies.

Taking seriously the challenge of nature-love as humility, one might imagine the practices and policies that could be instituted to stem the tide of ecological destruction, conserve natural resources, and ensure that future generations (our neighbors-to-be?) might also be able to enjoy the rich and diverse goodness of creation.[36] To be effective, such a challenge would require a multilevel and collective approach. For example, on a macro level, this approach would mean proposing "green taxes" to ensure that the real cost—including to the environment—of producing a good for consumption would be actually represented by the retail price.[37] Significant changes in industry,

---

35. James Nash, *Loving Nature*, 156.

36. Jürgen Moltmann speaks of "longitudinal" responsibility to future generations in addition to vertical and horizontal duties. He explains, "Because children are the weakest members, and because coming generations have no say in today's decisions, the costs of present profits are shuffled off on to them. This contravenes the justice of the kingdom of God." See *Jesus Christ for Today's World*, trans. Margaret Kohl (Minneapolis: Fortress, 1994), 26–27.

37. On these and other examples for business, see Paul Hawken's *The Ecology of Commerce: A Declaration of Sustainability* (New York: HarperBusiness, 1993).

such as higher prices for consumers, would occur, but higher prices should not be denounced out of hand, as consumers already pay the price for the pollution, waste, and other forms of environmental degradation in other ways, from sharing the cleanup costs passed on through national and local taxes to paying higher prices for goods and services made scarce by environmental change, dwindling resources, and species extinction.

Another level of neighborliness would include legal work to ensure that public lands, resources, and the species that dwell in these habitats are not susceptible to private interests or sacrificed in the name of economic progress or profit.[38] Being neighborly to nature means advocating for sustainable commerce for both producers and consumers. True, citizens vote every time they make a purchase as a consumer, and more ecologically responsible goods are available because of increased demand. Government-sponsored projects (like tax credits for energy-efficient appliances or remodeling) are helpful, but more laws and incentives could be developed for middle- and lower-class Americans who have less expendable income to make environmentally responsible purchases, which are invariably more expensive.

The discussion now comes to the individual person, whose practical reasoning will help him or her move from abstract moral principles to prudentially discern how to be neighborly to NHC and other human neighbors in need. Such neighborliness may often involve the principle of "preferential option for the poor," because poor, vulnerable, and marginalized people are often the first and most seriously affected by ecological devastation.[39] There is a link not only between love of neighbor and respect for nature but also love of neighbor *through* love of nature and vice versa.

---

38. Kevin O'Brien raises up the legal protection provided specific species thanks to the Endangered Species Act of 1973, and also cites how controversial this legislation has been, because these protections have come at the cost of economic and civic development. This example reinforces the need for conversion among Americans who still view economics and the environment in terms of a zero-sum struggle, rather than as interdependent features of the same *oikos*, or home (the Greek root that these two words share). See Kevin J. O'Brien, *An Ethics of Biodiversity: Christianity, Ecology, and the Variety of Life* (Washington, DC: Georgetown University Press, 2010), 114–118.

39. For a valuable treatment on the relationship between preferential option for the poor and care for creation, see Leonardo Boff, *Cry of the Earth, Cry of the Poor,* trans. Philip Berryman (Maryknoll NY: Orbis, 1997).

Being a neighbor means proactive care, leaving well enough alone when that's best for certain species or ecosystems, or taking a stand against attitudes and actions that detract from integral right-relationship and flourishing. To be neighborly means living with humility and in simplicity as a consumer and citizen, accountable to the sacramental commons of all creation and not just the human common good. As the "green movement" momentum grows, there are more and more organizations and associations, Web sites, and resources to help individuals find concrete ways to reduce one's carbon footprint, take advantage of one's power as a consumer or investor, and orient oneself away from cultural propaganda that encourages overconsumption, unsustainable production, irresponsible waste, and the consolidation of wealth into the hands of a few individuals or corporations.[40]

Though certainly there are many more ways one can be neighborly to nature, as a general rule, the more one descends to matters of detail, the matter of what is right will not be known to all, nor will it be applicable to all. So though universal precepts can be helpful (as popes exhort disciples to practice love of neighbor and respect and responsibility for nature), what this means at lower levels (from middle axioms down to concrete moral norms) will vary by context and situation. In the end, perhaps it is enough to state that to be neighborly is to practice an ethic of humble, respectful love for and with the people and environment with which one is in relationship.

CONCLUSION

The aim of this essay has been to better appreciate and understand why and how human responsibility to NHC is an essential part of the Christian faith and how this affects discipleship: Use was made of the parable of the Good Samaritan as a paradigm to unpack the depth and breadth of what it means to love one's neighbor and,

---

40. See, for example, E. F. Schumacher's *Small Is Beautiful: Economics as If People Mattered* (New York: Harper & Row, 1975) and Ellis Jones's *The Better World Shopping Guide: Every Dollar Makes a Difference* (New York: New Society, 2010); and the Web sites *http://www.catholicsandclimatechange.org/* and *http://www.greenamerica.org/*.

more than this, to be a loving neighbor. The Samaritan models compassion and mercy to break barriers between humans in a way that reflects God's merciful love for every person. Hart argues that the expansive spirit of this parable, when read through the lens of ecological concern, means that vertical love of God ought to be complemented by horizontal love of neighbor *and* nature. Human love for nature is not as easily tenable as Hart and others propose, however. Finally, how a chastened anthropocentrism honors the ontological and moral asymmetry between humans and NHC, protecting against a simplistic collapse of neighbor-love into nature-love has been examined.

Despite significant differences between humans and nonhumans, loving relationships between them are not an impossible ideal. In light of the Samaritan being moved to act by compassion, Robert Murray proposes that compassion is a way for disciples to cultivate the "proper feeling for fellow-creatures, [which] is indeed fundamental and is seen as a religious duty."[41] To be neighbor to humans and nonhumans—a similar orientation but worked out differently—is not a matter of competing causes but part of an integral ethic of covenantal fidelity striving for vertical and horizontal right-relationship.

To be neighborly to nature is to practice a humble, respectful love for nature that "mirrors the creative love of God" through the gift of grace. To be neighborly is to "go and do likewise," in following the example of the Samaritan by breaking the boundaries of what is owed to whom or what. Read in light of the "essential" matter of responsibilities to NHC, Christians can understand the horizontal dimension of covenantal right-relationship to extend beyond human neighbors to include all creation. Doing so requires being good neighbors and building good neighborhoods through love of God, neighbor, self, and humble, respectful love for NHC too.

---

41. Moreover, compassion with NHC leads toward action on behalf of NHC, which is part of the biblical message that humans have duties to the rest of creation and are answerable to God for how their covenant partners fare. See Robert Murray, *The Cosmic Covenant: Biblical Themes of Justice, Peace, and the Integrity of Creation* (Piscataway, NJ: Tigris, 2007), 114, 174.

QUESTIONS FOR REVIEW

1. What are the three key insights into the parable of the Good Samaritan that this chapter highlighted?
2. On what basis does this parable offer a framework for understanding and practicing right-relationship with NHC?
3. What are some limitations or obstacles to extending neighbor-love to nature-love?
4. What are some examples of being neighborly to nature? How do they demonstrate a desire for right-relationship with God and others?
5. What significance does compassion have for "green discipleship"?

IN-DEPTH QUESTIONS

1. Do you think the parable of the Good Samaritan offers a legitimate basis for extending neighbor-love to include nature-love? Why or why not?
2. If Jesus were healing and teaching today, would you expect his ministry to include more direct engagement with ecological issues? Explain.
3. In what ways and times can you recognize that NHC is neighborly to you? Do you consider yourself to be a neighbor to NHC? What are a few concrete ideas and practices that can demonstrate your neighborliness to nature?
4. What do you appreciate about what "respect" and "love" involve for Christian discipleship with regard to the environment? What are their limitations? What other norms or requirements would you add?
5. Give at least one example of how Jesus' command to "go and do likewise" challenges you to integrate right-relationship with God, other humans, and the rest of creation.

SOCIAL ETHICS

CHAPTER 12

CATHOLIC SOCIAL TEACHING AND CREATION

Christopher P. Vogt

KEY TERMS

anthropocentric
authentic development
common good
dominion
encyclical
episcopal conferences
magisterium
preferential option for the poor
solidarity
subsidiarity
sufficiency
superdevelopment
universal purpose of created things

INTRODUCTION

This chapter will introduce the rich tradition of reflection on social justice that is Catholic social teaching, first by explaining its origins and then by examining how it has addressed questions of environmental ethics. In particular, it will highlight the concept of authentic human development and explain how it can provide both a personal and a social framework for making economic decisions in a way that can best serve the good of humanity and the rest of creation.

WHAT IS CATHOLIC SOCIAL TEACHING?

Catholic social teaching is not concerned primarily with environmental ethics, but the question of how humans should relate to the rest of creation is one of the many issues the teaching addresses in its attempt to describe the shape of a just and well-ordered society. Modern Catholic social teaching can be traced to the year 1891, when Pope Leo XIII issued the encyclical *Rerum novarum* (On Rights and Duties of Capital and Labor). An encyclical is a formal letter on a matter of morals or doctrine addressed by a pope to the entire church and often to all people of goodwill as well.[1] Pope Leo wrote this particular encyclical out of concern for the economic, social, and political upheaval happening in European society during the second half of the nineteenth century.[2] In particular, Leo was concerned about "the misery and wretchedness pressing so unjustly on the majority of the working class" and the need to articulate "the relative rights and mutual duties of the rich and of the poor, of capital and of labor."[3]

What began with Leo XIII's encyclical has become a rich tradition of official teaching. Several of the popes who succeeded Leo XIII and many conferences of Catholic bishops from around the world have added their contributions to this collection of official statements on social, economic, and political questions. Of course, Christians were writing and speaking out about these issues long before 1891; in fact, they have been doing so since the very origins of the church. Profound wisdom and reflection on social questions is embedded in theological writings, the lives of the saints, mysticism, the liturgy of the church, and the religious practices of

---

1. Michael O'Keefe, "Encyclical," in *The HarperCollins Encyclopedia of Catholicism*, ed. Richard P. McBrien (San Francisco: HarperCollins, 1994), 465.

2. Thomas A. Shannon, "Commentary on *Rerum novarum*," in *Modern Catholic Social Teaching: Commentaries and Interpretations*, eds. Kenneth R. Himes, et al. (Washington, DC: Georgetown, 2004), 128–131.

3. Pope Leo XIII, *Rerum novarum* (On Capital and Labor), nos. 2–3. *http://www.vatican.va/holy_father/leo_xiii/encyclicals/documents/hf_l-xiii_enc_15051891_rerum-novarum_en.html*, accessed January 26, 2011.

Christians. Catholic social teaching should be understood to be a subset of this much richer, broader, and more extensive tradition.[4]

What distinguishes Catholic social teaching from other Christian sources of social reflection is its authorship. Catholic social teaching is a collection of texts written by the magisterium (official teaching

METHODIST SOCIAL PRINCIPLES

The Roman Catholic Church is not the only Christian church to have a vibrant body of teaching and reflection on matters of social justice. The United Methodist Church has a similar tradition known as the "social principles," which date at least to the publication of the Methodist Social Creed in 1908. Like Catholic social teaching, the Methodist social principles originally focused on securing justice for all people, especially workers, but over time, the tradition has expanded and now includes attention to a range of issues, including environmental ethics. In the section pertaining to the natural world, it states, "Let us recognize the responsibility of the church and its members to place a high priority on changes in economic, political, social, and technological lifestyles to support a more ecologically equitable and sustainable world leading to a higher quality of life for all of God's creation."[5] The United Methodist Church understands the authority of its social principles differently from the way the Catholic Church understands the authority of Catholic social teaching. The Methodist social principles are "a call to faithfulness and are intended to be instructive and persuasive in the best of the prophetic spirit; however, they are not church law."[6]

---

4. Christine Firer Hinze, "Catholic Social Teaching and Ecological Ethics," in *And God Saw That It Was Good*, eds. Drew Christiansen and Walter Grazer (Washington, DC: United States Catholic Conference, 1996), 166.

5. United Methodist Church, "Natural World." *http://archives.umc.org/interior.asp?mid=1701*, accessed March 24, 2010.

6. United Methodist Church, "Social Principles," *http://archives.umc.org/interior.asp?ptid=1&mid=1686,* accessed March 24, 2010.

authority) of the Roman Catholic Church. As such, it is understood to have some authoritative claim on all Roman Catholics.

Even though Catholic social teaching is particularly important for Catholics, it has also been explicitly addressed to all people of goodwill since the pontificate of John XXIII (1958–1963). In its social teaching, the Catholic Church seeks to call attention to pressing moral issues that are of concern to everyone and "to invite all people to do all they can to bring about an authentic civilization."[7]

THE CORE CONTENT OF CATHOLIC SOCIAL TEACHING

Initially, Catholic social teaching focused exclusively on human concerns without considering the implications of human choices for the rest of creation. Thus, it was a decidedly anthropocentric ethic (one that considers humanity to be the central and most important part of the world or even the universe and which measures the worth of everything in terms of its value for humans). It was concerned with how people should work together to build societies that protect the well-being and dignity of all humans. These concerns remain its primary focus, but it has increasingly come to recognize that the good of humanity cannot be separated from the good of the planet as a whole. As Pope Benedict XVI remarked in his 2010 message for the World Day of Peace, it is a practical and moral imperative that humankind develop a renewed understanding of economic and human development that is cognizant of the relationship between humans and the rest of creation. [8]

Many documents of Catholic social teaching that deal with the environment begin by expressing the concern that environmentally reckless actions are negatively affecting the quality of human life. For

---

7. Pontifical Council for Justice and Peace, *The Compendium of the Social Doctrine of the Church* (Vatican City: Libreria Editrice Vaticana, 2004), no. 3. Also available online at *http://www.vatican.va/roman_curia/pontifical_councils/justpeace/documents/rc_pc_justpeace_doc_20060526_compendio-dott-soc_en.html*, accessed July 9, 2009.

8. Pope Benedict XVI, "If You Want Peace, Protect Creation: Message for the 2010 World Day of Peace," (Message of His Holiness Benedict XVI for the celebration of the World Day of Peace, January 1, 2010), 5, *http://www.vatican.va/holy_father/benedict_xvi/messages/peace/documents/hf_benxvi_mes_20091208_xliii-world-day-peace_en.html*, accessed June 9, 2011.

example, the bishops of the Dominican Republic note that "the sin of humanity against nature always has its repercussions against humanity itself" (no. 1).[9] Similarly, the U.S. Catholic bishops wrote that "the whole human race suffers as a result of environmental blight, and generations yet unborn will bear the cost for our failure to act today."[10] In short, it is the concern for human well-being in Catholic social teaching that has led the tradition to begin to turn to questions of environmental ethics. Later in this chapter, the tendency to consider environmental questions primarily from the point of view of human well-being will be revisited.

Catholic social teaching has developed a sophisticated set of concepts that it draws on to describe what a good society should look like and how humans should relate to one another politically and socially. Catholic social teaching has used these same concepts to analyze environmental issues. In what remains of this discussion of the core content of Catholic social teaching, readers will find a description of some of these concepts and an explanation of how each has been used to analyze questions of environmental ethics.

The Common Good

To understand contemporary Catholic social teaching, it is essential to understand the concept of "the common good."[11] The common good is not a uniquely Catholic concept; its roots can be traced to ancient Greek philosophy, most notably to Aristotle, who maintained that the good of each individual was inseparably linked to the quality of the common good of the society in which they lived.[12] Aristotle and Catholic social teaching both maintain that humans are social

---

9. Dominican Episcopal Conference, "Pastoral Letter on the Relationship of Humans to Nature," in *And God Saw That It Was Good*, eds. Drew Christiansen and Walter Grazer, 259–274.

10. United States Conference of Catholic Bishops, *Renewing the Earth: An Invitation to Reflection and Action on Environment in Light of Catholic Social Teaching* (Washington, DC: USCC, 1991), section I.B. *http://www.usccb.org/sdwp/ejp/bishopsstatement.shtml*, accessed July 8, 2009.

11. Todd David Whitmore, "Catholic Social Teaching: Starting with the Common Good," in *Living the Catholic Social Tradition: Cases and Commentaries*, eds. Kathleen Maas Weigert and Alexia K. Kelly (Lanham, MD: Rowman & Littlefield, 2005), 59.

12. David Hollenbach, *The Common Good and Christian Ethics* (Cambridge: Cambridge University Press, 2002), 3. See Aristotle's *Nicomachean Ethics*, 1094b.

creatures who can develop to their full potential and achieve a deeply satisfying, good life only when they participate actively in the life of a good society. People flourish when they are able to contribute to the common good and when they have access to all of the social goods they need to thrive.

Catholic bishops from all over the world articulated the classic definition of the common good in contemporary Catholic social teaching when they gathered for the Second Vatican Council. In the Council document, *Gaudium et spes* (Pastoral Constitution on the Church in the Modern World), *the common good* is defined as the "sum total of social conditions which allow people, either as groups or as individuals, to reach their fulfillment more fully and more easily" (no. 26). The logic of the common good goes something like this: Humans need access to many things to survive and to realize their full potential. A good society facilitates universal access to all of those goods—known as the common good. Think about how much one's life would be diminished if one did not have access to a good educational system or if one could not go to a hospital when extremely ill or if one did not have access to art or literature or if one lived in a place in which the economy was so underdeveloped that no jobs were available. The common good includes all of those concrete goods plus other "social conditions" that are conducive to a good human life, including the very existence of a community that provides these goods. It is the responsibility of everyone in a community to build up the common good.

As may be apparent, the notion of the common good was traditionally anthropocentric. It was typically used to describe what should be universally available to all *people* and to condemn unjust situations in which people were deprived of anything they need to live a dignified human life. However, in the last several decades, the common good has been expanded and has come to be an important concept for addressing environmental concerns from a Catholic perspective as well. A crucial step has been the explicit recognition in Catholic social teaching that a safe and healthy natural environment is an important component of the common good.[13] Every person has a right to live in a place in which the environment has not been degraded, in which people are not exposed to dangerous toxins, and

13. Pontifical Council for Justice and Peace, *Compendium*, no. 468.

in which clean water is readily available. In addition, every individual and every society has an obligation to promote and protect the vibrant health of the natural environment. The responsibility stems from humans' duty to protect and build up the common good.

Another important development has been an expansion of the Catholic understanding of who is responsible for the common good and for whom it exists. Traditionally, the common good was meant to foster the well-being of a local community. However, in his 1963 encyclical letter, *Pacem in terris* (On Establishing Universal Peace in Truth, Justice, Charity, and Liberty), Pope John XXIII expanded the idea of the common good from the local level to the global level. He recognized that individual groups or nations, by themselves, cannot protect some goods that are nevertheless essential. The U.S. bishops adopted John XXIII's global understanding of the common good when they wrote, "Some of the gravest environmental problems are clearly global. In this shrinking world, everyone is affected and everyone is responsible."[14] Protecting the ozone layer, preserving clean freshwater sources, controlling greenhouse gas emissions, and so on are all critical actions for sustaining life on Earth; they are part of the global duty to protect the common good.

Pope Paul VI (in *Populorum progressio* [On the Development of Peoples], no. 17) and later John Paul II (*Centesimus annus* [On the Hundredth Anniversary of *Rerum novarum*], no. 37) expanded a Catholic understanding of the common good in another important way when they insisted that every generation has an obligation to ensure the existence of the common good for future generations. In making this claim, both popes were building on another important concept in Catholic social teaching called the universal purpose of created things (sometimes also known as the universal destination of goods).[15] This term refers to the Catholic belief that the bounty of Earth's natural resources exists for sustaining life on Earth and should be used for the benefit of all.[16] This is a

14. United States Conference of Catholic Bishops, *Renewing the Earth*, III C.

15. Pontifical Council for Justice and Peace, *Compendium*, no. 171.

16. Pope Paul VI, *Populorum progressio* (On the Development of Peoples), no. 22. *http://www.vatican.va/holy_father/paul_vi/encyclicals/documents/hf_pvi_enc_26031967_populorum_en.html*, accessed July 12, 2009.

EPISCOPAL CONFERENCES

The episcopacy (from the Greek term *episkopos*, or *overseer*) refers to the office of bishop (the pastoral leader of a particular geographic region or diocese). Thus, an "episcopal conference" is a conference of bishops. Episcopal conferences originated in the nineteenth century as a structure that allowed all of the Catholic bishops of a particular nation to present a united front in their dealings with national governments.[17] The importance and legitimacy of episcopal conferences was recognized in the *Christus Dominus* (Decree Concerning the Pastoral Office of Bishops in the Church), issued by the Second Vatican Council no. 37 and no. 38). Since then, conferences of bishops have convened in various places around the world to address innumerable issues of public policy and social concern, including environmental ethics. A substantial portion of Catholic social teaching on creation was written by episcopal conferences. For example, in 1988, the Guatemalan Catholic Bishops' Conference issued a pastoral letter titled, "The Cry for Land," which addresses issues of land use, ownership, and stewardship; that same year the Catholic Bishops Conference of the Philippines published "What Is Happening to Our Beautiful Land?" These writings were addressed primarily to the Church and people of goodwill living in the region under the bishops' jurisdiction, but they also found much wider circulation and can be considered part of the body of Catholic social teaching that belongs to the entire Church.

complicated principle, but in short, it holds that natural resources must be used not only for humans' private good but also in ways that respect humans' deeper purpose of supporting the common good and the viability of life for future generations. This point is summarized nicely in "The Columbia River Watershed: Caring for Creation and the Common Good," a pastoral letter authored by the Catholic bishops of

17. Thomas J. Reese, *Inside the Vatican: The Politics and Organization of the Catholic Church* (Cambridge, MA: Harvard University Press, 1996), 33.

the region. (See also the discussion of this pastoral in chapter 2.) That document states, "The watershed is the common home and habitat of God's creatures, a source of human livelihood, and a setting for human community. The commons belongs to everyone, and yet belongs to no one. We hold this land for our present use, for future generations, and ultimately for God, from whom all good things come. It is intended by God to be used for the well-being of all its human inhabitants, present and future."[18]

Catholic social teaching holds that when humans use the goods of Earth for their own advantage at the expense of the common good, they are going against the intrinsic purpose of those natural resources. It may seem odd to think of mineral deposits, or forests, or any natural resource as having an intrinsic purpose. Some might think these things are merely objects that do not have any purpose until humans assign them one or might ask whether the purpose of any good is a matter to be established strictly by its owner. Catholic social teaching has a nuanced understanding of private property that can be helpful for sorting out these questions.

On the one hand, Catholic social teaching has long recognized the importance and legitimacy of the private ownership of goods. Pope Leo XIII maintained that the ability to hold private property was one of the things that would lift the working class out of poverty; he even went so far as to say that people have a natural right to hold private property.[19] At the same time, Catholic social teaching has long recognized that private property rights are not absolute; rather, those rights are always tempered by the principle of the universal purpose of created things. Pope John Paul II put it this way: there is a "social mortgage" on private property. One's property does not exist to serve one's interests alone; one has a moral obligation to use what one has to build up the common good.

Drew Christiansen, SJ, has argued that the common good ought to sustain and serve the ecological or biotic community as well as

---

18. "The Columbia River Watershed: Caring for Creation and the Common Good—an International Pastoral Letter by the Bixhops of the Region" (Seattle: Columbia River Pastoral Letter Project, 2001), 3, at *http://thewscc.org/columbia-river/*, accessed March 10, 2010.

19. Pope Leo XIII, *Rerum novarum*, no. 5

humans.[20] Catholic social teaching ought then to require humans to use natural resources to benefit not only themselves, but also society and the rest of creation.

Solidarity

People are increasingly interconnected around the globe. A call to a customer service number may be answered at a call center in India. The products people buy and the foods they eat often are produced in various places around the globe. The political and economic choices they make affect others in various parts of the world, and vice versa. Solidarity is a principle and a virtue that speaks to how people should respond to that interdependence. Pope John Paul II wrote that when humans strive to make interdependence a "moral category," the result is solidarity.[21] By this, he meant that humans must do more than simply recognize that they are connected to people in various ways; they must commit themselves to shaping those interconnections in mutually beneficial ways. Humans must have a sense of moral concern for all people, no matter where they live in the world, but they must do more than feel concern, because solidarity is also a "persevering determination to commit oneself to the common good; that is to say to the good of all and of each individual, because we are all really responsible for all."[22] More recently, Pope Benedict XVI has emphasized that solidarity must extend across both space and time; it must be intragenerational (with others now living, no matter where in the world) and intergenerational (with future generations).[23]

The Catholic viewpoint is that humans are social by nature. Simply as fellow members of the human race, they are bound to others in a web of mutual responsibilities. As Catholic social teaching

20. Drew Christiansen, "Ecology and the Common Good: Catholic Social Teaching and Environmental Responsibility," in *And God Saw That It Was Good*, eds. Drew Christiansen and Walter Grazer (Washington, DC: United States Catholic Conference, 1996), 185.

21. Pope John Paul II, *Sollicitudo rei socialis* (On Social Concern), no. 38, *http://www.vatican.va/holy_father/john_paul_ii/encyclicals/documents/hf_jp-ii_enc_30121987_sollicitudo-rei-socialis_en.html*, accessed July 23, 2009.

22. Ibid.

23. Pope Benedict XVI, "If You Want to Cultivate Peace," accessed March 13, 2010.

has begun to devote more attention to environmental ethics, there have been signs of a deepening solidarity within the tradition that has also begun to recognize how humans are connected to the rest of creation. For example, John Paul II maintained that economic development must always include "respect for the beings which constitute the natural world."[24] Although it is certain that John Paul II did not think that people should accord precisely the same respect to nonhuman life that they accord to their fellow humans, nevertheless his words make clear the need to consider humans' interdependence with all of creation as a moral category. The Canadian Conference of Catholic Bishops made this principle clear when they wrote that "all serious solutions to the ecological crisis demand that human beings change our thinking, relationships and behaviors in order to recognize the interconnectedness of all creation."[25]

A Preferential Option for the Poor

Concern for poor people has always been a central feature of Catholic social teaching. In contemporary Catholic teaching, this has been called "a preferential option for the poor." The name can be misleading, because having a deep concern for the poor is not actually considered "optional" for Roman Catholics. Catholic social teaching affirms individual responsibility for acts of mercy and caring for poor people but takes the preferential option for the poor further by asserting that societies will be judged by a similar standard. As the U.S. Catholic bishops put it, "We know that our faith is tested by the quality of justice among us, that we can best measure our life together by how the poor and the vulnerable are treated."[26]

A strong concern for poor people has also been a central element of Catholic social teaching on environmental ethics in at least three respects. First, it has called attention to the poor as

---

24. John Paul II, *Sollicitudo rei socialis,* no. 34.

25. Canadian Conference of Catholic Bishops' Social Affairs Commission. *A Pastoral Letter on the Christian Ecological Imperative* (October 4, 2003), no. 14, *http://www.cccb.ca/site/Files/pastoralenvironment.html*, accessed July 12, 2009.

26. United States Conference of Catholic Bishops, *Economic Justice for All: Pastoral Letter on Catholic Social Teaching and the U.S. Economy*, in *Catholic Social Thought: The Documentary Heritage*, eds. David J. O'Brien and Thomas A. Shannon (Maryknoll, NY: Orbis, 1992), 572–680, no. 8.

more likely than other people to suffer the effects of environmental degradation; the lands, neighborhoods, and drinking water of the poor are more likely to be polluted.[27] For example, Keith Warner, assistant director for education at the Center for Science, Technology & Society at Santa Clara University, has noted that the state of California chose some of the state's poorest rural communities for the disposal of hazardous waste.[28] Second, Catholic social teaching has pointed to poverty as one of the leading causes of environmental degradation. For example, the Catholic bishops of the Dominican Republic have claimed that lack of access to adequate fuel sources among the poor "all but forces them to destroy nature" by scavenging for wood for charcoal in the island's forests, which in turn has disastrous effects in terms of soil erosion.[29] One need only look to the other side of the island of Hispaniola to see an extreme example of the problem that the Dominican bishops have described. Haiti has seen massive deforestation and subsequent soil erosion. The Dominican bishops maintain that it will be impossible to develop a coherent environmental policy without simultaneously addressing problems of human poverty. Finally, Catholic social teaching consistently holds that efforts to protect the environment by reducing economic growth and production must always be weighed against the need to provide sufficient economic opportunities for the poor. This last theme will be taken up in the section "Authentic Human Development."

Subsidiarity

Subsidiarity is the principle of Catholic social teaching that explains how responsibility for upholding the common good should be shared by individual people, local organizations, community groups, non-governmental organizations (NGOs), and various levels of government. Pope Pius XI is credited with adding this term (which derives from the Latin word for help or assistance) to Catholic social

27. United States Conference of Catholic Bishops, *Renewing the Earth*, I.B.

28. Keith Douglass Warner, "Poverty and Environmental Justice in Franciscan Perspective," *http://webpages.scu.edu/ftp/kwarner/FranciscanEJ.pdf*, accessed March 11, 2010.

29. Dominican Episcopal Conference, "Pastoral Letter on the Relationship of Humans to Nature," no. 5.

teaching in 1931.[30] Subsidiarity holds that responsibility for the common good should be maintained at the most local level possible; individuals and local groups should be empowered to take responsibility for the common good of their own community. At the same time, it is important not to confuse subsidiarity with some form of libertarianism. Catholic social teaching has a preference for local empowerment and local control, but whenever individuals and local groups are not able to protect the common good on their own, groups and governments beyond the local community are obligated to step in.

In terms of protecting the environment, the principle of subsidiarity implies that every level of society has a role in environmental stewardship.[31] Individuals and local groups should not sit back and wait for the government or "someone else" to address the problem. They have a duty to uphold the common good, which includes care for the natural environment. At the same time, given the complexity of many environmental problems and the impossibility of addressing them at a strictly local level, the principle of subsidiarity points to the need for a higher authority to address these problems. Of course, no international authority has responsibility to coordinate environmental policy; one can merely say that Catholic social teaching suggests the possible need for such an authority or at least for nations to cooperate to address these issues and to be mutually accountable.[32]

AUTHENTIC HUMAN DEVELOPMENT

Having established some of the basic principles and concepts of Catholic social teaching, this chapter now turns to a more complicated idea that builds on them: authentic human development. This theme seeks to answer questions that many people do not even think to ask: What is the purpose of economic development? Why are people trying to "grow" the economy? Do their efforts to accumulate

30. Thomas Massaro, *Living Justice: Catholic Social Teaching in Action*, rev. ed. (Lanham, MD: Rowman & Littlefield, 2008), 89.

31. Jeanne Heffernan Schindler, "Catholic Social Thought and Environmental Ethics in a Global Context," in *Gathered for the Journey: Moral Theology in Catholic Perspective*, eds. David Matzko McCarthy and M. Therese Lysaught (Grand Rapids, MI: Eerdmans, 2007), 342.

32. Ibid.

wealth and material goods interfere with their ability to lead a good, authentically human life? High levels of consumption by people in the Northern Hemisphere are a massive threat to the ecological security of the planet. Crucial in addressing this threat is to face the underlying questions that the Catholic notion of authentic human development addresses very well.

One of the most sustained reflections on authentic human development in recent Catholic social teaching can be found in John Paul II's encyclical, *Sollicitudo rei socialis*. There, the pope questioned what he perceived to be the widespread assumption that expanding economic activity is always a good thing, and he cast doubt on the idea that economic growth will automatically lead to increased human happiness (no. 27). He was not opposed to economic growth and development per se. Instead, he merely cautioned that economic development, science, and technology must be "guided by a moral understanding," or else they may actually cause more harm than good (no. 28).

John Paul II used broad strokes to paint a picture of two sides of the contemporary problem of development. On the one hand, millions of people today suffer from debilitating underdevelopment. They do not have the material resources necessary to realize full human development (no. 28). On the other hand is the problem of "superdevelopment," which is "an excessive availability of every kind of material goods" (no. 28). In other words, some have too little to live a good life while others have too much.

Although it may be clear that living in utter destitution would negatively affect one's quality of life, one might ask how the superabundance of goods can be a problem. After all, having things is not bad in itself. Caught up in the quest to have things, however, one can forget that the acquisition of goods is not the most important task in life.[33] John Paul II described this problem as valuing "having" over "being."[34] One's ultimate goal in life should be to become a particular kind of person. To use traditional Christian language, one should strive to become a virtuous person—someone who embodies charity (love of God), compassion (empathy and love for others), faith, hope, justice, and many other virtues (see also chapter 9). All of these virtues

33. Pope Paul VI, *Populorum progressio*, no. 19.

34. Pope John Paul II, *Sollicitudo rei socialis*, no. 28.

describe a particular mode of *being* that is an essential dimension of Catholic theological ethics and Catholic social teaching. Many people in American society and in other "superdeveloped" nations, however, neglect the task of becoming a virtuous person in favor of possessing more and more objects. John Paul II maintained that such a life—that values having over being—will be unsatisfying and unhappy because it is centered on things rather than more authentic goods, such as relationships with others and with God. Instead of organizing one's life around the acquisition of things, one should use things in such a way that is most helpful for becoming a good person.

The traditional Christian concepts of sufficiency and community are helpful for understanding the personal implications of authentic human development.[35] People should manage their own pursuit of material goods on the basis of sufficiency; in other words, they should seek to acquire what they need to live a good, dignified life but not seek to have more than they legitimately need. They should direct the surplus toward the common good and toward ensuring that others have a sufficient share of material goods to live a dignified life. At the social level, the model of authentic human development suggests that the ideal of global economic development programs should not be to replicate the materialistic excesses of superdeveloped nations but to develop a global economy in which there is a more widespread access to sufficiency.

Earth simply will not be able to support a superdeveloped lifestyle for every human. Catholic social teaching calls for a moral reassessment of the way of life enjoyed by the privileged classes in the global north.[36] Pope Benedict XVI has encouraged all people to pursue new lifestyles "in which the quest for truth, beauty, goodness, and communion with others for the sake of common growth are the factors that determine consumer choices, savings and investment."[37] Moving from a lifestyle of high consumption to one of simplicity will require material sacrifice. However, Catholic social teaching also holds out the hope that a more simplified life

---

35. Christiansen, "Ecology and the Common Good," 187.

36. Pope Benedict XVI, *Caritas in veritate* (On Integral Development in Charity and Truth), no. 51. *http://www.vatican.va/holy_father/benedict_xvi/encyclicals/documents/hf_ben-xvi_enc_20090629_caritas-in-veritate_en.html,* accessed July 12, 2009.

37. Pope Benedict XVI, "If You Want to Cultivate Peace," no. 11.

may nevertheless be full and satisfying. In short, living according to the norms of sufficiency and community would actually be more conducive to human happiness and more beneficial for the well-being of the rest of creation.

CATHOLIC SOCIAL TEACHING AND ANTHROPOCENTRISM

In a 1967 article that has become a classic, Lynn White Jr. argued that Christian beliefs (especially the Christian understanding that humankind has a calling to exercise dominion over creation) have had devastating ecological effects.[38] In short, he accused Christianity of being hopelessly anthropocentric and argued further that such anthropocentrism was incompatible with a viable environmental ethic.

Catholic social teaching does not respond directly to White's charges, but it addresses the question of what should be the proper relationship between humanity and the rest of creation. In resounding fashion, Catholic social teaching affirms that humans occupy a special place in the world and have a unique vocation to act as stewards over the rest of creation. In the social encyclical *Caritas in veritate*, Pope Benedict XVI affirmed that "it is contrary to authentic development to view nature as something more important than the human person."[39] That remark was echoed in his 2010 World Day of Peace message, in which he declared that ecocentric or biocentric approaches to environmental ethics are erroneous "because such notions eliminate the difference of identity and worth between the human person and other living things. In the name of a supposedly egalitarian vision of the dignity of all living creatures, such notions end up abolishing the distinctiveness and superior role of human beings."[40]

Similarly, the Catholic bishops of northern Italy affirmed that the "spiritual quality" of humanity and humans' ability to use reason and technology to transform nature suggest that it is only proper for humanity to exercise dominion over nature; indeed, it

38. Lynn White Jr., "The Historical Roots of Our Ecologic Crisis," *Science* 155, no. 3767 (1967), 1203–1207.

39. Pope Benedict XVI, *Caritas in veritate*, no. 48.

40. Pope Benedict XVI, "If You Want to Cultivate Peace, Protect Creation," no. 13.

is central to their vocation as humans. They see the question to be not *whether* humans will act as stewards of creation, but *in what manner* "human activity [should] alter the dynamic ecological balances."[41] Interestingly, they believe that it is natural for humans to exercise this kind of dominion: "The mediation of human liberty is essential in order that God's creation should realize the destiny assigned to it."[42]

Dominion and Stewardship

Catholic social teaching unabashedly affirms that humans are called by God to exercise dominion over the rest of creation. This belief is rooted in the biblical creation stories, especially Genesis 1:26, in which God specifically grants humankind dominion over all of the planet's creatures. Some critics of this view hold that any notion of human dominion over creation is problematic; humans are part of creation, not standing above it. Humans should not seek to control creation but must accommodate themselves to it. Catholic social teaching rejects that viewpoint, however, holding instead that it is the misuse and abuse of human power over creation that is at the root of the problem rather than the exercise of dominion per se.

Catholic social teaching maintains that humanity has confused its right and duty to exercise dominion over creation with a license to dominate creation. *Domination* and *dominion* sound almost alike but have two very different meanings. Domination is the use of power without restraint and without regard for the integrity of that over which power is exercised. Humans dominate creation when they "make arbitrary use of the earth, subjecting it without restraint to [their] will, as though it did not have its own requisites and a prior God-given purpose, which [humanity] can indeed develop but must not betray."[43] Creation is never to be seen merely as an instrument or as an object to be exploited for the

---

41. Catholic Bishops of Northern Italy, "Ecology: The Bishops of Lombardy Address the Community," in *And God Saw That It Was Good*, eds. Drew Christiansen and Walter Grazer (Washington, DC: United States Catholic Conference), 1996), 299–300.

42. Ibid., 302.

43. Pontifical Council for Justice and Peace. *The Compendium of the Social Doctrine of the Church*, no. 460.

benefit of humankind; such is the view of creation that leads to immoral domination.[44]

In exercising dominion, by contrast, humankind may draw on natural resources for its own well-being and development but must do so while respecting the integrity of creation as also always a good in itself. As John Paul II explained, "the dominion granted to [humanity] by the Creator is not an absolute power, nor can one speak of a freedom . . . to dispose of things as one pleases."[45] Humans are not free to simply manipulate creation according to their own whims and wishes. It is necessary to recognize that the natural world is a delicate system that must be respected and which humans cannot really control.[46] To be a good steward is to use natural resources and exert influence over creation in a way that is simultaneously for the good of both humanity and the rest of creation.

An Assessment

Daniel Cowdin, a Catholic theologian who teaches at Salve Regina University, has offered a nuanced response to the question of whether it is legitimate to continue to claim a special place for humanity as a species set apart from the rest of creation. On the one hand, he affirms that it is wrong to make an absolute distinction between humanity and other creatures because "we exist within a continuum of life, sharing degrees of consciousness, mobility, and vitality" with other species.[47] On this point, he offers a critique of Catholic social teaching; for example, he would likely question the validity of the *Compendium*'s desire to insist upon an "ontological and axiological" difference between humans and other creatures. In other words, he would likely reject claims that humans are categorically different from other life on Earth (ontology is the philosophical reflection on the nature of being), and he would also reject any claim that humans are so precious that their value cannot really be compared with the worth of other creatures.

44. Ibid, no. 461.

45. Pope John Paul II, *Sollicitudo rei socialis*, no. 34.

46. Pope John Paul II, *Sollicitudo rei socialis,* no. 34.

47. Daniel M. Cowdin, "Toward an Environmental Ethic," in *Preserving the Creation: Environmental Theology and Ethics*, eds. Kevin W. Irwin and Edmund D. Pellegrino (Washington, DC: Georgetown University Press, 1994), 129. Cited in Hinze, 168.

On the other hand, Cowdin is skeptical about claims that humanity is simply one species like any other. He maintains that it would be factually inaccurate to say that humans do not play a unique role in the world because their actions have a much more substantial effect on the rest of creation than those of most other species. As Catholic theological ethicist Christine Firer Hinze has put it, "human interaction with nature is ubiquitous and human action or inaction will inevitably have an impact on the future of non-human nature. The 'is' of our entanglement with and unavoidable impact on nature leads to a moral 'ought': humans, because of who we are within nature, have particular responsibilities in relation to nature."[48] Thus, humans occupy a place of unique importance in the ecosystem due to our capacity to shape and nurture it.

Although it would be wrong to say that humans have a worth that cannot even be compared with that of other creatures, it would be equally wrong to underplay the immense importance and value of human life. It is easier to say that humans and the rest of creation have equal worth when one imagines it might be possible to harmonize the good of every creature in the biosphere. However, the fact is there is sometimes a struggle for survival among species as they compete for habitat and other vital resources.[49] In such a situation, would humans really say that the survival of their race is not more important than the survival of another species? Surely, the best route would be to avoid such conflicts, but considering the possibility of their own death or the extinction of humankind might lead them to think more deeply about whether favoring the human species is always misguided. Exactly how the value of human life should be understood in relation to other species is something that must be worked out more satisfactorily as Catholic social teaching on creation continues to mature. It is likely that debate about the validity of its anthropocentric leanings will continue well into the future.

---

48. Hinze, 169. Hinze's statement seems very close to the view put forward by the bishops of northern Italy when they argued that the question is not whether humanity will exercise power over nature but rather how and according to what moral guidelines it should exercise that power.

49. Hinze, 169.

ACCESSING OFFICIAL TEXTS OF CATHOLIC SOCIAL TEACHING

All of the encyclicals that make up Catholic social teaching can be accessed freely via the Internet. Official English translations (as well as translations in some other languages) can be found on the Vatican's Web site (*http://www.vatican.va*). Usually, it is most effective to search for an encyclical by using its Latin title (e.g., *Rerum novarum*). Another convenient access point is a site maintained by the Office of Social Ministry in the Archdiocese of Minneapolis-Saint Paul, Minnesota. It offers a full list of the major documents of Catholic social teaching (including those written by the U.S. Catholic bishops). A brief description of each document and a link to its full text is included along with a few other helpful resources. For access, visit *http://www.osjspm.org/social_teaching_documents.aspx*.

CONCLUSION

Since the nineteenth century, Catholic social teaching has provided moral guidance on questions of social justice. It is still only beginning to integrate environmental ethics into its vision of a just society. Nevertheless, the principles of Catholic social teaching already provide a set of concepts that can help one understand how people should relate to one another and to the rest of creation. Some of these principles have already been put into action. The Vatican has taken small but important concrete steps to bear witness to its vision of green discipleship. For example, it has begun replacing roof tiles on some Vatican buildings with solar panels and taken other steps to honor its stated commitment to become the first carbon-neutral state.[50]

Catholic social teaching does not provide the most radical vision of green discipleship. When placed on a spectrum alongside other

50. "Vatican continues initiatives to go green," *Catholic News Agency*, November 18, 2008, *http://www.catholicnewsagency.com/news/vatican_continues_initiatives_to_go_green/*, accessed January 30, 2011.

approaches to environmental ethics, Catholic social teaching might appear to some to be timid. However, if one places the understanding of authentic human development found in Catholic social teaching alongside the typical American lifestyle of superabundance, Catholic social teaching looks challenging or even radical. By providing a clear explanation for why people should aim for lives of simplicity and strive to be in solidarity with one another and the rest of creation, Catholic social teaching can contribute substantially to contemporary conversations about ecological ethics.

QUESTIONS FOR REVIEW

1. Catholic social teaching originally ignored environmental ethics and focused exclusively on human concerns. What led this tradition to engage environmental ethics?
2. Briefly define each of the following: common good, preferential option for the poor, subsidiarity, universal destination of goods. What is the relevance of each for environmental ethics? How should these concepts or principles guide our response to environmental challenges, according to Catholic social teaching?
3. Explain the distinction between dominion and domination.
4. What constitutes "authentic" development, according to Catholic social teaching? What might be some examples of development that is not authentic?

IN-DEPTH QUESTIONS

1. What concrete goods would you include in a list of those things that every human needs to live a good, dignified life? Would you agree with the claim that a society is good and just to the degree that it makes those concrete goods widely available? Why or why not?
2. Catholic social teaching encourages individuals to see their wealth as a social good. One's money, talent, and assets should be used not merely to enrich oneself but also to build up the common good. Do you agree that there is a "social mortgage" on private property? Why or why not?

3. Do you think you would be genuinely happy living a life of material sufficiency? Why or why not? Describe the changes you would have to implement in your personal life to embrace a lifestyle of sufficiency.
4. How does one live in a way that values being over having?
5. Catholic social thought claims that the typical American lifestyle (superdevelopment) is neither ideal nor sustainable. Do you agree? How would you convince someone to see things from your point of view?
6. Catholic social teaching insists on a special role for humans in exercising stewardship over creation. Is this ongoing anthropocentrism problematic or is it justified? Why? Does the notion of human dominion inevitably lead to human domination of nature? Why or why not?

CHAPTER 13

GOD, CREATION, AND THE ENVIRONMENT: Feminist Theological Perspectives

Kari-Shane Davis Zimmerman

KEY TERMS

ecofeminism
ecojustice
patriarchal
ecological theology
ecological economics
functional cosmology
ecological literacy
ecological anthropology

INTRODUCTION

This chapter explores the work of three prominent feminist theological thinkers from across the Christian theological spectrum. In particular, the reader will see how each author explores the relationship between Christian beliefs about God, creation, and humans and the domination of nature (and for some, especially women).

FROM FEMINISM TO ECOFEMINISM

The term *global warming* is nowadays part of most people's working vocabulary. Everyone from politicians to environmentalists to TV producers is talking about the "threats" and "dangers" that loom if humans as a global society fail to heed the warning signs nature is providing. In the U.S. Congress, for example, politicians, along with scientists, debate the evidence regarding climate change. On television, such channels such as Discovery Channel and the History Channel are drumming up new ways to talk about the environment. Shows highlight the wonders and perils of nature, such as Discovery Channel's eleven-part miniseries *Planet Earth*, which, producers Penny Allen and Jonny Keeling explain, took more than five years and two thousand days in the field to film, or *Life Without People*, a History Channel program that addressed what would happen to planet Earth if suddenly humans were to disappear forever.

Despite these and other attempts to address what is really going on in nature, for many people, the issue is not *if and when* climate change will become a reality we all must face, but rather what one should do given the changes *already* taking place in the environment. Whether one sits in a college classroom or perches atop one of Earth's breathtaking mountain peaks, there is no easy answer. Some reflect on this question by asking what the Christian tradition has to say regarding climate change, global warming, and other such environmental concerns. Among the latter are Christian feminist theologians.

Each of these theologians—Rosemary Radford Ruether, Elizabeth Johnson, CSJ, and Sallie McFague—has particular concerns; however, each believes Christian theology must attend to the changes taking place both within the environment (e.g., global warming) and within the academic discipline of environmental studies. In addition to a discussion of their concerns, this chapter will look briefly at the Green Sisters movement to see one "on-the-ground" example of how some with Christian theological commitments are addressing the challenges posed by changes in the environment.

One more caveat: the focus of this chapter is narrow; there are many voices in addition to these three, both within and outside the American context. Feminist theologians around the globe have been speaking and continue to speak from their particular social-economic-political location, offering crucial insights for this growing field within feminist theology that many label "ecofeminism." For some feminist thinkers, ecofeminism is feminism's third wave. For others, it is merely a logical conclusion that an environmental perspective is necessary for feminism. Thus, none of the authors discussed in this chapter presumes to speak either for all women across the globe or for all women who identify themselves as part of the Christian tradition.

ROSEMARY RADFORD RUETHER

Rosemary Radford Ruether (b. 1936) is a central figure within feminist theological circles inside and outside the United States and also within the Catholic tradition. In Ruether's first major work in the area of ecofeminism, *Gaia and God: An Ecofeminist Theology of Earth Healing*,[1] she makes clear in her introduction (as she does in later essays on the subject) that the heart of ecofeminism concerns joining two explorations, ecology and feminism. That is, ecofeminism seeks to investigate how male domination of women and of nature interconnects both in their perception of culture and within the construction and shaping of social structures themselves.[2] In other words, Ruether draws a connection between the cultural and social roots that promote not only destructive relations between men and women or between ruling and subjugated human groups but also between humans and the entire biotic community of which humans are one part. More important, she contends that dominating and destructive relations with Earth are interrelated with gender, class, and racial domination. As a result, Ruether does not believe technological "fixes" can heal the many rifts that continue to expand between humans and the environment. Rather, she calls for a social reordering that enables access to the means of life for all men and women, races and nations, and stratified social classes. That is, humans must speak of ecojustice and not simply of domination of Earth, as if the latter happens unrelated to issues of social domination.

Rosemary Radford Ruether

1. Rosemary Radford Ruether, *Gaia and God: An Ecofeminist Theology of Earth Healing* (San Francisco: HarperCollins Publishers, 1992).

2. Ibid., 2.

ROSEMARY RADFORD RUETHER

Rosemary Radford Ruether is an internationally acclaimed theologian, writer, and teacher. She is the author of nearly five hundred articles and more than thirty books. A self-proclaimed ecofeminist, Ruether's work represents a significant contribution to contemporary theology, especially in the area of women and the church. Ruether formerly was Carpenter Professor of Feminist Theology at the Pacific School of Religion and Graduate Theological Union. She also served as the Georgia Harkness Professor of Applied Theology at Garrett-Evangelical Seminary in Evanston, Illinois, and was a faculty member in the joint doctoral program with Northwestern University. In addition, she has lectured at colleges and universities in the United States and the United Kingdom. Currently she is Visiting Professor of Feminist Theology at Claremont School of Theology and Claremont Graduate University. She and her husband have three children.

Ruether also claims that people's consciousness must change for healing to take place between men and women and between humans and the planet. Related to this healing, a corresponding change is needed in how one symbolizes the interrelations of men and women, humans and Earth, humans and the divine, and the divine and Earth.[3] Such is the case for Ruether, because ecological healing is both a theological and psychic spiritual process. Given this dual process, a brief look follows at what ecofeminism is not according to Ruether.

On the one hand, Ruether criticizes the view of the self, developed especially in the West, as against all that is nonhuman. She also criticizes a concept of "nature" as that which is nonhuman and nondivine. Ruether finds both these constructions problematic and needing reevaluation. Similarly, she finds attempts by some Christian scholars to replace the term *God* with the term *Gaia*, the word for

3. Ibid., 4.

the Greek earth goddess, problematic. Merely replacing the image of a male transcendent deity with an immanent female deity does not provide a sufficient response to the "god problem."

In contrast, Ruether claims an adequate ecofeminism is concerned with two levels: the cultural-symbolic level, in which the connection between sexism and ecological exploitation go hand in hand, and the socio economic level. More often than not, the former is an "ideological superstructure that reflects and ratifies" the latter, particularly within the social patterns coming out of ancient Near Eastern culture. Ruether argues these social patterns are deeply rooted in the distortion of gender relations and lead to the subjugation of women. In the ancient Near East, a social system that includes the domination of women has its roots in a larger patriarchal, hierarchical social system of priestly and warrior-king control over land, animals, and slaves, which in turn, further monopolizes wealth, power, and knowledge.[4] As this system of domination takes shape socially, ideological tools are constructed to validate the social system as a reflection of the "nature of things" and the "will of God/the gods."[5] From this social system come law codes that define women, slaves, animals, and land as property, as well as creation stories that depict this hierarchical social order as a reflection of the entire cosmos.

According to Ruether, the Hebrew creation story in the book of Genesis (chapters 1–3) is an example of the previously mentioned process at work. The story "posits a patriarchal God who shapes an original chaotic matter into cosmos through his word-command during a six-day work week, culminating in sabbatical rest. The human, created male and female on the sixth day and given the command to rule over Earth and its plants and animals, is not created as a slave, but as a royal servant, or administrator, of Earth as representative of God, or 'in God's image.'"[6] Although the story itself contains no explicit mandate for the domination of some humans over others, implicit in the narrative (and explicit in

4. Rosemary Radford Ruether, *Christianity and Ecology: Seeking the Well-Being of Earth and Humans*, eds. Dieter T. Hessel and Rosemary Radford Ruether (Cambridge: Harvard University Press, 2000), 97.

5. Ibid., 97.

6. Ibid., 100.

Hebrew law and exegesis) remains the belief that Adam—a generic human—embodies the male patriarchal class. This social class represents dependent humans (women, slaves, and children) and its purpose is to rule over God's creation.

In Genesis 2–3, the male is identified with the original male human out of which the female is created by the male God and handed over to be the male's wife-servant, says Ruether. In her judgment, the narrative does not depict an egalitarian relationship. This "derivative female" initiates disobedience to God's command. Her act causes both man and woman (otherwise known as Adam and Eve) to be thrown out of paradise (the Garden of Eden) and forced to live a life of hard labor (for the man) and to endure painful childbearing and subjugation to her husband (for the woman). Even though Hebrew thought suggests that once humans (Israel's patriarchal class) turn to and obey God, paradise will be restored and violence between man and woman and between man and nature will cease, Ruether notes that this hope for a future paradise is "earth- and mortality-bound." That is, redeemed humans will live a long, healthy life, but it is now a *mortal* life on a peaceful and bountiful yet *mortal* Earth.[7]

For Ruether, early Christianity loses much of the previously mentioned explanation for women's inferiority. That is, some early Christian movements suggest a subversive liberation in Christ from all relations of subjugation, for example, women to men, slaves to masters, conquered to ruling nations. However, once Christianity becomes institutionalized within both the patriarchal family and the political order, it leaves behind any such radical interpretation of redemption in Christ. Thus, although women are granted equal access to heavenly redemption, any sense of future hope is not allowed to subvert the flourishing of patriarchal relations on Earth in the newly forming Christian church and society of the first and second centuries.

Moreover, Ruether believes Saint Augustine's commentaries on the book of Genesis (written over the years 401 to 414/415 CE), especially the creation story itself, add to the already existing levels of patriarchal domination of women by men. According to Augustine, woman is created in her female nature to be subordinate to the male in the sexual and social roles of wife and child-bearer. For Augustine,

7. Ibid.

femaleness represents the inferior bodily nature, whereas maleness represents the intellect that rules over both the man and woman's body. As a result, Augustine views the male as the collective Adam made in God's image, while the woman does not possess the image of God in herself but rather images God through the male. In other words, woman is "in the image of God" only when taken together with the male "who is her head."[8]

Compounding matters further for Ruether is Augustine's belief that Eve initiates disobeying God's command in the Garden of Eden. Because Adam consents to Eve's prompting, he concedes to his lower self, thus resulting in the whole of humankind falling into sin. Augustine understands woman as created subordinate to man but also rightly placed in a state of forced subjugation due to her original insubordination. This means redemption in Christ does not liberate woman from subordination; rather, only through voluntary acceptance of her subordination does woman, in Augustine's analysis, make herself obedient to God and fit for heavenly bliss.

For Ruether, these and other kinds of patriarchal patterns reign steady until modern times. However, there are challenges to this doctrine of male domination. For example, Ruether notes the work of a few "maverick feminist humanists" and Quakers in the sixteenth and seventeenth centuries that argue all humans are created equal in the original creation. Moreover, they claim the domination of woman (as well as other forms of domination) comes about from the sin of dominant males who distort the original harmony and not because of woman's sin. In this view, Christ overcomes all such dominations and restores equality between men and women. Redemption, therefore, includes a social struggle to overcome unjust domination of women by men (as well as masters over slaves) here on Earth. Ruether points out this latter theology of original and redeemed equality over patriarchal "slavocracy" is developed further by some abolitionist feminist thinkers of the nineteenth century such as the Grimké sisters (nineteenth-century American Quakers) and Lucretia Mott (1793–1880). In more recent decades, Ruether highlights modern feminist theology's critique of patriarchal views of human nature.

---

8. Ibid., 101.

Despite these and other challenges, Ruether insists ecofeminism must continue to challenge the view of the self that operates in Christian thought and suggests a separation between soul and body, and associates mind with maleness and body with femaleness. This latter picture of the human person distorts how humans are related to each other as well as how they stand in relation to life on Earth and the cosmos as a whole. Put differently, Ruether believes men and women must shift their view of humans and their place in the cosmos. In her view, humans are descendents of a long evolutionary process; consciousness does not set them radically apart from other forms of life on Earth. Instead, humans must understand that there is a "continuity of matter-energy dynamics on different levels of organization, moving from inorganic energy to life, then to awareness of life, and then to self-reflecting consciousness in organisms with progressively more complex brains."[9] Humankind's job is not to dominate and rule Earth. Earth has governed itself well and better for millions of years berfore the arrival of humans! Moreover, stewardship is not a primal command but rather the effort of dominant males to correct overabuse and become better managers of what they have presumed to be their own. In other words, human consciousness does not magically fall from a heaven that is outside Earth; human destiny is of and for this Earth. Human immortality, therefore, lies not in the preservation of individual consciousness as some sort of separate substance, but on the contrary, in the miracle and mystery of endlessly recycled matter-energy out of which humans come and into which humans shall one day return.

Practically thinking, then, Ruether believes humans need to use their special capacity for thought to celebrate the wonder of the whole cosmic process and to be the place in which this cosmic process comes to celebrative consciousness (versus imagining themselves as ruling over others, believing themselves to be superior to others, and escaping their common mortality). Similarly, she argues humans must use their capacity for consciousness in such a way as to contemplate further how they can better harmonize their lives with the life of the whole Earth community. This demands, in Ruether's view, articulating a spirituality and ethic of mutual

9. Ibid., 104.

limitation and of reciprocal life-giving nurture rather than a spirituality of separation and domination.

ELIZABETH A. JOHNSON, CSJ

Like Rosemary Radford Ruether, feminist scholar and Catholic theologian Elizabeth Johnson (b. 1941) also takes up the challenge of responding to the environmental crisis in her scholarly work. For Johnson, humans stand currently within a unique dialectic she characterizes as "wonder" and "wasting."[10] Contemporary science has deepened most people's sense of wonder when it comes to the intricate workings of Earth; yet, at the same time, many are lamenting at how quickly humans also are spoiling the natural world. Within this dual ecological context, one of Johnson's contributions is to reawaken and reaffirm an ancient theme within Christian theology, namely, the presence and action of the creative Spirit of God throughout the natural world. In her mind, ecological theology (as she calls it) needs to work on two fronts, the Spirit and the natural world.

IMAGE COURTESY SISTERS OF ST. JOSEPH OF BRENTWOOD, BRENTWOOD, NY

Sister Elizabeth Johnson

According to Johnson, if one thinks about the image of Earth from space, at least four aspects of this planet and its place in the universe become glaringly apparent.[11] First, both Earth and universe are very old. The current scientific consensus suggests a "Big Bang" approximately fourteen billion years ago, followed by continued expansion as galaxies and stars have come and gone. Most scientists estimate Earth's sun and the planets emerged five billion

10. Elizabeth A. Johnson, *Quest for the Living God: Mapping Frontiers in the Theology of God* (New York: Continuum, 2007), 182.

11. Ibid., 183.

ELIZABETH JOHNSON

Elizabeth Johnson is a leading scholar in the field of Christian systematic theology and feminist theology. Both a readable author and inspiring teacher and public lecturer, Johnson's main areas of research focus on the mystery of God, Jesus Christ, the Holy Spirit, the communion of saints (including Mary), the dialogue with science and ecological ethics, and the problem of suffering and issues related to justice for women. She currently serves as Distinguished Professor of Systematic Theology at Fordham University (New York). Beyond the classroom, Johnson serves as a theologian on the national Lutheran-Catholic dialogue. In addition, she is a consultant to the Catholic Bishops' Committee on Women in Church and Society, a theologian on the Vatican-sponsored dialogue between science and religion, a member of the Vatican-sponsored study of Christ and the world religions, and a core committee member of the Common Ground Initiative started by Cardinal Joseph Bernardin to reconcile polarized groups in the church. She is a religious sister in the Congregation of St. Joseph (Brentwood, New York).

years ago, and life first appeared on Earth about four billion years ago. Second, the universe is incomprehensively large, and humans on Earth are but a speck in it. Third, the universe is "complexly interconnected, everything being related to everything else to some degree."[12] In other words, the story of biological evolution confirms that humans share with all other living creatures a common genetic ancestry tracing back to the original single-celled creatures in the ancient seas. Fourth, Johnson notes the profound dynamism of the universe and credits this dynamism with the emergence of the human species itself. She writes, "Human thought and love are not something injected into the universe from without, but are the flowering in us of deeply cosmic energies, arising out of the very physical dynamism

12. Ibid., 184.

of the cosmos, which is already self-organizing and creative."[13] In other words, humans are not aliens deposited within a strange physical world, but rather they are an intrinsic part of the ever-evolving storyline. It also means humans are distinctive but not separate, or as Johnson puts it, "a unique strand in the cosmos, yet still a strand *of* the cosmos."[14]

Unfortunately, however, there is another version of this storyline—a story not of wonder, but of distress. According to Johnson, overconsumption, unbridled reproduction, exploitative use of resources, and burgeoning pollution are quickly depleting life-supporting systems on land, in the sea, and in the air.[15] Planet Earth is undergoing a massive assault by humans (whether intended or not), which is wreaking ecological havoc of the greatest magnitude. In Johnson's view, the unholy litany is known well: global warming, holes in the ozone layer, clear-cut forests, drained wetlands, denuded soils, polluted air, poisoned rivers, overfished seas, and over all, the threat of nuclear conflagration.[16] Humans now live in a time of great dying-off.

Johnson also warns that the picture continues to darken if one further attends to the deep-seated connection between social injustice and ecological devastation. Poor people, in particular, suffer disproportionately; not only are they ravaged personally but so also is the land on which their survival depends. For example, in the Amazon basin, rural peoples are pushed to the edge of rain forests where they are forced to practice slash-and-burn agriculture for lack of land-reform policies. In contrast, those more economically well off choose to live amid acres of green while the poor within wealthy nations are housed near factories, refineries, or waste-processing plants that pollute the environment and are linked to birth defects and general ill health. Moreover, feminist analysis clarifies further how the plight of poor women "becomes exemplified in poor women whose own biological abilities to give birth are compromised by toxic environments, and whose nurturing of children is hampered at every

13. Ibid., 185.

14. Ibid.

15. Ibid.

16. Ibid., 186.

turn by lack of clean water, food, and fuel."[17] For Johnson, the remedy for overcoming poverty has an ecological face.

Given this dual context of wonder and wasting, Johnson is most concerned with how people think about God in relation to the world. That is, she seeks to find new ways to talk about divine presence. Most discussions of divine presence center on the Spirit of God, but for Johnson, ecological theology maps yet another new frontier when it comes to imaging and describing divine presence. She believes the best way to explore divine presence is through the following three rubrics: it is *continuous*; it is *cruciform*; and it *abides in the mode of promise*.

Regarding what Johnson refers to as *continuous*, she contends that one must understand the Spirit of God neither at nor beyond the apex of being but rather "within and around the emerging, struggling, living, dying, and renewing circle of life and the whole universe itself."[18] With this understanding of divine presence, the natural world is no longer divorced from the sacred world; instead the latter takes on what Johnson calls a sacramental character, that is, the entire physical world is the matrix of God's gracious indwelling. However, the natural world, despite its beauty and harmonies, contains great suffering and death. Both predation and death are an inescapable part of the pattern of biological life. Moreover, Johnson reminds her readers that the history of life itself depends on death, and without death, there would be no evolutionary development.

Divine presence also must be understood as *cruciform*. According to Johnson, for those who believe Jesus Christ is the wisdom of God made flesh, there is no better lens through which to interpret the character of the living God. Through this particular lens, one glimpses a merciful love that knows no bounds. At the same time, Johnson argues that Christ's unjust execution on the cross links divine compassion with the sinful condition of the world, that is, with the world's painful suffering and terrifying death. As a result, ecological theology seeks to cross the species line and extend divine solidarity to all creatures. Ecological theology proposes that the Creator Spirit "dwells in compassionate solidarity with every living being that suffers. . . . "[19]

17. Ibid., 187.

18. Ibid., 189.

19. Ibid.

The claim here is not to glorify suffering but rather to emphasize the Creator Spirit's relation to an evolutionary and suffering world.

Lastly, Johnson believes it fully reasonable to understand further divine presence as *abiding in the mode of promise*. The scientific account of the expanding cosmos, along with the evolution of life on this planet, makes abundantly clear that the universe is understood best as an "open-ended adventure" instead of a settled phenomenon.[20] In other words, Johnson contends the universe is "seeded with promise, pregnant with surprise" and that this sense of unfinished openness places the world firmly within the parameters of biblical faith.[21] If one reflects on the world's evolutionary history along with the biblical stories of faith, then ecological theology suggests that the Creator Spirit be understood as the "generous wellspring of novelty not only for humans, but also for the whole natural world."[22] Put differently, Johnson believes the Creator Spirit not only provides the world with creative power but also sets off the world's grand adventure, "saying at the Big Bang, in effect, 'Go, become, explore, bring forth the new, because more is still possible.'"[23]

In summary, Johnson believes ecological theology suggests that the Creator Spirit is understood best as dwelling at the heart of the natural world and thus graciously energizing its evolution from within. However, what is the role of divine agency? If the scientific picture of the universe suggests that nature always is organizing itself into new forms of life at all levels, then how does God act in an evolutionary, emergent universe? The answer to this question is fiercely contested between some scientists and religious adherents of "intelligent design," with the former arguing no trace of divine activity exists and the latter positing some sort of direct action and overall plan. According to Johnson, neither view is adequate. Instead, ecological theology proposes that the divine creativity of the Creator Spirit "is the source not just of cosmic order but also of the chance that allows novelty to appear."[24] The Creator

20. Ibid., 190.

21. Ibid., 191.

22. Ibid.

23. Ibid.

24. Ibid., 195

Spirit has made possible lawful regularities, yet, at the same time, embraces what Johnson refers to as the "chanciness of random mutations and the chaotic conditions of open systems . . . "[25] It should come as no surprise to find divine creativity hovering very close to turbulence.

In conclusion, Johnson asserts that this theology of the Creator Spirit undergirds an ethic of responsible and assertive care for Earth. Therefore, humans can no longer conceive of a moral universe as limited to them. If, as Johnson and ecological theology suggest, Earth is indeed a sacrament of divine presence, a locus of divine compassion, and a bearer of divine promise, then its ongoing destruction is a deeply sinful desecration.[26] As a result, Johnson argues the response of people of faith needs to become both prophetic and challenging. All the techniques of active nonviolent resistance must be employed to halt aggression against those most vulnerable. "One stringent criterion must now measure the morality of our actions: whether or not these contribute to a sustainable life community on Earth."[27] For Johnson, ethical attention must turn away from humans alone and instead focus on the whole community of life. In other words, an ecological ethic of life seeks to redefine Jesus' Great Command to love your neighbor as yourself to extend it beyond human life to include all members of the life community. In Johnson's view, the new moral goal is as follows: to ensure a vibrant life in community for all because the great, incomprehensible mystery of God, as both utterly transcendent and beyond the world, is the same dynamic power at the heart of the natural world and its evolution.

SALLIE MCFAGUE

No overview of feminist theology's response to the environment is complete without also highlighting the work of Sallie McFague, a noted Protestant theologian (b. 1933). McFague has been engaging how theology and questions on the environment intersect since the late 1980s. These issues are addressed in a preliminary manner in

25. Ibid.

26. Ibid., 197.

27. Ibid.

Sallie McFague

Models of God (1987), followed by a more explicit engagement in *The Body of God* (1993). Five years later she returned to the subject matter in *Super, Natural Christians: How We Should Love Nature* (1997). In this latter work, she suggests ways in which Christians can better love nature. She argues for a shift in sensibility, that is, a shift in how Christians view nature, because most Christians do not know how to relate to nature, or they do so as Western culture does, as merely an object for human use. McFague believes that a change in sensibility can produce significant and meaningful consequences. For instance, she believes such a change can assist Christians in feeling more integrated and whole because they would have *one way* of being, knowing, and doing in relation to God, other people, and nature. Put differently, Christians would have a "functional cosmology," that is, an understanding of who they are in the natural world, and a practice toward the natural world that was on a continuum with Christian understandings of and action toward God and other people. Moreover, with this shift in sensibility, McFague believes things "would hold together, be of one piece, as they have not been for Christians for several centuries." That is, the concepts of being, knowing, and doing fit together. Who people believe they are influences what they think about others and how they act toward them. If, in *all* relations, including those with nature, people believe they are subjects relating to other subjects, then they might treat them that way.[28]

McFague's concern with merging the fields of feminist epistemology and process theology with the ecological model of the self and world is the focus of her follow-up publication, *Life Abundant:*

28. Sallie McFague, *Super, Natural Christians: How We Should Love Nature* (Minneapolis: Fortress, 1997), 2.

SALLIE MCFAGUE

Sallie McFague currently acts as Distinguished Theologian in Residence at the Vancouver School of Theology in British Colombia, and the Carpenter Professor of Theology Emeritus at Vanderbilt Divinity School in Nashville, Tennessee. McFague is best known for her analysis of how metaphor is central to how one speaks about God. More recently, she has applied this approach in particular to ecological issues, writing extensively on care for Earth as if it were God's "body."

Rethinking Theology and Economy for a Planet in Peril (2001). In this book, she attempts to rectify what she refers to as the "inadequacies" present within *Super, Natural Christians.* She contends in *Life Abundant* that North American middle-class Christians need to try to live differently to better love nature, as well as think differently about themselves and who they are. However, by thinking differently, McFague explains she does not mean humans' "conscious, 'for publication' thoughts" about themselves, but rather what she calls the largely unconscious picture of who people are, because this silent partner most influences people's behavior and decisions.[29] That is, the current dominant American worldview (whose legacy, for McFague, can be traced back to the Protestant Reformation, the Enlightenment, and eighteenth-century economic theory) suggests Americans have the right to happiness, especially the happiness of a consumer-style "abundant life."[30] Moreover, she believes men and women are told they are consumers with a life goal of making money. McFague admits that a more thorough analysis of the role of economics, more specifically the assumptions and results of a consumer-oriented economic theory, needs to accompany any analysis of how to better love nature. Without such analysis, middle-class Americans find difficulty in knowing or acknowledging

29. Sallie McFague, *Life Abundant: Rethinking Theology and Economy for a Planet in Peril* (Minneapolis: Fortress, 2001), xi.

30. Ibid.

that they live on a path unjust to others and unsustainable to the planet. McFague explains that the task she set out for herself in *Life Abundant* imagines another kind of abundant life, which requires reimagining the good life in just and sustainable ways or what she calls the "ecological economic model."[31] What, then, are some basic premises of McFague's ecological economic model?

For McFague, the focus of ecological economics is the well-being of the community, but what she means by *well-being* is as follows. Ecological economics is neither concerned with fulfilling the desires of persons (as in neoclassical economics) nor simply with humans. Rather, ecological economics concerns itself with community, justice, and sustainability. One of its primary claims then is that "we cannot survive (even to *be* greedy) unless we acknowledge our profound dependence on one another and on the earth."[32] In other words, human need encompasses more than human greed because humans are relational beings from the moment of conception. Therefore, ecological economics begins with the viability of the whole community and assumes the survival of all community members is necessary. McFague writes:

> Before all else the community must be able to survive (sustainability), which it can do only if all members have the use of its resources (distributive justice). Then, within these parameters, the allocation of resources among competing users can take place.[33]

She is stating that ecological economics is not value-free; it prefers the well-being and sustainability of the household and planet Earth.

Furthermore, as a human enterprise, ecological economics seeks to maximize the optimal functioning of the planet's gifts and services for everyone. As a result, ecological economics, first of all, provides a vision of how humans *ought to live* on planet Earth in light of the perceived reality of *where and how they live*. Given this, McFague argues humans need to reconceive themselves, that is, think differently about who they are. Among other things, they need to recognize that

31. Ibid., xii.

32. Ibid., 99.

33. Ibid., 100.

they have choices and that they belong to the earth or are embedded in nature. Ecological economics insists humans view themselves as inalienable members of the Earth community. At the same time, they must understand that the individual exists only within the community, and the community is composed of these individuals. As a result, the individual and the community are not in conflict with each other. They need and thrive on each other.[34]

In summary, the ecological economics model is concerned with individuals; however, that concern looks at the individual as always part of the community and claims, in fact, the individual cannot survive apart from the well-being of the community as a whole just as the whole cannot survive apart from the well-being of individuals. This is why, argues McFague, issues of sustainability and distributive justice precede any discussion of allocation of resources. The latter "is a decision made on the basis of what it takes to achieve a just and sustainable society."[35] According to ecological economics, the maintenance of a healthy community is the goal rather than simply the satisfaction of individual desires.

Nearly eight years later, however, the questions that haunted McFague at the close of *Life Abundant* have led to her most recent work, *A New Climate for Theology: God, the World, and Global Warming* (2008). This time around, McFague believes that the threat of global warming is quickly moving humanity further away from what many want, that is, a vision of the banquet at which all are invited to the table and at which all can experience an abundant life of justice and sustainability. McFague, therefore, sees the need now to do theology within the context of climate change. This means focusing on deconstructing and reconstructing two key doctrines: who humans are and who God is. Trying to deconstruct and then reconstruct who God is, for McFague, is a limited and linguistic task, but in her view, global warming "is the empirical evidence that different ways of envisioning ourselves and God are necessary."[36] So, how does McFague suggest humans reenvision themselves and God?

---

34. Ibid., 104.

35. Ibid., 105.

36. Sallie McFague, *A New Climate for Theology: God, the World, and Global Warming* (Minneapolis: Fortress, 2008), 3.

On the one hand, humans' need to reenvision themselves stems from humans acting according to who they think they are. Their unconscious and subconscious assumptions about who they are shape their behavior. For McFague, climate change and the consequences that follow from it demand humans not only live differently but also that they reshape their anthropology, that is, who they think they are. Thus, McFague speaks now in terms of an "ecological anthropology" relating this to her view that climate is the "broadest, deepest, most intricate system on earth" because it controls everything else such as water, land, the sun, food, and so on. That is, the "quality" of the space for humans and other life-forms all depends on climate. Humans must begin to rethink who they are, because global warming is illustrating that even the slightest change in Earth's temperature can place living creatures in jeopardy. "Regardless of where one lives on the earth, and regardless of one's status, everyone, and everything will be affected."[37] As a result, McFague believes humans are called to see themselves not as self-sufficient individuals who can barricade themselves in gated communities but as creatures (like all living things) dependent on a temperate global climate.

To bring about this shift in thinking, McFague argues that humans need to develop their ecological literacy. McFague explains that the latter is not some "newfangled secret knowledge" but more simply, a reminder of where humans come from and where they belong (from nature and in nature). One consequence of developing one's ecological literacy is discerning a functional creation story that can teach humans about themselves and their Earth. McFague believes the sciences provide them with such a story, and interestingly enough, it meshes well with the oldest and deepest Christian creation story. She writes,

> This theological story also asks us to broaden our perspective from 'the soul and God' to the whole earth: in Christian faith, the redeemer is also the creator. Hence, ecological theology is not a New Age fad; rather, it returns this tradition to its cosmological roots. God is God of all creatures.

37. Ibid., 48.

> We are not the only ones who matter: God cared for the sparrow and the lilies.[38]

This kind of refocusing of knowledge is not, according to McFague, sentimental nature worship. Rather, it is the recognition, rightly so, of the three contexts in which Christian theology has been and should be done: the cosmological (Earth as a whole), the political (the world of human oppression), and the psychological (the inner life of the individual).[39]

Related to this is another kind of shift in thinking that McFague believes is necessary given climate change, a shift from asking "why" and "where" kinds of questions about God to better articulating the most basic relationship between God and the world. She writes, "Christianity has traditionally been focused on the why questions rather than turning our eyes to the beauty, concrete details, processes, and uniqueness of our home, planet Earth."[40] For McFague then, it is necessary, given climate change, to pay more attention to the world humans inhabit. Among other things, it requires rethinking the issues of creation and providence in light of the world as internally related to God. It also means understanding Christian doctrines about creation and God's providence as "offshoots" of our deepest beliefs about the nature of God's relation to the world rather than as simply stand-alone doctrines. In other words, how humans understand God and the world directly shapes how they see their relationship. If humans believe God and the world are wholly other, then McFague believes they will see creation and providence in that light. However, if they believe God and the world are intrinsically intimate, they will understand creation and providence from within that perspective.[41]

CONCLUSION

As indicated at the start of this chapter, more can be said in reference to feminist theological responses to the environment. The aim of this

38. Ibid., 49.

39. Ibid.

40. Ibid., 62.

41. Ibid., 63.

chapter has been to introduce readers to three prominent voices in the field. However, talking about the relationship between theology and the environment is one thing and asking the more potent question, "How shall people live?" given the dialogue taking place between these two disciplines is an entirely different, albeit related-concern. In what follows, a brief look will be given at one particular group of women that is taking to heart the conversations taking place between those concerned with the environment and those who also profess a belief in the Christian God.

Meet the Green Sisters. Referred to as "green nuns," "eco-nuns," or "green sisters," these women religious merge two similar yet different worlds: the world of Catholicism and the world of environmentalism. As Sarah McFarland Taylor notes in her study, *Green Sisters: A Spiritual Ecology* (2007), green sisters all across the United States are beginning the ecological repair of planet Earth on communal land right in their own backyards.[42] Their commitment can appear somewhat simple, yet at the same time, one can already foresee change: these vowed women religious are taking on the challenge of committing themselves to addressing the most pressing environmental concerns confronting both human and nonhuman life today. The green sisters movement is now expanding globally into such areas as Australia, Ireland, the Philippines, the Netherlands, Peru, and Africa. In North America, they are building new "earth ministries" and finding more ecologically friendly ways of reinhabiting their communal lands.

For example, some sisters are replacing the sod that envelops many of their motherhouses with community-supported organic gardens to engage in "sacred agriculture" and "contemplative gardening." Others are building alternative housing structures and hermitages from renewable materials such as straw bales, rammed earth, and cob materials instead of traditional forest products. Everywhere across the United States, composting toilets, solar panels for heating, and solar ovens for cooking are springing up. Other green sisters are placing their community lands into land trusts or creating wildlife sanctuaries on their properties. Some of the more daring disrupt

---

42. Sarah McFarland Taylor, *Green Sisters: A Spiritual Ecology* (Cambridge, MA: Harvard University Press, 2007).

shareholder meetings of corporate polluters and locally contest the construction of garbage incinerators, genetically modified organisms, and irradiated food. Moreover, many are developing "green" liturgies that strive to honor the entire life of the community. Creating ecological learning centers, community-supported farms, and other kinds of earth ministries, more than fifty of these centers and ministries are now active in the United States and Canada. Although the bulk of these ministries are located either in the Midwest or on the East Coast, every region of the United States is represented today, as well as some parts of Canada.

In conclusion, the Green Sisters are one small example of religiously committed people actively seeking to put into practice what Ruether, Johnson, and McFague each writes, about in her own unique way: how can one begin to bridge the divide between theological claims about God, creation, and humanity's place within God's creation, with today's understanding of the inner workings of nature and the changes that are already taking place in the natural environment. As all three authors indicate in their work, feminist theologians have a stake in helping bridge this divide, because at times doctrinal claims about God, creation, and the human person have fostered not only the domination of nature but also women. Ruether, Johnson, and McFague each in their own way advocate for both intellectual and practical change, that is, a change in self-consciousness (Ruether and Johnson) or a shift in sensibility (McFague) and a transformation in how one approaches one's daily living practices. Regarding the latter claim, all three authors agree that changes in personal and communal behavior are a priority, whether one is advocating for ecojustice (Ruether), ecological theology (Johnson), or ecological economics (McFague). How these changes play out on the ground will differ locally, regionally, and nationally among differing communities and geographic regions. Nevertheless, as Johnson indicates strongly in her work, the Christian command to love one's neighbor as oneself must be expanded to include all of creation. Moreover, given McFague's poignant claim regarding the necessity of theology now to be done within the context of climate change, every person and every living thing on Earth has a stake in finding a new way of approaching love of God and love of creation.

QUESTIONS FOR REVIEW

1. What would an adequate understanding of ecofeminism look like, given Ruether's concerns and theological commitments?
2. According to Ruether, how is the Hebrew creation story in Genesis 1–3 an example of sexism and ecological exploitation working hand in hand? In addition, how does she think Saint Augustine's commentaries on these stories add to the already existing levels of patriarchal domination of women?
3. Johnson suggests that there are two storylines operating when it comes to what is transpiring on Earth, one of "wonder" and one of "waste" and "distress." What are some of the features of each?
4. What connection does Johnson see operating between instances of social injustice throughout the world and ecological devastation?
5. Johnson suggests exploring the notion of divine presence through three different yet overlapping rubrics. Give a brief description of each rubric.
6. How does Johnson's view of divine agency contrast with the view of some scientists and religious adherents of "intelligent design"?
7. What does McFague mean by "ecological economics"? Describe any local, regional, national, or international examples of the term.
8. Why does McFague think it is important to develop one's ecological literacy? How does this relate to her understanding of the Christian creation story?
9. How is the threat of climate change leading McFague to reconceive her understanding of ecological economics? What is the new term she wants to use?

IN-DEPTH QUESTIONS

1. Ruether insists that ecofeminism must challenge the view of the self that operates in Christian thought. Do you agree? Why or why not?

2. According to Johnson, people of faith must begin to evaluate the morality of their actions based on whether they contribute to "a sustainable life community on Earth." Do you agree? Why or why not? How would one begin to evaluate one's actions given Johnson's request?
3. Do you think Ruether would agree with McFague when McFague argues that the most recent scientific story of creation "meshes well with the oldest and deepest Christian creation story"?
4. All three authors suggest that humans must begin the process of rethinking how they think about themselves and view themselves in relation to God and creation. Is this approach adequate? What are its strengths? Weaknesses?

CHAPTER 14

GREEN SOLIDARITY:
Liberation Theology, the Ecological Crisis, and the Poor

Kathryn Lilla Cox

KEY TERMS

ecology
environment
liberation theology
Second Vatican Council
structural sin
social ecology

INTRODUCTION

This book discusses various aspects surrounding the connection between creation and ethics and, specifically what has become, in the eyes of many, an ecological crisis. One population profoundly affected by this crisis is the poor. This chapter explores that effect, and also what a theological movement known as liberation theology has had to say about it. The chapter begins with a brief discussion of poverty, and then uses stories to connect poverty and environmental degradation, explains the origins of liberation theology and its theological foundations, and finally, examines the contributions of a few liberation theologians in helping readers think about caring for creation and transforming poverty.

A few caveats are in order before beginning this exploration. First, poverty has different faces, and the context can and does influence how poverty manifests itself and a community's response to it. Second, while the chapter uses the term *liberation theology* in a particular way, this term has many meanings. It frequently is used to refer to theology written from the context of Latin America. However, liberation theology also functions as an umbrella term for various theological approaches concerned with exploring how theology can address various types of oppression and bring about change in the world. Issues related to gender, race, culture, and sexuality are examined in theological approaches classified as feminist, mujerista, womanist, black, Asian, African, GLBT (gay, lesbian, bisexual, and transgendered), and environmental, to name a few.[1] In many instances, theologians writing in the area of liberation theology have overlapping concerns. For example, Ivone Gebara, a Brazilian theologian, is concerned with the intersection of women's oppression, poverty, the destruction of creation, and human views of race and culture. This chapter will focus on poverty and theological responses from Latin America, that is, Latin American liberation theology. Third, given the first two caveats, this chapter could be considered as one possible introduction to an area within theology that one could study for a lifetime.

POVERTY

What comes to mind when someone says "poverty"? Do you think of material poverty, spiritual poverty, or some other type of poverty? *Poverty* can be defined in many ways. It can mean a "deficiency, dearth, scarcity; smallness of amount." For example, a person could have a dearth of kindness and a lack of compassion or be in need of spiritual resources. *Poverty* also may be defined as "the condition of having little or no wealth or few material possessions; indigence, destitution"[2]; in other words, *poverty* can be understood as economic or material poverty. One might also consider ecological and environmental poverty: a scarcity of the environmental conditions necessary for human flourishing. These types of poverty—economic and ecological—have varying faces around the world—what is poor in

1. Alfred Hennelly, SJ, *Liberation Theologies: the Global Pursuit of Justice* (Mystic, CT: Twenty-Third Publications, 1995).

2. *Oxford English Dictionary*, "Poverty." Online version, *http://www.oed.com,* accessed April 14, 2011.

North America might be wealthy in Southeast Asia or parts of Latin America. Even in the United States, poverty can be relative to the region in which one lives, because similar salaries do not go as far in, say, New York City as they would in rural Montana or Mississippi.

Despite these general differences, the economically and environmentally poor exist on every settled continent. In the past, scholars divided the world into the developed world (first-world country) and the developing world (second- and third-world). It was often assumed that the first world was wealthy, the third world poor, with the second world somewhere in between. However, growing globalization and an increasing global gap between the rich and poor has caused some theological scholars to begin shifting their perspective. Rather than speak just of first-, second-, and third-world nations, scholars are now discussing a global north and south, while recognizing that many nations have their material elite and their poor.[3] Nonetheless, extreme poverty afflicts certain regions of the globe more than others. As a result, there exists both a local and a global aspect to questions surrounding how the ecological crisis affects the world's poor.

POVERTY AND ENVIRONMENTAL DEGRADATION: A FEW STORIES

Film

The 2008 movie *Slumdog Millionaire*, set in Mumbai, India, tells the story of Jamal Malik, a young man from the slums, who wins a game show. During a series of flashbacks, the viewer receives a window into Jamal's life and the poverty in which millions like him live. In one scene, Jamal uses a primitive latrine and subsequently falls into the human waste himself. In other scenes, children scrounge garbage heaps for food and other "reusable" materials. This kind of poverty is inconceivable for many in developed countries, who take indoor plumbing and grocery stores for granted. They might cringe as these scenes—one hopes—expand their horizons and challenge

3. Leonardo Boff and Virgil Elizondo, eds. *Ecology and Poverty: Cry of the Earth, Cry of the Poor* (London; Maryknoll, NY: SCM Pr; Orbis, 1995); David G. Hallman, ed. *Ecotheology: Voices from South and North* (Maryknoll, NY: Orbis, 1994).

their worldviews. The film can raise many questions, as well: How does living in and around a garbage heap affect a person's long-term health? How is the usable water supply affected by the open, public toilet system? How does one's comparatively comfortable life in the United States or in another similarly developed country contribute to the economic poverty in India?

Personal Experience

In mid-August 1990, I finished orientation for the Jesuit Volunteer Corps and traveled with my five housemates for our upcoming volunteer year in Camden, New Jersey. We had just spent a week in the Blue Ridge Mountains of Pennsylvania, surrounded by mountains, trails, trees, and wildflowers, breathing fresh, crisp air, admiring the vast span of stars at night, while preparing for the next twelve months. As we entered Camden, located just across the river from Philadelphia, we were greeted with the sight of its poverty—concrete, little vegetation, burned-out houses, vacant lots, graffiti—and an odor like none I had smelled before. In the humid summer, the city reeked of rotting food and decaying organic matter. The stench permeated everything as it emanated from a nearby waste disposal plant that burned waste. The type of day—hot and humid or cold and dry—and the prevailing winds determined how much one noticed the smell. Yes, the plant kept waste out of the landfills and created some jobs for an impoverished community. However, it did not beautify the city or contribute to a healthy lifestyle. Instead, it contributed to the city's poor air, which often resulted in increased asthma, burning eyes, irritated lungs, and an inability to be outside for the city's residents.

The olfactory introduction to Camden and subsequent experiences with its residents over the year—people whose asthma or simple breathing were made more difficult on the days the plant operated or received more trucked-in waste—led to my first nontheoretical conversion and also two insights related to this chapter. One, our environment matters. Two, environmental concerns and concerns about poverty intersect. Furthermore, people with money, political power, or connections can keep facilities such as waste incinerators out of their neighborhoods, inflicting them instead on other, poorer communities.

Current Events

In November 2008, the public television program *NewsHour with Jim Lehrer* ran a story about a dispute between local farmers and a Coca-Cola plant in Rajasthan, an Indian state. The dispute centered on Coca-Cola's use of ground water to make its product. The local farmers in this arid state said Coca-Cola was responsible for lowering the water table faster than the normal rate and for polluting the water. A decreased and polluted water supply had ramifications for the farmers, as they drew from the same water reservoir as the Coca-Cola plant. Less groundwater meant less water for crops, potentially affecting yields, while polluted water meant less drinking water. This story highlights the connection among local environmental and ecological concerns, the global economy, and the ability to provide food for one's community. Coca-Cola needs water to make its product, which it hopes to sell at a profit around the world. The farmers need the water to grow their crops, for food both to eat and to sell. This story raises questions about the relationship between international corporations and local communities that might have different goals. Which goals take priority—those of the local community or the international corporation? What would a responsible use of the water supply look like in Rajasthan?[4]

Hope and a Model of Transformation

Wangari Maathai, the 2004 Nobel Peace Prize winner, founded the Green Belt Movement in Kenya in 1977. Her purpose was to begin breaking the links among poverty, environmental degradation, and people's despair. Maathai saw the relationship among deforestation, poor soil for planting due to soil runoff when rain fell, poor water quality in the rivers, and hunger. Working primarily with local women, she began by planting trees to help hold topsoil in place. With more topsoil in place, farming is possible, and with reduced soil runoff, rivers run cleaner. Biodiversity increases. As land and water are rejuvenated, people can grow food, hunger diminishes, and health improves. This return to health and wholeness in turn leads to less

4. PBS, *NewsHour*, "Water Wars," December 2008, *http://www.pbs.org/newshour/bb/asia/july-dec08/waterwars_11-17.html*, accessed March 1, 2010.

IMAGE © MICHELINE PELLETIER/CORBIS

Kenyan environmentalist and human rights campaigner Wangari Maathai was awarded the Nobel Peace Prize in 2004, "for her contribution to sustainable development, democracy and peace." In 1977, she founded the "Green Belt Movement" where, for nearly thirty years, she mobilized poor women to plant thirty million trees. She was the first African woman to win this prize. In this 2004 photo, she is pictured with militants of the Green Belt Movement. Maathai died Sept. 25, 2011.

conflict over scarce resources. Maathai also recognized that empowering people to transform where they live is crucial, because then they become invested in, and take ownership of, the projects. Therefore, from the beginning of her project she engaged local women's help.[5]

LIBERATION THEOLOGY: ORIGINS, AIMS, PURPOSES, AND THEOLOGICAL GROUNDING

Clodovis and Leonardo Boff point out that "in Latin America . . . there have always been movements of liberation since the early days of the Spanish and Portuguese conquests."[6] While this may be true, Gustavo Gutiérrez (b. 1928), a Peruvian priest and theologian,

5. Wangari Maathai, *Unbowed: A Memoir* (New York: Alfred A. Knopf, 2006).

6. Leonardo and Clodovis Boff, *Introducing Liberation Theology*, trans. Paul Burns (Maryknoll, NY: Orbis, 1987), 6.

is considered the father of contemporary Latin American liberation theology. His book *A Theology of Liberation: History, Politics, Salvation* (1971) has been pivotal in raising global awareness about Latin American liberation theology, as well as the poor's plight in that region of the world. Additionally, a gathering of Catholic bishops in Medellín Colombia, is historically important in the development of liberation theology. The Catholic bishops of Latin America met in Medellín, in 1968, less than three years after the close of the Second Vatican Council. They produced a series of documents that—reading the signs of the times in their countries—called for changes in political structures and sought to make the Christian gospel message more relevant in addressing the needs of the poor. The plan was to develop a theology premised on pastoral concerns and Christian action.[7] In other words, there was a concerted effort and desire to bring theology and social concerns together at three levels: local, national, and international.[8]

Theological Grounding

The Judeo-Christian Scriptures, through many narratives, say that believers are to be concerned with and care for the poor and marginalized. Therefore, many Christians feed the hungry, clothe the naked, visit the imprisoned, and provide other aid to the poor. However, liberation theologians argue that feeding, housing, and clothing the poor with little or no attention to correcting the underlying causes for their poverty is insufficient.[9] Liberation theologians advocate a changed relationship with the poor that should affect the behaviors and practices by the nonpoor and should transform unjust worldly structures into just ones. This transformation of structures can begin with the recognition that poverty is not solely the result of individual action. Rather, one must acknowledge the interplay between individual actions and societal structures, institutions, and processes. Therefore, to address poverty at its roots means a multipronged approach must address all aspects of the problem. For Christians, attention to this interplay of individual and communal causes of

7. Ibid., 66–77; Philip Berryman, "Latin American Liberation Theology," *Theological Studies* 34 no. 3 (1973): 357, 364.

8. Berryman, "Latin American Liberation Theology," 357, 364.

9. Boff, *Introducing Liberation Theology*, 22–42.

poverty ultimately requires Christians to propose courses of action premised on moving from "what is" to "what could be."

Theologically, the foundation for this transformation, or conversion, is scriptural. Jesus Christ preached and lived from his belief in the coming kingdom of God, whereby one sees evidence in the present of this new heaven and new Earth. In seeking to inaugurate the kingdom of God, Jesus did not take a top-down approach to his ministry. Rather, the Gospels witness repeatedly to a Jesus who speaks to and heals the leper, the crippled, and the blind; who eats with and converses with the outcast, the marginalized, and the sinner; and who challenges the rich to give away what they own to follow him. Jesus is in solidarity with the marginalized people of his day.

Liberation theologians challenge Christians today to identify the marginalized, oppressed, and outcast in societies and then be in solidarity with them in a manner like Jesus. Jesus' solidarity with the poor should frame Christian attempts to live the gospel message. Solidarity requires more than simply "helping" the poor. Feeding the hungry and clothing the naked should not be the final goal; instead, these are the first measures toward changing a system. Many liberation theologians argue that because the poor are the most affected by distortions in political and economic systems, they are in the unique position of understanding what most needs changing and ways to accomplish this change. The poor are meant to be agents in this worldly transformation, advocates for what they need and how change can be implemented. In other words, the oppressed and dispossessed should be present and have a voice at policymaking tables; they should be empowered so that they can be the agents of their own lives and enact their moral agency by teaching others. The challenge for those in power is recognizing when the adage "teach a man to fish" needs recasting as "ask a man how he would fish" or "say to a man, 'teach us how you would fish.'" In sum, liberation theologians recognize the interconnectedness among people and want to eliminate the systems of oppression that lock people into cycles of poverty and hunger. When people are given the basic necessities to survive, they can be honored and respected as creative agents that contribute to the broader society.[10]

---

10. Leonardo Boff, *Ecology and Liberation: A New Paradigm,* trans. John Cumming, (Maryknoll, NY: Orbis, 1995), 95.

Clodovis and Leonardo Boff articulate three basic theological ideas, in addition to the kingdom of God motif, that lie behind liberation theology: compassion, the Suffering Servant—Jesus Christ, and reflection on faith leading to action. The Boffs define *compassion* as "suffering with another." Given the focus of this chapter, *suffering with another* means "entering into the situational reality of the starving, homeless, and others on society's margins and more deeply understanding what poverty entails." Suffering with the marginalized entails following the Suffering Servant who is Jesus. The Boffs believe the ability to follow the Suffering Servant springs from one's spirituality. Theology that advocates for social justice has as its counterpart prayer, contemplation, and introspection. However, this prayerful reflection on one's faith is not primarily for the individual's edification but should also be when God draws one's attention to the world's suffering, a suffering that demands response. According to the Boffs, "In the light of faith, Christians see in them [the poor and oppressed] the challenging face of the Suffering Servant, Jesus Christ." Referencing Matthew 25:31–46, they argue for action that raises the Crucified to life. This Gospel pericope dares the listener to see Jesus in the hungry, naked, and imprisoned. Connecting this passage to the suffering of Jesus can call one to ask, Where is God working today? Where can suffering be transformed into new life? Who are the crucified and suffering ones? Stated differently, this brief reflection on the Suffering Servant is an example of how Christians are called to be inspired and challenged by Scripture and their faith to help make Jesus' good news relevant to today's world.[11] How does one carry out the mission of the gospel in this historical era? Because Christians believe in a God who acts in and through history, a God who chose to become Incarnate and enter history, this question is relevant.

According to the Boff brothers, the challenge to make the gospel relevant today is not just the responsibility of professional theologians but also of every Christian. However, how Christians understand this task depends on their social location. Liberation theology is carried out in three interconnected arenas: professional, pastoral, and popular.

11. Boff, *Introducing Liberation Theology*, 6–8.

The professional sphere is the arena of the academic theologian, the professor, and the teacher. The pastoral arena comprises pastoral ministers, religious sisters and brothers, and priests. The popular sphere is made up of those in the communities seeking liberation.[12] Although the members of the communities seeking liberation are often the poor and oppressed, this does not mean that a middle-class Christian has no responsibility to advocate for liberation. All Christians have a role to play in living out the gospel message of liberation and salvation; responsibility, obligation, and conversion lie with everyone. It is possible to argue that one does not fit the categories outlined by the Boff brothers and, therefore, to say these concerns do not affect him or her. Yet, Christianity argues that what affects one in the Body of Christ, affects all.

Juan Luis Segundo (1925–1996), a Jesuit priest from Uruguay, highlighted the role of the middle class in advocating for social change in a 1985 lecture at Regis College, Toronto. In this lecture, Segundo argued that historically the seeds of liberation theology, as it eventually became known, were simultaneously being sown in various countries and places within Latin America even before the Second Vatican Council. He notes that documents such as *Gaudium et spes* (the Church in the Modern World) were "used afterwards as an official support for the main views of this liberation theology."[13] According to Segundo, during the 1960s and 1970s, one place where seeds were being sown was in the university. The university, which asked the university student to be a thinker and analyzer of structures, cultures, and ideologies, helped facilitate liberation theology. Christian students examined how they understood their Christianity in relation to the ideologies of the culture. As a result of this analysis a few insights emerged for some Christian students in Latin American universities: (a) they recognized how their privilege made them oppressors, even if unintentionally; (b) the current structures supported their interests; (c) various ways they comprehended and lived their faith impeded their growing desire to advocate for liberation of the poor and marginalized; and (d) there was

12. Ibid., 11–21.

13. Juan Luis Segundo, "The Shift within Latin American Theology," *Journal of Theology for Southern Africa,* no. 52 (S, 1985), 17–29.

a need to find a way to incorporate the "new theological vision of faith" to "engage a new type of Christian commitment to liberation, even against their own material interests and privileges."[14] Thus, Segundo claims, some of the initial thrusts of liberation theology began with the middle-class university students. Those with privilege and economic security let the lives of the poor affect and change their operating framework for engaging the world and for understanding the connection among Christian faith, spirituality, and action in the world.

For systems that oppress and disenfranchise some persons to be disassembled, the poor need to be empowered to claim their moral agency and voice, while those with privilege need to recognize and convert their hearts and actions. This can be a tough challenge for both the middle class and the wealthy. Jesus states that it is easier for a camel to pass through the eye of a needle than for a rich person to enter the kingdom of heaven (see Matthew 19:24). The particular challenge this scripture poses for the middle class is to ask which perspective they take—are they poorer than the materially wealthy or richer than the materially poor?

Theological Challenges for Liberation Theology

If the initial waves of liberation theology appeared in the 1960s and 1970s, where is it today in the first decade of the twenty-first century? Often Latin American liberation theology is associated with Catholic theologians, although it is and has been an ecumenical endeavor from the start.

Within Catholic circles, the latter half of the twentieth century saw various pronouncements from the Vatican office of the Congregation of the Doctrine of the Faith (CDF) that have criticized aspects of liberation theology, in general, and more specifically, the work of particular theologians. The CDF in some instances has approved ecclesial sanctions or theological correction of a theologian's work. See, for example, the 1984 "Instruction on Certain Aspects of the Theology of Liberation," and the notification issued by the CDF in 2007 regarding Christological errors

14. Ibid., 21.

JOSÉ MÍGUEZ BONINO

José Míguez Bonino was born in March 1924 in Argentina. His family was Methodist, and he became an ordained minister in 1949. He received theological training in both Argentina and the United States. Bonino was copresident of the World Council of Churches (WCC) between 1975 and 1983. His research and writing engages Trinitarian theology, Christianity and Marxism, theology and politics, historical theology, analysis of Roman Catholic social teaching, and liberation theology. Like other liberation theologians, Míguez Bonino worked with the poor and oppressed, was politically active, and put his life at risk during times of political persecution.

that the CDF reports are in the work of Jesuit liberation theologian Jon Sobrino.[15]

One common misconception is that because the CDF has sanctioned theologians or critiqued aspects of liberation theology, one can ignore or dismiss it as a viable theological option. However, despite their critique and sanction of particular theologians, the CDF and other Vatican offices have advocated for the preferential option for the poor and have, in some instances, critiqued certain types of economic and political structures. In fact, Pope John Paul II in various encyclicals spoke against the abuses of both capitalism and communism and stressed the need to examine how economic systems exploit humans and damage human dignity. More recently, Pope Benedict XVI, in *Caritas in veritate* (Love in Truth), looks at charity, truth, and love, as well as at distortions in economic systems that lead to hunger, death, and a decrease in human dignity. He affirms that Christians have a moral obligation to be concerned with the effects of their economic systems, locally and globally, on the poor within their midst and with whom they are connected internationally.

15. Both documents can be found on the Vatican's Web site at *www.vatican.va*.

MAGISTERIAL, ECUMENICAL, AND INTERFAITH REFERENCES

See Pope John Paul II's address for the World Day of Peace 1990, "The Ecological Crisis: A Common Responsibility," in *And God Saw That It Was Good: Catholic Theology and the Environment*, eds. Drew Christiansen and Walter Grazer, (Washington DC: United States Catholic Conference, 1996), 215–216. Other Christian denominations and religions have also issued various statements on care of creation and Earth. Many of these statements can be found on GreenFaith: Interfaith Partners for the Environment Web site: *www.greenfaith.org*. Harvard University's forum on Religion and Ecology is also a good resource for interfaith work on the environment, see *www.emergingearthcommunity.orgforum-on-religion-and-ecology*. Finally, Earth Ministry is a nonprofit organization, whose mission is to help foster the Christian community's environmental stewardship. In addition to their ecumenical work, they perform interfaith work. See *www.earthministry.org*.

John Paul II and Benedict XVI are referenced here to support the claim that while expressed differently and in a different format, many of the issues and concerns raised by Latin American liberation theology can also be found in some writings of the two most recent Catholic popes. Furthermore, support for the issues and concerns highlighted by liberation theology can be found in Catholic social teaching—especially teaching surrounding human dignity, economic justice, and the preferential option for the poor (see chapter 12 for more information on these themes).

CARING FOR CREATION, TRANSFORMING POVERTY

Liberation theologians over the decades have expanded how they define the poor, oppressed, and marginalized to include the voices of the indigenous peoples of Latin American and elsewhere, women, and creation. This section will explore more directly how liberation theologians argue that the preferential option for the poor cannot be severed from concerns about creation. A few caveats are in order: First, the concern for the connection between the preferential option for the poor and ecological issues must be contextualized because different homes (places) have different ecological needs and poverty concerns. Second, even though there are many Latin American theologians who address the connection between poverty and ecological concerns, time and space necessitate limiting such a discussion. Therefore, this section will feature the work of Leonardo Boff. Of the "fathers of liberation theology," Leonardo Boff, a Brazilian theologian, has looked most directly at the links between how humans care for Earth and how they try to eliminate poverty. He does this in two major books, *Ecology and Liberation: A New Paradigm* (1995) and *Cry of the Earth, Cry of the Poor* (1997). Boff wants readers to recognize that humans are deeply connected to, and dependent on, their environment. He uses the term *social ecology* to illuminate the reality that humans are not outside of the ecological web of relationships studied by scientists but that their history is tied with how they treat each other and the planet.[16] For example, Boff asserts that the destruction of Earth and local environments affects humans. Polluted water can lead to disease; polluted air creates smog, making breathing difficult; and poisoned soil yields poisoned food.

As a consequence of inadequate care, Boff contends in *Cry of the Earth, Cry of the Poor,* the "earth is ill." For Boff, as a Brazilian, this means that the Amazon is ill. Images of the Amazon often vividly portray the lush foliage and vegetation, the brightly colored, exotic-looking animals, and the pristine-looking waters. Other pictures, however, showcase soil erosion, burning vegetation, brown, muddied waters from soil runoff, and barren abandoned land, not to mention vast crowds of impoverished people; absent from these photos will be the plants, animals, insects, and birds that have disappeared. The fragile equilibrium in the Amazon is easily disrupted because the Amazon ecology requires interconnectedness among the diversity of life forms to prevent soil erosion. The soil is suited to certain types

16. Boff, *Ecology and Liberation*, 88.

IMAGE © GUENTERMANAUS/SHUTTERSTOCK.COM

A destroyed tropical rainforest in Amazonia

of vegetation and other life forms, such as fungi, all of which help hold the soil in place. If someone changes one piece of the Amazon ecological web without understanding all the ripple effects, devastation results. Humans are not separate from, or outside of, their habitats. Rather, as Boff argues, they need to see themselves as a part of an ecological habitat, whereby they work in the best interest of the whole.[17]

Boff gives examples of different types of explorations and economic development projects in the Amazon that have failed and wrought various forms of ecological and personal destruction. These projects include the 1967 attempt by American billionaire Daniel Ludwig to farm rice and soybeans, raise cattle, and transplant African trees to manufacture wood pulp; and the 1975 attempt to raise cattle by a company established by Volkswagen of Brazil. Both projects failed because they destroyed the delicate ecological balance of the Amazon by clear-cutting land, and bringing in trees, crops, and animals not suited to the soil or climate of the region.[18] The project designers did not work with the forest, they worked against

17. Leonardo Boff, *Cry of the Earth, Cry of the Poor*, trans. Phillip Berryman, (Maryknoll, NY: Orbis, 1997), 104–139.

18. Ibid., 89–92.

it. They ignored the ecosystem in place by trying to transplant an ecosystem from another part of the globe and failed. The result was soil erosion, loss of forest habitat, a decreased food yield, an increase in rates of poverty among certain segments of the population, and the disappearance of certain indigenous communities. In addition to the two projects just noted, Boff catalogues the destruction caused by roads carved through the Amazon, trees cut for lumber, hydroelectric projects like the Balbina dam built near Manaus, and various mining operations for minerals and precious metals that raze the forest while poisoning the air, water, and soil.[19] Local and international monies fund the various projects; thus, the global community is complicit in the Amazon's destruction.

Even though there are political and economic reasons facilitating the Amazon's ecological devastation, Christianity also bears some responsibility for the ecological crisis. This responsibility is well documented elsewhere. However, Christianity also teaches that destruction of Earth is a sin against God's creation. Boff looks at three resources within Christianity to address the crisis and help humans envision a changed relationship with Earth that welcomes and protects the created world's diversity.[20] First, the second creation story in the first chapter of the book of Genesis includes the image of God as creator of all, supporting the insight that Earth belongs first and foremost to God not to humanity. Therefore, humans are simply caretakers of a gift that, if well cared for, will sustain humanity. Second, Christian belief in the triune God (the Trinity) draws attention to the relationality of life and the coexistence of all humans and all creation. This insight lends support to the contention that humans are not at the top of an ecological system but are imbedded in a web of relationships. What humans do affects other aspects of the ecosystem. Third, the Christian exemplar Francis of Assisi functions as a model for his time in integrating love for the poor, oppressed, and marginalized—human and all creation.[21]

To elaborate on this third point, Francis of Assisi exemplifies the "spirit that acts in kinship, one that is filled with compassion

19. Ibid., 89–103.

20. Boff, *Ecology and Liberation*, 55–78.

21. Boff, *Cry of the Earth*, 140–220.

and respect before each representative of the cosmic and planetary community."[22] Francis also illustrates how one can connect one's inner and outer ecologies. For Francis, humans' inner ecology refers to their spirituality. Their outer ecology refers to their participation in a variety of relationships. Christian spirituality, faith, and actions must be integrated toward health and wholeness. This integration is with other humans and with all creation.[23] Humans depend on the rest of creation for their lives. Careful cultivation and use of the rest of creation are crucial because of creation's inherent sacredness and because its destruction is also inevitably humans' destruction. Key to this cultivation is the need to listen and learn from those who might have overlooked sources of wisdom and knowledge for ecological sustainability, such as the indigenous peoples of the Amazon forest.[24]

Working in the Amazon—Sister Dorothy Stang

Dorothy Stang was a Sister of Notre Dame de Namur, born in 1931. Although born in the United States, she initially served as a missionary to Brazil and eventually "became a naturalized Brazilian in order to be more radically dedicated to the people." Her work began in the Brazilian state of Maranhão and ended in the Amazonian region of Pará, more specifically Anapu. She was involved in the Sustainable Development Project. This project "aims basically to cultivate 20 percent of the land and to preserve 80 percent as forest" while "respecting its incalculable biodiversity, with extractive cultivation and increasing the native species of trees that produce fruits and other harvests." Stang worked with and advocated for the natives of the forest and their way of living. The forest provided food and sustenance, and the people integrated themselves into the ecosystem. This way of life clashed with the "agri-business project, concerned with exporting timber, minerals, meat, and soya."[25] It was

22. Ibid., 204.

23. Ibid., 216–219.

24. Ibid., 98.

25. Luiz Carlos Susin, "Sister Dorothy Stang: A Model of Holiness and Martyrdom," in *Eco-Theology*, eds. Elaine Wainwright, Luiz Carlos Susin, and Felix Wilfred, (London: SCM Press, 2009), 109–113, at 110–111.

this work with the poor and the Sustainable Development Project that led to Stang's death on February 12, 2005, when two hired gunmen murdered her. She was not the first to be murdered for her work in this area, and she will probably not be the last, as the work to bring sustainable development to the Amazon continues. However, she continues to inspire the people she worked with and stands as a witness to the need to care for all creation with her love of God that manifested itself in her love for "the people and the forest, biodiversity and justice."[26]

CONCLUSION

Though most of this chapter focused on liberation theology and its proponents' attention to the economic, material poverty in the world, the awareness that poverty and ecological destruction are connected is increasing. One valuable insight from liberation theology is that one's location influences what one perceives about reality, the way things work in the world. A single perspective is not enough for addressing issues and concerns and for implementing transformative change. If humans truly want to understand the implications of their work, inventions, and ecological and environmental policies, they need to speak with and listen to a broad cross section of people, especially the poor and the oppressed—indeed the very people who are often most at risk and affected by environmental threats and degradation of creation. Humans need to see fellow humans—the poor, the vulnerable, the ones who look and speak differently from them—as their brothers and sisters. Boff follows Francis of Assisi and argues that humans need to see Earth and all its creatures as their brothers and sisters.[27] When they can do this, then they can begin to listen to how their actions affect others and begin to create policy that does not privilege one way of life or one set of lives over another. Lastly, liberation theology illuminates once again that faith and spirituality have implications for how one lives and acts in the world.

---

26. Susin, "Sister Dorothy Stang: A Model of Holiness and Martyrdom," 113. For more information, see the official Web site for the Dorothy Stang Center at *http://www.dorothystang.org/index.html*, accessed April 14, 2011.

27. Boff, *Cry of the Earth*, 213–219.

QUESTIONS FOR REVIEW

1. How would you define liberation theology after reading this chapter?
2. In the 1960s and 1970s, what was the primary focus of Latin American liberation theology?
3. What theological motifs do liberation theologians use to argue that Christians have a responsibility to advocate for and be in solidarity with the marginalized of society?
4. Why does Leonardo Boff make the connection between the human poor and the rest of creation as poor?

IN-DEPTH QUESTIONS

1. How does material poverty manifest itself in your community?
2. How is the environment in your area "ill"? What evidence can you provide of the ecological devastation in your community?
3. Is there a connection between the material poverty and the ecological destruction in your community? Why do you think this is or is not the case?
4. How would you begin helping heal the sick environment where you live?
5. Have you had any experiences with poverty that have changed the way you see the world or your faith? How did your actions change because of this experience? Please explain.
6. If you saw *Slumdog Millionaire,* what was your reaction to the film? Did your view of the connection between poverty and ecological degradation change because of the film? Explain.
7. How would you begin addressing structural sin in your community or the connection between ecological destruction and poverty?
8. What can you learn from other religions about care for creation? Visit one of the Web sites listed in the sidebar on page 278 to find information.

INSIGHTS FROM OTHER RELIGIONS

CHAPTER 15

Judaism and the Care for God's Creation

Hava Tirosh-Samuelson

CHAPTER 16

Greater than the Creation of Mankind (*Qur'an* 40:57):
Creation as the Divine Signature in *Qur'anic* and Sufi Revelation

June-Ann Greeley

CHAPTER 17

Why Does the Buddha Close His Eyes in My Eden?
A Buddhist Ecological Challenge
and Invitation to Christians

David Clairmont

CHAPTER 15

JUDAISM AND THE CARE FOR GOD'S CREATION

Hava Tirosh-Samuelson

KEY TERMS

Torah
rabbinic Judaism
Sukkot
festival of Tu B'shvat
Kabbalah
Hasidism
teshuvah
Eco-Kosher
Tikkun Olam

INTRODUCTION

The literary sources of Judaism—the Bible, the Mishnah, the Babylonian and Jerusalem Talmuds, Jewish philosophy, kabbalah and Hasidism, and modern Jewish thought—have much to say about the natural world and about humanity's obligation to care for God's creation. Although the Bible allows humans to use natural resources to benefit themselves, it sets specific limits on the use of natural resources, forbids wanton destruction, and spells out how to care for God's creatures. The concern for nature and respect for its inviolability characterize Jewish environmental ethics of responsibility, which sees a causal link between the moral and religious quality of human life and the well-being of the natural world. Throughout its long evolution under changing historical circumstances, the Jewish tradition has articulated deep ecological concerns that could inspire conservation policies and a distinctive Jewish ecotheology.[1]

THE PRINCIPLES OF JEWISH ENVIRONMENTAL ETHICS

The Hebrew Bible is the literary evidence of ancient Israelite religion and the canonic scripture of Judaism. It also reflects the agrarian conditions of ancient Israel,[2] even though the priests and scribes who composed it were not themselves farmers. The biblical text came into existence in a complex editorial process that lasted several centuries (roughly from the seventh century BCE to the first century CE). During the Second Temple Period (516 BCE–70 CE), even though the Jerusalem Temple functioned as the political, spiritual, and administrative center of the Jewish people in the land of Israel, the Jews came to accept the Bible as their canonic text, regarding it as divinely revealed. Thus, the Bible shaped the collective identity and culture of the Jewish people through ongoing interpretation, adaptation, and application to changing historical circumstances.

The biblical narrative of creation is the basis of Jewish attitudes toward the natural world. The book of Genesis includes two creation narratives that present different, but not necessarily contradictory, views of the relationship between humanity and the natural world.[3] The first creation narrative (Genesis 1:1—2:3) depicts the creation

---

1. For overviews of Jewish attitudes toward the natural world, see Hava Tirosh-Samuelson, "Judaism," in *Oxford Handbook of Religion and Ecology*, ed. Roger S. Gottlieb (Oxford: Oxford University Press, 2006), 25–64; Hava Tirosh-Samuelson, "Judaism," in *Encyclopedia of Religion and Nature*, vol. 2 (London: Continuum, 2005), 525–537, and other related essays in that encyclopedia.

2. See Daniel Hillel, *The Natural History of the Bible* (New York: Columbia University Press, 2006); Ellen E. Davis, *Scripture, Culture and Agriculture: An Agrarian Reading of the Bible* (Cambridge: Cambridge University Press, 2009); Evan Eisenberg, *The Ecology of Eden* (New York: Knopf, 1998).

3. For a good analysis of the two creation narratives that teases out the ecological differences between them, see Theodore Hiebert, *The Yahwist's Landscape: Nature and Religion in Early Israel* (New York and Oxford: Oxford University Press, 1996). For the theological implications of the biblical creation myth that distinguishes Israelite religion from its neighboring cultures, consult Jon D. Levenson, *Creation and the Persistence of Evil: The Jewish Drama of Divine Omnipotence* (Princeton, NJ: Princeton University Press, 1988).

of the material world as an act of ordering unordered chaos. This narrative sees creation as boundary formation, and it serves as the rationale for distinguishing the sacred and the profane, the permitted and the forbidden, such as clean and unclean foods, in the legal parts of the Bible and in postbiblical Judaism (see Leviticus 10:10–11; Leviticus 19; Deuteronomy 22:11).

In the first creation narrative, one animal, namely, the human, is presented as different from all others, because it was made in the "divine image" (*zelem elohim*) (see Genesis 1:26). By virtue of the divine image, the human receives the commandment to have dominion over other animals (see Genesis 1:28). The commandment clearly privileges the human species over others and calls the human to rule over other living creatures but does not give license to exploit Earth's resources, because Earth does not belong to humans but to God. The act of divine creation ends with rest on the seventh day, the Sabbath, imposing rest on nature.

The second creation narrative (Genesis 2:4—3:24) considers the origin of humanity through the Garden of Eden myth and highlights the link between the human earthling (*adam*) and the earth (*adamah*) from which the human comes and to which the human will return at death. God's breath transforms the earthling from the "dust of the earth" into a living being (*nefesh hayah*), thus establishing the direct link between humanity and God. This narrative places the human in the Garden of Eden "to serve and to keep it," or in a different translation "to till and protect it" (*le-ovdah u-leshomrah*), a command that implies farming activities such as tilling, plowing, and sowing, as well as the deep obligation toward the environment. This command is the basis of Jewish environmental ethics of responsibility that regards humans as stewards of nature, even though the term *stewards* does not appear in the Bible. The responsibility for the well-being of nonhuman creatures is manifested in broad legislation toward various aspects of nature.

Several land-based commandments in the Bible express the belief that "God is the rightful owner of the land of Israel and the source of its fertility; the Israelites working the land are but God's tenant-farmers who are obligated to return the first portion of the land's yield to its rightful owner in order to insure the land's continuing fertility and the farmer's sustenance and prosperity."[4] Accordingly, the first sheaf of the barley harvest and the two loaves of bread made from the new grain are to be consecrated to God.[5] The Bible articulates extensive protection of vegetation, especially trees. Leviticus 19:23 commands that during the first three years of growth, the fruits of newly planted trees or vineyards are not to be eaten (*orlah*), because they are considered to be God's property. Fruit-bearing trees are to be protected in wartime and must not be chopped down while the city is under siege (see Deuteronomy 20:19). Scripture thus recognizes the interdependence between humans and trees, on the one hand, and the capacity of humans to destroy natural things, on the other.

Also, when Israel conducts itself according to the laws of the Torah, the land is abundant and fertile, benefiting its inhabitants with the basic necessities of life—grain, oil, and wine—but when Israel sins, the blessedness of the land declines, and it becomes desolate and inhospitable (see Deuteronomy 11:6–11). Thus, the well-being of God's land and the moral quality of the people who live on the land are causally linked and both dependent on obeying God's will.

The Bible recognizes the diversity of species (literally "kinds") in the natural world (see Genesis 1:11–25). Biblical legislation expresses concern over the protection of diversification, such as Leviticus 19:19: "You shall not let your cattle breed with a different kind; you shall not sow your field with two kinds of seeds" (repeated in Deuteronomy 22:9–11). The Bible prohibits mixing different species of plants, fruit trees, fish, birds, and land animals, a prohibition clarified and further elaborated by the rabbis.

Limiting human consumption of animals and regulating all food sources is a major concern of the Bible and the Holiness Code. The laws of Leviticus 11 and Deuteronomy 14 are part of an elaborate system of purity and impurity affecting the sanctuary and the

---

4. Richard Sarrason, "The Significance of the Land of Israel in the Mishnah," in *The Land of Israel: Jewish Perspectives*, ed. Lawrence A. Hoffman (Notre Dame, IN: University of Notre Dame Press), 114.

5. On these and other agricultural commandments in the Bible, see Victor Raboy, "Jewish Agricultural Law: Ethical First Principles and Environmental Justice," in *Ecology & the Jewish Spirit: Where Nature & the Sacred Meet*, ed. Ellen Bernstein (Woodstock, VT: Jewish Lights, 2000), 190–199.

priesthood, as well as the lives of individual Israelites.[6] In general, the Torah prohibits eating the meat of certain living creatures that are classified as impure or unclean, the ingestion of blood of any animals, the consumption of animal fat, and the eating of meat of the carcass of dead animals and fowls. The differentiation between clean and unclean animals, which is the core of Jewish dietary laws, has generated a lot of discussion about their internal logic. Some scholars explained that the unclean animals were those regarded as deities in neighboring cultures. Still others considered the means of locomotion as the crucial classificatory principle. However, the prohibition on consuming certain animals is also possible to explain as ecologically motivated.[7]

Animals (horse, mule, camel) that were domesticated could be kept by farmers for transportation and work on the field but not for consumption. The cow was used for work, milk, and meat, and the sheep and goat for milk and meat only. Water animals that could be eaten must have fins and scales (i.e., fish) but frogs, toads and newts were not to be eaten, perhaps because the authors of the Bible were aware that they benefit the ecosystem and control mosquitoes. Lobsters, oysters, and mussels are also forbidden, most likely because the coast of Palestine is not suited for them. All birds of prey, including owls, were forbidden for human consumption as well as all storks, ibises, herons, and species of bats. Once one realizes that many of the forbidden species were actually common in the land of Israel, it is possible to look at these prohibitions as extended protection of birds that are important to "maintaining the ecological equilibrium and serve as the most efficient control agents of species."[8]

Another deep ecological concern of the Bible is the perpetuation of life of nonhuman animals: "If you come on a bird's nest, in any tree or on the ground, with fledglings or eggs, with the mother sitting

---

6. See Jan J. Boersma, *The Torah and the Stoics; On Humankind and Nature; A Contribution to the Debate on Sustainability and Quality* (Leiden, Boston, Köln: Brill Academic, 2001), 113–188; Bryan David, *Cosmos, Chaos and the Kosher Mentality* (Sheffield: Sheffield Academic, 1995).

7. This approach is the gist of Aloys Hüttermann, *The Ecological Message of the Torah: Knowledge, Concepts, and Laws Which Made Survival in a Land of "Milk and Honey" Possible* (Atlanta: Scholars Press, 1999).

8. Ibid, 76.

on the fledglings or on the eggs, you shall not take the mother with the young. Let the mother go, taking only the young for yourself, in order that it may go well with you and you may live long" (Deuteronomy 22:6–7). By saving the mother, the Torah enables the species to continue to reproduce and avoid potential extinction. In addition, cruelty toward animals is prohibited because it leads to other forms of cruelty.[9] The ideal is to create a sensibility of love and kindness toward animals to emulate God's attribute of mercy and fulfill the commandment "to be holy as I the Lord am holy" (Leviticus 19:2). Thus, in Deuteronomy 22:10, yoking an ass and an ox together is prohibited, because the uneven size could cause unnecessary suffering. The prohibition on "seething a kid in its mother's milk" (see Exodus 23:19; Exodus 34:26; Deuteronomy 14:21), which is the basis for an elaborate system of ritual separation of milk and meat products in rabbinic Judaism, is explained by the rabbis as an attempt to prevent cruelty in humans (*Deuteronomy Rabbah* 6.10). While Scripture does not forbid slaughtering animals for consumption or sacrifice or using eggs for human use, it curtails excess cruelty. Kindness to animals is a virtue of the righteous person, which is associated with the promise of heavenly rewards (see Proverbs 12:10).

The most distinctive feature of Jewish environmental legislation is the causal connection between the moral quality of human life and the vitality of God's creation. The corruption of society is closely linked to the corruption of nature. In both cases, the injustice arises from human greed and the failure of humans to protect the original order of creation. From the Jewish perspective, the just allocation of nature's resources is a religious issue of the highest order. The treatment of the marginal in society—the poor, the hungry, the widow, the orphan—must follow the principle of scriptural legislation. Thus, parts of the land's produce—the corner of the field, the gleaning of stalks, the forgotten sheaf, the separated fruits, and the defective cluster—are to be given to those who do not own land. By observing the particular commandments, the soil itself becomes holy, and the person who obeys these commandments ensures the religiomoral purity necessary to live in God's land. A failure to treat

9. See Ze'ev Levy, "Ethical Issues of Animal Welfare in Jewish Thought," *Judaism: A Quarterly Journal* 45 (1996), 45–57.

other members of the society justly, so as to protect the sanctity of their lives, is integrally tied to acts extended toward the land. This aspect of Jewish ecological ethics is the foundation of the concept of "Eco-Kosher" promoted by contemporary Jewish environmentalists, as shown below.

The connection between land management, rituals, and social justice is most evident in the laws regulating the sabbatical year (*shemittah*).[10] The sabbatical year is an extension of the laws of the Sabbath to Earth. On the Sabbath, humans create nothing, destroy nothing, and enjoy the bounty of Earth. As God rested on the seventh day, the Sabbath is viewed as the completion of the act of creation, a celebration of human tenancy and stewardship. The Sabbath teaches that humans stand not only in relation to nature but also in relation to the creator of nature. Most instructively, domestic animals are included in the Sabbath rest (see Deuteronomy 5:13–14). Specific cases exist in which it is permissible to violate the laws of the Sabbath to help an animal in distress. Thus, one must alleviate the suffering of an animal that has fallen into a cistern or ditch on the Sabbath, to bring food or pillows and blankets to help it climb free. The normal restrictions against such labors on the Sabbath are waived. Cattle must be milked and geese fed, lest the buildup of milk in the cow or hunger in the geese cause suffering to a living being. The observance of the Sabbath is a constant reminder of the deepest ethical and religious values that enable Jews to stand in a proper relationship with God.

During the sabbatical year, it is forbidden to plant, cultivate, or harvest grain, fruit, or vegetables or even to plant in the sixth year to harvest during the seventh year. Crops that grow untended are not to be harvested by the landlord but are to be left ownerless (*hefqer*) for all to share, including poor people and animals. The

---

10. For discussion of the laws of the sabbatical year, consult Shlomo Riskin, "Shemitta: A Sabbatical for the Land; The Land Will Rest and the People Will Grow," in *Judaism and Ecology*, ed. Aubrey Rose (London: Cassell, 1992), 70–73; Gerald Blidstein, "Man and Nature in the Sabbatical Year," *Tradition: A Journal of Orthodox Thought* 8 (1996): 48–55. On modern attempts to live by the laws of the Sabbatical year, see Benjamin Bak, "The Sabbatical Year in Modern Israel," *Tradition* 1, no. 2 (1959), 193–199. For reflections on the theological relevance of biblical legislation today, see Arthur Waskow, "From Compassion to Jubilee," *Tikkun Magazine* 5, no. 2 (1990), 78–81.

rest imposed during the sabbatical year helps restore nutrients and improves the soil, promotes diversity in plant life, and helps maintain vigorous cultivars. On the seventh year, debts contracted by fellow Israelites are to be remitted (see Leviticus 25; Deuteronomy 15:3), providing temporary relief from these obligations. In the Jubilee year, all Hebrew slaves are manumitted, regardless of when they were acquired (see Leviticus 25:39–41), to teach that slavery is not a natural state.

The laws of the sabbatical years were practically reversed in the rabbinic period when a written document (*prozbul*) assigned the debt to the court before the sabbatical year with the intention of collecting the debt at a later time. This reinterpretation indicates the broad transformation of ancient Israelite religion especially after the destruction of the Second Temple and the emergence of rabbinic Judaism.

THE SANCTIFICATION OF NATURE IN RABBINIC JUDAISM

The rabbis elaborated and expanded many biblical laws, including laws concerning the land, its flora and fauna, claiming the status of oral Torah to their legal deliberations. Together the written Torah and the oral Torah constituted the ideal way of life that all Jews should follow. By 600 CE, the Judaism of the rabbis would become normative so that to be Jewish meant to live the Torah as interpreted by the rabbis.[11] Rabbinic Judaism created a religious system aimed at making Jews holy as God is holy outside the precincts of the Jerusalem Temple and even without the Temple altogether. All aspects of life—space, time, the human body, and human relations—were sanctified by following a prescribed and all-encompassing way of life. These prescriptions, or commandments (*mitzvot*), capture the creative tension between nature and Torah in rabbinic Judaism. On the

11. The logic of rabbinic Judaism is best explained by the numerous writings of Jacob Neusner, including *The Way of Torah: An Introduction to Judaism*, 5th ed. (Belmont, CA: Wadsworth, 1993). Neusner insightfully speaks about the "ecology of Judaism," a phrase that highlights the intrinsic connection between the Jews and their natural environment.

one hand, the sacred texts as interpreted by the rabbis specify normative behavior, ethical values, and social ideals that shaped all aspects of Jewish life, including attitudes toward the natural world. On the other hand, the veneration of and dedication to the Torah caused the distancing of religious Jews from the natural world. Because studying Torah was presented as the most important commandment, equivalent in worth to all other commandments combined, a rabbinic text declared that Scripture regards the one who stops Torah study to appreciate the beauty of nature "as if he forfeited his soul" (Mishna, Tractate Avot 3.7).[12] Precisely because rabbinic Judaism placed Torah at the center of Jewish life, rabbinic Jews would experience the natural world through the prism of Torah.

Rabbinic Judaism posed an elaborate program for the sanctification of nature through observance of divine commandments.[13] In daily prayers, the Jewish worshipper sanctifies nature by expressing gratitude to the Creator "who in his goodness creates each day." The prayers recognized the daily changes in the rhythm of nature—morning, evening, and night—and recognized the power of God to bring about changes. Similarly, when Jews witness natural phenomena such as a storm or a tree blossoming, they are obligated to say a blessing that bears witness to God's power in nature. The observant Jew blesses God for the natural functions of the human body and for the food that God provides to nourish the human body. Through such blessings, acts from which the worshipper derives either benefit or pleasure are consecrated to God. To act otherwise is a form of theft (Tosefta, tractate Berakhot 6.3).

An example of the sanctification of nature in rabbinic Judaism can be seen in the festival of Sukkot (Tabernacles). Originally celebrated at the end of the summer harvest and the preparation for the rainy season in the land of Israel, Sukkot was associated with the redemption of Israel from Egypt (see Leviticus 23:24). Removed from the protection of their regular dwelling, the Israelites had

12. For analysis of this rabbinic text that attempts to overcome the tension, see Jeremy Benstein, "'One, Walking and Studying . . . ': Nature vs. Torah," *Judaism: A Quarterly Journal* 44 (1991–92), 25–35.

13. Michael Wyschogrod, "Judaism and the Sanctification of Nature," *The Melton Journal* 24 (Spring 1991), 5–7.

wandered in the desert, forced to live in temporary dwellings (the Hebrew *sukkah* [plural, *sukkot*] refers to this booth). Life in a *sukkah* compelled the Israelites to experience the power of God in nature more directly and become even more grateful to God's power of deliverance. In addition to dwelling in a *sukkah*, the Israelites were commanded to "take the fruit of majestic trees, branches of palm trees, boughs of leafy trees, and willows of the brook; and . . . [to] rejoice before the LORD your God for seven days" (Leviticus 23:40). In this manner, nature became a means for Israel's fulfillment of the commandment to rejoice before God.[14] After the destruction of the Temple, the complex ritual of this pilgrimage festival could no longer be carried out in the Temple. Hence, the rabbis elaborated the symbolic meaning of the *sukkah*, viewing it as a sacred home and the locus for the divine presence.

Another Jewish festival also celebrated the ritual transformation of nature. First mentioned in the Mishnah (Rosh Hashanah 1.1), the fifteenth day of the month of Shevat, which coincides with the beginning of bloom of almond trees after the period of dormancy during winter, was celebrated as "the new year for trees."[15] The celebration apparently originated in the secular activity of paying taxes on fruit trees, but it received a religious meaning when the day was interpreted as God's judgment of trees, analogous to the judgment of people at the beginning of the Jewish year. During the Middle Ages, when the Jews no longer dwelled in the land of Israel, the festival assumed a new symbolic meaning, with new prayers and new customs. Fruits grown in the land of Israel were eaten by Diaspora Jews, and a special set of Psalms was added to the daily liturgy. The most elaborate ritual for the holiday was constructed by kabbalists in the sixteenth century, for whom the land of Israel was no longer merely a

14. On the history of this festival and the symbolism of its rituals, consult Jeffrey L. Rubinstein, *The History of Sukkot in the Second Temple and Rabbinic Periods* (Atlanta: Scholars Press, 1995); and "The Symbolism of the Sukkah," *Judaism* 43 (1994), 371–387. On the significance of Sukkot for Jewish environmentalism, see "Sukkot: A Holiday of Joy," in *Ecology & the Jewish Spirit: Where Nature and the Sacred Meet*, ed. Ellen Bernstein (Woodstock, VT: Jewish Lights, 2000), 133–136.

15. For more on the history, significance, and transformation of the festival of Tu B'Shvat, consult Ari Elon, Naomi Mara Hyman, and Arthur Waskow, eds., *Trees, Earth and Torah: A Tu B'Shvat Anthology* (Philadelphia: Jewish Publication Society, 2000).

physical place but also a spiritual reality. Modeled after the Passover service, the kabbalistic ritual for the "new year for trees" endowed it with the capacity to restore the flow of divine energy to the broken world. The very fact that, for the kabbalists, everything in the world was a symbol of divine reality facilitated the creation of new rituals and endowed natural objects with a new spiritual meaning. Thus, nature was absorbed into the sacred narrative of Judaism. In modern times the festival of Tu B'shvat was revived in the State of Israel but with no reference to its religious meaning; instead, the festival was used to launch massive efforts of reforestation. By contrast, in North America, Jewish environmentalists in recent years have revived the kabbalistic ritual with its symbolic meanings to allow Jews to invest emotionally with the ecologically significant ancient practice.

In their attempt to create a holy society, the rabbis elaborated biblical ecological legislation though the Temple no longer existed. For example, the rabbis decreed that gifts to God are to be made only from produce grown by Israelites in the land of Israel, in contrast to all other cereal and animal offerings, which may be brought to the Temple also from outside the land (Mishnah Men 8:1; Mishna Parah 2:1). Some of the consecrated produce is to be given to the priests and Levites, whereas other produce is to be eaten by the farmer. Similarly, the rabbis elaborated on the biblical prohibition against mixing of species in Mishnah, Tractate Kil'ayim and in the Palestinian Talmud on that tractate. While rabbinic rulings about the main grains of the land of Israel—wheat, rye grass, barley, oats, and spelt—and about other species of vegetation do not indicate that the rabbis understood the principles of genetic engineering, it does suggest they were keen observers of the natural world and they respected diversification of nature.

The biblical prohibition on the cutting down of fruit-bearing trees during time of war (see Deuteronomy 20:19) was generalized by the rabbinic sages into the general prohibition against all forms of destruction, complete or incomplete, direct or indirect, of all objects that may be potential benefit to humans.[16] By invoking the principle of "do not destroy," the rabbis prohibited cutting off water supply

16. Eilon Schwartz, "*Bal Tashchit:* A Jewish Environmental Precept," *Environmental Ethics* 19 (1997), 355–74.

to trees; overgrazing the countryside; unjustified killing of animals or feeding them harmful foods; hunting animals for sport; species extinction and the destruction of cultivated plant varieties; pollution of air and water; overconsumption of anything; and the waste of mineral and other resources. These environmental regulations indicate that the Jewish legal tradition requires that one carefully weigh the ramifications of all actions and behavior for every interaction with the natural world; it also sets priorities and weighs conflicting interests and permanent modification of the environment.

The rabbis further extended the ethics of care by closely attending to the needs of animals.[17] On the basis of Deuteronomy 22:6, which forbids the killing of a bird with her young because it is exceptionally cruel, the rabbis articulated the general principle of *tza`ar ba`aley hayyim* (literally "distress of living creatures") that prohibits the affliction of needless suffering on animals. The rabbis considered this particular commandment one of seven commandments given to the sons of Noah and, therefore, binding on all humans, not just on Jews. The obligation to release the ass from its burden (Exodus 23:5), that is, to assist the owner in unloading merchandise or materials by a beast of burden and a similar obligation to come to the assistance of a fallen animal (see Deuteronomy 22:4) are understood by rabbinic sources (BT Baba Metzi`a 32b) as duties rooted in the concern for the financial loss that would be suffered by the animal's master were the animal to collapse under the weight of the burden. Although generally human needs take precedence over the suffering of animals, there are cases in which the rabbis privilege the needs of animals. Thus, Deuteronomy 1:15 is understood in rabbinic exegesis as forbidding a person to partake of any food unless one has first fed one's animal (BT Berakhot 41a; Gittin 62a). Similarly, one is permitted to buy animals only after one can assure that the animals could be fed (Yerushalmi, Yebamot 15:3; Ketubot 4:8).

The concern for future generations of nonhuman species is elaborated in *Deuteronomy Rabbah* 6.5, Babylonian Talmud, Tractate

17. Elijah Shochet, *Animal Life in Jewish Tradition: Attitudes and Relationships* (New York: KTAV, 1984); Noah J. Cohen, *Tza'ar Ba'ale Hayim: The Prevention of Cruelty to Animals, Its Bases, Development, and Legislation in Hebrew Literature*, 2nd ed. (New York: Feldheim, 1976).

Hullin 138b-42a, and *Sifre Deuteronomy* 2.27, specifying that the person who finds the nest is allowed to take the nestlings only if they are not fledged. Such concern intimates a notion of sustained use of resources and could provide Jewish support for the concept of sustainability. This reasoning led the rabbis to prohibit raising sheep and goats that graze, even though the rabbis were aware these animals generated a profitable business in the Roman Empire (Babylonian Talmud, Tractate Hullin 58b). The ban was imposed after the devastation of Judea in the Bar Kokhba revolt (132–135 CE) to enable the land to heal from the devastation of the war: thus short-term hardship was traded with long-term gains. This kind of environmental legislation was legitimated by appeal to the holiness of the land, but it also indicates attention to the particular physical conditions.

Although the rabbis speculated about the origin of the universe and reflected on the order of creation in Genesis, they were mainly concerned about nature as a source for moral lessons. For example, the Talmud notes that if the Torah did not prescribe certain virtues, Israel would have learned honesty from the ant, modesty from the cat, chastity from the dove, and loyalty from the cock (BT Erubin 100b). Conversely, some animals exemplify vices that humans must avoid. Anecdotes about individual rabbinic figures depict them either as observers of natural phenomena (e.g., Rabbi Shimon ben Halfta) or as people who have special sensitivity to their domestic animals (e.g., Rabbi Pinchas ben Yair). By parables and fables in which animals are employed allegorically, the rabbis inculcated their ethical outlook and the virtues they sought to cultivate in humans, especially modesty, self-control, and prudence.

The purpose of rabbinic legislation was to cultivate the upright moral personality that could stand in a relationship with God. On the one hand, the rabbinic interpretation of Scripture specified normative behavior, ethical values, and social ideals that shaped Jewish attitude toward nature, but, on the other hand, the dedication to Torah study distanced rabbinic Jews from the natural world. The Torah was believed to be the paradigm that God had consulted when creating the world. To know how God wishes Jews to behave, they must consult the Torah. Thus the sacred text and its ongoing interpretation both sanctified the natural world and called on Jews to aspire to transcend nature and its demands on humans. This is why rabbinic Judaism could be said to give rise to the "unnatural Jew."[18] The more Jews lived in accordance to the religious prescriptions of the rabbinic tradition, the less they were interested in the natural world for its own sake.

UNDERSTANDING GOD'S CREATION IN MEDIEVAL PHILOSOPHY AND KABBALAH

What does it mean for the Torah to be the paradigm of the created world? During the Middle Ages, two Jewish schools of thought addressed the question: rationalist philosophy and theosophic kabbalah. These intellectual programs presented themselves as the correct interpretation of the Bible, and they theorized about nature in their attempt to specify the relationship among creation, revelation, and redemption. As ideal paths for religious perfection, rationalist philosophy and theosophic kabbalah flourished simultaneously from the twelfth to the sixteenth centuries, cross-fertilizing each other.[19] Though each school of thought developed distinct conceptions of the natural world, it is only in these sources that the term *nature* (*teva*) appears as an abstract concept. In rabbinic sources, by contrast, the natural world is referred to only as "*beriah*," namely, *creation*. Thus, to speak about creation in Judaism is inherently ambiguous because the term *creation* denotes both the act of bringing the world into existence, as well as the outcome of the act: the physical world in its totality.

Rationalist Jewish philosophers—chief among them Moses Maimonides (1138–1204)—speculated about the origin of the world, viz., whether the world is created out of nothing or out of

18. Steven S. Schwarzschild, "The Unnatural Jew," *Environmental Ethics* 6 (1984), 347–362.

19. On the relationship between philosophy and kabbalah, see Hava Tirosh-Samuelson, "Philosophy and Kabbalah, 1200–1600," in *Cambridge Companion of Medieval Jewish Medieval Philosophy*, eds. Daniel H. Frank and Oliver Leaman (Cambridge: University of Cambridge Press, 2003), 218–257. On philosophy and kabbalah as programs for the attainment of religious perfection, see Hava Tirosh-Samuelson, *Happiness in Premodern Judaism: Virtue, Knowledge, and Well-Being* (Cincinnati: Hebrew Union College Press, 2003).

something.[20] To believe that the world was created by God entails that the world came into existence by a deliberate act of divine will. As a created entity, the world is contingent; it exhibits design and intentional order, and it manifests divine freedom. In contrast, to believe that the world is eternal means to believe that the world is an extension or an overflow of divine nature, which is itself eternal. The eternal world shares the characteristics of divine nature, even if only in a diminished way, that is to say, it exhibits an immanent and unchangeable order that constitutes its rational necessity. The eternality of the world entails the belief that the world's causation is natural and necessary. God and the world are coeval. Between these conflicting beliefs were the notions that God created the world from eternal, preexisting matter or that God creates the world eternally. By sorting out the precise meaning of these beliefs, medieval Jewish philosophers clarified the concept of creation, exploring notions such as action, power, causation, time, necessity, contingency and volition. These philosophical concepts had little to do with actual observation of the natural world.

Besides speculating about the origins of the universe, the rationalist philosophers sought to understand the structure of the created world by using the scientific standards of the day, namely, Aristotelian physics and cosmology. In medieval Aristotelian cosmology, all beings are arranged in hierarchical order, each occupying its natural place and acting in accord with its inherent *telos*, its goal or purpose. The hierarchical order of the universe ranges from the most spiritual of beings—God—to the most material. Humans stood just below God in this schema. The main task of the thoughtful human was to contemplate and comprehend the structure of the universe on the basis of empirical observation. It was through the study of nature that the philosopher could fathom the wisdom of God. Because God is absolutely one, in God there is no distinction between what God knows and what God does. Divine activities in the physical

20. See Barry Kogan, "The Problem of Creation in Late Medieval Jewish Philosophy," in *A Straight Path: Studies in Medieval Philosophy and Culture*, ed. Ruth Link-Salinger (Washington, DC: The Catholic University of America Press, 1988), 158–164. For analysis of Moses Maimonides's interpretation of the belief in creation, see Kenneth Seeskin, *Maimonides on the Origins of the Universe* (Cambridge: Cambridge University Press, 2005).

environment manifest divine wisdom, and God's continued care for the world, that is, divine providence. The philosophers studied the natural world to understand the mind of God, emphasizing the orderliness, stability, and predictability of nature. The human ability to understand how God works in nature was ascribed to the human capacity to reason, which the philosophers equated with the "image of God." The study of nature by means of the human sciences, culminating in metaphysics, was thus understood to be a religious activity: the better one understood the laws by which God governed the world, the closer one might come to God.

The philosophical discourse on the doctrine of creation generated very sophisticated arguments, but it had little to do with actual observation of the natural world or with concern for the protection of nature. Only in Italy, during the sixteenth century, did Jewish philosophers begin to exhibit interest in minerals, animals, and plants, especially those mentioned in the Bible,[21] but they framed the interest in nature within the theological assumptions of medieval Jewish rationalism: natural phenomena are to be understood in light of the Torah, because it functioned as the blueprint of creation. Because observation of natural phenomena must be consistent with a correct reading of the biblical text, interest in nature is ultimately a hermeneutical activity. For the medieval and early modern Jewish philosopher, there was no division between nature and Scripture: each made manifest an aspect of divine activity.

This point of view, which exacerbates the alienation between Jewish religious life and the experience of the natural world, is even more acute in medieval kabbalah, the mystical strain of Judaism. The kabbalists viewed the natural world as a linguistic construct, comprising the letters of the Hebrew alphabet in their infinite permutations. The one who possesses the knowledge of kabbalah (literally meaning "tradition") can decode nature, participate in God's life, and benefit from the blessing of God's creative energy.

21. On Jewish interest in the natural world during the sixteenth and seventeenth centuries, see Noah J. Efron, *Judaism and Science: A Historical Introduction* (Westport, CT: Greenwood, 2007); David Ruderman, *Jewish Thought and Scientific Discovery* (New Haven CT: Yale University Press, 1995). My interpretation differs from theirs, because I highlight the religious significance ascribed to nature in early modern Jewish philosophy.

According to kabbalah, the biblical narrative of creation relates how God emerged from utter concealment. The biblical text, therefore, pertains primarily to events that take place in God, a unity within plurality of ten forces known as *Sefirot*, and only secondarily in the world of corporeal nature and human history. Accepting the cosmological picture of the rationalist philosophers, the kabbalists also envisioned the universe as a Great Chain of Being arranged hierarchically from God to corporeal matter. However, unlike the philosophers, the kabbalists held that correct interpretation of scripture can enable humans to affect events in the corporeal world, as well as bring humans to participate in the rhythm of divine life. Because nature became a symbol of divine reality, decoding nature was the path for communion with God (*deve kut*).

The primary kabbalistic text was the *Zohar* (Book of Splendor), an extensive commentary on the Torah composed by a mystical fraternity in Castile, in Spain, toward the end of the thirteenth century but attributed to Rabbi Shimon bar Yohai, a second-century rabbi.[22] Similar to rabbinic homilies, the *Zohar* did not offer a consistent theory about the physical universe: in some Zoharic texts, everything that exists in the world was concealed in the heavens and the earth that were created on the first day, which means that the process of creation realized things that already existed in potentiality. In other texts, the heavens, Earth, and the water of the biblical narrative acted as artisans who assisted the Creator during the days of creation.

After the Jews were expelled from Spain (1492), the *Zohar* gradually emerged as a canonic text, second in importance only to the Talmud. In the town of Safed in the Galilee, a community of refugees from Iberia formed a mystical fraternity that made the study of the *Zohar* central to its messianic expectations and mystical practices.[23] Isaac Luria (d. 1572) led this group, and his mystical speculations on the origins of space, the physical universe, life, and the human

22. A good presentation of the *Zohar* is available in Pinchas Giller, *Reading the Zohar* (Oxford: Oxford University Press, 2005). On the Zoharic symbolic interpretation of the natural world, see Isaiah Tishby, *Wisdom of the Zohar*, vol. 2, trans. David Goldstein (London: Jewish Litmann Library, 1987), 549–586.

23. The communal life, religious practices, and theology of Lurianic kabbalah are best explained in Lawrence Fine, *Physician of the Soul, Healer of the Cosmos: Isaac Luria and His Kabbalistic Fellowship* (Palo Alto, CA: Stanford University Press, 2003).

soul offered the deepest exposition of the doctrine of creation and its relationship to revelation and redemption. Luria's theory of origins told a dramatic story about God's "self-contraction" or "withdrawal" (*tzimtzum*), the breakdown of the divine world (*shevirat ha-kelim*), and the responsibility of humanity, especially the Jews, to repair the broken world through performance of divine commandments with appropriate intentions. The task of the kabbalistic virtuoso, whose own soul has been healed by living the mystical way, is to repair the broken universe and the broken deity. In the mending or healing of the world and of God lies the messianic import of Lurianic kabbalah and its attractiveness to Jews.

The Lurianic insistence on human responsibility to repair the broken world will become a central principle of the Jewish environmental movement in the twentieth century, although kabbalah itself has little to do with concern for the physical world as championed by the environmental movement. In fact, because kabbalah conflated the belief in creation with an emanationist schema that viewed the created world as emanating, or flowing, from a divine source, kabbalah actually gave rise to conflicting and even paradoxical attitudes toward the natural world.[24] On the one hand, kabbalah gave rise to a negative attitude toward the corporeal world, because it was viewed as an obstacle to the attainment of spiritual ends. On the other hand, because the world was seen as a linguistic construct, the kabbalist who deciphers the code of elements, the Hebrew letters, knows the grammar of nature's language. If the observable world is a linguistic construct whose rules and grammar are accessible to the kabbalist, he can also attempt to manipulate nature by using linguistic formulas. This is why kabbalah was associated with magic and alchemy that flourished in the sixteenth century when scientists began to seek control of nature's occult (i.e., hidden) properties.[25]

24. Hava Tirosh-Samuelson, "The Textualization of Nature in Jewish Mysticism," in *Judaism and Ecology: Created World and Revealed Word*, ed. Hava Tirosh-Samuelson (Cambridge, MA: Harvard University Press, 2002), 389–404.

25. On the connection of kabbalah and magic, see Moshe Idel, *Golem: Jewish Magical and Mystical Traditions on the Artificial Anthropoid* (Albany NY: SUNY Press, 1990). This connection continues in Hasidism. See Moshe Idel, *Hasidism: Between Ecstasy and Magic* (New Haven CT: Yale University Press, 1995).

Lurianic kabbalah dominated Jewish intellectual life during the early modern period, giving rise to the messianic movement of Sabbatai Zevi in the seventeenth century and to the revival movement of Hasidism in the eighteenth century. Hasidism articulated a pantheistic worldview that accommodated diverse attitudes toward the natural world, ranging from control of nature by means of magic to denial of the cosmos' reality (i.e., a-cosmism). Hasidic theology saw all natural phenomena as ensouled: divine sparks enlivened all corporeal entities and not just humans. By means of ritual activity, the Hasidic master attempts to draw close to the divine energy, liberate the divine spark, and redeem reality by returning to its original, noncorporeal state. The worship of God through the spiritualization of corporeal reality (*avodah ba-gashmiyut*) was a central Hasidic value, complementing the deemphasis on formal Torah study. Hasidic tales (the major vehicle for the transmission of Hasidic teachings) were situated in natural, rather than urban, settings, encouraging the Hasidic worshipper to find the divine sparks in all created beings. However, the Hasidic masters were not necessarily concerned with the well-being of nonhuman creatures or with the protection of nature. In fact, the spiritualizing tendencies of Hasidism contributed to Jewish bookish culture that stood in tension with the emerging modern worldview of mechanistic material science that would eventually give rise to the environmental crisis.

NATURE AND RENEWAL IN MODERN JEWISH THOUGHT

Modernity spelled a major intellectual, political, and cultural challenge for Jews. In the premodern world, Jews suffered from persecution and discrimination; if they were not expelled from a given area, they were forced to live in ghettos, a concession to their unwanted presence in Europe. Jews were granted civil rights as individuals in France after the French Revolution in 1789, but another eight decades passed before Jews could become citizens in the rest of Western and Central Europe. With the spread of capitalism and the industrialization of Europe, Jews became even more associated with commerce, trade, and finance. With the opening of the liberal professions (e.g., law, civil service, journalism, and the arts) and the universities to Jews, many Jews left behind the traditional way of life and assimilated into European culture.

The prominent achievements of Jews created the false impression that they were the primary beneficiaries of modernity, a perception that fueled modern anti-Semitism now supported by the pseudoscientific theory of race and wedded to Social Darwinism. Once again, Jews faced discrimination, marginalization, and exclusion, culminating in the attempt to completely annihilate the Jewish people. The modern era witnessed not only the attempt to exterminate the Jews but also a profound cultural, political, and religious renaissance of the Jews who rose to face the challenges of modernity. Reform Judaism, Modern Orthodoxy (also known as Neo-Orthodoxy), and Zionism were the main modern reinterpretations of Judaism, and in all of these approaches nature plays a crucial role in the construction of modern Jewish identity.

Nature in Reform Judaism

Reform Jewish theologians in Germany during the nineteenth century did not focus on the religious significance of the natural world because for them, Judaism was a universal, spiritual religion that transcends nature. Only pagan religions identified God with nature, while rational Judaism based on the teaching of the prophets is the ultimate rejection of paganism. Instead, Reform Jewish theologians devoted their energy to defending the doctrine of revelation against historicism and biblical criticism by showing that revelation is logically plausible and that Judaism is the highest expression of universal, rational, and moral religion.

The theologians of the Reform movement concerned themselves with nature in the context of the debates about the doctrine of evolution, debates that pertained more to the nature of Judaism than to scientific theory per se. In America, the Jewish engagement with Darwinian evolution came mainly after the publication of Darwin's *Descent of Man* in 1871.[26] A rigorous dispute erupted

26. See Marc Swetlitz, "American Jewish Responses to Darwin and Evolutionary Theory, 1860–1890," in *Disseminating Darwinism: The Role of Place, Race, Religion, and Gender*, eds. Ronald L. Numbers and John Stenhouse (Cambridge: Cambridge University Press, 1999), 209–246; and Marc Swetlitz, "Responses to Evolution by Reform, Conservative, and Reconstructionist Rabbis in Twentieth-Century America," in *Jewish Tradition and the Challenge of Darwinism*, ed. Geoffrey Cantor and Marc Swetlitz (Chicago: University of Chicago Press, 2006), 47–70.

between leading Jewish theologians who promoted the reform of Judaism. Rabbi Kaufmann Kohler (d. 1926) endorsed Darwin's theory because he viewed it as a scientific proof for Reform Judaism: Judaism is a progressive religion that evolved over time, but Kohler ignored Darwin's theory of natural selection. His opponent, Rabbi Isaac Mayer Wise (d. 1900) understood natural selection to be a natural law in which survival of the strongest prevails, thereby robbing the moral law as taught by Judaism of all its legitimacy. Rejecting Darwin, Rabbi Wise developed his own theory about the history of life, which acknowledged that the Jewish religion, like nature, is bound by the law of evolution, that is, progression from lower to higher forms. However, Wise did not adopt the theory of progressive revelation and opposed the notion of gradual continuous transmutation of species.

The debate between those who appealed to evolution to explain the progressive nature of Judaism and the traditionalists, who rejected evolution because it challenged Jewish observance, resulted in the emergence of a new Jewish denomination, Conservative Judaism, which enabled millions of Eastern European Jewish immigrants to America to modernize while remaining loyal to traditional Judaism. In the 1930s, Rabbi Mordecai Kaplan (d. 1983) elaborated the notion of Judaism as an evolving civilization, even though he did not accept key elements of Darwin's theory of evolution.[27]

Nature and Observance of Torah in Modern Orthodoxy

The well-being of the physical environment did not matter to Reform theologians during the nineteenth and early twentieth century. Such concern appears in the writings of Neo-Orthodox or Modern Orthodox Jews who insisted (against their Reform opponents) that divinely revealed Torah is not susceptible to historical changes. Samson Raphael Hirsch (d. 1888), the founder of Neo-Orthodoxy, derived an ecologically sensitive theology from the doctrine of creation. Hirsch

27. For a succinct overview of Mordecai Kaplan's theology, see Rebecca T. Alpert and Jacob J. Staub, *Exploring Judaism: A Reconstructionist Approach* (Wyncote, PA: The Reconstructionist Press, 1988). For an elaborate analysis of his transnaturalism, see Meir Ben-Horin, *Transnature's God: Studies in Mordecai M. Kaplan's Theology* (Wilton, CT: Ada-Nisan Books, 2004).

held that the act of creation cannot be fathomed by human reason alone; humans learn about it only from divine revelation. Scripture makes known that the world was created because Scripture emanates directly from God, who is Absolute Mind. The Torah is the embodied form of the "Will of God" communicated through divine revelation. To act rightly humans must correlate their subjective will with the absolute Will of God, which, in turn, will actualize their potentialities in conformity with the divine will. By virtue of their free will, humans liberate themselves from the deterministic laws that govern the universe and regulate the involuntary behavior of nonhuman species.

The revealed Torah spells out how humans should treat the natural world. According to Hirsch, humans were indeed given the right to rule nature, but the God-given *right* to ownership comes with a *duty* to treat God's created order according to God's will. Hirsch reiterated the rabbinic ethics of responsibility toward nature, which teaches humanity "that the earth is not yours, but you were given to the earth, to respect it as Divine soil and to deem each one of its creatures a creature of God, your fellow being."[28] He saw humans as part of the natural world (i.e., a "brother to all creatures") but like a firstborn, the human also has special privileges and obligations. For Hirsch the status of the human as "first-born child" in the created world is analogous to the status of Israel among the nations: privilege that entails obligations. The Torah itself, God's revealed will, discloses how nature is to be treated with justice and respect. Hirsch highlighted the importance of the biblical command "do not destroy" as interpreted by the rabbis, insisting that heedless destruction of nature reflects human arrogance and rebellion against God. Instead, the Torah's laws about nature assure that humanity behave wisely and judiciously to protect the integrity of the natural world and its perpetuation. Hirsch explained the environmental legislation of the Torah as laws that are rooted in the act of creation when God separated his creatures "each according to its kind." Through the Torah, the Creator of the world functions as the "Regulator of the world"; the human who was appointed as

28. Samson Raphael Hirsch, *The Nineteen Letters on Judaism*, ed. Jacob Breuer (Jerusalem and New York: Feldheim, 1969), 37.

the "administrator" of God's estate executes the rules that ensure protection of nature. In Hirsch's analysis, nature serves as a model for observance of divine command and places its own demands or commandments on humans.[29] Hirsch elaborated on the significance of the Sabbath as a symbolic reminder of divine ownership, and the same logic is expressed in the laws of the sabbatical year that constitute humankind's "acknowledgement of God as the owner and master of the land."[30] The Sabbath becomes a source of Jewish spiritual renewal. These ideas were elaborated in the teachings of Hirsch's grandson, Isaac Breuer (d. 1946), who articulated a holistic understanding of the environment that links social justice, economics, and environmental concerns. His ideas are now receiving attention from religious environmentalists in Israel.

Nature and Renewal in Zionist Thought

The most comprehensive reflections on nature were articulated by Zionism, the Jewish nationalist movement that advocated the return of the Jews to the land of Israel. Zionism was revolutionary because it recognized the physical universe itself, particularly the land of Israel, as a source of spiritual renewal for the Jewish people, whose history Zionist thinkers interpreted anew by secularizing traditional categories. Zionism also advocated the development of the "muscular Jew" who will be a fearless, agile Jew rooted in the land and able to respond to physical attacks. The new Jew will be rooted in the soil rather than in the study of sacred texts and the performance of religious rituals. If the return to the land of Israel was to liberate the Jew from the negative traits acquired during the long exilic life, secular Hebrew culture was to highlight the agricultural basis of many Jewish festivals and celebrate the land without referring to God and without linking the abundance of the land to religious performance.

The most original reflections about the Jewish return to nature was articulated by Aaron David Gordon (d. 1922), the spiritual leader of

---

29. Shalom Rosenberg, "Concept of Torah and Nature in Jewish Thought," in *Judaism and Ecology: Created World and Revealed Word*, ed. Hava Tirosh-Samuelson (Cambridge, MA: Harvard University Press, 2002), 189–226, esp. 214–218.

30. Noah H. Rosenblum, *Tradition in an Age of Reform: The Religious Philosophy of Samson Raphael Hirsch* (Philadelphia: Jewish Publication Society, 1976), 246.

Labor Zionism who grew up in a traditional Jewish home but, as an autodidact, became conversant with European culture and was deeply influenced by Romanticism, the German *Lebensphilosophie*, the *elan vital* philosophy of Henri Bergson, the reinterpretation of Christianity by Leo Tolstoy, and the critique of Western culture by Friedrich Nietzsche. Settling in Palestine in 1904, Gordon joined the agricultural settlements to create a new kind of Jewish life and Jewish person.[31] He viewed humans as creatures of nature but warned that humans are in constant danger of losing contact with nature. For Gordon, the regeneration of humanity and of the Jewish people could come only through the return to nature and the development of a new understanding of labor as the source of genuine joy and creativity. Through physical, productive labor, humanity would become a partner of God in the process of creation. Rejecting the traditional Jewish focus on Torah study, Gordon viewed labor as redemptive act, provided that the means humans employ are in accord with the divine order of things, that is, with nature.

The key insight of Gordon was that humanity is part of an organic totality. The human must not stand outside of nature, either as a lover of nature's beauty (the artist) or an explorer of nature's mystery (the scientist or philosopher) or as an exploiter of nature's resources (the engineer). All of these postures are predicated on the denial that humans are part of nature. Instead humans must see themselves as part of nature and must strive "to live with and in nature." The universe is an organic totality enlivened by divine energy that pulsates through all levels of reality. The human species is part of that organic totality, which Gordon calls Being (*havayah*), while reaching the most developed state of being: culture and self-consciousness. The tragedy of the human species (about which the Bible speaks in the narrative of the Garden of Eden) is the tendency to alienate oneself from Being, by living as if nature is only to be controlled by humans to satisfy human needs. The human tragedy is especially severe in the case of Jews, because they seek to assimilate into Western Christian culture, denying their roots in the land of Israel, the Jewish nation, and the Hebrew language.

31. Eliezer Schweid, "A. D. Gordon: A Homeland That Is a Land of Destiny," in *The Land of Israel: National Home or Land of Destiny*, trans. Deborah Greniman (Rutherford/Madison/Teaneck, NJ: Fairleigh Dickinson University Press, 1985), 157–170.

The Zionist revolution means the return of the Jews to the land of Israel, the affirmation of the Jewish national existence, and the creation of new culture in the Hebraic language. For Gordon and all the pioneers who followed him, only agriculture and farming can reconnect modern, alienated Jews to the sources of cosmic creativity, enabling them to live most authentically as Jews, as well as humans. Although Gordon's ideas are little known outside of Israel, his interpretation of Zionism can serve as a source of inspiration for contemporary Jewish environmentalists who are seeking to find a balance between Jewish religiosity and secularism. If translated into English and reinterpreted in light of the science of ecology, Gordon's original thought could be extremely useful to Jewish environmentalists who seek to overcome the divide between secular and religious ways of being Jewish.

CONTEMPORARY JEWISH ENVIRONMENTALISM

The Zionist call for the return of the Jews to nature illustrates the traditional Jewish idea of *teshuvah*. The term is usually translated as "repentance," but its Hebrew stem connotes both "to return" and "to reply," so that *teshuvah* means "both a movement of return to one's source, to the original paradigm, and simultaneously a response to a divine call."[32] In America during the second half of the twentieth century, this concept gave rise to the Jewish Renewal Movement. This variant of contemporary Judaism is the primary context of Jewish environmental activism.

The Jewish environmental movement began in the late 1960s as an apologetic response to the charges of Lynn White Jr., who in a short article in *Science* magazine charged the Judeo-Christian tradition with responsibility for the current ecological crisis.[33] Defending Judaism and the Bible against White's charges, Orthodox,

---

32. Ehud Luz, "Repentance, " in *Contemporary Jewish Religious Thought: Original Essays on Critical Concepts, Movements, and Beliefs*, ed. Arthur A. Cohen and Paul Mendes-Flohr (New York, London, Sidney, Singapore: Free Press, 1988), pp. 785–793; quote is on p. 785.

33. Lynn White Jr. "The Roots of Our Ecologic Crisis," *Science* 155 no. 3767 (1967), 1204–1207.

Conservative, Reform, and Reconstructionist rabbis and educators responded that he misinterpreted the Bible and ignored the postbiblical rabbinic tradition. Moreover, Jewish theologians went further to mine the literary sources of Judaism for their ecological wisdom and environmental sensibilities, showing that Judaism advocates an ethics of stewardship toward the natural world, even though the word *stewardship* itself is never mentioned in the Bible.[34] In addition to the external challenge, Jewish environmental activism emerged as part of the societal and spiritual upheavals of the late 1960s in America and all over the world. In America, Jews witnessed a spiritual renewal and the call to return to the sources of Judaism wherein lie the answers to the societal and existential problems of Judaism in the post-Holocaust era.

The catalyst for the Jewish Renewal Movement was Rabbi Abraham Joshua Heschel (d. 1972). A Polish Jew born into a Hasidic family, Heschel also received modern university training. He managed to flee Nazi-occupied Poland and settled in America in 1941, where he inspired scores of alienated American Jews to find their way back to the sources of Judaism to heal the atrocities of modernity, which culminated in the Holocaust. [35] Heschel's ecologically sensitive Depth Theology, spoke of God's glory as pervading nature, leading humans to radical amazement and wonder, viewed humans as members of the cosmic community, and emphasized humility as the desired posture toward the natural world. The founder of the Jewish Renewal Movement, however, was Zalman Schachter-

34. For example, Robert Gordis, "Judaism and the Spoliation of Nature," *Congress Bi-Weekly* (April 2, 1971); Jonathan Z. Helfand, "Ecology and the Jewish Tradition: A Postscript," *Judaism* 20 (1971): 330–335; Norman Lamm, "Ecology and Jewish Law," in *Faith and Doubt* (New York: KTAV, 1971), 162–185; Evert Gendler, "On the Judaism of Nature," in *The New Jew*, ed. James A. Sleeper and Alan T. Mintz (New York: Random House, 1971); Bradley Shavit Artson, "Our Covenant with Stones: A Jewish Ecology of Earth," *Conservative Judaism* 44 (1991–1992): 25–35; Ismar Schorsch, "Tending to Our Cosmic Oasis," *Melton Journal* (Spring 1991).

35. On Heschel's biography, poetic theology, and impact on American Jewish culture, see Edward K. Kaplan, *Holiness in Words: Abraham Joshua Heschel's Poetics of Piety* (Albany NY: SUNY Press, 1996); Edward K. Kaplan, *Spiritual Radical: Abraham Joshua Heschel in America, 1940–1972* (New Haven, CT: Yale University Press, 2007); Edward K. Kaplan and Samuel H. Dresner, *Abraham Joshua Heschel: Prophetic Witness* (New Haven, CT and London: Yale University Press, 1998).

Shalomi (b. 1924), another product of Hasidism and a refugee from Nazi-occupied Europe. His creative reinterpretation of Judaism combined a "Gaia consciousness" with psychological interpretation of Lurianic kabbalah and New Age spirituality.[36]

Schachter-Shalomi urged a paradigm shift from monotheism to pantheism within Judaism but did not intend to revive neopagan pantheism. Instead, he offered contemporary Jews a new way to infuse Jewish life with rituals that envision "a God who is an integral part of all human civilization and all of humanity has a specific responsibility for that relationship."[37]

Schachter-Shalomi's ideas were systematized into Jewish ecotheology by Arthur Green (b. 1941), a major scholar of kabbalah associated with Reconstrucionist Judaism. Combining evolutionary theory with kabbalah and neo-Hasidism, Green suggests that the kabbalistic doctrine of *Sefirot* explains how "the bio-history of the universe" became "the only sacred drama that really matters."[38] In Green's progressive interpretation of evolution, the evolutionary process is "re-visioned not as the struggle of creature against creature and species against species, but as the emergence of a single life energy, a single cosmic Mind that uses the comparative adaptabilities of all forms it enters as a means of going forward into richer and more diverse forms of life. . . . This constant movement of the One, expansive in all directions at once, is at the same time a life form of fully realized self-consciousness."[39] Thus, Green presents a holistic view of reality in which all existents are in some way an expression of God and are to some extent intrinsically related to one another.[40] Contrary to those who hold that in Judaism nature per se is not sacred, Green wishes to obliterate the ontological gap between the

36. For example, see Zalman Schachter-Shalomi, *Paradigm Shift: From the Jewish Renewal Teachings of Reb Zalman Schachter-Shalomi*, ed. Ellen Singer (Northvale, NJ: Jason Aronson, 1993).

37. Shaul Magid, "Jewish Renewal, American Spirituality, and Post-Monotheistic Theology," *Tikkun Magazine* (May/June, 2006): 62–67, quote on p. 65.

38. Arthur Green, *EHYEH: A Kabbalah for Tomorrow* (Woodstock, VT: Jewish Lights, 2003), 111.

39. Ibid., 111–112.

40. Ibid., 118–119. Green further develops his ecotheology in *Radical Judaism: Rethinking God and Tradition* (New Haven, CT: Yale University Press, 2010).

Creator and the created and instead adopts the monistic and immanentist ontology of kabbalah, which blurs the distinction between creation and revelation. The world and the Torah are both God's self-disclosure, and both are linguistic structures that require decoding, an act that humans can accomplish because they are created in the image of God. From the privileged position of the human, Green derives an ethics of responsibility toward all creatures that acknowledges the differences between diverse creatures while insisting on the need to defend the legitimate place in the world of even the weakest and most threatened of creatures. For Green, a Jewish ecological ethics must be a *torat hayim*, namely, a set of laws and instruction that truly enhances life.

Even more famous and influential than Arthur Green is Rabbi Arthur Waskow (b. 1933), a left-leaning political thinker who found his way back to the religious sources of Judaism and became a disciple and partner with Schachter-Shalomi. Waskow is the most important Jewish voice in interreligious discourse about ecological matters, because he shows how to ground environmental concerns in the religious sources of Judaism. Waskow popularized the concept of "Eco-Kosher," which Schachter-Shalomi had coined, integrating a wide-ranging critique of unjust social practices with deep concern for Earth and its natural resources and compassion for the socially marginal.[41]

Waskow's environmental activism inspired many nonprofit Jewish organizations such as ALEPH: Alliance of Jewish Renewal, Shomrei Adama, Hazon, Teva Learning Center, Kanfey Nesharim, the Isabella Friedman Learning Center, Elat Chayyim Center for Jewish Spirituality, Tel Shemesh, the Shalom Nature Center, the Eden Village Camp and others. These rather small organizations offer four main types of activities: nature education, environmental awareness, advocacy on environmental legislation, and community building. These programs, in turn, are informed by the three values

41. For example, Arthur Waskow, *Down-to-Earth Judaism: Food, Money, Sex and the Rest of Life* (New York: Morrow, 1995); Arthur Waskow, "What Is Eco-Kosher?" in *This Sacred Earth: Religion, Nature, Environment*, ed. Roger S. Gottlieb (New York: Routledge, 1996), 297–300; Arthur Waskow, ed., *Torah of the Earth: Exploring 4,000 Years of Ecology in Jewish Thought* (Woodstock, VT: Jewish Lights, 2002).

of responsibility, interconnectedness, and Tikkun Olam (literally, "mending the world"). Derived from Lurianic kabbalah, as noted earlier, the value of Tikkun Olam now justifies a full-fledged program of environmental justice in regard to economic and racial inequity, unjust labor practices, and the causal connection between exploitation of Earth resources and unjust political policies. To achieve Tikkun Olam, one has to live by the ideal of "Eco-Kosher." Because environmentalism requires experiencing nature, Jews who are involved in environmental organizations leave human-built, urban settings and experience nature directly through outdoor activities. Some of these efforts are informed by the teachings of kabbalah and Hasidism, but the early Zionist pioneering ethos and its commitment to communalism often inspire the lifestyle.

In 1993, Jewish environmental organizations coalesced into the Coalition on the Environmental and Jewish Life (COEJL).[42] This umbrella organization (with a membership of about 10,000) has attempted to educate Jews about environmental matters, inspiring Jews to lead environmentally sound lives, beginning with the greening of synagogues, and calling Jews to lend their support to various legislative initiatives as well as to get involved in interfaith dialogue on environmental matters. One organization, Hazon, has attempted to take the concept of "Eco-Kosher" to the next step, creating symbiotic food-production chains, whereby synagogues and other Jewish institutions buy their food from local, organic farms. In New York, New Jersey, Washington, D.C., and Texas, synagogues contracted local farmers for all or a significant part of their harvest, giving the farmers financial support while encouraging their own members to use locally grown, organic produce. It is hard to predict whether American Jews, whose overwhelming majority does not observe the Jewish dietary laws, will adopt the concept of "Eco-Kosher," but this concept is a distinctive Jewish contribution to environmental discourse.

---

42. For a perspective on COEJL, see Mark X. Jacobs, "A Jewish Environmentalism: Past Accomplishments and Future Challenges," in *Judaism and Ecology: Created World and Revealed Word,* ed. Hava Tirosh-Samuelson (Cambridge, MA: Harvard University Press, 2002), 449–477.

Unfortunately the message that Judaism can be part of the solution to the current environmental crisis and offers a distinctive approach to environmental issues has been slow to spread. Jews either assume that Judaism has little to say about environmental matters or presuppose that Judaism and environmentalism are inherently incompatible. Among Jewish academics too, environmentalism is not yet viewed as an important topic, even though there is a significant and growing body of literature that enables one to teach a college-level course on Jewish environmentalism. In general, Jewish attitudes toward environmentalism attest a generational dimension: young Jews are more open to an environmental interpretation of Judaism than Jews who are 60 and older. To convince Jews that Judaism is environmentally wise and relevant will require a lot more work from historians of Judaism, environmental activists, rabbis, educators, theologians, and policymakers.

This issue is especially important in Israel, where there is a vibrant environmental movement but also a disturbing dichotomy between secular and religious approaches to environmentalism. Zionism, as previously noted above, was the concerted effort to produce the "natural Jew," but the complex situation in the modern State of Israel illustrates the paradoxes of Zionism. On the one hand, intimate familiarity with the landscape of the land, its flora and fauna, and the concern for the preservation of the physical environment are popular among secular Israelis, but they are not legitimized by appeal to the religious sources of Judaism. For secular Israelis attention to environmental issues has more to do with Western orientation and the environmental movements in Europe and North America than with Judaism. On the other hand, Jews who are anchored in the Jewish tradition tend to link their love of the land of Israel to a creation of religious nationalist vision that has little to do with environmental values and sensibilities. In fact, these religious-nationalist groups have no qualms committing various environmental sins (e.g., uprooting ancient olive groves) to advance their nationalist agenda (i.e., the settlement of Greater Israel) at the expense of the nationalist agenda of the Palestinians. The ongoing Israeli-Arab conflict and especially the Israeli-Palestinian conflict have exacerbated the environmental challenges in the land of Israel, but conversely, acute environmental problems such as water shortages that affect Arabs, Israelis, and Palestinians have actually inspired some promising Israeli-Arab-Palestinian collaboration.[43] The land that three world religions consider as Holy Land unfortunately suffers from serious environmental challenges.[44]

Today, the State of Israel has a thriving environmental movement that boasts two green parties and many nonprofit organizations that are engaged in advocacy, political action, legislation, and education.[45] The environmental movement in Israel, however, is decidedly secular and does not appeal to Jewish religious sources to make its case about soil degradation, waste disposal, air and water pollution, solar power, biodiversity, loss of habitats, and other environmental concerns. The science of ecology underscores the identification of certain problems and the solution to them, and Israel is at the forefront of many environmental initiatives, including desalination, alternative energy, electric cars, and others. All of these are justified by appeal to scientific data rather than to the Jewish tradition. Exceptions to this generalization are the Heschel Center for Education and Environmental Leadership, the small nonprofit organization *Le-Ovdah U-Leshomrah* (To Till and to Protect), and *Teva Ivry* (Hebraic Nature). These organizations justify their activities and educational efforts by appeal to the values of Judaism, and they deliberately try to bridge the gap between the religious and secular communities in Israel. The concern for the well-being of Israel's natural environment could become a shared project that bridges the cultural divide in Israel, and the need to solve pressing environmental issues, one hopes, could generate cooperation among Israel, the Palestinian Authority and the Arab nations.

By contrast, in the North American Diaspora, in which Jews have no legislative power, the Jewish environmental movement

---

43. Susan H. Lees, *The Political Ecology of the Water Crisis in Israel* (Lanham, MD: University Press of America, 1998); Miriam Lowi, *Water and Power: The Politics of Scarce Resources in the Jordan River Basin* (Cambridge, MA: Cambridge University Press, 1993); Jad Isaac and Hillel Shuval, eds., *Water and Peace in the Middle East* (Amsterdam: Elsevier, 1994). Alon Tal and Alfred Abed Rabbo, eds., *Water Wisdom; Preparing the Groundwork for Cooperative and Sustainable Water Management in the Middle East* (New Brunswick, NJ: Rutgers University Press, 2010).

44. See Alon Tal, *Pollution in a Promised Land: An Environmental History of Israel* (Berekely, CA, and London: University of California Press, 2002).

45. Alon Tal, "Israel and Environmentalism," in *Encyclopedia of Religion and Nature*, ed. Bron Taylor (London: Continuum, 2005), 887–891.

carries out its activities in religious settings and through decidedly religious idioms, including interfaith dialogue. The environmental activism of Arthur Waskow and the ecotheology of Arthur Green illustrate the religious nature of Jewish responses to the environmental crisis in North America. Of course, in the American environmental movement, many Jews have leading positions as activists and theorists—Murray Bookchin, the founder of Social Ecology,[46] is one obvious example—but traditional Judaism does not inform their activism or theoretical writings. Whether a commitment to environmentalism is a secular version of foundational Jewish values (e.g., responsibility, concern for the exploited, and justice) might be asked about others as well. These include leading ecofeminists like Starhawk (born Miriam Simon), the "priestess" of earth-based spiritual religion who is linked to Wicca and who promotes a neopagan religion of the Goddess, the Immanent Life Force,[47] and Riane Eisler, a Jewish refugee from Nazi-occupied Europe who is a human rights activist and a leader in the movement for peace, sustainability, and economic equality.[48]

CONCLUSION

Judaism has much to say about the current ecological crisis and could contribute to addressing contemporary environmental challenges. Elaborating the ecological wisdom of the Bible, the Jewish religious tradition highlights human responsibility toward the natural world, forbids wanton destruction, prevents unnecessary cruelty toward animals, and sees a link between moral integrity

---

46. See, for example, Murray Bookchin, *The Philosophy of Social Ecology: Essays on Dialectical Naturalism* (Montreal and New York: Black Rose Books, 1990); *Re-Enchanting Humanity: A Defense of the Human Spirit against Antihumanism, Misanthropy, Mysticism* (London and New York: Cassell, 1995); *Social Ecology and Communalism* (Edinburgh and Oakland, CA: AK Press, 2007).

47. Starhawk, *The Spiral Dance: A Rebirth of the Ancient Religion of the Great Goddess* (San Francisco: Harper & Row, 1979); *Webs of Power: Notes from the Global Uprising* (Gabriola, British Columbia: New Society Publishers, 2002).

48. Riane Tennenhaus Eisler, *The Chalice and the Blade: Our History, Our Future* (San Francisco: Harper & Row, 1987); *The Real Wealth of Nations: Creating a Caring Economics* (San Francisco: Berrett-Koeler, 2007).

and the well-being of the natural environment. The Jewish concept of the Sabbath as imposed rest can be extended to nature, urging humanity to protect parts of the natural world from human interference. The more Jews explore their own tradition, the more they can appreciate its diverse attitudes toward nature and the more they can engage members of other religious traditions in taking the necessary steps to protect nature from human destruction. The environmental challenges ahead are real, and the Jewish community in the Diaspora, as well as in the State of Israel, cannot afford to ignore them. The future of Jewish environmentalism depends not only on environmental activism by Jews but also on a creative involvement of Jewish scholars in exploring the complex relationship between Judaism and nature in light of the tensions between religion and secularism as well as the deeper involvement of Jews in interreligious environmental discourse. Judaism is not the cause of the environmental crisis but rather a viable path to mending an environmentally broken world.

QUESTIONS FOR REVIEW

1. What are the main principles of Jewish environmental ethics?
2. In what way did rabbinic Judaism elaborate biblical environmental legislation?
3. How did medieval philosophers and mystics interpret the doctrine of creation?
4. In what way was Zionism the return of the Jews to nature?
5. What does "Eco-Kosher" mean and what does it add to the global environmental movement?

IN-DEPTH QUESTIONS

1. Is *Jewish environmentalism* a contradiction in terms? What are the intrinsic challenges to Jewish environmentalism?
2. Are biblical environmental principles relevant to environmental policies today? If so, how could the biblical mindset be applied to contemporary ecological problems?

3. If nature is symbolically meaningful, does it generate interest in and concern for the physical environment or rather distance and alienation from it? Explain.
4. What are the differences between Jewish environmentalism in Israel and in the Diaspora? What will it take to bridge the two environmental communities?
5. Is Jewish ethics of responsibility toward nature necessarily religious? Can the concern for nature be justified on secular grounds?

CHAPTER 16

GREATER THAN THE CREATION OF MANKIND (*QUR'AN* 40:57):

Creation as the Divine Signature in *Qur'an*ic and Sufi Revelation

June-Ann Greeley

KEY TERMS

tawhid

khalifa

Qur'an

fitra

amanah

hima

aya

janna

The East and the West belong to God: wherever you turn, there is His Face. (*Qur'an* 2:115)

INTRODUCTION

This chapter introduces the relatively new study of environmental theology and the ethics of ecology in Islam, based primarily upon *Qur'an*ic teachings. The religious teachings of Islam have long advocated the natural obligation, based on beliefs of kinship, of humanity to protect creation and to encourage the health of all its natural cycles. The complex history of colonial rule in the Islamic world, combined with modern economic influences, has weakened those ecological teachings of protective kinship and the behaviors such teachings inspire. More recently, however, Muslim scholars, ethicists, and activists have begun to revisit the environmental principles of Islam and reassert the traditional Islamic perception of creation as encompassing *ayat*, or signs, of God, and the piously lawful practices toward the created world that Islam enjoins on its believers as an aspect of their obedience to God.

GREEN ISLAM?

It should not be surprising that conversations about the "greening" of the faith or about the ethical dimensions of "green discipleship" have seemed less vigorous within Islam than within, for example, Christianity, especially during the last few decades, as a more deliberate consciousness of environmental concerns has emerged from the work of scholars in Christian ethics and Christian theology. That ostensible lack of vigorous Islamic inquiry into environmental issues, however, is certainly not a question of Muslim uninterest or disregard for the natural world: in fact, quite the contrary is true. Yet, it can be argued that two critical factors particularly have contributed to the delay of the ecological conversation within the Muslim world, which only very recently has begun to address formally and publicly this most crucial matter.

On one hand, the impact of modernity, filtered through the presumptions of colonial domination, had significant repercussions upon the Islamic world, especially in the Middle East, Africa, and southeast Asia, and only now is the magnitude of that effect beginning to be understood as Muslim scholars and activists address the multilayered legacies of exploitation and sufferance long endured by those once-colonized nations. Self-interested values and self-aggrandizing demands of external powers assuming economic and social dominion over less materially advanced nations and peoples have always characterized the imprint of colonialization. Yet, through the latter half of the twentieth century, Western nations practiced a particular form of colonialism, in the Middle East and elsewhere, that was especially noted for its vigorous secularism and acquisitiveness, along with an enthrallment with efficiency and technology that resulted in an unapologetic misuse of Earth, its resources, and its potentialities. Thus, the effect of Western colonialization on the environment and ecological systems of the Muslim world was as severe and as devastating as its effect upon the cultural and spiritual identities of those Muslim nations.[1] The colonizing powers bequeathed to Muslim nations policies of austere secularization combined with relentless economic practices—involving models of consistent growth—that dismissed religious practices and beliefs, as well as environmental concerns, as peripheral, and likely detrimental, to material and political "progress."[2]

On the other hand, it is also true that some native governments and Islamic leaders themselves abetted the urgent promotion of colonial investment in oil and other natural resources and similarly advocated policies and projects that resulted in the degradation of the native environment. As one scholar has argued, the

> "modernizing" movement succeeded in producing an elite, including a Muslim elite, that wanted for themselves what the West wanted . . . the establishment of a global system . . . based on an institutional model run according to secular principles subscribing to a philosophy of endless economic growth.[3]

The trajectory of "endless economic growth" was especially problematic because the financial and corporate interests of the "Muslim elite" did more than encourage exploitation of natural resources and the local working force: they acted with complete disregard for a profoundly spiritual dimension of Islam, the defining faith of that region of the world.[4] As contemporary Muslim proponents of

---

1.See E. Kula, "Islam and Environmental Conservation," *Environmental Conservation* 28, no. 1 (2001), 2.

2. For example, Ali Mohamed Al-Damkhi, "Environmental Ethics in Islam: Principles, Violations and Future Perspectives," *The International Journal of Environmental Studies* 65 (2008): 20–21, in which he discusses the practice of wealthy nations of maintaining a "green" profile at the expense of abusing and exploiting dependent, poorer nations in the Middle East and Africa, dumping hazardous materials, reducing emission standards, and polluting native waters and land.

3. Fazlun Khalid, "Islam, Ecology, and Modernity: An Islamic Critique of the Root Causes of Environmental Degradation," in *Islam and Ecology: A Bestowed Trust*, editors Richard C. Foltz, Frederick M. Denny and Azizan Baharuddin (Cambridge, MA: Harvard University Press, 2003), 300.

4. Al-Damkhi, 25-26; Geoffrey Roughton, "The Ancient and the Modern: Environmental Law and Governance in Islam," *Columbia Journal of Environmental Law* 32, no. 1 (2007): 100; Sayed Sikandar Shah Haneef, "Principles of Environmental Law," *The Arab Law Quarterly*, 3, no. 17 (2002), 241–242.

ecological consciousness and environmental justice assert, such a ready exploitation (and degradation) of nature was, in fact, more than the customary assertion of capitalist values and demands; rather, for theologically grounded Muslim activists, the heedless acceptance of utter dominion over nature should be more properly understood as an arrogant rejection of what is believed to be the gift of creation, an obstinate act against God and against the lawful role sanctioned for humanity as stewards of Earth.

The international petroleum industry of the Middle East offers sobering examples—too many to recount—of this kind of (impious) anthropocentric extremism that was reinforced by the seductive lure of financial gain. However, one example might prove especially illuminating. In the 1990s, the substantial colonies of oil wells in Kuwait became the pivotal targets of hostile "ecoterrorism" tactics as Iraqi military forces set ablaze nearly all those oil wells, with horrific consequences, particularly for the area's native, civilian tribes. It has been estimated that this instance of Iraqi "scorching" of the Kuwaiti petroleum industry released more than 156 million barrels of crude oil into desert regions, polluting precious (because limited) supplies of local waters, emitting toxic vapors into the atmosphere, blighting the fertile soil within the devastated area (thus compromising greatly future agricultural production), and utterly laying to waste the biological systems throughout the region.[5] That one Muslim government deployed its forces so catastrophically against the natural environment of another Muslim nation was particularly dreadful—and infuriating, as, presumably, both nations adhered to similar *Qur'an*ic teachings.

In some instances, a Muslim nation has degraded its own environment with careless disregard for either ecology or piety. For example, Indonesia, considered one of the most biologically diverse lands in the world, allowed its excessive dependence on its natural resources to cause grave damage to its celebrated ecosystem—rapid and relentless deforestation; illegal logging; reckless expansion of

5. See Al-Damkhi, 11–12. That section of the article includes as well the chilling description of the relentless destruction by Saddam Hussein's government of the wetland and marshlands of southern Iraq during the 1980s, with an estimated 90 percent devastation of the wetlands area (12–13).

human habitation without consideration of its bionetwork or the resident animal populations, and persistent pollution of the clean water supply. By the 1990s, many Indonesians had to concede that the country's economic- and growth-driven practices and policies were becoming dangerously unsustainable.[6]

Such a disappointing historical trend of environmental degradation in Muslim nations has inspired Muslim scholars and activists to revitalize the inherent ecotheology of Islam, not merely as a reminder of but also as a guide to authentic Islamic devotion and observance. Those scholars insist that

> for the Muslim world, the answer to the current environmental dilemma lies in entirely going forward to the environmental ethics of Islam; in giving practical shape to the environmental dictates of the *Holy Qur'an* . . . and returning to the environmentally conscious traditions and lifestyles of Islam.[7]

Contemporary Muslim leaders, then, concerned about the degradation of the natural habitat, and conscious of the spiritual implications of ethical negligence and biological assault, are determined to reaffirm and articulate anew the ecological values of Islam that have their unquestionable foundation in the narrative and revelation of the most sacred text of Islam, the *Qur'an*.

THE *QUR'AN* AS THE PRIMARY GUIDE FOR ENVIRONMENTAL CONSCIOUSNESS

At the center of Islam and of Muslim identity abides the *Qur'an*, the sacred text of divine revelations to the Prophet Muhammad. The *Qur'an* is the Word of God, the ultimate source of meaning and signification, the compilation of wisdom and direction for living faithfully in the world, and the living engagement of the Almighty

---

6. For a more complete discussion, see Fachruddin Majeri Mangunjaya, "Developing Environmental Awareness and Conservation through Islamic Teaching," *Journal of Islamic Studies* 22, no. 1 (2011), 36–49.

7. Al-Damkhi, 26.

with the human, the gracious "text" of revelation made intelligible for humanity to come closer to God. The *Qur'an* exists for faithful Muslims as the perfect expression of Divine will and signification, and thus, for a Muslim, any consideration of nature and the natural world or the proper human response to the natural world or the appropriate relation between the human and nonhuman world, must be based on the primal authority of the *Qur'an*. As so many other sacred scriptures for their devotees, the *Qur'an* is for Muslims the direct discourse of revealed relation: it is the relational instrument that connects God with the entire created universe and especially with humanity. Muslims perceive the revealed messages in the *Qur'an* to be God's merciful encouragement to connection, the breaching once again of an impasse between the Divine and human realms with magnificent declarations—erupting with concern and frustration and love—of advice and warning, explanation and prophecy.[8] The teachings within those messages of the *Qur'an* offer the faithful the essential elements of proper being in the world and a guide to proper engagement with the world.

Yet, it is critical for non-Muslims to appreciate that Muslims experience the *Qur'an* and its divine disclosures as something distinct from the traditional model of the status and authority of the sacred texts in other religious traditions. That is to say, the *Qur'an* exists for Muslims not as the Bible does for most Christians, for example, but more accurately, the *Qur'an* exists for Muslims as does Jesus Christ for Christians.[9] Muslims understand the *Qur'an* to be the living word of God, the direct revelation made immediate to humanity through the agency of Muhammad as the chosen prophet. Muslims regard the *Qur'an* as pure, glorious, and miraculous, and not amended or modified by human interference or contextual interpretation, not conveyed as indirect accounts of a third articulation of the original. The *Qur'an* is the divine will made sentient, initially as sound, and then as sound transcribed into language: a textual incarnation. To be

---

8. On the wondrous origin and import of the *Qur'an*, see, for example, *Qur'an* 17:82–89; 26:192; 28:51; 46:11–14. Unless otherwise indicated, all citations from *Qur'an* are taken from the translation by M. A. S. Abdel Haleem (New York: Oxford University Press, 2005).

9. There is a great deal of literature about the unique status among religious texts of the *Qur'an* within Islam. Among the most accessible sources, see Seyyed Hossein Nasr, *Religion and the Order of Nature* (New York: Oxford University Press, 1996), 20.

sure, there are other testimonies of God's messages, other forms of understanding Divine disposition, such as the *Hadith* of Muhammad, collections of his own "extratextual" remarks and reflections on *Qur'an*ic teachings for pious devotion, as well as pragmatic practice in both private and public life.[10] That Muslims recognize the *Hadith* as the observations and deliberations of the Prophet himself ascribes to the material a certain moral credence and import; nevertheless, without exception, the *Qur'an* remains the principal authority in Islam and incomparable as the direct articulation of God's will. The *Qur'an* is thus unparalleled in ontology and stature among the sacred texts of the world's religions.

ENVIRONMENTAL THEMES IN THE *QUR'AN*

Creation as *Tawhid* (Absolute Unity of God)

> *He is Allah besides Whom there is no god; the Knower of the unseen and the seen; He is the Beneficent, the Merciful*
> *He is Allah, besides Whom there is no god; the King, the Holy, the Giver of peace, the Granter of security, Guardian over all, the Mighty, the Supreme, the Possessor of every greatness; Glory be to Allah from what they set up (with Him).*
> *He is Allah the Creator, the Maker, the Fashioner; His are the most excellent names; whatever is in the heavens and the earth declares His glory; and He is the Mighty, the Wise.*[11]

Among the defining tenets of Islamic theology, perhaps none is so vital and so central as the principle of *tawhid*, the fundamental Unity, the radical Oneness, of God. Islam shares with its Abrahamic cousins Judaism and Christianity the belief in a single Creator God, and for Islam, God's Absolute Singularity encompasses all reality—*is* Reality—and expresses the relational essence of all being, all life. *Tawhid*, of course,

10. A brief review of the vitality of the *Hadith* in the lives of Muslims can be found in S. Nomanul Haq, "Islam and Ecology: Toward Retrieval and Reconstruction," in *Islam and Ecology: A Bestowed Trust*, eds. Richard C. Foltz et al. (Cambridge, MA: Harvard University Press, 2003), 141–142.

11. *Qur'an* 59:22–24, translated by M. H. Shakir. Tahrike Tarsile Qur'an, 1983.

must never be construed as a kind of monism or, more darkly for Islam, a kind of pantheism; the essential dynamism of all existence is the continual expression of God's transcendence (*tanzil*) and immanence (*tashbih*). God is as remote as the expanse of the edge of the universe but as intimate with each individual as his own heart:

> . . . He is with you wherever you are; He sees all that you do;
> control of the heavens and earth belongs to Him . . .
> He makes night merge into day and day into night.
> He knows what is in every heart . . . [12]

Properly understood, particularity and diffusion only *seem* divisive and contrary: beyond the mortal, material quotidian abides the truth of final universality and essential interdependence of all things. As the first pillar of confession (*shahadah*) proclaims, the *Qur'an* teaches that there is no god but God and that that transcendent One encompasses all that is real.[13] As such, there is no authentic existence outside God, and creation—the natural world—cannot exist apart from God and does not operate according to a separate dynamic, but is, rather, an extension of the Divine Will, a consequence of Divine Mercy. It is the miraculous proof of God's presence. The *Qur'an* bears witness:

> It is the Lord of Mercy Who taught the *Qur'an*. He created man . . .
> The sun and the moon follow their calculated courses; the plants and trees submit to His designs; He has raised up the sky; He has set the balance . . . weigh with justice and do not fall short in the balance . . . [14]

The universe is ordered, purposeful, and inherently stable, intimately beholden to God. Surah (a section of the *Qur'an*) 55 continues with an elaboration of the marvels of creation, like pearls, saltwater and freshwater, fire and mountains, and proclaims that all exist as blessings because of God and *for* God, in submission (*islam*) to Him. God's

12. *Qur'an* 57: 4–6.

13. See, for example, *Qur'an* 2:255.

14. *Qur'an* 55:1–9.

will is the dynamism of the universe, the active agency of the Divine Unity (*tawhid*). It becomes then quite clear that the created world is an astonishing gift, a bestowed blessing that should inspire care and protection, not disregard and neglect, because it *is* of God, and humanity most perfectly can realize its own flourishing by remaining adhered to the universe. As one scholar has noted,

> . . . (the life desired) is a state of being where the human being lives in accordance with *fitra*, experiencing the divine presence both within the purified heart, and without, in harmony with nature.[15]

Creation, by its very nature as *created*, is significant and purposeful, not of itself singly and apart but in its capacity as the phenomenal expression of the One God, and the faithful, genuine life of every human is realized by the clear recognition of the One God within the serene purity of the soul linked to the peaceful unity of the created world.

Creation as *Ayat* (Signs) of God

> *To the eye of a discerning man, every leaf upon a growing tree is a book imparting knowledge of our Creator.*
>
> —Sa'adi[16]

Yet, the natural world is not simply a pleasant diversion or constant testimony to the utter majesty of God. Creation is appropriately understood to be a sign (*aya*) of God the Absolute Unity, and to consist of a multitude of signs (*ayat*) that point to the reality of God. As the *Qur'an* states,

> Another of His signs is the creation of the heavens and the earth,
> and the diversity of your languages and colors . . . among His signs are your sleep, by night and by day, and your seeking

15. Ron Geaves, *Aspects of Islam* (Washington, DC: Georgetown University Press, 2005), 40.

16. From *Poems from the Persian*, translated by J. C. E. Bowen (Oxford: Blackwell, 1958), 53.

> His bounty . . . among His signs, too, are . . . the lightening that terrifies and inspires hope . . . water that He sends down from the sky to restore the earth to life . . . [17]

Thus, all aspects of creation, including essential characteristics of humanity, manifest the reality of God and reveal His Will. All of creation, all that generates and all that destroys, are signatures of the Divine and, therefore, must be accorded the dignity such remarkable capacity possesses. Yet, the natural world—indeed, all of creation, including humanity—should be understood to be more than just demonstrative of God: creation does not consist merely of "things" that offer humanity ideas or suggestions about God's power and permanence. Creation, rather, consists of objects and categories and actions and events that are dynamically transformative of human understanding, that exist as traces (*athar*) of God's act of creation and of His constant presence.[18]

Creation, then, is *iconic* rather than imagic, which is to say that in Islam, the created universe signifies a Real Presence much as does an icon. An icon is a liminal object, a corporeal portal to spiritual Reality, and a participant in the duality of spiritual existence. It is, as object, the physical, material, and, therefore, corruptible, condition of being that it presents to external observation; yet, it embodies also the faultless, pristine spiritual presence of that which it indicates. Just so is creation in Islam. It is important to recall that the first mandate handed to Muhammad was "Read!" In that instruction he understood that the world around him, in fact, the entire universe, stands as a revelation of God, persists as a sacred text wherein one should "read" the signs (*ayat*) of God, of God's Mercy and Compassion, of the Truth of God, that exist everywhere.[19] It clearly follows, then, that creation is to be honored, cherished, even admired, regarded as one of the eternal sacred texts by which, and *in* which, communication with God may transpire.

17. *Qur'an* 30: 22–24.

18. For further discussion on this idea, see Aref Ali Nayed, "Ayatology and Rahmatology: Islam and the Environment," in *Building a Better Bridge: Muslims, Christians and the Common Good*, ed. Michael Ipgrave (Washington, DC: Georgetown University Press, 2008), 161–167.

19. Of course, Surah 96, the "first" revelation.

Read the "book of creation," God instructs humankind in *Qur'an* 88:17–20: "Do disbelievers not see how rain clouds are formed, how the heavens are lifted, how the mountains are raised high, how the earth is spread out?" To corrupt the "book" of nature—the signs of the created world—is to impede communication with God, to rupture the binding of *tawhid*.

There is also a moral dimension to the understanding of nature as singly and collectively *aya* of God; this dimension suggests a path the contemporary environmentalists in Islam choose to follow. Those who remain aware of creation as the vital "signs" of God appreciate that the wonders of creation must never be damaged or misused, regardless of the motivation. Thus, humanity is called on to discern its own will when encountering the natural world and to engage the world according to the piety not only of *islam* but also of *ihsan*: the faithfulness of submission and the righteousness of "doing what is beautiful," of remaining humble before the wonder of God's beneficence, and, above all, of being grateful for God's goodness.[20] If humanity stands before the created world in thankfulness for God's generosity and honors the handiwork of God's creation, then humanity will have begun to fulfill appropriately its assigned task, that of *khalifa*, or vice regent over the natural world.

Human as *Khalifa* (Vice Regent)

> *Allah named him khalif for this reason, since man guards His creation as treasure is guarded with the seal. As long as the seal of the King is on the treasure, no one dares to open it without his permission. He made him a khalif in respect of safeguarding the universe, and it continues to be guarded as long as this Perfect Man is in it.*[21]

As is true in both Judaism and Christianity, humanity in Islam is the privileged portion of creation: " . . . it was He Who created all that is on the earth for you . . . " (*Qur'an* 2:29). Yet, that lofty position

20. Nayed expresses this beautifully at 165–166.

21. Muhiyyi'd–din Ibn al-'Arabi, *The Seals of Wisdom* (*Fusus al-Hikam*), ch. 1, *http://bewley.virtualave.net/fusus1.html*, accessed February 17, 2011.

is not without grave responsibilities, for God's purpose is also for humanity to behave on Earth as God would will, with devotion and humbleness. "We have adorned the earth with attractive things so that We may test people to find out which of them do best" (*Qur'an* 18:7). Humanity does not have complete license to exercise its own will as each human wishes; rather, humanity is tasked with acting deliberately, with care. Indeed, the nobility of humanity is exemplified by the *Qur'an*ic understanding of the human as *khalifa*, the vice regent, over creation. A *khalifa*, in its root form, is understood to be someone who succeeds to a responsibility or a position when the original placeholder is no longer available, for a variety of reasons.[22] However, it is incumbent upon the successor, the *khalifa*, to honor the position since vacated by the predecessor and to execute all assigned tasks with complete dignity and gratitude. The *khalifa*, then, must accept his role as a trust (*amana*) that he will fulfill sincerely all obligations delegated to him and justly carry out all actions appropriate to the assigned position.

*Qur'an*ic revelation, however, underscores the tension inherent in humanity's vocation as *khalifa*, vice regent over Earth. Islam does believe that the natural world was bestowed as a gift to humanity: "It was He who created all that is on the earth for you, then he turned to the sky and made the seven heavens . . . " (*Qur'an* 2:29)[23]; yet, that gift was not conferred without concomitant accountability: "It is He who made you *khalifa* on the earth and raises some of you above others in rank, to test you through what He gives you" (*Qur'an* 6:165). Humanity enjoys great freedom in its access to the natural world, to utilize its resources and its treasures. Humans may build cities, sail the oceans, create industry, and develop agriculture. Still, humanity is obliged to temper such liberty with a humble consciousness of God as the supreme and ultimate authority and with a corresponding appreciation for the inherent limitations on the power of the vice regency. Earth and all its bounties are indeed resources but also are gifts to be honored, to be treated with the degree of dignity and respect appropriate for God's handiwork. Nothing on Earth, or in the universe, was created frivolously: "It was not without purpose that We created

22. See Al-Damkhi, 16.

23. There are many such verses; see also, for example, *Qur'an* 22:65–66.

the heavens and the earth and everything in between. That may be what the disbelievers assume."[24] All of creation has meaning and value, has been deliberately formed and generated in goodness and order, interconnected and interrelated, beautiful and wondrous—so wondrous, in fact, that the creation of the natural world overwhelms the creation of humanity. "The creation of the heavens and earth is greater by far than the creation of mankind, though most people do not know it."[25]

Exploitation of or damage to any dimension or aspect of the natural world would be, in effect, an affront against God and a rejection of God's mercy and care, as well as a usurpation of God's primacy and authority and a dangerous misapprehension of the human condition. God reminds humanity that, though vice regent, humankind is not so distinct from other animals: "All the creatures that crawl on the earth and those that fly with their wings are communities like yourselves."[26] The lives of animals are inherently worthy, just as the lives of humans are not autonomous or without obligation. Indeed, the *Qur'an* articulates a broad sensitivity to the generosity of nonhuman animals and the requisite gratitude and compassion humans are advised to demonstrate:

> . . . (a)nd livestock—He created them too. You derive warmth and other benefits from them: you get food from them; you find beauty in them when you bring them home to rest and when you drive them out to pasture. They carry your loads to lands you yourselves could not reach without great hardship—truly your Lord is kind and merciful.[27]

God constantly admonishes humanity to acknowledge the symbiotic relationship among the different aspects of creation and to live mindfully of that relationship, not only in submission (*islam*) to God's will and justice and with faith (*iman*) in God's mercy but as an expression of the beautiful deed (*ihsan*) of pious righteousness

24. *Qur'an* 38:27.

25. *Qur'an* 40:57.

26. *Qur'an* 6:38.

27. *Qur'an* 16:5–7.

and remembrance (*dhikr*) of the gentle blessings suffusing earthly existence. Humanity has the freedom to honor such blessings or to be heedless of the bestowed gifts and so fall into thoughtless disregard of the natural world.

The *Qur'an* avers consistently that humans are themselves responsible to read the signs bestowed by God throughout creation and acknowledge the proper conduct expected of ones so graciously gifted; however, humanity is also at will to renege on the assigned tasks at hand, and sadly, humanity has been guilty of just such folly. Humans have been ungrateful for the splendor of creation (*Qur'an* 40:61), humans have shed blood and caused unnecessary harm to nature (*Qur'an* 2:30), and humans have been arrogant about their stature on earth, "strutting about" and being blind to the truth of their position within creation (*Qur'an* 17:37). With such behavior, humans have, in effect, demonstrated their separation from God; in their frequent rejection of the responsibility to care for Earth and in their disavowal of the trust (*amana*) God bestowed on them to assume the authority as vice regent over the natural world with humility and graciousness, humans have displayed a forgetfulness of truth and an ingratitude to God that are soul-searing blunders. Yet, now, in their post-colonial status and endowed with certain freedoms that modern society offers, Muslims individually and also collectively enjoy opportunities to revive and realize the *Qur'an*ic models of environmental consciousness and ecological justice, models which are not the result of secular, modernist philosophy, but are, on the contrary, distilled from the very heart of Islam.

The Image of the Garden in the Ecotheology of Islam

> *And as for one who fears to stand in the presence of his Lord*
> *and forbids the soul from low desires,*
> *Lo! the Garden—that is the abode.*
>
> — *Qur'an* 79:40–41

Islam offers explicit guidance about the order of life within nature and the proper human response to its condition in the natural world, in the *Qur'an*ic exemplar of the garden. While there are several references to gardens and to garden imagery throughout the revelations, a remarkable parable merits consideration: A man was graced by God to enjoy two gardens rich with grapes, dates palms, and corn, and generously irrigated by flowing streams. One day, the man spoke to his neighbor and boasted that his wealth and property far exceeded that of his neighbor, arrogantly asserted that all such natural abundance was the result of his own effort, and that he could exert his will at his pleasure over the garden. His neighbor was astounded and scolded him:

> Have you no faith in Him Who created you from dust, from
> a small drop of fluid, then shaped you into a man? . . . if only,
> when
> you entered your garden, you had said, "This is God's will, there is
> no power not given by God."[28]

For his vanity, the man whose luxuriant and plentiful garden had been the source of such pride was destroyed by a divine thunderbolt. The parable illuminates not only the absolute majesty of God and the dangerous consequences of human frailty and folly, but also it suggests that there is nothing in creation that God has not set there, and any human attempt to assume primacy over the natural world deserves retribution.

The *Qur'an* also teaches that Paradise, the Abode of the Blessed, is a luxurious garden, a place of "thornless lote trees and clustered acacia with spreading shade, Constantly flowing water, abundant fruits, unfailing . . . "[29] Eternal life in Islam is conceived as Edenic splendor, in which the souls of the graciously pure may find peace amid the dense flourishing of verdant vegetation. It is a sanctified *locus amoenus* surpassing human imagination, and yet it remains a garden, the consecrated world of nature. In the afterlife, the pious and merciful will dwell within a garden, the Garden of Paradise: *janna* (garden) *al-firdaws* (paradise). Throughout the *Qur'an*, there are constant reminders that those who have lived lives of devotion, righteousness, and humility will rejoice to spend eternity in a "garden" that is variously described as a verdant site of repose lush with running streams of water, milk and wine and copious bounties of fruits from the trees:

---

28. *Qur'an* 18:37–39.

29. *Qur'an* 56:28–33.

SUFISM AND THE GARDEN

An illustration from a manuscript of "Gulistan" (Rose Garden) by the Sufi poet Sa'di (ca. 1184–ca. 1292). The text of the manuscript was copied by calligrapher Sultan Ali Mashhadi in 1468 and the illumination added in the early sixteenth century.

Come to the garden in
  Spring,
There is light and wine, and
  sweethearts
in the pomegranate flowers.

—Rumi[30]

Sufism is the name given to the dimension of Islam that expresses a more mystical, interior and subjective devotion than might be found in the more familiar forms of piety. The tenets of Sufism are sometimes contrasted with *shari'a*, or "the law" of Islam, a more formal dicta of human action and endeavor, so that among some Muslim constituencies, a tension exists, even an antagonism, between the outer (exoteric, *shari'a*) and inner (esoteric, *tasawwuf*, or Sufi) paths of religious piety. The more literal, legal-minded believers tend to regard with suspicion the less predictive, less conformist spirituality of the adept, and the many disciples of the internal journey of awakening insist that the essence of any faith must be the personal, immediate encounter with the Divine. Sufism declares that both forms of observance are necessary to an authentic life of devotion. As one scholar has explained,

continued

30. From *The Essential Rumi*, trans. Coleman Barks with John Moyne (HarperSanFrancisco, 1995), 37.

SUFISM AND THE GARDEN continued

> . . . the true Sufi hands over his affairs to guidance and illumination. This is *tariqa* . . . the fine balance between shari'a and the *haqiqa* (the mystical consciousness): the one is the science of the outward, and the other the science of the inward. *Tariqa* is balance and harmony: it is beyond mere religious significance—it is also socially and politically significant.[31]

The Sufi way, then, concentrates on detachment from the mundane and the pedestrian as a mechanism for spiritual advancement, and yet is not so dismissive of the common and the everyday that it does not attend in some measure to the daily life of humanity. It is not uncommon, for example, for the actual residences of Sufi masters to be at once central locations of religious education, spiritual training, infirmaries and hospices, and lodgings of hospitality.[32] Sufi shaykhs are as committed to the physical health of the seeker as to her spiritual health, and their understanding of the garden as the metaphor for the numinous place of the spiritual journey of the individual translates into a deep regard for the organic gardens of humanity that are themselves signs of Divine beneficence.

"So God will save them from the woes of that Day, give them radiance and gladness, and reward them . . . with a Garden . . . with shady branches . . . and clusters of fruit" (*Qur'an* 76:11–14) and "As for those who believe and do good deeds— . . . they will have Gardens of lasting bliss graced with flowing streams . . . " (*Qur'an* 18: 30). Although the idea of an afterlife in a paradisal garden is certainly not unique to Islam, the *Qur'an*ic revelations insist that eternal

31. Hashim Ismail Dockrat, "Islam, Muslim Society, and Environmental Concerns: A Development Model Based on Islam's Organic Society," in *Islam and Ecology: A Bestowed Trust*, editors Richard C. Foltz et al. (Cambridge, MA: Harvard University Press, 2003), 362 (parenthesis mine).

32. Ibid., 363.

HIMA, "THE PROTECTED PLACE"

The concept of *hima*, or "protected place," is as much about justice and piety as it is about ecological consciousness. The original, pre-Islamic idea was actually much more a problem of injustice and dominion: pre-Islamic tribal leaders would declare a particularly fertile or verdant area *hima* and, therefore, forbidden to external access. The tribal leader would, thereby, have sole authority over the use of the land, such as grazing, irrigation, and planting, as well as control over whatever goods the land would produce. However, with the ascent of Islam in the region, the idea of the *hima* changed with the Islamic notion of *tawhid:* all of creation belongs to God and must be treated with care and respect (*Qur'an* 11:64). The revelations to Muhammad ended the tradition of privately owned *hima* and Muhammad himself decreed that any *hima* was to be conserved for the public good and should be managed only for the public benefit. The *hima* cannot deprive any local community of necessary resources and should actually be of benefit to a wider population. The tradition of the *hima*, then, is an early model of conservation and reasonable use of resources, and environmental planners and activists in the Middle East have begun to encourage its wider revival.[33]

life is best understood as correlative to an almost perfect condition of the natural world: ripe, fecund, moist, and throbbing with generation. Such an image should not be surprising for a religion born out of the desert, yet the vibrant image of the garden is densely detailed: the portrait is one of order, balance, beauty, moderation, and sustenance.

The proper setting for humanity, then, has been idealized as within the garden, within nature, amid flowing waters and ripening vines—but it is not nature as disposable or at the mercy of human will. Rather, God *welcomes* humanity into the Garden as reward

33. See *http://www.muslimheritage.com/topics/default.cfm?articleID=916* for history of *hima* conservation, accessed April 15, 2011.

for having lived lives of righteousness and piety, and so, humanity enters the garden as a *guest*, with a grateful heart, conscious of the humbling responsibility that must be assumed. Even though humanity has freedom within the garden and much of what is there exists to delight and please the human soul, nonetheless, those within the garden live in harmony with the natural surroundings, appreciating the beauty and abundance of the natural world and acknowledging the compassionate munificence of God.

QUESTIONS FOR REVIEW

1. According to the *Qur'an*, what does it mean that humans are *vice regents* of creation? What rights does that suggest humans have? What responsibilities?
2. What does it mean in Islamic teaching that nature is a *sign* of God?
3. What is the concept of *tawhid?* Is there a similar concept in any other religion you know? Compare and contrast those similar concepts.
4. What is the Islamic concept of the garden, especially as Sufism understands it? How does that concept of the garden relate to broader themes of care for the environment?

IN-DEPTH QUESTIONS

1. Are any of the environmental teachings in Islam similar to the environmental teachings of other religions? Discuss with reference to at least one other religious tradition.
2. What is the difference, if any, between the term *creation* and the term *nature* in describing the nonhuman world which humans inhabit? Might the belief that something is *created*, perhaps even deliberately, inspire or diminish human care for its surroundings? Explain your response.
3. How might the concept of *tawhid* affect an understanding of human responsibility toward the natural world? How might it not?

4. In terms of the history of environmental degradation of countries within the Islamic world, do you think that colonial influences or native governmental policies were more responsible? Why?

CHAPTER 17

WHY DOES THE BUDDHA CLOSE HIS EYES IN MY EDEN?

A Buddhist Ecological Challenge and Invitation to Christians

David Clairmont

KEY TERMS

Siddhartha Gautama
Buddha
Theravada
Mahayana
Four Noble Truths
Noble Eightfold Path
Law of Dependent Co-Origination
Dhamma
Sangha
engaged Buddhism

INTRODUCTION

Buddhism is the name given to the tradition of stories, philosophical writing, meditation instruction, and devotional practices that developed in response to the life and teachings of Siddhartha Gautama, a man from northern India who lived sometime between 600 and 400 BCE. Étienne Lamotte (1903–1983), a Catholic priest from Belgium and one of the greatest scholars of Indian Buddhism of his era, once suggested that "Buddhism cannot be explained unless we accept that it has its origin in the strong personality of its founder."[1] Indeed, the personalities one encounters tend to exert a strong pull on the form of life toward which one is attracted. Yet, studying the significant moral issues of current times—especially the threats to global ecology—requires something other than charismatic examples or retreats to small agrarian communes or myths about human origin. That "something other" is a thoughtful engagement with the world's many moral problems (each of which has its own story and web of influences), as well as with the world's religious traditions (each of which also has a story and a mixed history of questions and tentative answers).

The tradition of Buddhist concern for the natural world, the world's harmonious functioning, and the place of humans within the world is at least as complicated for practicing Buddhists as hearing the call for "green discipleship" is for contemporary Christians. Just as the Christian churches have, over many years, struggled to come to a greater appreciation of their responsibilities to creation, so too have Buddhist communities struggled to understand their proper relationship to the world. Yet, the study and practice of Buddhism, in North America and Europe especially, has often focused on emulating an idealized personality of the Buddha and his practice of meditation or on selecting elements of his teachings as building blocks for a verdant Buddhist utopia. In reality, Buddhist communities around the world continue to struggle with problems similar to those faced by Christians who want to engage their tradition on difficult questions that admit of no easy solutions.

Caution becomes necessary on a number of fronts as one enters a discussion of Buddhist views about nature, creation, and ecological ethics from the perspective of Christian theology. First, such Christian expeditions into Buddhist thought are often undertaken with the idea that some modest consensus might eventually appear around practical strategies for confronting global environmental degradation. Even if such common commitments were to emerge, Christians must

1.Étienne Lamotte, *History of Indian Buddhism from the Origins to the Śakya Era* (Louvain, 1988), 639, cited in Rupert Gethin, *The Foundations of Buddhism* (Oxford and New York: Oxford University Press, 1998), 15–16. On Lamotte, see Heinz Bechert, "In Memoriam Étienne Lamotte (1903–1983)," *Numen* 32, no. 1 (1985): 119–129.

remain cautious that their reasons for committing themselves to a course of action will not necessarily be the same as those of members of other traditions. Second, when Christians fail to live by the highest standards of their tradition, standards that for Christians, as well as Buddhists (and perhaps others), are still unfolding, the modes and reasons for their failures will likely also differ. Cultural differences and social and economic complexities will make different religious responses to ecological ethics even more difficult. However, Christian theologians who hope to think and act responsibly in the face of growing ecological concerns, in a world in which religious and other cultural diversities are becoming ever more evident, must always keep before them one question: Why should we think with other people from different religious backgrounds about these common moral challenges? Don't Christians have enough to do just to understand the many teachings of their own tradition about ecologically sensitive discipleship? Is there something additionally important, internal to the activity of thinking about other religious readings of the natural world and other traditions' histories of approaching ecological ethics that can make them better Christian thinkers and more responsible Christians? These questions should be kept in mind while reading the following pages.

This chapter will examine some of the early teachings that have become central to Buddhist approaches to moral problems, how such teachings relate to Buddhist interpretations of the natural world, and how Buddhist critiques about ideas of God and creation relate to Buddhist ecological teachings. Most of those teachings come from ancient Buddhist sources (although what is oldest should not necessarily be equated with what is best), texts still revered as "canonical" in those Southeast Asian countries such as Sri Lanka, Burma/Myanmar, Cambodia, and Thailand that follow the so-called *Theravada* ("way [*vada*] of the elders [*thera*]"). Although the other main branches of Buddhist teaching (*sasana*), the *Mahayana* ("great [*maha*] vehicle [*yana*]," which includes the famous Chan/Zen communities), and the *Vajrayana* ("diamond vehicle," which features the well-known Tibetan Buddhist teachings of the fourteenth Dalai Lama), have much to say about contemporary environmental problems, this chapter will focus on those earliest teachings that, with a few exceptions, all Buddhists share. Although the comparison is not entirely apt (especially because such ideas were never formulated as articles of belief demanding assent), these Buddhist teachings do exhibit the same general consensus as the creeds of the early Christian churches.

BUDDHIST VIEWS AND BUDDHIST WORLDS

In one way, Lamotte's comment about the person of the Buddha is quite helpful, insofar as a particular series of events in the life of Siddhartha Gautama (the one referred to as the Buddha or the enlightened one) are closely connected to what the Buddha had to teach, how he taught, and what place he perceived himself to play in what he taught. The bare outlines of the Buddha's story suggest that he was a man of a well-established, if not noble, family who became dissatisfied with his world, its allures, promises, and disappointments. The story is frequently told of Siddhartha taking a series of chariot rides during which he encountered three disturbing images: an old man, a sick man, and a man who had died. On his fourth ride, he encountered a wandering ascetic whom Siddhartha took to have discovered some important truth about the nature of life. However, neither could this one give an answer to how one should respond to age, sickness, and death. Thus, Siddhartha vowed to sit in meditation under a tree until he discovered freedom from the disturbances of this life. What Siddhartha discovered, the Buddhist tradition tells, is some deep insight into the nature of the world, an insight commonly called the Four Noble Truths:

1. All of life is unsatisfactory/suffering (*dukkha*).
2. Craving (*tanha*) is the cause (*samudaya*) of this unsatisfactoriness.
3. The cessation (*nirodha*) of craving is the cessation of unsatisfactoriness.
4. There is a path (*magga*) that leads to the cessation of this unsatisfactoriness.

The Buddha was interested in knowing the root cause of this unsatisfactoriness and, although the Four Truths isolate craving as the primary cause, the Buddha also suggested that this craving has three "roots": greed (*raga*), delusion (*moha*), and hatred (*dosa*).

The path the Buddha taught was, he said, a practical path, intended as a training in practices, rather than as an exercise in speculative thinking, about the nature of the universe. The path has been commonly referred to as the Noble Eightfold Path and is divided into three kinds of training:

- *Morality* (*sila*) is a preparatory stage, intended both to prevent suffering by not hurting others and also to free one from thinking too much about morality, that is, to free one for higher meditative attainments. It has three parts:
    1. right speech
    2. right action
    3. right livelihood
- *Concentration* (*samadhi*) pertains to developing focused, single-minded thought about a meditation subject. The point is to eliminate distraction from the mind so it will eventually be free to see reality as it truly is. It has three parts:
    1. right effort
    2. right mindfulness
    3. right concentration
- *Insight Wisdom* (*pañña*) has to do with the attainment of truths about reality through immediate awareness of the three characteristics. It requires the calm mind and sustained attention that concentration develops. It includes two parts:
    1. right thought
    2. right understanding

What comprises this third kind of training—insight wisdom? This is difficult to answer, in part because its answer is not something the Buddha assumed could be formulated in propositional statements. Although there are various interpretations of this wisdom, at least three of the components—although conceptually stated—must be tested experientially and fostered through practices if they are to be "known" in the full sense.

First, the wisdom described consists in knowledge of the characteristics of all things in this and any other world.

Three Characteristics of All Reality:

1. not-self (*anatta*)
2. unsatisfactory, suffering (*dukkha*)
3. impermanent (*anicca*)

Second, the wisdom consists in knowing how, in many obvious and subtle ways, humans' actions and the events humans encounter are related to their prior choices and other factors in a way that renders these experiences unsatisfactory. This is formulated as the object of the Buddha's insight about the nature of reality and is sometimes called the Law of Dependent Co-Origination (*paticcasamuppada*), or more commonly dependent origination, and depicted as a circle of linked elements in a chain.[2]

1. ignorance (*avijja*)
2. mental formations (*sankhara*)
3. consciousness *(vinnana)*
4. mind-body (*nama-rupa*)
5. six-sense bases (*salayatana*)
6. contact (*phassa*)
7. feeling (*vedana*)
8. craving (*tanha*)
9. clinging (*upadana*)
10. becoming (*bhava*)
11. birth (*jati*)
12. old age and death (*jara-marana*)

2. The twelve elements in the chain of dependent origination also account for the traditional Buddhist belief in the round of rebirth through successive lives (*samsara*). The first and second elements account for one life, which in a single moment of consciousness (the third element) is reborn into a momentary unity of mind and body (the fourth element), which then itself undergoes the processes of life and moves again to death and rebirth (the eleventh and twelfth elements). See Mark Siderits, *Buddhism as Philosophy: An Introduction* (Indianapolis IN, and Cambridge: Hackett, 2007).

The same insight can be reformulated in terms of the object of humans' craving. The Buddha supposed that humans crave not just the things they see but also an uninterrupted sense of ease or completeness when they have grasped and held tight to whatever thing they seek for satisfaction. In other words, the root of their attachment is a wrong view, namely, that they can be fulfilled by the acquisition of what they crave. More puzzling perhaps, the Buddha suggested that what they crave is not, most important, the union with or satiation by something they desire but instead the notion of a self that can experience satisfaction at all. They crave to be selves, able to be completed and fulfilled by unchanging things. However, he taught that if they scrutinize their experience closely enough, they will find no evidence of such unchanging things. Indeed, if they look closely enough, they will find nothing in their "selves" that is a permanent, unchanging place from which to experience satisfaction or to be content.

Third, the Buddha explained that all things humans might view as solid or permanent are really only a combination of five aggregates, or *khandhas*. These are the most basic units by which one can analyze one's experiences and what one takes to be separable realities that give rise to one's experiences:

1. name-form (material; *nama-rapa*)
2. feeling (mental; *vedana*)
3. perception (*sanna*)
4. mental formations/active thinking (*sankhara*)
5. consciousness (*vinnana*)

It is important to realize, regarding each of these teachings, that the Buddha assumed a distinction between the mere fact of being able to list these factors (that is, to know what they are and to see some rough way in which they could explain the reality they confront) and being able to know them experientially, through the rigors of mental training. So to know that all of reality is well described by the three characteristics is quite different from being able to analyze every thought and experience one has in a way that convinces one of their truth. Moreover, to see how the links in the twelvefold causal chain of dependent co-origination work means something quite different from merely knowing of them. The Buddha is said to have seen the chain in the depths of meditation, and likewise, he advises his followers not to accept what he says but also to test it in their experience. These teachings, and others of the Buddha, are commonly known as his *Dhamma* (or in the more familiar Sanskrit word, *Dharma*, meaning variously "way" or "truth" or "law").

Members of a Buddhist community are said to have "taken refuge" in the "threefold jewel" (*tiratana*): the *Buddha* (that is, the person who discovered these truths), the *Dhamma* (his teaching or truth), and the *Sangha* (the monastic community to whom he entrusted his teaching to be passed on to those who wish to know the cessation of suffering in this life).

The Buddha bequeathed to his community of followers some practical moral guidance, as well, that flows from his root judgments about the nature of the world and of the trials and disappointments of life. The following five precepts (known as the *pañcasila*) are expected of all Buddhists, whether monks, nuns, or laypersons:

1. refrain from taking life
2. refrain from taking what is not given
3. refrain from wrong conduct in sexual matters
4. refrain from false speech
5. refrain from intoxicants that are the occasion for reckless behaviors

Three more precepts extend to monks and to laypersons who are willing to observe them, especially at certain times of the year:

6. refrain from eating at the wrong time (that is, after noon)
7. refrain from attending musical and theatrical performances and from wearing jewelry and perfumes
8. refrain from sleeping in large, high, or otherwise fancy beds

For monks only, the same eight precepts hold, slightly reformulated, and two are added:

9. refrain from accepting gold and silver

10. refrain from wearing clothing in an ungraceful or undignified way[3]

Broadly speaking, all of these elements—the personal example of the Buddha, his teaching about the nature of reality and humans' relation to it, and the moral precepts of his community—form the outlines of what might be termed a basic Buddhist ethic. Yet, one must also ask how this rudimentary Buddhist ethic is related to Buddhist teaching about the natural world (that is, all material things but especially plants, animals, and humans), to Buddhist judgments about God and creation, and to attempts by contemporary Buddhists to address ecological concerns.

THE BUDDHA'S TEACHING ON NATURE AND ECOLOGICAL ETHICS

Just as Christians have gradually developed a coherent ecological ethic and a set of practices through which to live their commitments, so too have Buddhist communities undertaken challenges in coming to an understanding of how their heritage and practices as Buddhists ought to influence their thinking about ecological issues. Given the basic points of the Buddha's teaching outlined previously, it should not be surprising that Buddhists have debated what these teachings ought to mean for ecological ethics. Indeed, in recent discussions, scholars of Buddhism, among them practicing Buddhists, have disagreed over how to interpret the teachings of the Buddha and also how the earliest Buddhists understood the natural world and actually practiced their beliefs. For just as Christians, both early in their history and still today, do not always match their actions to what the Gospels or the church community says they ought to be doing, so too Buddhists.

Some scholar-activists, such as Joanna Macy, have argued that the Buddha's teaching about dependent co-origination is the central lens through which to read other aspects of early Buddhist history,

3. These precepts are found in various early Buddhist writings. One convenient point of reference is the *Brahmajala Sutta*, in the collection of longer discourses. For an English translation, see *The Long Discourses of the Buddha: A Translation of the Dagha Nikāya*, trans. Maurice Walshe (Boston: Wisdom Publications, 1995), 67–90.

including Buddhist literature about animals, plants, and other aspects of the natural world. Macy argues that accepting the Buddha's teaching on dependent co-origination commits contemporary Buddhists to view all beings (humans and other animals, indeed, all aspects of the natural world) as interconnected, deserving of equal dignity, respect, and protection. Here, this central Buddhist teaching is taken to mean not only that all beings are related through a complex series of causes but also that they ought to interpret all their actions in light of their effect on beings with whom they are interconnected.

Macy sees in the Buddha's teachings a wellspring from which to draw insights about environmentally responsible living. However, these wellsprings center particularly on the Buddha's teaching about *anatta* (not-self) and *anicca* (impermanence or change), which Macy describes as overlapping, interconnected fields of influence rather than separate entities. Macy sees destructive consequences for societies that view themselves as isolated actors competing for resources. She sees a common wisdom in Buddhist teaching and recent scientific theories: a "'conventional notion of the self' is being replaced by wider constructs of identity and self-interest—by what you might call the ecological self or the eco-self, co-extensive with other beings and the life of our planet. It is what I will call 'the greening of the self.'"[4]

Other scholars have argued that to interpret the Buddha's teaching on dependent co-origination and not-self in this way is to miss, perhaps even misrepresent, the earliest Buddhist teachings about the natural world and the practices through which early Buddhists navigated their values and commitments. Ian Harris, one such opponent, has suggested that interpretations such as Macy's do not give due weight to the genuinely ambivalent, even hostile or fearful, relationship that many premodern societies, including the Buddha's, had to their physical surroundings. Moreover, Harris argues, eco-Buddhists like Macy have, in their particular interpretations of dependent co-origination, added onto traditional Buddhist teaching a "principle of emergent purpose," that is cooperative activity by humans sensitive to the intrinsic balance of

4. Joanna Macy, "The Greening of the Self," in *Dharma Gaia: A Harvest of Essays in Buddhism and Ecology*, ed. Allan Hunt Badiner (Berkeley, CA: Parallax, 1990).

nature. According to Harris, eco-Buddhism is guilty of adding new and distinctively non-Buddhist elements "to a traditional Buddhist core" in an attempt to show Buddhism's natural affinity with modern ecological sensitivity, "which is incapable, without modification, of responding to the present environmental crisis."[5]

Lambert Schmithausen has noted that the variety in positions of what now has come to be called "green Buddhism" or "eco-Buddhism" stems at least in part from the ambivalent attitude of Buddhists toward the natural world and the challenges that arise when one speaks of the "natures" of different living beings. He suggests that the earliest strata of the Buddhist tradition allow for, at best, a "largely passive ecological attitude," one based on the values of "intact nature and . . . natural diversity."[6] Although the focus on right action as part of the Eightfold Path and the Five Precepts precludes aggression toward or abuse of living creatures, dependent co-origination does not ground an all-purpose ecological sensitivity.

THE BUDDHA'S TEACHING ON CREATION AND GOD(S)

Given the fundamental teachings of the Buddha outlined previously and the diversity of approaches to ecological matters among Buddhists and scholars of Buddhism hinted at in the preceding section, one must add one more important topic to the conversation. Both old and unsettled, this topic may be roughly posed as a question: What did the Buddha teach about God and about creation? This question is closely related to another frequently cited: Is Buddhism a religion? Given the diversity of responses by Buddhists about the status of the natural world and advice about how to live responsibly in it, that the Buddhist response to the question of a creator God is equally divided should not be surprising.

The Buddha's discourses record his arguing against those of his contemporaries who believed in a single, all-powerful creator God.

---

5. Ian Harris, "Buddhist Environmental Ethics and Detraditionalization: The Case of EcoBuddhism," *Religion* 25, no. 3 (July 1995): 206.

6. Lambert Schmithausen, "The Early Buddhist Tradition and Ecological Ethics," *Journal of Buddhist Ethics* 4 (1997): 7.

The basis for the Buddha's argument, across its various forms, is that one should not cut off at some artificial time the logical question of prior causes. Unlike theologians in many other traditions, the Buddha found that an account of an eternal sequence of interrelated causes—as he saw them through meditation, which led to his teaching on dependent co-origination—would fully explain all the physical and mental events one could possibly experience.[7] Therefore, he supposed, there was no need to posit a creator God understood to be the first cause of all that exists or a particular moment when the world began. Such a creator would represent, at best, an artificially inserted stopping point in a causal sequence that has no logical beginning; one can always ask the further question: What gave rise to that allegedly first cause?

Although not immediately discounting the idea of an all-powerful God (the Buddha, like his contemporaries, saw a world filled with superhuman, even divine, beings), he was critical of those who accepted the idea of a single, ruling creator God (that is, the *issara-nimmana-vada,* or "belief [*vada*] in creation [*nimmana*] by a lord" [*issara*]), especially if their belief was based on the testimony of other people without fully scrutinizing it themselves. Moreover, the Buddha suggested that such a deeply felt need to find an origin to this sequence of causes was, if submitted to the rigors of meditative analysis, really just another (particularly strong) example of craving that leads to attachment that in turn eventuates in suffering. However, even though the Buddha suspected that such belief or attachment to a view (*ditthi*) could lead to great violence, he was aware that those holding such views could also lead exemplary lives, much like the lives he hoped that his followers would lead. As Nyanaponika explains, "God-belief . . . is not placed in the same category as those morally destructive wrong views which deny the

7. For a very helpful summary of the Buddhist objections to a creator God, see the essay by Nyanaponika Thera, "Buddhism and the God-Idea," *The Wheel Publication* No. 47 (Kandy: Buddhist Publications Society, 2008 [1962]). For three of the frequently cited discourses on the subject, see the Brahmajala Sutta and the Tevijja Sutta, both in the *Digha NiKaya* (trans. Walshe, 67–90, 187–195), and the Casakuludāyi Sutta in *The Middle Length Discourses of the Buddha: A Translation of the Majjhima NiKaya*, trans. Bhikkhu Nyanamoli and Bhikkhu Bodhi (Boston: Wisdom Publications, 1995), 654–662.

karmic results of action, assume a fortuitous origin of man and nature, or teach absolute determinism. These views are said to be altogether pernicious, giving definite bad results due to their effect on ethical conduct."[8]

This reveals an interesting criterion for Buddhist evaluations of various religious beliefs: they must ultimately be tested through the kinds of lives they enable those holding them to lead. So although the Buddha rejected belief in a creator God, his mode of rejecting it—affirming that those who believe in God are likely to live morally praiseworthy lives, even as they are in constant danger of becoming excessively and even violently attached to what they say they believe—makes the Buddha's teaching on God and creation both inviting and problematic for those considering it from a theological point of view.

At least two things should now be clear: First, though Buddhist teachings about the natural world and how people ought to live within it are of significant depth and firmly rooted in Buddhist history, there continues to be significant disagreement about how those teachings should be interpreted and to what extent the values and practical guidance communicated in them can support an environmental ethic appropriate to the modern world. For the Buddha, like Jesus five hundred years later, offered guidance to his followers at a time when the scope and complexity of environmental challenges were neither foreseen nor understood. It was left to the communities that inherited the teachings of the Buddha and Jesus to examine and debate how those teachings could and ought to be interpreted in light of present problems.

Second, in many ways, Buddhism should and does remain one of the most, if not *the* most, significant dialogue partners for Christians on many contemporary moral issues, including global ecological problems. This is due to a peculiar feature of Christian-Buddhist dialogue—namely the ability of these two communities to share so many commonalities in how they diagnose moral problems and the solutions they present, despite their nearly opposite judgments about the centrality of a creative, loving God to human history.

---

8. Nyanaponika Thera, "Buddhism and the God-Idea," *The Wheel Publication* No.47 (Kandy: Buddhist Publications Society, 2008 [1962]):1.

Practicing Buddhists perform many noteworthy efforts to address the ecological challenges and crises humans face in the modern world. Although recounting all of them here is not possible, a few examples provide a sense of the depth and breadth of Buddhist activities in environmental affairs. Such examples also offer points of initial comparative explorations for those interested in cultivating an interreligious and cross-cultural moral sensitivity about the natural world.

CONTEMPORARY BUDDHIST ECOLOGICAL MOVEMENTS

Among contemporary Buddhists in Asia and elsewhere, efforts to effect social change grounded in Buddhist teachings have come to be known as "engaged Buddhism." Scholars of these "Buddhist liberation movements" have noted some similarities with allied Christian movements, in which the former are characterized by "a fundamental commitment to making Buddhism responsive to the suffering of ordinary Buddhists."[9] The origin of the phrase "engaged Buddhism" or "socially engaged Buddhism" is usually attributed to the contemporary Vietnamese monk Thich Nhat Hanh, writing at the time of the Vietnam War to explain the actions of Buddhist monks protesting the treatment of the Vietnamese people.[10]

Various expressions of engaged Buddhism arose across the countries of Asia and elsewhere in response to both social and political difficulties, many of which predated the Vietnam War and still continue in some form today. Yet engaged Buddhism was also a response to the contact between Asian Buddhists and European intellectuals, some of whom saw deep affinities between the modern search for a true religion based not in tradition and superstition but in science and reason. For example, in a address to the World's Parliament of Religions held in Chicago in 1893, an Sinhalese Buddhist, Angarika Dharmapala (1864–1933), suggested a deep affinity between the Buddhist emphases on the causal interrelatedness of

9. See Christopher S. Queen and Sallie B. King, eds., *Engaged Buddhism: Buddhist Liberation Movements in Asia* (Albany, NY: SUNY Press, 1996), x.

10. Ibid., 2, 34 (n. 6).

reality, the rational interrogation of experience, and a critical view toward traditional religious forms, with what he judged to be similar values grounding modern scientific investigation.[11] In a different way, Bhimrao Ramji Ambedkar (1891–1956) became an influential legal and political thinker in India in part by turning to Buddhism to envision new ways to liberate people in his society from material need and oppression by those holding economic and political power. However, as with Dharmapala, Ambedkar's interpretation of Buddhism sought to trim away its traditional religious heritage to find a core of "social freedom, intellectual freedom, economic freedom and political freedom."[12] His critics worried that he was reducing Buddhism to "a merely social system" and loosing it from its proper context and community that ought to focus on release from, rather than transformation of, worldly realties.[13]

This balance between social and political liberation and liberation from excessive attachment to this world plays out in the more ecologically focused engaged Buddhist movements as well. For example, in Thailand, the *Theravada* monk Buddhadasa Bhikkhu (1906–1993) established the rural Suan Mokkh ("Garden of Liberation") monastery in 1932 so he and other young monks would have a place to study the Buddha's teaching away from the politically aligned monastic communities in the busy city of Bangkok.[14] From this retreat, Buddhadasa became one of the foremost preachers in the Thai *Theravada* tradition, hoping that his return to central aspects of Buddhist teaching (especially the truth of *anatta* that opposes selfishness and attachment) might bring about a peaceful unification of different religious paths and political liberation to the oppressed of his country. More recently, Buddhadasa's student, Santikaro Bhikkhu, has founded Liberation Park on a 70-acre site in southwest Wisconsin. Based on the model of his mentor's Suan Mokkh, Santikaro teaches an "ecumenical, socially progressive, non-patriarchal,

11. David L. McMahan, *The Making of Buddhist Modernism* (New York and Oxford: Oxford University Press, 2008), 91–97.

12. Queen and King, eds., *Engaged Buddhism*, 47.

13. Ibid.

14. Santikaro Bhikkhu, "Buddhadasa Bhikkhu: Life and Society through the Natural Eyes of Voidness," in Queen and King, eds., *Engaged Buddhism*, 147-193.

pragmatic and creative" interpretation of Buddhist Dhamma, "dedicated to fostering a community of liberatory practice; providing a natural setting for personal meditation retreats and study; and living out a Buddhist ethic of ecological healing, social responsibility, and right relationship."[15] Similar communities in the *Theravada* lineage exist around the United States, with many such as Metta Forest Monastery in California also serving as centers for both spiritual retreat and Buddhist and more broadly ecological education.[16]

Many similar movements throughout Asia and elsewhere that display more directly ecological concerns have been coordinated through or affiliated with the Alliance of Religions and Conservation (ARC).[17] For example, in traditionally *Theravada* countries, the Mlup Baitong or "Green Shade" movement has arisen. Cambodian monks work to cultivate trees and other shade plants around their pagodas and elsewhere. The monks also attend and then present educational workshops in local towns and villages. Cambodia is also the home for the Association of Buddhists for the Environment (ABE), which coordinates conservation and educational activities throughout the region.[18]

In Sri Lanka, the Sarvodaya Shramadana organization, founded by A. T. Ariyaratne in the 1950s, coordinates a diverse set of programs that place local communities, community empowerment, and ecological sustainability at the heart of their work. Whether the work is tsunami relief, aiding refugees from the Sinhalese-Tamil civil war, or fostering community tourism, this organization has tried to develop a coordinated plan of action for addressing the country's

15. See *http://www.liberationpark.org/index.htm.*

16. See *http://www.watmetta.org/.* In other Buddhist communities in the United States, the connection between spiritual practice and ecological sensitivity has moved in other directions. For example, the San Francisco Zen Center's Green Gulch Farm has forged connections with local farmers' markets and offers education in organic gardening and food preparation. See *http://www.sfzc.org/ggf/.*

17. For a summary of the ARC and the many projects sponsored by or affiliated with this organization, see their Web site: *http://www.arcworld.org/*, accessed March 18, 2011.

18. For more information on the ABE, see their Web site: *http://www.sanghanetwork.org/index.php?option=com_content&task=view&id=100&Itemid=69*, accessed July 21, 2009.

multiple moral problems while retaining its Buddhist heritage. In a more focused effort in Thailand, the *phra nak anuraksa,* or "ecology monks," have undertaken work to educate local farming communities and to protest certain commercial and government projects. These acts have led to some novel interventions, such as the practice organized by Phrakhru Pitak Nanthakhun to ordain trees to protect them from destruction. As Susan Darlington relates, this practice involved much local participation, with the result that those attending the ceremony were less likely to carry out work that would destroy the very trees whose ordination they had witnessed.[19]

To be sure, such practices have often pitted religious communities against local and national governments and have even sometimes been occasions for division within religious communities. Yet a consideration of these movements allows one to return to the question posed at the beginning of this chapter: Why should we think with other people from different religious backgrounds about these common moral challenges? There are a number of possible answers to this question, and a few will be addressed here: First, the range of possible activities that might be undertaken by religious communities to foster ecological sensitivity and more sustainable practices can only be fully envisioned when people open themselves to the practices that have arisen in religious histories other than their own. Their problems are not the problems of Thai or Cambodian monks, but someday these, or problems like them, might be those of all people. It would be wise to begin to draw inspiration from other religious communities.

Second, it should come as some small consolation to Christians—who, as a group, seem to have remained rather behind the times in cultivating ecological sensitivities—that these are challenges all human communities face and to which they will not easily adapt. However, they should find equal consolation for the difficulties they face in discerning how the Christian tradition ought to meet these challenges from a cultivation of its own theological land. Buddhist communities have engaged in debates about the very meaning of their teacher's guidance as it relates to ecological ethics. One should expect the Christian tradition, in all its variety, to have it no easier,

19. For a more developed description of this practice and the history leading up to it, see Susan M. Darlington, "The Ordination of a Tree: The Buddhist Ecology Movement in Thailand," *Ethnology* 37, no. 1 (1998): 1–15.

as Christians strain to see how the life of Jesus and the witness of the early disciples ought to inform present ecological ethics and its attendant practices.

Third, and perhaps most seriously, these kinds of issues—complex moral issues such as global ecological degradation—return people to serious engagement with their theological traditions with renewed strength, commitment, and critical reevaluation. Buddhist communities have preserved their founder's teaching in a particularly profound and even prophetic way, including to other religious communities, Christians among them. For the Buddha taught that the origin of human trials is to be found in the threefold rotten root of greed, anger, and delusion. So it would be well for Christians to ask: What are the distinctly Christian manifestations of greed? What are the characteristically Christian angers? What are the common Christian delusions about oneself, one's communities, and one's faith? How are these manifestations of wrong Christian view, and what Christian cravings must one silence to respect and enhance God's creation?

QUESTIONS FOR REVIEW

1. What are the Four Noble Truths that the Buddha taught?
2. What are the three characteristics that, according to the Buddha, characterize all reality?
3. What central Buddhist teaching has been reinterpreted by the tradition to mean a kind of general interconnectedness of all beings?
4. On what basis does the Buddha judge that belief in a creator God is a belief unsupported by experience?
5. What are three of the environmental activities with which contemporary Buddhist communities are involved?

IN-DEPTH QUESTIONS

1. What are the most important similarities and differences between Buddhist and Christian views about the inherent goodness of the natural world?

2. What are the most important similarities and differences between Buddhist and Christian views about human responsibility to the natural world?
3. Do you think that Buddhists and Christians have basically the same view about the central moral problem that affects ecological issues, or do they identify fundamentally different problems?
4. How does one know when a religious tradition is departing from its traditional teachings, and how does one discern when such departures are responsible innovations that remain true to that tradition's basic value judgments?
5. What would be an example of such an innovation in a religious tradition from the Buddhist and the Christian side?

ISSUES AND APPLICATIONS

CHAPTER 18

TOWARD A JUST WAY OF EATING

Julie Hanlon Rubio

KEY TERMS

carbon footprint
local food
organic food
whole food

INTRODUCTION

Our food choices affect the environment. Furthermore, the conventional production, distribution, and consumption of food harm Earth and its creatures. Beginning from these premises, this chapter argues that people, in caring for creation, ought to adopt an ethical approach to food characterized by a just way of eating. This chapter also offers practical guidelines for a more ethical way of eating that ordinary families can adopt.

CONNECTING ENVIRONMENTAL ETHICS AND FAMILY ETHICS

In the midst of the current "green revolution," there is no shortage of attention to just eating. The attention is warranted because the way we eat has a huge effect on the environment, accounting for one third of our carbon footprint and using more fossil fuel than any sector of the economy except transportation.[1] Changing the way we eat has

1. See *texas.sierraclub.org/dallas/conservation/take-action/sustainable-food.pdf,* accessed December 15, 2010.

great potential to reduce not only our carbon footprint but also the broader effect on the planet. The food system that sustains the way people eat—one dominated by industrial agriculture, factory farming, and processed foods—is damaging to the environment, unsustainable, and unfair to future inhabitants of Earth.

The changes recommended by ardent environmentalists, however, can be unrealistic and contradictory. Some environmentalists advocate eating as much organic food as possible to support more sustainable farming methods. Advocates of a local diet argue that buying from local farmers to avoid transporting and storing foods (when food travels an average of more than 1,000 miles to stores) is more important. Philosopher Peter Singer and followers, in contrast, advocate striking a blow to factory farming by switching to an all-vegan diet. The omnipresent Michael Pollan opines, "Eat food. Not too much. Mostly plants," putting his emphasis on less meat and more whole, sustainably raised foods. *New York Times* food writer Mark Bittman tries to inspire readers to avoid processed foods and animal products and provides instructions for cooking from scratch but declares buying local, organic foods optional. One can easily become confused and overwhelmed by such contradictory information.[2]

Sales of organic products still account for only 2 percent of all U.S. food sales.[3] Meat consumption remains high in the United States and is growing elsewhere in the world. Most produce is far from local. One trip to a Whole Foods or a local farmers' market (where organic produce can cost two to three times as much as conventionally grown) is enough to convince most families that they cannot afford to eat differently. Food ethics debates are a concern of an elite minority, some believe. Meanwhile, the vast majority of Americans continue to buy most of their food from conventional

2. Recent books addressing the ethical dimensions of food include: Michael Pollan, *The Ominvore's Dilemma: A Natural History of Four Meals* (New York: Penguin, 2007); Nina Planck, *Real Food: What to Eat and Why* (NY: Bloomsbury USA, 2007); Marion Nestle, *Food Politics: How the Food Industry Influences Nutrition and Health*, rev. ed. (Berkeley, CA: University of California Press, 2007); Peter Singer and Jim Mason, *The Ethics of What We Eat: Why Our Food Choices Matter* (Rodale, 2006); and Mark Bittman, *Food Matters: A Conscious Guide to Eating with More than 75 Recipes* (New York: Simon & Schuster, 2008).

3. Singer and Mason, *Ethics of What We Eat*, 198.

grocery stores and discount chains, supporting the very systems most environmental analysts agree are responsible for the worst environmental damage. Clearly, people are not convinced that their behavior is unethical, and even those who want to be "green" are unable to imagine a more just way of eating that will work for them.

To effectively address this issue from the perspective of Christian social ethics, it is necessary to (1) make the connection between Christian faith and concern for creation and its most vulnerable inhabitants, (2) show the harmfulness of conventional food systems, and (3) suggest solutions that fit the context of our eating, which is, for the vast majority, some kind of family. I have argued elsewhere that Catholic social teaching will never penetrate the Church unless it goes through the family.[4] The Catholic tradition calls for families not only to care for their own but also to work for the transformation of society. How families live matters, because families are the smallest unit of society, thus familial actions shape society from the ground up. Accordingly, my approach in this chapter will be to pursue environmental ethics through family ethics. I will argue that concern for Earth and its most vulnerable inhabitants requires all Christian households to begin to break away from conventional food systems to eat more justly.

WHY IS "GOING GREEN" A CHRISTIAN ISSUE?

In a letter to the patriarch of Constantinople on September 1, 2007, Pope Benedict XVI wrote with passion of the beauty of the Amazon River. "This immense region, where waters are an incomparable source of harmony and riches, is presented as an open book whose pages reveal the mystery of life. How is it possible not to feel, both as individuals and as communities, urged to acquire a responsible awareness that is expressed in consistent decisions to protect such an ecologically rich environment?"[5] Earth, Benedict suggests, is God's creation presented to humans as full of God's majesty and love. A duty to protect creation

---

4. Rubio, "A Familial Vocation beyond the Family," *CTSA Proceedings* 63 (2008), 71–83.

5. Pope Benedict XVI, "Letter to the Patriarch of Constantinople," September 1, 2007. *www.zenit.org/article-27700?l=english*, accessed April 9, 2010.

flows directly out of an awareness of its power and beauty. Support for environmental causes "stems from contemplation of the eternal Word of God, the Author, Model and End of all things."[6] All who experience Earth's riches should be moved "to safeguard the *habitat* that the Creator has made available to the human being, in whom he has impressed his own image."[7] Environmental concern comes to many affectively, because their experiences in nature convince them that Earth is good and worthy of preserving. A love for creation implies a commitment to be good stewards of its resources.

According to Catholic social teaching, creation is given not to one but to all, so Christians are obligated to use and enjoy Earth in ways that safeguard the rights of others to do the same. Pope Leo XIII famously wrote that humans come into property by their labor or working the land, though they owe to others charity from their excess.[8] In the last century, however, Catholic teaching has seriously qualified Leo's approach, as shown in chapter 12. Pope John XXIII repeated Leo XIII's claim of a natural right to private property, but he immediately softened it by claiming that "the goods which were created by God for all men should flow to all alike, according to the principles of justice and charity."[9] In contemporary Catholic teaching, the reach of private property has been further modified by the principle of the universal destination of material goods and the social mortgage. John Paul II wrote, "God gave the earth to the whole human race for the sustenance of all its members, without excluding or favoring anyone." Though individuals make a portion of Earth their own through work, they "must cooperate with others so that together all can dominate [or exercise stewardship over] Earth."[10] The social mortgage on private property means that one cannot do whatever

6. Ibid.

7. Ibid.

8. Leo XIII, *Rerum novarum*, 1891, no. 22, *www.vatican.va/holy_father/leo_xiii/encyclicals/documents/hf_l-xiii_enc_15051891_rerum-novarum_en.html*, accessed April 9, 2010.

9. *Mater et Magistra*, 1951, nos. 43 and 121, *http://www.vatican.va/holy_father/john_xxiii/encyclicals/documents/hf_j-xxiii_enc_15051961_mater_en.html*, accessed April 9, 2010.

10. *Centesimus annus*, 1991, no. 31, *http://www.vatican.va/holy_father/john_paul_ii/encyclicals/documents/hf_jp-ii_enc_01051991_centesimus-annus_en.html*, accessed April 9, 2010.

one wants with what is owned. Rather, consumption and use of property must be in accord with broader human needs. Good stewardship of Earth requires humans to protect the environment by approaching property with a view to the common good. Catholic teaching brings to environmental ethics a long history of exhorting followers of Christ to embrace simple living. The Church "has always urged restraint and moderation in the use of material goods, so we must not allow our desire to possess more material things to overtake our concern for the basic needs of people and the environment."[11]

Christian environmental action is rooted not only in love for Earth and a moderate approach to property but also in deep concern for the poor. Climate changes affecting the planet (i.e., weather shifts, droughts, rains, and flooding) burden the poor disproportionately. Yet, the poor are often in the worst position to act.[12] More-privileged populations have a weighty responsibility to economically poor populations. The U.S. bishops warn that Americans cannot blame the environmental problem on industrializing nations, because American consumerism is a key cause of the problem, and it makes no sense to blame others for aspiring to live as Americans do. Instead, Americans need to draw from Catholic social teaching and seek "authentic development" for all, which means that progress must respect nature and the good of all people, especially the most vulnerable.[13]

Responsibility for Earth is also warranted by a concern for future generations. In a speech outlining ten Catholic ecological commandments, then-Bishop Giampaolo Crepaldi of the Pontifical Council for Peace and Justice affirmed, "The question of the environment entails the whole planet, as it is a collective good. Our responsibility toward ecology extends to future generations."[14] Though this

---

11. U.S. Conference of Catholic Bishops (USCCB), *Global Climate Change: A Plea for Dialogue, Prudence, and the Common Good,* June 15, 2001, *http://www.usccb.org/sdwp/international/globalclimate.shtml#change*, accessed April 9, 2010.

12. William S. Skylstad, "Stewards of Creation: A Catholic Approach to Climate Change" *America* 200, no. 13 (April 20, 2009): 13, *http://www.americamagazine.org/content/article.cfm?article_id=11600*, accessed February 24, 2011.

13. USCCB, *Global Climate Change.*

14. Giampaolo Crepaldi, "Ten Commandments for the Environment: A Christian View of Man and Nature," June 10, 2008, *http://www.catholic.net/index.php?id=499&option=dedestaca#*, accessed April 9, 2010.

principle is not often invoked in Catholic social teaching, it is especially important to environmental ethics, as small choices Christians make today may seem innocuous but, in reality, may be vastly harmful to Earth's future and the shape of the lives of "those who come after us."[15] The common good extends to future generations, so passing along problems created today is unjust.

In recognition of the duty to protect Creation for the sake of the common good, contemporary Catholic teaching affirms the necessity of conversion. A Vatican spokesperson recently stated, "The world needs an ecological conversion so as to examine critically current models of thought, as well as those of production and consumption."[16] Authentic conversion has both personal and social dimensions and is an ongoing process.[17] For Christians in America faced with the problem of global climate change, the U.S. bishops place the heavier responsibility on "those with power to act" but counsel prudence, which "allows us to discern what constitutes the common good in a given situation."[18] Conversion, then, ought to include political engagement for some, but all citizens can exercise restraint in their personal lives. Christians are asked "not [to] allow our desire to possess more material things to overtake our concern for the basic needs of people and the environment."[19] Embracing moderation "can ease the way to a sustainable and equitable world economy in which sacrifice will no longer be an unpopular concept."[20] Moderation may not be as painful as people think, say the bishops. In fact, it may bring about better, simpler lives centered on people rather than on things.[21]

Today the Church is joining with others in the struggle for the environment out of an understanding of Earth as God's creation given

---

15. Ibid.

16. H. E. Monsignor Celestino Milglore, *Intervention of the Holy See*, October 25, 2006. *http://www.vatican.va/roman_curia/secretariat_state/2006/documents/rc_seg-st_20061025_sustainable-development_en.html*, accessed April 9, 2010.

17. John Paul II, *Ecclesia in America*, nos. 27–28, *http://www.vatican.va/holy_father/john_paul_ii/apost_exhortations/documents/hf_jp-ii_exh_22011999_ecclesia-in-america_en.html*, accessed April 9, 2010.

18. USCCB, *Global Climate Change.*

19. Ibid.

20. Ibid.

21. Ibid.

to all, concern for the poor who are disproportionately harmed by environmental destruction, and a responsibility to future generations. In linking a traditional Catholic economic vision to the green agenda, Church leaders are calling Christians to convert to a new way of living. Examining and shifting our food choices is a good place to begin.

HARMFULNESS OF CURRENT FOOD SYSTEMS

To work effectively for conversion to a new way of life, Christians have to understand the current habitat or context that shapes how most people eat. The Christian habitat for eating is usually the family or household.[22] Among the most significant trends within this habitat are a movement away from regular family meals, decreasing commitment to cooking from scratch, and increasing meat consumption. These trends support the problematic current food system.

How People Eat

According to a 2005 longitudinal study by the Center on Addiction and Substance Abuse at Columbia University, the percentage of adolescents eating with families actually increased 23 percent between 1998 and 2005, probably due in part to public campaigns linking declining family meals to health and social problems.[23] Still, only about 55 percent of 12-year-olds and 26 percent of 17-year-olds report that they regularly eat meals with their families.[24] Because more women are in the workforce, professionals are more likely to work late, adults holding service jobs work more evening hours, children and teens engage in more extracurricular activities, and fewer families have an adult at home who is free to make a meal each day, sitting down to an evening meal has become much more difficult.

---

22. U.S. Census Bureau, "America's Families and Living Arrangements: 2003," *www.census.gov/prod/2004pubs/p20-553.pdf*, accessed August 10, 2010.

23. Nancy Gibbs, "The Magic of the Family Meal," *Time* (June 12, 2006), 50. The CASA study, *National Survey of American Attitudes on Substance Abuse XII: Teens and Parents,* found at *www.casacolumbia.org/absolutenm/articlefiles/ImportanceofFamily-Dinners*, accessed September 4, 2009.

24. Gibbs, "The Magic of the Family Meal," 50.

Unsurprisingly, even when people do eat at home, fewer people are eating meals they have cooked from scratch. A 2005 survey found that 58 percent of Americans questioned ate last night's meal at home (32 percent of them prepared dinner from scratch; 22 percent, with premade ingredients), while 17 percent ate takeout and 23 percent ate in a restaurant.[25] Most studies show that Americans spend 13 percent of their income on food, but only 33 percent of that amount goes to groceries, far less than 50 years ago.[26]

Most people are also eating more processed foods at meals or instead of meals. One third of their calories come from nutrient-poor foods such as sweets, snacks, and fruit drinks.[27] According to analysts of the most recent Consumer Expenditure Survey, an average family's spending on sweets, bakery items, and beverages accounts for 20 percent of Americans' budgets, versus 7 percent on fresh fruit and vegetables.[28] Even these averages are deceiving. Researchers identify one quarter of households (most upper-middle class) that rely more on restaurant and takeout but eat relatively healthily. Another quarter (more lower-income households) are high users of frozen and fast foods. A "balanced" category accounts for another quarter of families, but even these households consume large amounts of sweets, cereal and bakery items, meat, and alcohol.

Rising meat- and animal-product consumption is another key trend. Americans eat about one half pound of meat per day, or 180–200 pounds per year (versus one ounce per day in Africa). Beef consumption has been stable since the 1950s, though chicken and dairy consumption is rising, and meat consumption in the developing world has tripled since the 1970s.[29] "Global meat consumption is expected to double within the next 40 years."[30] Many families

25. A. Elizabeth Sloan, "What, Where, and When America Eats," January 2006, *http://members.ift.org/NR/rdonlyres/65A7B82E-0AFF-4639-95B2-733B8225D93A/0/0106americaeats.pdf*, accessed April 9, 2010.

26. Jessie X. Fan, et al., "Household Food Expenditure Patterns: A Cluster Analysis," *Monthly Labor Review*, April 2007, *http://www.bls.gov/opub/mlr/2007/04/art3full.pdf*, accessed May 20, 2009.

27. Bittman, *Food Matters*, 13–14.

28. Fan, "Household Food Expenditure Patterns."

29. Bittman, *Food Matters*, 11.

30. Ibid., 9.

find it difficult to imagine a meal without meat. Reliance on animal products, along with prepared and processed foods, shapes an eating habitat that supports Americans' conventional food system, a system that is harmful to the environment and unsustainable.

Industrial Agriculture

The farming practices that currently dominate American agriculture are the source of most foods on dinner tables. These practices rely on large quantities of fossil fuels, strip the soil of its nutrients, and contribute to land and water pollution and a loss of biodiversity. In her analysis of "big agriculture," Christian ethicist Rebecca Todd Peters shows that large farms typically rely on pesticides, fertilizers, and mass production of a few crops to maximize yield and profits.[31] These practices have several negative effects: Big corporations with access to machinery, fuel, and chemicals (not to mention government subsidies) produce food so cheaply that small farmers with more environmentally friendly farming methods are unable to compete. The practices themselves are unsustainable, because they rely on nonrenewable fossil fuels instead of the sun, cover crops, and crop rotation to enrich the soil. The result is significant topsoil erosion. Currently, 90 percent of U.S. farmland is losing topsoil above replacement rates, which means eventually, crop yields will drop.[32] Big, industrialized farms also contribute to water pollution when rain washes excess fertilizer into local water sources. Herbicides and insecticides kill worms and microorganisms that nourish the soil and discourage birds and insects that contribute to biodiversity.[33]

In addition, industrial agriculture relies on specialization that necessitates moving crops long distances, requiring even more fossil fuel.[34] A local label alone does not ensure that a product has a low

---

31. Rebecca Todd Peters, "Supporting Community Farming," in *Justice in a Global Economy: Strategies for Home, Community, and World*, eds. Pamela K. Brubaker, Rebecca Todd Peters, and Laura A. Stivers (Louisville, KY: Westminster, 2006), 18–19.

32. Wes Jackson, "Farming in Nature's Image: Natural Systems Agriculture," in Andrew Kimball, *Fatal Harvest* (Washington, DC: Island Press, 2003), 68.

33. Jackson, "Farming in Nature's Image," 70.

34. See *www.foodroutes.org and www.localharvest.org*, accessed May 1, 2009.

ecofootprint, because transportation accounts for only a small percentage of the energy cost of food.[35] Still, transport based on fossil fuels is unsustainable, as are the other practices detailed previously. For all of these reasons, industrial agriculture is a major source of harm to the environment.

Factory Farming

Even in the most recent Catholic teaching on the environment, the Church places humanity at the center of creation and allows for the use of animals for human nourishment and enjoyment, whether they are necessary to human health or not.[36] Though Christians ought to be concerned enough with animal suffering to buy humanely raised products, in the view of most Christian ethicists, they need not avoid all food from animals.

However, current consumption levels are unsustainable. Because raising meat places such high demands on land, energy, and water, "It is simply not possible for everyone in the world to eat as much meat as people in the affluent world now eat."[37] Beef is a particularly problematic choice because its production contributes to global warming through the release of methane gas and because it requires 13 pounds of grain (and corresponding amounts of chemical fertilizers and fossil fuels to grow the grain) to produce one pound of food compared to three pounds of grain for poultry.[38] This is an extremely inefficient way to acquire the protein humans need. From an environmental perspective, eating less beef is one of the most significant choices a person can make. Limited amounts of humanely and sustainably raised chicken and eggs are a better choice and are generally more affordable than pasture-raised beef and, thus, more in keeping with a Christian commitment to living simply.

---

35. James Randerson, "The Eco-Diet . . . and It's Not Just about Food Miles," *The Guardian*, June 4, 2007, *www.guardian.co.uk/uk/2007/jun/04/lifeandhealth.business*, accessed May 1, 2009.

36. Crepaldi, "Ten Commandments."

37. Singer and Mason, *Ethics of What We Eat*, 232.

38. Ibid.

Processing and Packaging

One of the more recent insights in food ethics is that the kind of food humans eat may be more important than how far it has traveled. Some environmental scientists are proposing a complex calculation of the ecological footprint of particular foods that would take into account the amount of energy used to produce, package, store, and ship each product.[39] Some estimates suggest that most of the energy cost is in production (83 percent), rather than the transportation (11 percent) of products.[40] New web sites attempt to make these calculations easier for the average person.[41] In response to this information, many contend that people should strive to eat whole foods and only then worry about the local and organic issue.[42] Because packaging and processing alone account for 37 percent of the energy cost of food, reducing consumption of these foods is key.[43]

In sum, the environmental damage of modern agriculture and food production is considerable, and Christians need to find ways to lessen their cooperation with these systems. Their responsibilities to Earth, the poor, and Earth's future inhabitants require more of them. They must find a just way to eat that is possible for ordinary families. In *Sharing Food: Christian Practices for Enjoyment*, ethicist Shannon Jung urges readers to work toward "a deeply satisfying way to eat."[44] The recommendations that follow are directed toward this end. They represent not absolute rules but rather suggestions for a more just eating practice.

SOLUTIONS FOR A FAMILIAL CONTEXT

Because food choices involve competing goods, it is difficult to discern precisely what constitutes just eating, but I propose the following guidelines:

---

39. Randerson, "The Eco-Diet," *www.sustainableagriculture.com*.

40. Christopher L. Weber and H. Scott Matthews, "Food Miles and the Relative Climate Impacts of Food Choices in the United States," *Environmental Science & Technology* 42, no. 10 (April 16, 2008): 3508–3513.

41. See *www.eatlowcarbon.org*.

42. Bittman, *Food Matters*, 10.

43. Ibid., 17.

44. L. Shannon Jung, *Sharing Food: Christian Practices for Enjoyment* (Minneapolis: Fortress, 2006), 6.

1. *Regular, shared evening meals*. Getting this practice right not only provides a context for making other just choices but also trains family members to be in community with others. According to Jung, "Not to share at home constitutes a loss of our mutuality."[45] When families fail to eat together, they practice a problematic kind of individualism in which personal tastes and priorities trump the value of community. According to anthropologists, family meals are a primary means of "civilizing children. It's about teaching them to be a member of their culture."[46] Around the table, a family shares the stories, jokes, and concerns that become central to its identity. Children learn how a conversation is structured, how to ask others about their day, how to respond to questions or to extend a discussion. Moreover, in sharing food that is not always their preference, children and adults learn compromise and tolerance, for "meals together send the message that citizenship in a family entails certain standards beyond individual whims."[47] The practice of eating civilizes and stretches people because it teaches them to participate in something larger than themselves.

Christian families are called to be schools of virtue in which communal bonds are forged and the sociality of humans is taught via experience.[48] When a majority of families do not sit down together for an evening meal, they lose an opportunity to be schooled in solidarity. It is unsurprising that so many are unable to contemplate eating more justly. Choosing to cook and eat together is a practice with formative power. The groundwork for more just eating is making the countercultural choice to prioritize evening meals. "Children," Peters insightfully points out, "do not learn simply by listening to what we say; their moral formation is shaped and formed by the actions in which we participate together as a family and as a community."[49] Eating, especially, has formative power, because families can engage in it every single day. Few other activities offer this kind of consistent, ongoing opportunity for forging a family's identity as a Christian community oriented to a larger good.

---

45. Ibid., 42.

46. Ibid.

47. Ibid.

48. John Paul II, *Familiaris consortio* (On the Role of the Christian Family in the Modern World), (Washington, DC: USCCB, 1981), no. 42.

49. Peters, "Supporting Community Farming," 25.

2. *More whole foods and cooking from scratch.* This is important because much of the energy that goes into producing food is at the processing, packaging, and storing stages. Bittman argues, "To reduce our impact on the environment, we should depend on foods that require little or no processing, packaging, or transport, and those that efficiently convert energy to calories."[50] More complex calculations enable measurement and comparison of different foods. Analysts now know that whole foods generally have much lower energy costs than processed foods. So, for instance, producing potato chips takes more energy than producing eggs, and apple juice has a higher eco-footprint than milk.[51] Many foods sold in organic stores are highly processed in small quantities with excess packaging. Choosing these foods may be healthier than choosing nonorganic frozen dinners or pasta in a bag, but the energy costs could be just as high. The alternative is to buy whole foods such as rice, beans, lentils, pasta, and vegetables that are easy to cook at home.

3. *Less meat and fewer animal products.* This is a response to concerns that current consumption levels are unsustainable because factory-farming methods use too much energy, water, and land and contribute to water pollution via fertilizer runoff during rains and to global warming via the release of methane gas. Households should opt to spend most of the portion of their budget devoted to meat on chicken and wild-caught fish. Sustainably raised beef should be an occasional indulgence. If families could aim to cut their weekly meat consumption from the average of 3 pounds per person to 1 pound per person, the industrialized world would come closer to the developing world's levels and would constitute a fairer, more sustainable sharing of resources.[52]

Cutting out all meat and animal products is not necessary from a Christian environmental standpoint. No doubt, meat is a luxury with a large environmental footprint. However, so are many

50. Bittman, *Food Matters*, 19.

51. Singer and Mason, *Ethics of What We Eat*, 237.

52. Anthony J. McMichael, et al., "Food, Livestock Production, Energy, Climate Change, and Health," *The Lancet*, September 13, 2007, *www.thelancet.com*, accessed April 9, 2010.

other things people value, including professional sporting events, movies, and airplane travel. In the face of the environmental crisis, Christians are called to live simply but not to avoid all unnecessary harm to Earth. The problem is similar regarding wealth.[53] Generally, people should avoid excess, and always, they should question cultural standards, but celebration is a part of a good life. While people should cultivate consciousness of the effect of their food choices, they need not let go of all cultural traditions. Eating less meat and dairy is a reasonable and moderate strategy that most should be able to embrace.

Moving closer to a vegetarian diet need not be painful. Grains and legumes are essential to Hispanic, Middle Eastern, and Asian meals, and they were central to the cooking styles of European American and African American families just a generation ago. Popular American cookbooks from the first half of the twentieth century include many meatless or less-meat recipes that could be revived and adapted for a broad audience. It is possible for all Americans to use fewer meat and animal products, lower their effect on the environment, and still make satisfying meals.[54]

4. *More organic produce.* Buying organic produce is an important way to assure that no synthetic fertilizers, genetically engineered seeds, growth hormones, antibiotics, and most pesticides are used and that crop rotation and cover crops to restore the soil are employed.[55] Organic farmers are doing their part to maintain soil quality, foster biodiversity, and reduce water pollution, and their methods use 35 percent less energy per unit of crop production than conventionally grown produce.[56] Organic growing methods use less energy overall even if the products are transported longer distances than local products.[57] Singer concludes that "in most cases buying organic means less chemical fertilizer runoff, fewer herbicides and pesticides

---

53. See Julie Hanlon Rubio, *Family Ethics: Practices for Christians* (Washington, DC: Georgetown University Press, 2010), 164–189.

54. Weber and Matthews, "Food Miles."

55. Singer and Mason, *Ethics of What We Eat*, 99.

56. Ibid., 202–204.

57. Ibid., 201.

in the environment, more birds and animals around the farm, better soil conservation, and, in the long run, sustainable productivity."[58] Most food analysts agree that when it comes to the environment, organic matters.[59]

The "gold standard" for some is local, organic produce. However, it is difficult to feed a family all local and organic foods. Buying into a local Community Support Agriculture (CSA)—purchasing a share in local farm production and receiving a weekly "basket" of its produce—is costly and entails working with large quantities of seasonal produce. The sorts of fruits and vegetables that children commonly eat (i.e., bananas, apples, oranges) will rarely be included. During the winter, many areas would be limited to greens, squash, and root vegetables. Most families would have to supplement their basket with additional produce from the grocery store. Peters claims that living within the boundaries of what the local area produces may be a legitimate sacrifice, and in view of the environmental damage agribusiness imposes, buying local and organic produce should be a goal of Christian families.[60] Yet, it is more difficult to impose this sacrifice on children, especially considering their need for nutrients and lack of willingness to try new foods. In addition, considerations about how much money a family ought to spend on food are legitimate, especially considering that local-organic products can cost several times as much as conventional ones.[61]

How could average families afford more organic produce? Consider first that the average family spends only 7 percent of its food budget on fresh produce. If they paid twice as much for all that they currently buy, they would not see a major increase in their food budget. Transferring some of the food budget from snack and fast food to produce would provide extra money. Beginning with cheaper organic items, such as carrots, potatoes, salad and winter greens, bananas, and root vegetables could allow families to increase demand for a more sustainable way of farming.

---

58. Ibid., 277.

59. Marion Nestle, quoted in Singer, 221. See also, Bittman, *Food Matters*, 25.

60. Peters, "Supporting Community Farming," 26.

61. See Planck, *Real Food*, 154, and Bittman, *Food Matters*, 101–104.

Some ask whether the money spent on organic produce would be better given to the poor. It is important to remember that sustaining Earth's soils and waters benefits all people but especially the underprivileged, today and in the future. Second, few families actually make this sort of trade-off. Since the 1950s, real incomes have risen and real food costs have dropped, but donations to charity as a percentage of income have remained relatively constant.[62] Moreover, the percentage of income given to charity does not vary considerably with income, suggesting that extra income rarely goes to charity.[63] A Christian family should strive to give away a percentage of their income *and* adjust their food bill so that their choices support better farming methods.

5. *More local, seasonal produce.* This is important, though not as important as eating less meat and dairy and more whole and organic foods. For families, eating local may be even more challenging than eating organic, as noted previously. Organic or conventional produce from another state is sometimes a better option. Efficient shipping methods sometimes mean that less fossil fuel is used for transport by big growers than by small farmers who drive their food to multiple local markets and sell to customers who travel long distances to get to them. The transparency that comes from knowing farmers and their growing practices is valuable, and it is hard to deny the pleasure involved in patronizing a farmers' market, but, as Singer notes, "not everyone has the time for that, and trust and understanding need not be exclusively local."[64] Moreover, Christians have obligations to the rural poor in developing countries, not just to local farmers.[65]

Perhaps most important, though many sources claim that local farmers are more likely to use sustainable, if not certifiably organic,

---

62. For data on income, see *www.econlibrary.org/library/Enc/DistributionofIncome.html*, accessed November 1, 2008. On charity, see Dean Hoge, Charles Zeck, Patrick McNamara, and Michael J. Donahue, *Money Matters: Personal Giving in American Churches* (Louisville, KY: Westminster, 1996).

63. See "Patterns of Household Charitable Giving by Income Group, 2005," Center on Philanthropy at Indiana University, Summer 2007, *www.philanthropy.iupui.edu*, accessed September 15, 2008.

64. Singer and Mason, *Ethics of What We Eat*, 142.

65. Ibid., 150, 147.

practices, it is not clear that this is always the case. In a recent article titled, "How the Myth of Food Miles Hurts the Planet," Robin McKie of the British newspaper *The Observer* quotes several sources that now believe food miles are an unhelpful measure that may mislead customers.[66] She cites one study in which researchers found that for the British, green beans from Kenya had a lower ecofootprint than local beans. In 2008, scientists Christopher L. Weber and H. Scott Matthews used a total life-cycle approach to measure energy impact of various food choices, including production, transport, and distribution. They calculated the impact of a family of four switching to all local foods and found that if the family substituted chicken, eggs, or vegetarian protein instead of beef for just one day a week, the family would have a much greater energy impact.[67] Weber and Matthews were criticized by fellow scientists for assuming that the only benefit of local farms was food miles, that is, for failing to assume that local farmers would be much more likely to use organic methods.[68] Weber and Matthews responded by noting that their critics presented no evidence for their claims, which they could not do because there is little nonanecdotal data proving their contention. Although there is local, sustainably grown food that is worth buying, eating lower on the food chain is far more important from an environmental perspective.[69]

Families ought to try to buy local, seasonal produce from farmers committed to sustainable farming, and if possible, they should make more local produce available by gardening. However, limiting one's shopping to items grown within a 100-mile radius is not necessary, or even optimal, for just eating.

---

66. Robin McKie, "How the Myth of Food Miles Hurts the Planet," *The Guardian,* March 23, 2008, *http://www.guardian.co.uk/environment/2008/mar/23/food.ethicalliving*, accessed May 1, 2009.

67. Weber and Matthews, "Food Miles."

68. Steven L. Hoop and Joan Dye Gussow, "Comment on 'Food-Miles and the Relative Climate Impacts of Food Choices in the United States'" *Environmental Science Technology*, April 23, 2009. *http://pubs.acs.org/doi/full/10.1021/es900749q*, accessed May 25, 2009.

69. Weber and Matthews, "Response to Comment on 'Food Miles and the Relative Climate Impacts of Food Choices in the United States,'" *Environmental Science Technology*, April 23, 2009, *http://pubs.acs.org/doi/full/10.1021/es901016m*, accessed May 25, 2009.

CONCLUSION: MORE JUST EATING

Christians cannot ignore the demands of environmental stewardship. Because they see creation as God's gift to humanity now and in the future, they have an obligation to protect this gift, enjoying their share, but leaving enough for others. Given the reality of environmental harm caused by the current system and the difficulty of changing the system through legal channels, just eating can be considered a crucial practice of resistance and a viable way of participating in social change.[70] Just eating involves competing goods, and families may legitimately differ in their approach to this practice. Still, it seems that all families must first commit to eating together and then balance concerns for enjoyment, health, sustainable farming practices, and cost. In particular, eating home-cooked whole foods, limiting meat and dairy consumption, buying more produce from organic and local sources, and avoiding heavily packaged, processed foods seem warranted.[71] Caring for the environment and the world's poor will mean trying to eat more simply and saving more environmentally and financially costly foods for celebrations. In coming together to make these choices, families have the potential to reshape the social order from the grassroots, as Catholic social teaching has always called them to do.

QUESTIONS FOR REVIEW

1. What theological claims ground Christian concern for just eating?
2. How does the Christian duty to live simply give a distinct shape to the "ecological conversion" called for by Pope Benedict XVI?
3. Name three trends that are important to the way American families currently eat.
4. How are conventional eating practices harmful to the environment?

---

70. See Michael Pollan, "Why Bother?" *www.michaelpollan.com*, accessed May 1, 2009.

71. Bob Schildgen, "10 Ways to Eat Well," *www.sierraclub.org/sierra/200611/tenwaysasp*, accessed May 1, 2009.

5. Why is eating whole foods more significant than eating a local diet, according to Rubio?

IN-DEPTH QUESTIONS

1. Should responsibilities to the poor and to future generations shape eating practices, even if it means that families will have to spend more money on food?
2. Is the attention to everyday actions like eating misguided? If everything we do (breathing included) has an effect, isn't it impossible to avoid damaging creation?
3. Does focusing on food place too much importance on issues that are ultimately not significant? Would it be better to focus on reforming agriculture from the top down?
4. Are the recommendations given in this chapter for just eating realistic?
5. What guidelines would you suggest for a Christian practice of eating? Would you argue that vegetarianism or localism should receive more emphasis than the chapter gives them?

CHAPTER 19

THEOLOGY H_2O:
The World Water Crisis and Sacramental Imagination

Mark J. Allman

KEY TERMS

sacramental imagination
pastoral circle
access
sanitation
symbol
means
sanctification
commodity
right
privatization
baptism
universal destination of goods
lex orandi
lex credendi
lex agenda

INTRODUCTION

This chapter explores the most serious humanitarian-ecological crisis today: the world water crisis. Moving beyond mere analysis, the chapter argues that Christians have a unique moral obligation to address this crisis precisely because of the prominent role water plays in Scripture (the Bible) and in Christian worship. The scope and intensity of the world water crisis, coupled with the role of water in Christianity, makes action on behalf of the poor and thirsty an essential obligation of the Christian faith.

RELIGION AND POLITICS?

Water is the most pressing humanitarian, ecological, and political crisis in the world and will be for the next century, if not the next millennium. Consider the current situation: 3.575 million people die annually from water-related disease. Forty-three percent of those deaths are due to diarrhea, including 1.5 million children under the age of five.[1] These numbers translate to approximately 4,900 deaths every day or one child every 15 seconds.[2] Hearing this, people often respond, "This is tragic, but it's not like I can do anything about it. I'm only one person," or they may ask, "But what does any of this have to do with religion?"

Far too many Christians fail to connect their faith with their politics. Some object, "But what about the separation of church and state?" To suggest that being a disciple of Jesus Christ does not have practical, real-life implications, however, is ludicrous. This is not an argument for theocracy. Rather, it is simply to counter the popular "crossless Christianity," a spirituality that makes few demands and heavily emphasizes God's unconditional love. This "warm and fuzzy Jesus who loves us no matter what" theology bears little resemblance to the Jesus of history, a man whose preaching and actions were so radical he was executed. Even a cursory review of Scripture reveals that the Christian life requires more than feelings and prayer. The idea that justice is a requirement of living the covenant runs throughout the Hebrew Bible.[3]

1.Annette Prüss-Üstün, Robert Bos, Fiona Gore, and Jamie Batram, *Safer Water, Better Health: Costs, Benefits and Sustainability of Interventions to Protect and Promote Health* (Geneva: World Health Organization Press, 2008), 7; United Nations Children's Fund (UNICEF) and the World Health Organization, *Diarrhea: Why Children Are Still Dying and What Can Be Done* (Geneva: United Nations' Children's Fund/World Health Organization Press, 2009), 9 and Water.org, "Water Facts," *http://water.org/learn-about-the-water-crisis/facts*, accessed January 11, 2011.

2. UN Human Development Programme (UNHDP), *Human Development Report 2006: Beyond Scarcity—Power, Poverty and the Global Water Crisis* (New York: Palgrave MacMillan, 2006), 6.

3. For more on the biblical idea of justice see John Donahue, "Biblical Perspectives on Justice" in *The Faith that Does Justice*, ed. John Haughey, SJ (Mahwah, NJ: Paulist Press, 1977), 68–112.

> "Give justice to the weak and the orphan; maintain the right of the lowly and the destitute. Rescue the weak and needy; deliver them from the hand of the wicked." (Psalm 82:3-4)

> Is not this the fast that I choose: to loose the bonds of injustice . . . to let the oppressed go free and to break every yoke? Is it not to share your bread with the hungry, and bring the homeless poor into your house, when you see the naked, to cover them? (Isaiah 58:6–7).[4]

In the Gospel parable of the sheep and the goats, Jesus identifies himself with the hungry, thirsty, imprisoned, naked, sick, and stranger and goes so far as to say, "Just as you did it to [cared for] one of the least of these who are members of my family, you did it to me" (Matthew 25:31–46). When asked about the greatest commandment, Jesus responds, "You shall love the Lord your God with all your heart, and with all your soul and with all your mind," to which he couples, "You shall love your neighbor as yourself" (Matthew 22:23–40).[5] When asked about what one must do to inherit eternal life Jesus answers, "Go sell what you own, give the money to the poor, and you will have treasure in heaven; then come, follow me" (Mark 10:17–31).[6] Jesus and Scripture assert: the Christian life requires some kind of action, for "faith by itself, if it has no works, is dead" (James 2:17).

But what kind of action? How do Christians know what they are supposed to *do?* The World Synod of Catholic Bishops provides one answer, "Action on behalf of justice and participation in the transformation of the world fully appear to us as a constitutive [absolutely essential] dimension of the preaching of the Gospel, or in other words, of the Church's mission for the redemption of the human race and its liberation from every oppressive situation."[7] Social justice work is inherently political and is as important to the Christian life as prayer and worship.

4. See Amos 5:21–24.

5. See Mark 12:28–31 and Luke 10:25–37.

6. See Matthew 19:16–30 and Luke 18:18–30.

7. World Synod of Catholic Bishops (1970), "Justice in the World," no. 6, in *Catholic Social Thought: The Documentary Heritage*, eds. David J. O'Brien and Thomas A. Shannon (Maryknoll, NY: Orbis, 2003), 289.

Another way to address the question of personal responsibility is to employ a longstanding method of ethical discernment called, "the pastoral circle." This three-step approach for addressing injustices involves seeing, judging, and acting (see diagram).[8]

The Pastoral Circle

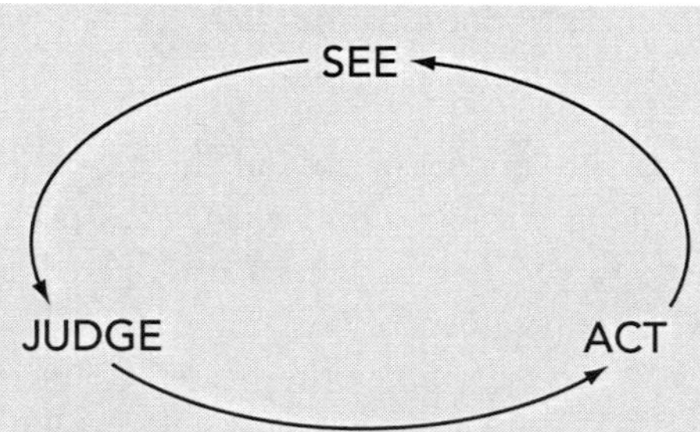

SEE: Begin by asking "What is going on?" This task is descriptive. It involves gathering information, history, and data in order to understand the social, cultural, political, and economic context.

JUDGE: Once the information has been gathered, one must decide the relevance and relationship of the information, evaluate options for addressing the injustice, and set a course of action.

ACT: One then puts this plan into action, which in turn yields a new experience, returning full circle to the first step whereby one now "sees" the situation in light of having acted on it, and the process begins anew.

Using the pastoral circle, one can begin to analyze the world water crisis (*see*), evaluate (*judge*) the crisis, and finally identify a course of (*act*)ion to address the crisis. Though numerous social justice issues deserve attention (war and peace, hunger, poverty, racism,

8. It is sometimes called "the hermeneutical circle" or "the circle of praxis." See Thomas Massarro, *Living Justice: Catholic Social Teaching in Action* (Franklin, WI: Sheed and Ward, 2000), 102–107.

sexism, and so on), Christians can easily understand the ethical obligation to advocate for global water justice due to the role water plays in Christian Scriptures and liturgy; as such, Christians have a unique responsibility to address it.

See

Building on the basic facts about the world water crisis provided earlier, now one can paint a more detailed picture. Development and relief agencies usually analyze the world water crisis by focusing on two areas: access (which includes cost and use) and sanitation.

Access

- About one billion people lack access to safe water (approximately 18 percent of the global population). By the year 2025, it is estimated that one third of the global population will face severe and chronic water shortage.[9]
- Less than 1 percent of the world's freshwater is easily accessible for direct human use (lakes, rivers, and shallow underground sources).[10]
- A person needs 13.2 gallons/day of water for drinking, sanitation, and hygiene.[11] The average person in developing countries uses 2.64 gallons/day. The average person in the United Kingdom uses 35.66 gallons/day. The average person in the United States uses 100–175 gallons/day.[12]

---

9. United Nations Children's Fund (UNICEF) and World Health Organization (WHO), *Water for Life: Making It Happen* (Geneva: WHO Press, 2005), 40 and *Progress on Drinking Water and Sanitation: Special Focus on Sanitation* (New York and Geneva: UNICEF and WHO Press, 2008), 23; and USAID, "The Global Water Crisis," *http://www.usaid.gov/our_work/environment/water/water_crisis.html*, accessed January 11, 2011.

10. World Health Organization, "Health in Water Resources Development," *http://www.who.int/docstore/water_sanitation_health/vector/water_resources.htm*, accessed January 11, 2011.

11. Water Encyclopedia, "Survival Needs," *http://www.waterencyclopedia.com/St-Ts/Survival-Needs.html*, accessed January 11, 2011.

12. Blue Planet Foundation, "The Facts about the Global Drinking Water Crisis," available online at *http://blueplanetrun.org/water/facts*, accessed January 11, 2011, and United Nations Office of Partnerships, "Some Statistics on Water and Sanitation," *http://www.un.org/partnerships/Docs/Statistics.doc*, accessed January 11, 2011.

- A person in the United States taking a 5-minute shower uses more water than a typical person in the developing world uses in a day.[13]
- The urban poor often pay five–ten times more per liter of water than their wealthy neighbors in the same city.[14]
- Millions of women and children spend 4–8 hours a day fetching water.[15]
- An investment of U.S. $11.3 billion per year is needed to meet the Millennium Development drinking water and sanitation goals. On average every U.S. dollar spent in water and sanitation provides an economic return of eight U.S. dollars.[16]

Sanitation

- Roughly 2.5 billion people (38 percent of the world's population) lack access to facilities that ensure hygienic separation of human excrement from human contact, including 1.2 billion who have no facilities at all.[17]
- Waterborne disease claims more lives annually than war.[18]
- Half of the world's hospital beds are filled with people suffering from water-related illness.[19]
- Poor sanitation is a major source of absenteeism at work and school and, thus, is one of the leading obstacles to overcoming entrenched poverty.[20]

---

13. United Nations Human Development Programme (UNHDP), *Human Development Report 2006: Beyond Scarcity—Power, Poverty and the Global Water Crisis* (New York: Palgrave MacMillan, 2006), 35.

14. Ibid., 10.

15. Ibid., 23.

16. UNICEF and WHO, *Water for Life: Making It Happen*, 2.

17. UNICEF and WHO, *Progress on Drinking Water and Sanitation: Special Focus on Sanitation* (2008), 2

18. UNHDP, *Human Development Report 2006*, 1.

19. Ibid., 45.

20. UN International Year of Sanitation (2007), no. 6.

MILLENNIUM DEVELOPMENT GOALS: A COST COMPARISON

World leaders met at the United Nations in 2000 and adopted the Millennium Development Goals (MDGs) aimed at reducing abject poverty worldwide. The MDGs are scheduled to be met by 2015. One target, to reduce by half the proportion of people without sustainable access to safe drinking water and basic sanitation, has a projected annual cost of $11.3 billion. By way of comparison, during the 2008–2009 financial crisis, the U.S. government bailouts included $400 billion for Fannie Mae/Freddie Mac; $280 billion for CITI Group; $180 billion for AIG Insurance; and $142 billion for Bank of America.[21] The cost of funding the entire MDGs for water is equal to 1.6 percent of the Troubled Asset Relief Program ($700 billion). Another comparison is also enlightening and ironic: Wholesale bottled water sales in 2008 were $11.2 billion, with most sales occurring in the United States and other developed nations in which potable water is readily available. That figure is nearly identical to what is needed to meet the Millennium Development Goals. [22]

Right or Commodity?

The world water crisis is not a problem about too much demand and not enough supply. As the 2006 UN World Water Development Report notes, "There is enough water for everyone. The problem we face today is largely one of governance: equitably sharing this water while ensuring the sustainability of natural ecosystems."[23] This is

21. Pro-Publica, "History of U.S. Gov't Bailouts," *http://www.propublica.org/special/government-bailouts,* accessed January 11, 2011.

22. John G. Rowdan, "U.S. and International Bottled Water Developments and Statistics for 2008," *Bottled Water Reporter*, annual report of the International Bottled Water Association (April/May 2009), 13, *http://www.bottledwater.org/public/2008%20Market%20Report%20Findings%20reported%20in%20April%202009.pdf*, accessed January 11, 2011.

23. United Nations Educational, Scientific and Cultural Organization (UNESCO), *Water: A Shared Responsibility* (executive summary of the UN World Water Development Report 2), (New York: Berghanh Books, 2006), 3.

a crisis of governance due to a lack of interest in solving the water crisis and political and economic systems ill equipped to address it. The principal debate rages over privatization of water supplies. In the developed world, water management is usually the responsibility of the local, regional, or national government. In the developing world, water is often managed or owned by a handful of multinational corporations (e.g., Suez, Vivendi/Venolia, SAUR, Thames Water, United Utilities).[24]

The proprivatization model views water as a commodity and holds the market is the most efficient mechanism for delivering water to people because it yields greater access, is more equitable, results in better management, improves sanitation, and leads to lower prices than government-run systems. In *Water for Sale: How Business and the Market Can Resolve the World's Water Crisis*, Fredrik Segerfeldt notes when a water supply is government run, it can be used as a political tool to reward those who support the ruling party, often resulting in the poor receiving the worst service and the middle and upper classes receiving the best.[25] He also notes that government-subsidized water programs are highly inefficient because they fail to provide incentive to reduce water waste and fail to invest in the infrastructure needed to make water management more efficient. Finally, he argues government-run systems are unjust. "Public water utilities cover only 30 percent of their cost. The remaining 70 percent is made up with subsidies from taxation revenue,"[26] but because most of the poor do not have access to public water supplies (while the wealthy do), the poor are essentially subsidizing the water consumption of the rich.

---

24. This is due to International Money Fund (IMF) and World Bank policies in the 1980s. When many of the poorest countries could no longer service their debt, the IMF and World Bank, the two leading international lending agencies addressing questions of global poverty, required many of these nations to privatize their water supplies under contentious "structural adjustment programs," in order for these countries to service their debt. For more on this situation, see Gary L. Chamberlain, *Troubled Waters: Religion, Ethics and the Global Water Crisis* (Lanham, MD: Rowan and Littlefield, 2008), 116–124.

25. Fredrik Segerfeldt, *Water for Sale: How Business and the Market Can Resolve the World's Water Crisis* (Washington, DC: Cato Institute, 2005). See also "Private Water Saves Lives," *Financial Times* (August 25, 2005), *http://www.cato.org/pub_display.php?pub_id=4462*, accessed January 11, 2011.

26. Segerfeldt, 52.

Many proprivatization advocates are not crass profiteers seeking to "make a buck" off the back of the poor. They genuinely believe that privatization is the most efficient, effective, and equitable solution to the world water crisis.

Antiprivatization advocates argue water is a human right, not a commodity, and access to water should not depend on ability to pay. This is a principled argument. Water is essential for life, and thus, it should not be left to corporations, which are profit-seeking entities rather than public servants. Water is part of the global commons, it cannot be owned by any one entity; everyone has a right to water. Second, the local community typically loses control over this vital resource when water is privatized. In an era of free-trade agreements, nations often cannot restrict who bids on water contracts. The private water sector is dominated by a handful of key players and when privatized, it most often falls under the control of a large multinational corporation. In many instances, the price of water increased anywhere from 60 to 600 percent after privatization and often led to significant decreases in water quality.[27] In short, antiprivatization advocates argue that water is far too important a resource to be left to the whims of the market.

The debate over privatization leads to an interesting question regarding the nature of water. Three natural resources are necessary to sustain human life: air, food, and water. Air is not a commodity, but food is bought and sold. The privatization debate is about whether water is a commodity (like food) or a free resource (like air). The difference lies in the infrastructure and labor needed to make these resources useful. Air requires no processing. Food, however, requires labor and infrastructure. Seeds are sown, fields are watered and fertilized, plants harvested, and animals reared and slaughtered. For food to reach people, it has to be processed, packaged, and shipped. Food is labor intensive, and the price includes distribution costs. Water, like air, simply exists. However, for most people to use water, it needs to be purified (filtration plants) and delivered (piping). Distribution requires an expensive infrastructure and labor. Thus when talking about water privatization, one is not simply discussing the element H_2O per se, but the element and all that is necessary to make it potable and available.

27. Chamberlain, 119–120.

Judge

Facts and figures are necessary for making informed judgments about what ought to be done regarding water, but ethics involves more than data. For Christians, Scripture, tradition, and the liturgy are deep wells for discerning ethical obligations.

Scripture

Considering the arid region in which both Judaism and Christianity developed, it is not surprising that water plays a significant role in both the Hebrew Bible and the New Testament.[28] The word *water* appears nearly six hundred times in the Hebrew Bible. It can refer to an actual body or source of water or serve as a metaphor for God or God's activity. God is described as "the fountain of living waters" (Jeremiah 2:13) and God's charity "is like the waves of the sea" (Isaiah 48:18). The Hebrew Bible stresses two attributes of water: it is necessary for life and has cleansing properties. These two attributes are metaphorically reinterpreted to emphasize God is the source of life (both earthly and eternal) and explain how God can transform what is profane into something holy. Thus water is both a *symbol* and a *means* for sustaining life (corporeal and eternal) and for making people and things holy (purification or sanctification).

Water as a Symbol and Means of Life in the Hebrew Scriptures

Water as a source of life is especially prominent in the two creation accounts, the story of Noah and in the Exodus accounts. The first creation story (Genesis 1:1—2:4a) opens with the spirit of God hovering over the waters. God brings order out of chaos by separating the waters. Water is the primordial "stuff" from which all of creation flows.[29] On the second day, God commands, "Let there be a dome in the midst of the waters, and let it separate the waters from the waters. So God made the dome and separated the waters that were under the dome [ocean] from the waters that were above the dome [rain]"

---

28. Most of this section is drawn from Gerald A. Klingbeil, "Water," in *New Interpreters Dictionary of the Bible* vol. 5, ed. Katharine Doob Sakenfeld (Nashville: Abington Press, 2009), 818–821.

29. Chamberlain, *Troubled Waters*, 40–42. See Isaiah 35:4–8 for an alternative account of creation.

(Genesis 1:6–8). On the third day, God creates dry land and seas and, on the fifth day, populates the seas with living creatures. The second creation story (Genesis 2:4b–225) opens with dry and desolate land "for the Lord God had not caused it to rain" (Genesis 2:5). God's first act of creation in this account is causing a stream to rise up from the earth and "water the whole face of the ground" (Genesis 2:6). The account goes on to describe four rivers flowing out of the garden to the four corners of Earth (Genesis 2:10–14). The effect of God's creative activity in Eden spreads to the whole world via the life-giving and life-sustaining waters of Eden. In both creation stories, water plays an essential role in the first act of creation.

Inversely, water serves as an agent of decreation in the story of Noah (Genesis 6—9). When humankind's wickedness is too great, God destroys all living creatures (except for those in the ark) by a great flood. This story in many ways is the antithesis of the Genesis accounts. What was once a blessing becomes a curse. It is also a story of re-creation and includes parallels to the creation accounts. When Noah and his family emerge from the ark, they are given the same command that Adam and Eve received, "Be fruitful and multiply and fill the earth" (Genesis 9:1).[30]

In the central event of the Hebrew Bible, the Exodus, water plays a key role in the liberation of the Israelites: Moses' life is spared when he is plucked from the river; the first plague is turning the Nile (Egypt's primary water source) into blood; the Israelites escape by the miraculous splitting of the sea, only to have it close in on and drown Pharaoh's army; and when dying of thirst in the desert, Moses strikes a rock and water gushes forth. Water is both a means of sustaining life and a symbol of God's protection and favor.

The notion of water as a blessing and its absence as a curse runs throughout the Scriptures. In an arid region dependent on rain and dew for water supplies, rain is viewed as a blessing[31] while droughts are interpreted as punishments for failing to keep God's law,[32] thus making water a sign of God's judgment for and against the people.

30. See also Genesis 1:22, 1:28, and 8:17.

31. See Ezekiel 34:26; Isaiah 35:7, 41:18, and 49:10; Zechariah 10:1; and Micah 2:10.

32. See 1Kings 18; 2 Chronicles 6:26–31, 20:9. See also Psalm 18:16, 29:10, 65:5-8, 89:9, and 93:3; Isaiah 24:1–5 and 43:2; Jeremiah 3:1–3 and 14:22.

When the Israelites are in good standing with God, they are blessed with the primary source of corporeal life; when they have turned their back on God, they are deprived, until they repent.

Water as a Symbol and Means of Purification and Blessing in the Hebrew Scriptures

Water's ability to clean renders it a natural symbol for religious purity or holiness. Water transforms what is sullied into something clean. Ancient Judaism included numerous purification rituals: priests washed themselves before offering sacrifices and prayers; ordination rituals involved bathing; women were required to purify themselves after menstruation; and hospitality rites involved washing of feet.[33] Bodily cleanliness was associated with purity of heart or holiness. Water, which is necessary for washing, became a crucial link to God. To have "clean hands" meant to have a clear conscience.[34] In the context of ritual, water serves as both a *symbol* and a *means* of transformation. "I will sprinkle clean water on you, and you will be clean; I will cleanse you from all your filthiness and from all your idols" (Ezekiel 36:25).

For water to function as a symbol of life, it must be clean. Water can take what was once profane (or just ordinary) and make it into something new, good, holy, and pure. Water in the Hebrew Scriptures has no potency of its own. Its ability to give life, purify, bless, curse, create, or destroy comes from God. God uses water as a means of relating to humanity. The symbolic value of water comes from God's choosing to act through it, reflecting the ancient belief that water, like all natural resources, is a thing created by God for humans.

Water as a Symbol and Means of Life in the New Testament

In the New Testament, the life-giving attributes of water are again emphasized. It is also a tool for demonstrating Jesus' authority and ethics. Twice in the Gospel of John, Jesus uses water as a metaphor for himself and his mission. Jesus' conversation with the

---

33. For sacrifices and prayers, see Exodus 30:18–21, 40:30–31, and Deuteronomy 21:6. For ordination rituals, see Exodus 29:4 and Leviticus 8:6. For women, see Leviticus 15:19–24. For hospitality, see Genesis 18:4, 19:2, 24:32, and Judges 19:21.

34. See Deuteronomy 21:6, 2 Samuel 22:21, and Psalm 18:21.

Samaritan woman at the well starts about obtaining water but quickly turns theological (John 4:1–42). Jesus proclaims,

> If you knew the gift of God and who is saying to you, "Give me a drink," you would have asked him and he would have given you living water. . . . Everyone who drinks this water will be thirsty again; but whoever drinks the water I shall give will never thirst; the water I shall give will become in him a spring of water welling up to eternal life. (John 4:11–14)

In John 7:37–38, Jesus declares, "Let anyone who is thirsty come to me, and let the one who believes in me drink. As the scripture has said, 'Out of the believer's heart shall flow rivers of living water.'" He says this during a harvest festival (Sukkot) in which the community prays for rain and is linked to the hope for the coming of a messiah.[35] Both passages use water to make the point that Jesus is the long-awaited messiah, the one who will usher in a new age, a time of perfect harmony between God and humanity, between all humans and between humans and creation. In this eschatological age, death will be no more; thus Jesus, "the living water," doesn't just satiate thirst, he also brings eternal life. The final book of the New Testament (Revelation) draws on the first book of the Bible (Genesis) in its description of how the fecundity of Eden spreads to the four corners of Earth. It speaks of a new heavens and new Earth that will come at the end of time, and how the "river of the water of life" will flow from "the throne of God and the Lamb" (Revelation 22:1) and bring new life to the world.

Water as a Symbol and Means of Purification and Blessing in the New Testament

The notion that Jesus Christ brings new or eternal life is the cornerstone of the Christian faith and is ritually expressed in baptism. The contemporary ritual of baptism will be addressed shortly; here, the focus is baptism in the New Testament. John the Baptist called the people to a baptism of repentance in expectation of the coming of the messiah. Jesus comes to John and is baptized, during which God reveals, "This is my Son, the Beloved" (Matthew 3:17). After his

35. Henry Knapp, "The Messianic Water Which Gives Life to the World," *Horizons in Biblical Theology* 19 (1997): 109–110.

Resurrection, Jesus commands his disciples to preach and baptize, and the epistles are replete with references to baptism.[36] The first Christians adopted and adapted the Jewish interpretations of water as life-giving and purifying to their initiation ritual. Baptism comes to be interpreted as a washing away of sin; as a death and resurrection to new life; and as membership in a community, making water the primary symbol of the Christian faith from its earliest days.

Water as a Symbol and Means of Jesus' Authority and Ethics

The gospels record three instances in which Jesus' authority is revealed with water. Jesus' first miracle is changing water into wine (see John 2:1–11). Jesus' quieting of the storm is a demonstration of raw power (see Mark 4:37–41, Matthew 8:23–27, and Luke 8:22–25); and Jesus walks on water (see Mark 6:47–51 cf. Matthew 14:22–23 and John 6:16–21), which bears linguistic similarities to the Israelites' crossing the sea, suggesting that the author wanted to portray Jesus like Moses, as one who delivers his people through water.[37] In the gospels, the ability to manipulate water is provided as evidence of Jesus' divine power.

Jesus also used water to illustrate his ethics and his understanding of ministry: he describes discipleship saying, "Whoever gives even a cup of cold water to one of these little ones because he is a disciple will never lose his reward" (Matthew 10:42); he identifies himself with the thirsty, "I was thirsty and you gave me a drink" (Matthew 25:31–46); and he uses water to heal (see Mark 8:22–26 and John 9:1–11). Finally, John's account of the Last Supper includes the washing of the disciples' feet, which serves as the occasion for a lesson on servant-leadership and an example of Christian humility (John 13:1–20). God incarnate stoops to wash the filth from human bodies. God's glory is revealed in service.[38]

It is not coincidence that many of these biblical passages (Exodus, woman at the well, foot washing) are proclaimed during Lent

36. See Matthew 28:17, Romans 6, Ephesians 5:26, 1 Peter 3:20–21, and Hebrews 10:22.

37. William Richard Stegner, "Jesus' Walking on the Water: Mark 6:45–52," in *Gospels and the Scriptures of Israel*, eds. William Richard Stegner and Craig Evans (Sheffield, England: Sheffield Academic, 1994), 217.

38. Thomas Robinson, "Seeing God's Glory through Dirty Water," *Leven* 14 (2006), 26.

and the Triduum liturgies (Holy Thursday, Good Friday and Easter). Lent is the final period of preparation for adults seeking baptism. It is a time of intense scrutiny of the candidates and a period for those previously baptized to reflect on the meaning of their own baptism and to renew their faith. These "wet readings" are reserved for this pinnacle period of the liturgical calendar, reflecting the central role of water in Scripture and liturgy.

Tradition

Christians rightly turn to Scripture for guidance in discerning their moral obligations. They also look to tradition. How others have faithfully answered the challenges of their day can be illuminating for how Christians ought to respond to the challenges of today. While the Christian churches have only recently begun to directly address the global water crisis, there is a long and rich tradition on poverty, human rights, and private property that proves helpful in addressing it. In recent years, church statements on poverty have begun to explicitly identify access and sanitation as essential factors in alleviating global poverty.

The World Council of Churches (WCC), which includes more than 340 Christian denominations from around the world with approximately 500 million members, recognizes "water is the condition of all life on the planet—plants, animals and human beings. Water is an essential gift of God for all living beings. Water resources must, therefore, be protected for the whole of creation."[39] Initially the WCC placed the world water crisis in a larger ecological framework that includes the whole of creation, but the remainder of their analysis is exclusively anthropocentric (human centered). "Humans are part of the creation. Human society can only exist within the bio-system; its survival depends of the survival of the whole. . . . As far as human society is concerned, our starting point is that the access to water is a fundamental human right."[40]

39. World Council of Churches Water Working Group, "Waters of Life" (May 13, 2005), *http://www.oikoumene.org/resources/documents/wcc-programmes/justice-diakonia-and-responsibility-for-creation/climate-change-water/waters-of-life.html*, accessed January 11, 2011.

40. Ibid.

Thus water sanitation and access to water are examined insofar as these goods serve humans. The statement goes on to decry the privatization and commodification of water. "Water must not be treated as a commercial good . . . [nor] should it be subject to the rules of profit making."[41] They also advocate that management of water resources should be publicly administered at the most local level in a transparent manner.

The Catholic Church offers an alternative analysis of the world water crisis, which also reflects the larger Christian anthropocentric focus. Like the WCC statement, the Catholic Church's *Compendium of the Social Doctrine of the Church* identifies water as both a gift and a human right.

> "As a gift from God, water is a vital element essential to survival; thus, everyone has a right to it." Satisfying the needs of all, especially of those who live in poverty, must guide the use of water and the services connected with it. . . . For a suitable solution to this problem, it "must be set in context in order to establish moral criteria based precisely on the value of life and the respect for the rights and dignity of all humans."
>
> By its very nature, water cannot be treated as just another commodity among many, and it must be used rationally and in solidarity with others. The distribution of water is traditionally among the responsibilities that fall to public agencies [government], since water is considered a public good. If water distribution is entrusted to the private sector, it should still be considered a public good. The right to water, as all human rights, finds its basis in human dignity and not in any kind of merely quantitative assessment that considers water as a merely economic good. Without water, life is threatened. Therefore, the right to safe drinking water is a universal and inalienable right.[42]

---

41. Ibid.

42. *Compendium of the Social Doctrine of the Church*, no. 484–485. Internal quote from John Paul II, Message to Cardinal Geraldo Majella Agnelo on the occasion of the 2004 Brotherhood Campaign of the Brazilian Bishops' Conference, January 19, 2004: *L'Obsservatore Romano*, English Edition, March 17, 2004, 3.

Calling access to water a "human right" is significant because, as the Pontifical Council on Justice and Peace recognized, "A rights based approach places the human at the center of development. Access to safe water is made a legal entitlement rather than a service or commodity provided on a humanitarian basis."[43] It also recognized the right to water includes "means and mechanisms for holding governments accountable for the access of their citizens to safe water."[44]

Rights language in the Catholic tradition is robust. To call water a "universal and inalienable right" means everyone everywhere has a legitimate claim to it *and* that those in positions of wealth and power (especially governments) have the obligation to ensure all enjoy this right. Within the Catholic tradition, all rights have concomitant duties. The right to water comes with the obligations to use water responsibly and to ensure all other humans have access to water.

Pope Benedict XVI has raised the profile of water in the Catholic Church's social teachings to unprecedented levels. He describes water as a material good, an immaterial good, and as part of the common good.

> Those who consider water today to be a predominantly material good, should not forget the religious meanings that believers, and Christianity above all, have developed from it, giving it great value as a precious immaterial good that always enriches human life on this earth. . . . The full recovery of this spiritual dimension is ensured and presupposed for a proper approach to the ethical, political, and economic problems that affect the complex management of water.[45]

43. Pontifical Council for Justice and Peace, *Water, An Essential Element for Life, An Update* (March 2006), no. 3, *http://www.vatican.va/roman_curia/pontifical_councils/justpeace/documents/rc_pc_justpeace_doc_20060322_mexico-water_en.html*, accessed January 11, 2011.

44. Ibid.

45. Pope Benedict XVI, "Papal Message at International Expo of Saragosa" Message to Cardinal Renato Raffaele Martino (July 15, 2008), *Catholic Social Principles Towards Water and Sanitation*, ed. Dennis Warner (Baltimore, MD: Catholic Relief Services, 2009), 10, *http://crscollege.org/wp-content/uploads/2009/03/catholic-social-principles-towards-water-and-sanitation-_revised-209.pdf*, accessed January 11, 2011.

Benedict does not deny that water is a material good that affects economics and politics. He is critical of reducing its value to these dimensions *only*, however, while failing to recognize the religious significance of water.

On World Water Day 2007, Pope Benedict drew on the rich tradition of Catholic social thought to analyze this crisis in terms of human rights, the common good, the preferential option for the poor, solidarity, stewardship, and participation.

> Water, a common good of the human family, constitutes an essential element for life; the management of this precious resource must enable all to have access to it, especially those who live in conditions of poverty, and must guarantee the livability of the planet for both the present and future generations. Access to water is in fact one of the inalienable rights of every human, because it is a prerequisite for the realization of the majority of other human rights, such as the rights to life, to food and to health . . . [Sustainable water management] should be faced in accordance with the principle of subsidiarity, that is, through the adoption of a participatory approach that involves both the private sector and above all the local communities; the principle of solidarity, a fundamental pillar of international cooperation, which requires a preferential attention to the poor; the principle of responsibility to the present generation and those to come, from which derives the consequent need to re-examine the models of consumption and production.[46]

At first, such language appears platitudinous. Read carefully, however, it reveals guiding principles for ethical water management: participation of all sectors of society (public, private, wealthy, and poor) in decisions about how water should be managed; coordinated global solutions (not merely a patchwork approach by local communities); and sacrifices, particularly from the wealthy on behalf of the poor.

---

46. Pope Benedict XVI, "Message of the Holy Father Benedict XVI on the Occasion of the Celebration of World Water Day 2007," *Catholic Social Principles Towards Water and Sanitation*, ed. Dennis Warner (Baltimore, MD: Catholic Relief Services, 2009), 11–12.

While Catholic teachings define water as a human right, they do not oppose water privatization per se. The teachings do not speak about ownership as much as they speak about "access to water," neither do they reject the idea of water as a commodity—only the notion that water is "just another commodity among many" or a "material good." Water "runs the risk of becoming a mere consumer product . . . [but] water cannot be treated as a mere product of consumption among others since it has an inestimable and irreplaceable value. . . . Water therefore must be considered a public good, which all citizens should enjoy, but within the context of duties, rights and responsibilities."[47] This argument points to the Catholic Church's teaching on private property, which includes a concept known as the "universal destination of goods," and distinguishes between "use" and "ownership."

The universal destination of goods refers to the notion that God originally intended all the goods of Earth (including water) to satisfy human needs.

> Water is a natural resource vital for the survival of humans and all species on earth. As a good of creation, water is destined for all humans and their communities. God intended the earth and all it contains for the use of all, so that created things would be shared fairly by humankind under the guidance of justice tempered by charity. . . . Access to safe water and sanitation is indispensable for life and full development of all humans and communities in the world. . . . Water is a universal common good, a common good of the entire human family. Its benefits are meant for all and not only for those who live in countries where water is abundant, well managed and well distributed. This natural resource must be equitably at the disposal of the entire human family.[48]

It is worth noting that while this statement acknowledges water is necessary for "all species on earth," it also reflects the anthropocentric bias of most Christian teachings on creation. Water, like all things

47. Pontifical Council for Justice and Peace, *Water, An Essential Element, an Update*, no. 5.

48. Ibid., no. 2. The *Compendium of the Social Doctrine of the Church* explicitly identifies water as part of the universal destination of goods (no. 484).

in nature, is intended for human consumption; it is not considered a worthy end in itself and has no intrinsic value.

For centuries, the Catholic Church has defended the right to private property but has attached a significant caveat. All private property is held under a social mortgage, namely private property is permitted so long as it contributes to the common good because ultimately "private property" is a misnomer. Only God, as creator and sovereign, holds all titles of ownership. Anything humans claim as theirs traces its origin back to God. God allows them to *use* the things of Earth to meet their needs and fulfill their wants. Thus, there is a difference between owning and using.

This understanding of private property influences the teachings about water, which tend to speak of *access* to water as opposed to *ownership* of water.

> Governance is therefore perhaps the most important requirement for solving problems of access to safe water and sanitation. . . . An essential component of good management is community participation and ownership. . . . Public private partnership can play an important role in providing access to safe water provided that the different stakeholders work together for a common objective: that of guaranteeing access to safe water and sanitation for all.[49]

Thus, privatization is not inherently wrong. The ethical litmus test of water management is "access to safe water and sanitation for all." The document goes on to note that water pricing is the most contentious and controversial issue and requires that

> Users pay the true costs of services. . . . If however it is acknowledged that access to safe water and sanitation is fundamental to the alleviation of poverty, then water and sanitation cannot be treated as a commodity among other commodities . . . there exist important human needs which escape the market logic and water is precisely one of these. It cannot be used solely as a means for profit

49. Ibid., no. 6.

> because it is essential to the survival of the human person and thus cannot be transformed into a good reserved to the exclusive advantage of only those who can afford to pay for it. [50]

These teachings chafe between asserting water is a universal and inalienable right and the right to private property. In the end, the teachings could be summed up: all private property is held under a social mortgage, but water ownership is unique because it is not like other goods. Water is essential to human life and a primary symbol within the Christian tradition. The right to access trumps private property claims. Privatization of water can be legitimate if access and sanitation for all is ensured—with particular attention to the needs of the poor.

Liturgy

The connection between liturgy and ethics is often touted in theory; but in practice, namely Sunday services, ethical concerns rarely extend beyond vague references to caring for the poor and vulnerable and occasional sermons, often on abortion and same-sex marriage. There are exceptions to this characterization, but Sunday worship is devoted primarily to personal piety and building community. Most contemporary ethical issues are complex, politically divisive, and difficult to present and explore in a liturgical setting. The global water crisis is an exception.

Christian worship is soaking wet. The actual element—water—can be used in nearly every ritual: baptisteries, holy water fonts at the doors of churches, sprinkling rites, mixing of water with wine, washing of hands, all of which are accompanied with prayers that speak of how water purifies and gives life.

An ancient theological maxim, *lex orandi, lex credendi* (the law of prayer is the law of belief; or more colloquially: we pray what we believe; we believe what we pray) applies here. Looking to the actual prayer texts reveals what the church holds as true. For example, in the Catholic rite of baptism, the presider says over the water:

---

50. Ibid., no. 6.

> In baptism we use your gift of water, which you have made a rich symbol of the grace you give us in this sacrament. At the very dawn of creation your Spirit breathed on the waters, making them the wellspring of all holiness. The waters of the great flood you made a sign of the waters of baptism, that make an end of sin and a new beginning of goodness. Through the waters of the Red Sea you led Israel out of slavery to be an image of God's holy people, set free from sin by baptism. In the water of the Jordan your Son was baptized by John and anointed with the Spirit. Your Son willed that water and blood should flow from his side as he hung upon the cross. . . . By the power of the Holy Spirit give to this water the grace of your Son.[51]

In the celebration of the Eucharist, water is used in the sprinkling rite option. When blessing the water, the presider says,

> Hear our prayers and bless (+) this water which gives fruitfulness to the fields, and refreshment and cleansing to man. You chose water to show your goodness when you led your people to freedom through the Red Sea and satisfied their thirst in the desert with water from the rock. Water was the symbol used by the prophets to foretell your new covenant with man. You made the water of baptism holy by Christ's baptism in the Jordan: by it you give us new birth and renew us in holiness.[52]

Scripture, tradition, and the liturgical texts highlight two salient features of water: it is necessary for life, and it cleanses. These features

---

51. *Rite of Baptism*, "Blessing and Invocation of God over Baptismal Water," in *Catholic Rites Today*, ed. Allan Bouley (Collegeville, MN: Liturgical Press, 1992), 152.

52. Order of Mass, "Rite of Blessing and Sprinkling Holy Water" (options C) in *Catholic Rites Today*, ed. Allan Bouley, 267. The presider has two other options, both emphasizing the life-giving and sanctifying properties of water. Option A: "God our Father, your gift of water brings life and freshness to the earth; it washes away our sins and brings us eternal life. . . . Renew the living spring of your life within us and protect us in spirit and body." Option B: "Lord in your mercy give us living water, always springing up as a fountain of salvation: free us, body and soul, from every danger" (Bouley, 266–267).

ORTHODOX CHRISTIANITY AND THE GREAT WATER BLESSING

IMAGE © VASSIL DONEV/EPA/CORBIS

A boy holds up a cross as men perform the national dance "Horo" in the icy waters of the river in the town of Kalof er, some 100 miles from Sofia, Bulgaria, during celebrations of the Epiphany Day on January 6, 2011. Epiphany is a Christian feast originating in the Eastern Christian churches.

For Orthodox Christians the Feast of the Epiphany is one of the most important celebrations in the liturgical year because it commemorates the baptism of Jesus in the Jordan River. According to Rev. Thomas Fitzgerald, "When Christ was baptized, it not only marked the beginning of his public ministry and revealed the Trinity, but also signified that the entire creation is destined to share in the glory of redemption in Christ. While Christ entered into the Jordan to be baptized, two things were happening: He was identifying Himself with the people He had come to save; and He was identifying Himself with the whole of Creation, which was represented by water. Through His baptism, the Lord revealed the value of the created world and He redirected it toward its Creator. Creation is good and it belongs to God."[53] The Orthodox theology of creation is markedly less anthropocentric than the Catholic and Protestant interpretations.

continued

53. Thomas Fitzgerald, "Special Feasts and Blessings," Greek Orthodox Archdiocese of America, *http://www.goarch.org/ourfaith/ourfaith7113*, accessed January 11, 2011.

ORTHODOX CHRISTIANITY AND THE GREAT WATER BLESSING continued

For Orthodox Christians, water is the central symbol for all of creation and is considered hallowed because Jesus Christ was immersed in it. This is liturgically celebrated on the Feast of the Epiphany during the "Great Water Blessing" with the words, "The voice of the Lord cries over the waters, saying: Come all you, receive the Spirit of wisdom, the Spirit of understanding, the Spirit of the fear of God, even Christ who is made manifest. Today the nature of water is sanctified . . . "[54] The faithful may then drink the Epiphany water as a reminder of their baptism and take some to bless their homes.

parallel how the aid agencies emphasize the twofold nature of the world water crisis: access and sanitation. To inspire Christians to "take ownership" of this crisis, the use of water in liturgy simply needs to be strengthened and explicitly highlighted but not in a catechetical fashion. Instead, a sense of responsibility can be stoked imaginatively through the senses, by using water more often and generously and by talking about those who thirst. Facts and information are important, but they are not enough to inspire. Liturgy and ethics work not only on a cognitive level but also through the subconscious. To inspire Christians to act for water justice, the facts need to be laid out, the element has to be used in the context of communal prayer, and then, individuals need to discern their moral responsibilities.

Act

Christians have an additional reason to make the global water crisis a primary concern: sacramental stewardship. Water is the primary symbol of salvation. However, as Thomas Berry questioned, what happens when water, which is supposed to be a symbol of cleansing and life, becomes in the day-to-day experience of most people

54. "Great Water Blessing," in Konrad Onasch and Annemarie Schnieper, *Icons: The Fascination and the Reality* (New York: Riverside, 1997), 107.

a source of disease, filth, and death? For many, the concept of "holy water" is an oxymoron; perhaps it is better to speak of "sinful water," or more accurately "waters of social sin."[55] If water is to function as a symbol of life and holiness, then it must be kept clean and readily accessible. Water is in a state of crisis. It is increasingly scarce, more polluted, and more expensive. If Christians don't enter the fight for water, they will quickly see its symbolic meaning redefined by the marketplace. How can water symbolize the washing away of sin or eternal life in a world in which it is most often a source of disease and death or so expensive that it is unattainable?

John J. O'Brien aptly notes, "The sacramental imagination and a culture of water are the basis for a new spirituality. The church, refreshed at the water-bath and nourished at the supper table, is sent forth as a people with a mission. *Lex orandi, lex agenda!*"[56] This agenda must extend beyond feelings, pious prayers, and statements by bishops. It has to include concrete action. The first step in this action must be raising a sense of awareness followed by efforts to elicit a sense of responsibility, which is where liturgy can be effective. A symbiotic relationship exists between liturgy and ethics that is especially strong in water. Action on behalf of the world's thirsty augments understanding of scripture and baptism, and an active sacramental life can be an impetus for social-justice advocacy, namely some kind of concrete charitable, political action or both. No greater ecological-humanitarian crisis lays claim to the collective Christian conscience than this one, because: it is the single most-pressing ecological-humanitarian crisis facing the world today; water plays a prominent and indispensable role in scripture and liturgy; and the connection between the global water crisis and the Christian life is so easy to make.

---

55. Pope John Paul II spoke of social sin as institutionalized evil, which is "the accumulation and concentration of many personal sins. It is a case of the very personal sins of those who cause or support evil or who exploit it; of those who are in a position to avoid, eliminate or at least limit certain social evils but who fail to do so out of laziness, fear or the conspiracy of silence, through secret complicity or indifference; of those who take refuge in the supposed impossibility of changing the world and also of those who sidestep the effort and sacrifice required" (*Reconciliatio et Paenitentia* [Reconciliation and Penance], no. 16).

56. John J. O'Brien, "Baptismal Waters and the Waters of Life," *Proceedings of the North American Academy of Liturgy* (2007), 157.

CONCLUSION

Christians are called not simply to be educated about injustice, but also to act. Information and sympathy don't bring water to the 1.1 billion who are thirsty today. In the time it took to read this chapter, approximately eighty children have died because of filthy water. Identifying concrete steps for water justice is difficult to do in a book such as this, because the needs of the world's thirsty are constantly changing. To learn more about concrete steps Christians and others can take to alleviate human suffering, log on to one of the Web sites that follow. The choice is ours.

- Catholic Relief Services is the official international development agency of the U.S. Catholic bishops and one of most respected aid agencies in the world. *http://crs.org/water-sanitation/world-water-day/index.cfm)*
- Ecumenical Water Network is a network of churches and Christian organizations promoting people's access to water around the world. *http://www.oikoumene.org/en/activities/ewn-home.html*
- Tap Project is sponsored by UNICEF. This project asks restaurant patrons to donate to global water projects. *http://www.tapproject.org/*
- Water Advocates is the first U.S.-based nonprofit organization dedicated solely to increasing American support for worldwide access to safe, affordable, and sustainable supplies of drinking water and adequate sanitation. It is an advocacy organization. It does not implement projects. *http://www.wateradvocates.org/*
- Water.org is a nonprofit organization founded by Gary White and Matt Damon addressing the water crisis in Africa, Asia, and Latin America. *http://water.org/*
- The Water Project is a nonprofit organization that brings relief to communities around the world by building wells, dams, and rain-harvest systems. *http://thewaterproject.org/*
- Water for Waslala is a nonprofit organization started by college students that builds clean-water delivery systems for the rural region of Waslala, Nicaragua. The organization has brought

clean water to more than 3,000 people. *http://www.waterfor-waslala.org/*

- World Water Council is a collection of more than 300 governmental and nongovernmental organizations working to address the world water crisis. They sponsor the World Water Forums. *http://www.worldwatercouncil.org/*

QUESTIONS FOR REVIEW

1. What is the author's critique of "crossless Christianity"? Do you agree with him? Why or why not?
2. Explain the pastoral circle, and use examples of the global water crisis to illustrate each step.
3. What does it mean to say that water is a right? What does it mean to say that water is a commodity? What is the Catholic Church's position on the right vs. commodity debate?
4. What roles or functions does water play in the Hebrew Bible? What roles or functions does it play in the New Testament? Provide concrete examples for each role or function.
5. What is the Catholic Church's teaching regarding private property, and how does it relate to the world water crisis?
6. What is the connection among the world water crisis, sacramental imagination, and sacramental stewardship?

IN-DEPTH QUESTIONS

1. The author argues "the Christian life requires more than feelings and prayer" and that "social justice work is inherently political and is as important to the Christian life as prayer and worship." Do you agree or disagree with him? Why?
2. The official teaching of the Catholic Church is that water is a right and that it can also be treated as a commodity, so long as access is guaranteed for all. Critique this position by identifying at least two strengths and two weaknesses.
3. The author appeals to Scripture, tradition, and liturgy (worship) to make the case that Christians have a unique responsibility

to address the world water crisis. Do you find his argument compelling? Why or why not?

4. The final step of the pastoral circle is action. The chapter ends by noting "information and sympathy don't bring water to the 1.1 billion who are thirsty today" and lists several water advocacy organizations. What did you do when you finished reading this article? Why?

CHAPTER 20

NO PEACE ON EARTH:

War and the Environment

Matthew A. Shadle

KEY TERMS

anthropocentrism
ecological intervention
intrinsic value
just war theory
***jus ad bellum* criteria**
***jus in bello* criteria**
***jus post bellum* criteria**
just cause
noncombatant discrimination
proportionality

INTRODUCTION

From the mountain pass of Thermopylae and the plain of Gaugamela to the jungles of Vietnam and the deserts of Iraq, the natural environment has had an inescapable role in warfare. Military leaders have planned their strategies based on the physical features of the battlefield and have tried to use them to their advantage. In their efforts to defeat the enemy, generals have also wreaked destruction on the environment by burning agricultural lands and forests and poisoning or diverting water sources.

In modern times, however, war's potential to harm the natural environment has increased exponentially. This is the result primarily of the development of more powerful weapons. Militaries and other groups engaged in violence have developed ways of bringing about environmental destruction as a means of warfare, such as the incendiary gel napalm, which can be used to destroy vegetation. Even when the destruction of the environment is not an intentional tactic of war, in many cases serious damage nonetheless results, as in the bombing of a chemical plant. Imagine the horrific consequences another use of nuclear weapons would have for the environment.

The intersection of war and environmental destruction is a fertile field for ethicists. Both religious and secular ethicists have written numerous works on these as independent threats, but rarely have they examined how war and environmental destruction interrelate. Such an examination helps one to better understand each of the two as ethical issues. This chapter will focus on some of the ways that war and environmental destruction are linked and the problems these links raise for ethical reasoning. In addition, it will point out resources from both Christian tradition and contemporary writers that can help to develop solutions to these problems.

THE JUST WAR THEORY

The just war theory is a set of moral guidelines for government and military officials when they make decisions about war and for citizens as they morally evaluate the actions of their government and military with respect to those decisions. For Christians, the just war theory is an attempt to balance Christ's command to love one's neighbors, and even one's enemies, with the responsibilities of government to protect its citizens and promote public order. For example, according to Saint Augustine, a just war is waged out of love for those the enemy is harming; if it is waged out of hatred of the enemy, it cannot be just. Not all Christians have subscribed to the just war theory. Most Christians in the first centuries of Christianity rejected military service, and today, a handful of groups, particularly those known as the Peace Churches (such as Anabaptists and Quakers), promote pacifism, or the total rejection of war. Most Christian denominations, however, including the Catholic Church, advance some form of the just war theory, although many individuals and groups in these denominations may also support pacifism or some other position on war. Because of its predominance then, the just war theory will provide the framework in this chapter examining the effect of war on the environment.

The just war theory morally analyzes war from beginning to end. In most accounts of the just war theory, the *jus ad bellum* (right

SAINT AUGUSTINE OF HIPPO

Augustine of Hippo (354–430), perhaps the most influential early Christian theologian, was the Bishop of Hippo in North Africa and the author of many polemical works. In his early life, Augustine belonged to a religious group called the Manichees, who denied the goodness of material creation. He gradually returned to the Catholic faith of his childhood, however, and later was appointed a bishop. Augustine is considered the originator of a Christian theory of the just war, which he outlined in his *Against Faustus*, a work written against the Manichees, and in his Letter to Boniface, a letter to a governmental leader with questions about the compatibility of his Christian faith and his political position.

to wage war) criteria are distinguished from the *jus in bello* (justice in war) criteria. The *jus ad bellum* criteria describe five conditions that must be met for a decision to go to war to be just.

- First, one must have a just cause for war.
- Second, the cause must be proportionate, that is, serious enough to warrant going to war, and there must be a reasonable chance of successfully remedying the just cause for the war.
- Third, one must have the legitimate political authority for waging war.
- Fourth, one must turn to war only as a last resort, meaning all other reasonable alternatives of resolving the dispute must be tried first.
- Fifth, one must have the right intention, that is, the stated reasons must be the real reasons for waging the war, and one must wage the war in ways consistent with those reasons.

The *jus in bello* criteria govern the way a war is to be fought once it has begun. They include the principle of noncombatant discrimination, meaning that civilians and civilian-related structures cannot be intentionally targeted during war, and the principle of proportionality, meaning that when a legitimate military target is attacked, any unintended civilian deaths or destruction of civilian structures that result must be minimized and be justified by the importance of the target.

Recently, some ethicists have also attempted to revive what could be called the *jus post bellum* (justice after war) criteria dealing with the restoration of justice after a war. Early just war theorists had emphasized matters such as compensation for lost property and punishment for unjust aggression, but in the twentieth century, these issues were mostly neglected. Although *jus post bellum* criteria are less defined than the others, theologians Mark J. Allman and Tobias L. Winright have proposed four criteria.

- The first is that, if possible, the victorious side must ensure that the cause justifying the war is rectified but must not go beyond that cause. For example, in a war to prevent a genocide, the victors should not leave behind political chaos that will likely lead to further violence, but neither should they engage in punitive violence against the earlier perpetrators.
- Second, in a process of reconciliation, both sides in a conflict must admit any wrongdoing, including the injustices that led to the war.
- Third, those responsible for wrongdoing should pay some form of compensation, and the guilty should be punished for war crimes.
- Fourth, those who are able should work to restore what was damaged during the war and to reform political and social life to avoid further injustices and conflict.[1]

The intersection of war and environmental destruction raises questions for each of these three sets of criteria: *jus ad bellum, jus in bello,* and *jus post bellum.*

1. Mark J. Allman and Tobias L. Winright, "*Jus Post Bellum*: Extending the Just War Theory," in *Faith in Public Life*, College Theology Society Annual vol. 53, ed. William J. Collinge (Maryknoll, NY: Orbis, 2008): 241–64. Allman and Winright develop *jus post bellum* further in their *After the Smoke Clears: The Just War Tradition and Post War Justice* (Maryknoll, NY: Orbis, 2010).

ENVIRONMENTAL DESTRUCTION AS A CAUSE OF WAR

Within the *jus ad bellum* criteria, the intersection of war and environmental destruction particularly raises questions about environmental destruction as a cause for war. Regarding war, the word *cause* has a double meaning, as both the origin of a war and the moral justification for a war. It is important to look at environmental destruction as a cause for war in both senses of the term.

Scholars have identified several ways in which the environment has or could possibly contribute to conflict.[2] Rising temperatures as a result of climate change could lead to conflicts over newly emerging sea lanes at the poles. Refugees could flee from areas becoming uninhabitable because of changing climate, only to come into conflict with the residents of their destination. Countries could come into conflict over water supplies or about upstream water pollution in a shared river. For example, in Arab-Israeli conflict, the shortage of water in that region has often been a source of contention.[3] A decrease in the food supply because of the degradation of farmland could lead to conflict between different groups within a country. Moreover, a worldwide decline in the food supply could lead to the use of food as a "weapon," that is, an instrument for bending the will of food-scarce countries.

As Thomas Homer-Dixon, probably the leading scholar of environmental causes of conflict, points out, even if environmental factors contribute to a conflict, the origin of that conflict cannot be reduced to those factors; for these variables always act in combination with more social factors.[4] The interaction of environmental and

---

2. Thomas F. Homer-Dixon, "Environmental Changes as Cause of Acute Conflict," in *Conflict after the Cold War: Arguments on Causes of War and Peace*, 3rd ed., ed. Richard K. Betts (New York: Pearson Longman, 2008 [essay originally 1991]), 607.

3. John K. Cooley, "The War over Water," *Conflict after the Cold War: Arguments on Causes of War and Peace*, 3rd ed., ed. Richard K. Betts (New York: Pearson Longman, 2008 [essay originally 1991]), 596–606; Kimberley Kelly and Thomas F. Homer-Dixon, "The Case of Gaza," in *Ecoviolence: Links among Environment, Population and Security*, eds. Thomas Homer-Dixon and Jessica Blitt (Lanham, MD: Rowman & Littlefield, 1998 [essay originally 1995]), 67–107.

4. Thomas F. Homer-Dixon, *Environment, Scarcity, and Violence* (Princeton, NJ, and Oxford: Princeton University Press, 1999), 16.

social factors reveals the complex causes of war. For example, the environmental degradation of agricultural land combined with population growth and social inequalities contributed to the rise of the Sendero Luminoso (Shining Path) insurgency in Peru in the 1980s and 1990s.[5] Although humans are necessarily a part of the natural world and dependent on it, they also create social institutions to govern their common life and create identities for themselves—all of which can contribute to a war.

Clearly environmental degradation contributes to conflicts, but can it ever be a just cause for war? The seventeenth-century Dutch Protestant Hugo Grotius provides a good starting point for reflection on this question. One passage from his classic *The Rights of War and Peace* suggests that environmental degradation in one's land could not justify a war to seek better living conditions in another's: " . . . the desire of emigrating to a more favourable soil and climate [cannot] justify an attack upon a neighbouring power."[6] Elsewhere, however, Grotius says that waging war to preserve one's life is morally

HUGO GROTIUS

Hugo Grotius (1583–1645), a Dutch Protestant jurist, or scholar of the law, was arrested and given a life sentence in 1618 for his support of the Dutch government overthrown in a religious conflict in the 1610s. With the help of his family, Grotius escaped from prison in a book chest and fled to Paris. There, Grotius wrote *The Rights of War and Peace*, which ensured his legacy as one of the great modern interpreters of the just war theory and the founder of international law. Grotius was never able to return to Holland, his home country, because he refused to ask for pardon, which would have meant admitting he had been guilty for supporting the government.

5. Ibid., 151–152.

6. Hugo Grotius, *The Rights of War and Peace*, trans. A. C. Cambell (Washington, DC, and London: Dunne, 1909), bk. 2, ch. 22, nos. 7–8.

acceptable.[7] Likewise, he claims that in cases of necessity and under certain conditions, a person or group can use the property of another.[8] Therefore, in a case in which there is no other remedy and a people is in extreme need (as opposed to merely seeking "more favorable soil"), it seems Grotius might approve forcibly appropriating the property of others who are better off.

Grotius provides a useful starting point, but contemporary ethicists might have some problems with his view. First, the modern means of war are much more destructive than in Grotius's time, and that must weigh into any consideration of whether a war to escape environmental scarcity could be justified. Second, contemporaries would be more uncomfortable than Grotius because those who are attacked by those seeking to escape scarcity are most likely not at fault for that scarcity. Finally, modern ethicists would be more concerned with finding ways to avoid conflict before it breaks out.[9] Despite these caveats, in extreme cases it seems reasonable that the justice of a war to escape scarcity should at least be considered.

In some cases, environmental damage in one country might be more directly caused by the actions of another and, therefore, present a more clear-cut case of a just cause. A country could potentially claim that such environmental destruction caused by another country is a just cause for war. Richard B. Miller, in fact, makes this case.[10] He even argues for "ecological intervention," analogous to humanitarian intervention, "to rescue natural goods from ongoing, systematic tyranny or undue exploitation."[11] So, in what cases could environmental destruction justify war?

One helpful contribution to this question is Catholic moral theologian Kenneth R. Himes's suggestion that the environment should be included as an element of national security. The destruction of the environment is a serious national-security concern because

---

7. Ibid., bk. 1, ch. 2, no. 1.

8. Ibid., bk. 2, ch. 2, nos. 6–9.

9. Richard B. Miller, "Just War Criteria and Theocentric Ethics,"in *Christian Ethics: Problems and Prospects*, eds. Lisa Sowle Cahill and James F. Childress (Cleveland, OH: Pilgrim Press, 1996), 345.

10. Ibid., 339.

11. Ibid., 346.

of its great potential for generating conflict.[12] Most contemporary ethicists agree that self-defense and intervention to prevent massive human-rights violations are the only causes that could justify war; if the environment is a part of national security, then harm to the environment might justify a claim of self-defense. It is easy to see how environmental destruction could rise to such a level that a society's continued existence is at stake, justifying that society in defending itself against harm. If a war could be waged in a proportionate way to prevent such harm, it might be justified. This would be true in cases in which responsibility for the environmental destruction is clear and immediate. In cases such as climate change in which responsibility is diffuse and less immediate, it is harder to see how a war could be justified in self-defense, even if the harm to a nation is severe, because there is little chance that a war could remedy the situation. In any situation in which policymakers contemplate environmental degradation as a cause for war, they must consider the likelihood that war could remedy the behavior that is causing the degradation; if the degradation is irreparable, then there is little justification for war, no matter how unjust the situation.

ENVIRONMENTAL DESTRUCTION AS A TACTIC OF WAR

Environmental destruction can be a cause for war, but it can also be a deliberate tactic of war. In these cases, it would fall under the *jus in bello* criteria of the just war theory. Such tactics are as old as warfare. Typically, such tactics were intended to make continued living difficult, if not impossible, for the enemy's people, and included poisoning wells, burning crops, and cutting down fruit trees. Grotius is surprisingly lenient when it comes to such tactics: "When punishment is lawful and just, all the means absolutely necessary to enforce its execution are also lawful and just, and every act that forms a part of the punishment, such as destroying an enemy's property and country

12. Kenneth R. Himes, OFM, "Environment and National Security: Examining the Connection," in *The Challenge of Global Stewardship: Roman Catholic Responses*, eds. Maura A. Ryan and Todd David Whitmore (Notre Dame, IN: University of Notre Dame Press, 1997), 191.

by fire or any other way, falls within the limits of justice proportionable to the offence."[13] He does provide some limits, though, on this brutal view. The destruction must be proportionate to the cause, and while the destruction of property might be permissible if it is necessary for a crucial war objective, objectives are often not as crucial as they first appear. He further states that in many cases it is possible to prevent the enemy from using property during the course of the war without destroying it.[14]

Grotius's position is a good starting point for thinking about environmentally destructive war tactics, but contemporary ethicists would also raise some serious questions. For one, Grotius's view of the environment is very anthropocentric; in the first place, the environment can be destroyed as a means toward human ends; and in the second place, the environment is understood entirely as property, that is, as serving the needs of humans. According to this view, the environment and nonhuman organisms have no intrinsic value, a position to which many environmental ethicists would object. Additionally, modern military technology has made severely damaging the environment much more possible.

Three well-known cases illustrate the modern capability of severely damaging the natural environment as a war tactic. During the Vietnam War, U.S. troops used napalm, a gasoline jelly, to destroy vegetation used as cover by the Viet Cong. For the same purpose, they also used Agent Orange, a chemical defoliant that also causes cancer, birth defects, and death among humans. These tactics brought the issue of deliberately using environmentally destructive war tactics to the world's attention.[15] In addition, in 1991, the Iraqi army deliberately created oil spills into the Persian Gulf and set Kuwaiti oil wells on fire, severely harming animal life in the area, ruining beaches, hampering Saudi desalinization efforts, and releasing toxic gases into the air above Kuwait.[16] The Allies in both World War I

---

13. Grotius, *Rights of War and Peace*, bk. 3, ch. 1, no. 2.

14. Ibid., bk. 3, ch. 12, nos. 1–2.

15. Karen Hulme, *War Torn Environment: Interpreting the Legal Threshold*, International Humanitarian Law, eds. Christopher Greenwood and Timothy L. H. McCormack (Leiden and Boston: Nijhoff, 2004), vol. 7, 5.

16. William A. Wilcox Jr., *The Modern Military and the Environment: The Laws of Peace and War* (Lanham, MD: Government Institutes, 2007), 135–136.

An American Black Hawk helicopter flies above a burning Kuwaiti oil well on March 12, 1991. Saddam Hussein's forces ignited many of the wells when Iraq's defeat was imminent.

and World War II used a similar tactic when they burned oil fields in Romania to keep them from falling into enemy hands.[17] A third example of a tactic of war that purposefully damages the environment would be a biological, chemical, or nuclear attack by terrorists. For example, in 1995, the Japanese religious group Aum Shinrikyo released sarin gas into the Tokyo subway system, using the contamination of the natural environment as a weapon. Terrorists could also release biological agents into a city's water supply or detonate a radioactive "dirty bomb," making an area uninhabitable for humans.

The just war criteria of noncombatant discrimination and proportionality can help discern when environmentally destructive tactics can be justified and when not. The principle of noncombatant discrimination has traditionally been used to prohibit militaries from intentionally targeting innocent persons, who possess inherent dignity. If the natural environment has intrinsic value apart from its usefulness to humans, however, then at least some intentionally environmentally destructive tactics could also be said to violate the principle of noncombatant discrimination.[18] Michael N. Schmitt lays

17. Christopher D. Stone, "The Environment in Wartime: An Overview," in *The Environmental Consequences of War: Legal, Economic, and Scientific Perspectives*, eds. Jay E. Austin and Carl E. Bruch (Cambridge, MA: Cambridge University Press, 2000), 87.

18. Miller, "Just War Criteria and Theocentric Ethics," 352.

out three possible perspectives on this question: In the "anthropocentric" view, intentionally environmentally destructive tactics could be used if they served any legitimate military purposes whatsoever. In the "moderate intrinsic value" view, the environment has some value apart from human uses but could be damaged or destroyed if there is sufficient reason. Finally, in the "radical intrinsic value" view, the environment has just as much intrinsic value as human life and, therefore, could never be directly or intentionally destroyed through military means.[19] Recent Catholic views of the environment are probably most similar to the "moderate intrinsic value" view, affirming the intrinsic value of the natural environment but attributing a special dignity to humans. The moderate view also has a practical advantage over the radical view, which could be taken to absurd extremes: for example, prohibiting chopping down a tree to build a bridge across a river. In the moderate view, a sense of proportionality must come into play when coming to judgment on the deliberate destruction of the environment during war. For example, during the Persian Gulf War, the Iraqi leadership claimed that the spillage of oil and the burning of oil wells served legitimate military purposes, but those purposes were clearly not proportionate to the damage caused.[20] The criterion of proportionality is also necessary in cases in which environmental destruction is an unintended side effect of war.

ENVIRONMENTAL DESTRUCTION AS A SIDE EFFECT OF WAR

Cases in which the environment is unintentionally harmed as a side effect of war are probably much more common today than cases in which the environment is deliberately harmed. One example involves the use of depleted uranium in ammunition by American soldiers in the Kosovo War of 1999 and the Iraq War of 2003. Depleted uranium, because of its high density, is used in ammunition designed

19. Michael N. Schmitt, "War and the Environment: Fault Lines in the Prescriptive Landscape," in *The Environmental Consequences of War: Legal, Economic, and Scientific Perspectives*, eds. Jay E. Austin and Carl E. Bruch (Cambridge, MA: Cambridge University Press, 2000), 118–119.

20. Wilcox, *Modern Military*, 154.

to pierce armor, but it is also weakly radioactive and, therefore, poses a health hazard after use. Another example is that during the 2003 Iraq War, American bombs hit chemical factories, releasing dangerous chemicals onto the ground and toxic particles into the air as the factories burned.[21] In both of these cases, the contamination of the environment was not the intended result. Yet, the question remains: to what extent was the U.S. military morally blameworthy for the side effects of its actions? Environmental destruction is often not constrained by borders, and so war tactics may have a detrimental effect on the environment in neighboring countries that are not involved in the war. How should these side effects be factored into one's moral reasoning?

When environmental destruction is a side effect of war, the traditional principle of proportionality comes into play. The classical authors like Grotius provide little guidance here. Although these authors do put limits on the intentional destruction of the environment as a means of harming the enemy population, they hardly consider the unintended consequences war has for the environment. This can partially be explained because war was less destructive in their time and partially by their clear anthropocentrism. Contemporary writers are divided on the question. The problem is that making proportionate judgments with human targets is difficult enough, and adding nonhumans to the mix only makes it harder: "We can put ourselves in the shoes of a hostage, perhaps, but we cannot put ourselves in the hooves of a horse—or ask, how would we feel if we were a species or a mountain top?"[22] According to William A. Wilcox Jr., restrictions on military tactics will often lead to greater loss of human lives.[23] "So long as a commander has a legitimate military objective, and legitimate military means are employed to achieve that objective, the commander should be able to act with impunity."[24] In this view, the principle of proportionality primarily excludes only the wanton destruction of the environment that serves no legitimate military purpose. Richard B. Miller, however, argues that the effects

21. Ibid., 137.

22. Stone, "Environment in Wartime," 20.

23. Wilcox, *Modern Military*, 153–154.

24. Ibid., 141–143.

of military actions on the natural world should always be included when considering whether the destruction necessary to achieve an objective outweighs the importance of the objective.[25] This is probably the better option, and after all, human losses would also be factored into the considerations, taking care of Wilcox's concern.

RESPONSIBILITY FOR THE ENVIRONMENT AFTER WAR

In the past few years, just war ethicists have revived what could be called the *jus post bellum* criteria, that is, considerations of what justice requires after a war. These requirements are often linked to the causes that justified the war in the first place. According to Allman and Winright's criterion of just cause, the victors in a war must ensure that whatever conditions served as the cause for the war must be rectified. In a war in which environmental destruction, such as the pollution of water sources, served as a just cause, this would mean that the victors must remove that source of pollution. This criterion also states that victors should not go beyond what the just cause requires. Clearly, this would mean, for example, that in a war of self-defense, once the country is successfully defended, that country's military could not then go on and ravage the other country's environment. Allman and Winright's second criterion of reconciliation could also apply in cases in which the parties in a war admitted how their disregard for the environment contributed to the conflict or how their tactics during the war were needlessly harmful to the environment.

There are historical precedents for applying Allman and Winright's third criterion, punishment, to cases of environmental destruction during war, although they are not very helpful. In his treatment of the aftermath of war, Grotius briefly mentions compensation for lost property. He is very clear that neither side in the conflict is responsible for compensating for the environmental side effects of war.[26] Citizens also have no recourse to their own government for lost property, because "being united in the same cause, [they] ought to share the common losses, which happen to them in supporting

25. Miller, "Just War Criteria and Theocentric Ethics," 352.

26. Grotius, *Rights of War and Peace*, bk. 3, ch. 20, no. 15.

the privileges of their society."[27] Grotius does not write specifically on compensation for deliberate harm to the environment that serves no legitimate military purpose, although it is reasonable to expect that he would conclude that one side could demand compensation for such damage.

Modern approaches to the *jus post bellum* would be more willing to expect compensation for damage to the environment. First, remember that Grotius sees all environmental destruction resulting from legitimate military tactics as permissible, whereas most modern writers would put limits on this destruction. Therefore, compensation could be demanded for environmental destruction beyond what was absolutely necessary. Second, modern citizens typically see the government as their servant and believe it their right as citizens to demand compensation from their government. Some difficulties with demanding compensation for environmental destruction, however, are that it is hard to foresee what the extent of the damage will be in the long term; it is hard to put a monetary amount on environmental destruction even when its extent is known; and sometimes it is difficult to know precisely who should be compensated. A further difficulty is that a defeated country often faces economic hardship, and whatever compensation can be extracted from it will likely be in return for the destruction of human life and infrastructure rather than for environmental destruction.[28]

There is also the possibility that environmental destruction during war could be considered a war crime prosecutable under international law or as a new type of international crime. As Mark A. Drumbl points out, the Rome Statute of 1998, which established the International Criminal Court (the body responsible for prosecuting war crimes), includes environmental destruction as a possible war crime. The statute, however, has a very high threshold for the extent of damage necessary for it to be considered a war crime and also stipulates that the damage must be intentional, which could be hard to prove at a trial. Drumbl also notes that it is unlikely that the International Criminal Court would ever hear such a case, given that cases of humanitarian war crimes will always be a higher priority. He

27. Ibid., bk. 3, ch. 20, no. 8.

28. Stone, "Environment and War," 31–33.

suggests that a separate environmental court could be established to deal solely with environmental crimes committed during both wartime and peacetime.[29]

Allman and Winright's final *jus post bellum* criterion is restoration, which is also particularly helpful when thinking about the environment in the aftermath of war. Limiting belligerents' postwar responsibility for the environment to compensation hearkens back to the older anthropocentric view of the environment as merely property. If the natural environment has value of its own, then a belligerent's responsibility is not simply to its owners but to the environment itself. In such a case, restoration of the environment would be the just course of action. For example, the United States should take responsibility for cleaning up chemical contamination that resulted from the destruction of factories during the Iraq War. Of course, often an environment cannot be restored to exactly the way it was before damage was inflicted, but those who have responsibility for its restoration should take care to restore ecological harmony as close as possible to its previous state.

THE SPIRITUAL ROOTS OF WAR AND ENVIRONMENTAL DESTRUCTION

Both war and environmental destruction are violations of harmony: war is a violation of harmony between human communities, and environmental destruction is a violation of the harmony between humanity and the nonhuman world. In his 1990 World Day of Peace message and in his social encyclicals *Sollicitudo rei socialis* (On Social Concern) and *Centesimus annus* (On the Hundredth Anniversary of *Rerum novarum*), Pope John Paul II claims that there is a fundamental link between the attitudes that lead to both war and the destruction of the environment. According to John Paul II, both involve the use of things that have intrinsic value solely for humans' benefit, and in turn, both involve humans putting themselves in the place of God.

---

29. Mark A. Drumbl, "Waging War against the World: The Need to Move from War Crimes to Environmental Crimes," in *The Environmental Consequences of War: Legal, Economic, and Scientific Perspectives*, eds. Jay E. Austin and Carl E. Bruch (Cambridge, MA: Cambridge University Press, 2000), 620–646.

Therefore, not only do war and environmental destruction intersect in terms of causes and effects, they also share the same spiritual root.

In his encyclicals, John Paul claims that ultimately war has its roots in our sinful tendency to use others for our own benefit. In *Sollicitudo rei socialis*, written in 1987, John Paul is critical of the division of the world into two blocs, communist and democratic capitalist, during the Cold War. He is especially critical of the way the two superpowers, the Soviet Union and the United States, manipulated poorer and weaker countries for their own benefit, both through economic exploitation and through the wars sponsored by the superpowers that ravaged many of these countries.[30] Just as it is wrong to use another individual for one's own purposes rather than treating that individual as a person, it is also wrong for one country to use another country. The Cold War was only one example of how countries use one another for their own benefit, and this manipulation of other countries is ultimately the cause of wars.

John Paul finds the source of this tendency to use others in humanity's desire to put itself into the place of God. In modern times especially, wars have been "attempts to impose the absolute domination of one's own side through the destruction of the other side's capacity to resist, using every possible means, not excluding the use of lies, terror tactics against citizens, and weapons of utter destruction."[31] People believe they can take others' lives in their own hands in this way because they are convinced they possess "the secret of a perfect social organization" for which others can be sacrificed.[32] Humanity unjustly assumes for itself God's power and responsibility.

John Paul makes a similar argument concerning the destruction of the environment. A useful place to start for understanding his attitude toward environmental destruction is his description of consumerism. In *Centesimus annus*, John Paul states that although there is nothing wrong with seeking better material conditions for oneself, what is wrong is the reduction of the good life to having more and more stuff.[33] Consumerism in turn leads to disrespect for

30. John Paul II, *Sollicitudo rei socialis*, no. 22.

31. John Paul II, *Centesimus annus*, no. 14.

32. Ibid., no. 25.

33. Ibid., no. 36.

the environment as resources are consumed, and the environment is polluted by waste.[34] Just as the manipulation of other humans leads to a lack of respect for life through war, consumerism leads to a lack of respect for nonhuman life through overconsumption.[35]

Ultimately the lack of respect for nonhuman life stems from humanity's rejection of the order of God's creation. Christianity teaches that humans have an obligation to recognize and respect the order of the universe that has been established by God.[36] John Paul endorses the view that to some extent nonhuman life has intrinsic value: " . . . one cannot use with impunity the different categories of beings, whether living or inanimate—animals, plants, the natural elements—simply as one wishes, according to one's own economic needs. On the contrary, one must take into account the nature of each being and of its mutual connection in an ordered system."[37] Destroying the environment means turning one's back on nature's order, which is turning one's back on God, its creator.[38] Humanity's tendency to turn its back on God has roots in Adam and Eve's original rejection of God's plan, one of the results of which was the breaking of harmony between humanity and the earth.[39]

Pope John Paul's reference to Adam and Eve suggests that both war and environmental destruction have spiritual roots. Both stem from a spiritual alienation in the hearts of all humans. Because both share the same spiritual roots, then ultimately both have the same solution. In *Sollicitudo rei socialis*, John Paul says that the solution to the disruption of harmony represented by war and other political divisions is solidarity, which he defines as the virtue of committing oneself to the common good of the human race. Through solidarity, one recognizes the dignity of each person created in the image of God and redeemed by Christ.[40] Likewise, in his 1990 World Day

---

34. Ibid., no. 37.

35. John Paul II, "1990 World Day of Peace Message," no. 7.

36. Ibid., no. 15.

37. John Paul II, *Sollicitudo rei socialis*, no. 34.

38. John Paul II, "1990 World Day of Peace Message," no. 5.

39. Ibid., no. 3.

40. John Paul II, *Sollicitudo rei socialis*, no. 40.

of Peace message, John Paul emphasizes that through his death and Resurrection, Christ has reconciled all of creation, restoring the breach between humanity and the rest of the natural world.[41] In both cases, Christ restores lost harmony.

Pope John Paul's insights into the spiritual roots of war and environmental destruction appear to be becoming part of the Catholic tradition, as they were taken up by John Paul's successor, Pope Benedict XVI, in his 2010 World Day of Peace message. Benedict makes the connection between war and the environment clear in his theme: "If you want to cultivate peace, protect creation."[42] Like John Paul, he also traces both the lack of harmony between people and between humanity and the earth to Adam and Eve's original sin.[43] If humans saw creation as God's gift rather than a product of chance, they would respect one another and the earth.[44] Although humankind is in conflict with itself and with the earth, Christ brings reconciliation and will bring about "new heavens and a new earth."[45]

CONCLUSION

War and environmental destruction increasingly intersect, and the points of intersection illuminate the important ethical problems associated with each. Looking at the environmental causes of war and environmental destruction caused during war helps to expand one's understanding of the traditional just war criteria. Examining the moral problems of war helps Christians to better understand the intrinsic value of nonhuman life and their responsibility for restoring the environment. Finally, understanding the ethical issues of war and environmental destruction can provide insight into issues of spiritual alienation from God as well as the Christian vocation to be peacemakers and stewards of God's creation.

---

41. John Paul II, "1990 World Day of Peace Message," no. 4.

42. "If You Want to Cultivate Peace, Protect Creation," (message of His Holiness Benedict XVI for the celebration of the World Day of Peace, January 1, 2010), no.1. *http://www.vatican.va/holy_father/benedict_xvi/messages/peace/documents/hf_ben-xvi_mes_20091208_xliii-world-day-peace_en.html*, accessed June 12, 2011.

43. Ibid., no. 6.

44. Ibid., no. 2.

45. Ibid., no. 12.

QUESTIONS FOR REVIEW

1. What are the two senses in which environmental degradation could be a cause for war, and how do these senses differ?
2. What does Richard B. Miller mean by the term *ecological intervention*?
3. What does it mean to say that the environment has "intrinsic value" when considering the destruction of the environment as a tactic of war?
4. What are some of the difficulties in requiring compensation for environmental destruction that occurs during a war?
5. According to John Paul II and Benedict XVI, what is the ultimate source of both war and environmental destruction?

IN-DEPTH QUESTIONS

1. Do you think environmental degradation could ever be a just cause for one country to go to war with another? Why or why not?
2. Can aspects of the environment be intentionally damaged or destroyed as a tactic of war, and if so, what limitations should be placed on such tactics?
3. Should a country be held responsible for environmental damage that occurs as a side effect of tactics used in a just war? Why or why not?
4. Should environmental destruction during a war be considered a war crime that could be punished by international law? Why or why not?
5. Do you agree with John Paul II and Benedict XVI that war and environmental destruction share the same roots?

CONCLUSION

"GO FORTH IN PEACE TO LOVE AND SERVE THE LORD"

Tobias Winright

Whether the reader is Christian, agnostic, Muslim, atheist, Jew, seeker, Buddhist, or other, it is important to be informed about how and why religions are going green. Currently there are more than 1.3 billion Muslims, 2.1 billion Christians (including 1.1 billion Roman Catholics), 15 million Jews, 362 million Buddhists, and 830 million Hindus in the world.[1] That's a significant portion of the planet's population—and imagine what might happen if all of these people began living in ways that are Earth-friendly! Roger Gottlieb argues that religion "is now a leading voice telling us to respect the earth, love our nonhuman as well as our human neighbors, and think deeply about our social policies and economic priorities."[2] Indeed, similar to Michael Agliardo, SJ, in chapter 2 of this volume, Gottlieb compares this emerging ecological consciousness among the world's religions to other progressive religious social activist movements in the past, including the abolitionists in the nineteenth century and the civil rights movement of the twentieth century.

---

1. These numbers are rounded off from those given in Warren Matthews, *World Religions*, 6th ed. (Belmont, CA: Wadsworth, 2010), 66, 103, 237, 279, 325.

2. Roger S. Gottlieb, *A Greener Faith: Religious Environmentalism and Our Planet's Future* (Oxford: Oxford University Press, 2006), 9.

At the same time, the environmental problems we face can seem daunting and insuperable. What can we do, individually and collectively, to protect and heal the planet? Where should we start? Here Gottlieb offers both encouragement and a challenge: " . . . We need not be paralyzed by the scope of what lies before us. We will not be able to fix everything, for the only one responsible for 'everything' is God. Nevertheless, it is up to us to do our part."[3] The contributors to this volume offer many suggestions, guidelines, principles, virtues, and practices that should help equip and enable persons of faith to do their share. Addressed in these chapters are a range of topics with application to green discipleship, among them: sustainability, stewardship, Eco-Kosher, right-mindfulness, the social mortgage on private property, solidarity, the ecological common good, the preferential option for the poor, the universal destination of goods, ecological intervention, *tawhid*, neighbor-love, subsidiarity, sufficiency, ecojustice, green worship, temperance, *kenosis*, covenant, integral human development, conservationism, preservationism, interconnectedness, prudence, and more. In short, a framework for green discipleship is proposed.

As Pamela Smith observes, "The convergent themes in environmental ethics seem, then, to be largely visional."[4] A general worldview—one that includes a particular understanding of God, humankind, and the rest of creation—emerges that yields a basic orientation or fundamental direction for how one should think about who one ought to be and how one ought to live. Gottlieb corroborates this when he writes that religion offers a "comprehensive vision in which care for the earth and care for people go hand in hand."[5] Yet, although a fair amount of agreement is evident among the contributors about general principles (e.g., several highlighted sustainability or the common good), there remains legitimate room for differences with regard to the concrete applications of these principles to specific questions (e.g., about eating meat or chopping down trees in the Amazon). This volume does not purport to provide a one-size-fits-all solution to every environmental problem.

3. Ibid., 12.

4. Pamela Smith, *What Are They Saying about Environmental Ethics?* (New York and Mahwah, NJ: Paulist Press, 1997), 90.

5. Gottlieb, 13.

In making this point, I am following the moral methodology of the U.S. Catholic bishops in their statements on social-ethical issues such as war, economics, immigration, or the environment. As social ethicist Charles Curran has noted in connection with the 1983 pastoral letter *The Challenge of Peace*, the bishops employ the traditional Catholic distinction between universal moral principles and their particular application.[6] Citing the Second Vatican Council's *Gaudium et spes* on "how to relate principles to concrete issues," the bishops admit that their treatment of "many concrete questions concerning the arms race, contemporary warfare, weapons systems, and negotiating strategies" do not "carry the same moral authority as our statement of universal moral principles and formal Church teachings."[7] Differences of judgment are permitted regarding applications of principles in issues that, as Curran puts it, "by their very nature are so complex and specific that one cannot achieve a certitude that excludes the possibility of error."[8] Accordingly, Celia Deane-Drummond rightly emphasizes the importance of the recovery of prudence, which Nancy Rourke explores in her chapter on the virtues.[9] This reminder actually goes back to Thomas Aquinas, who held that as one moves from the level of general moral norms to the level of making particular judgments about applications to concrete issues, the virtue of prudence is necessary, and the degree of certitude ascribed to these judgments is less than what is ascribed to the general principles themselves.[10] Thus, there is room for disagreement

6. Charles E. Curran, "The Moral Methodology of the Bishops' Pastoral," in *Catholics and Nuclear War: A Commentary on The Challenge of Peace*, ed. Philip J. Murnion (New York: Crossroad, 1983), 53-54.

7. National Conference of Catholic Bishops, *The Challenge of Peace: God's Promise and Our Response* (Washington, DC: United States Catholic Conference, 1983), nos. 8-9; see also nos. 10-12. See also National Conference of Catholic Bishops, *Economic Justice for All: Pastoral Letter on Catholic Social Teaching and the U.S. Economy* (Washington, DC: United States Catholic Conference, 1986), no. 134. The bishops cite the Second Vatican Council, *Gaudium et spes*, in *The Documents of Vatican II*, ed. Walter M. Abbott, SJ (Piscataway, NJ: New Century, 1966), no. 1, n. 2.

8. Curran, 55.

9. Celia Deane-Drummond, *Eco-Theology* (Winona, MN: Anselm Academic, 2008), 184-185.

10. See Patricia Lamoureux and Paul J. Wadell, *The Christian Moral Life: Faithful Discipleship for a Global Society* (Maryknoll, NY: Orbis, 2010), 237–238.

and space for multiple possible solutions, which is why students, as they draw on these principles, virtues, and practices, triangulating from these a basic vision and direction, also are encouraged to study treatments of environmental issues in other disciplines, including economics, earth and atmospheric sciences, and political science.

As Gottlieb notes: "Difficulties and contradictions do not invalidate ecotheology any more than they do the idea of human rights, though they do mean that environmental ethics may be a lot harder than it looks. At the very least, general principles—about human rights and about the value of our kinship with nature both—can help establish the expectation that hurting or using other beings is a moral matter that requires reflection, honest self-assessment, and at times public justification."[11] Establishing such an ethical starting point that compels one to be a certain kind of person who lives a certain kind of way vis-à-vis others and creation itself would be a significant step in the right direction, countering antithetical worldviews (such as anthropocentric or individualistic ones) and overcoming their negative effects on creation.

In my view, the theological-ethical term that encompasses most everything that the contributors have proposed in these pages is *shalom*, usually translated from the Hebrew as "peace," but which refers more expansively to "the fullness of life and well-being that God wants for all creatures."[12] Alternatively, as the Mennonite theological ethicist John Howard Yoder beautifully put it, peace among God, humankind, and creation happens when we live "with the grain of the universe."[13] Therefore, "the protection of creation and peacemaking," in Pope Benedict XVI's view, "are profoundly linked."[14]

11. Gottlieb, 53.

12. Patricia Lamoureux and Paul J. Wadell, *The Christian Moral Life: Faithful Discipleship for a Global Society* (Maryknoll, NY: Orbis, 2010), 201. See Tobias Winright, "Peace to God's People *and* Earth," *The Cresset* 74, no. 2 (Advent/Christmas 2010): 30–33.

13. John Howard Yoder, "Armaments and Eschatology," *Studies in Christian Ethics* 1, no. 1 (1988): 58; also, John Howard Yoder, *The War of the Lamb: The Ethics of Nonviolence and Peacemaking*, eds. Glen Stassen et al. (Grand Rapids, MI: Brazos, 2009), 62. Also see Michael S. Northcott, *A Moral Climate: The Ethics of Global Warming* (Maryknoll, NY: Orbis, 2007), 278; and Stanley Hauerwas, *With the Grain of the Universe: The Church's Witness and Natural Theology* (Grand Rapids, MI: Brazos, 2001).

14. Benedict XVI, "If You Want to Cultivate Peace, Protect Creation," no. 14.

During the Catholic Mass, worshippers sing the "Gloria," which includes the line, derived from the angelic host's song of praise about the birth of Jesus (see Luke 2:14), "Glory to God in the highest, and peace to God's people on earth." Perhaps this should be amended, though, to sing instead, "Glory to God in the highest, and peace to God's people *and* earth." Peace, or *shalom*, is God's will for all creation, and the Christian vocation entails "that if we really desire to follow Christ, then we will act responsibly towards the environment. In other words, ecology . . . is also a mark of discipleship."[15] The principles, virtues, and practices—from sustainability to ecojustice, from right mindfulness to temperance—are the tools to equip and enable green disciples to, as the benediction at the end of most Christian worship services theocentrically commissions, "Go forth in peace to love and serve the Lord."

15. Deane-Drummond, 181.

APPENDIX

FROM THE REFERENCE LIBRARIAN:

A Practical Guide to Doing Research

Ronald Crown

The preceding chapters offer an array of topics for further research. The aim of this appendix is to offer a few tips on how to go about conducting that research. Possible topics range broadly, and every research project is in some way unique, making it impossible to offer a clear-cut process to follow in doing research. By applying some basic principles of how to use a library, however, your research will be a lot easier.

Perhaps the most difficult part of researching a topic is just getting started. Maybe you begin by asking a question. For example, what is the impact of war on the environment and how does the theory of just war relate to a Christian approach to the environment? What are the ethical implications of food consumption? How does (or should) a biblical view of creation influence human treatment of the environment? What contribution can be made to attitudes toward the environment by the theological views of classic theologians such as Thomas Aquinas, Saint Francis of Assisi, or Duns Scotus? How do Islam, Buddhism, and other religions view the environment? Whatever the topic, just getting started is a major hurdle. Even if you have a general notion about a topic, you will probably need to refine it into a workable subject to research and write. The library can help you get started with your research and refine your topic.

The library offers at least two major resources to help you start your research. The first resource is, of course, the librarian, and in particular the reference librarian, a professional who works in your library's reference department, or "information commons," and is trained in library research. The main job of a reference librarian is to assist people needing to use library resources. Most reference librarians also specialize in certain subjects and so are familiar with the resources specific to a particular field of study such as theology, history, science, business, and so on. Reference librarians are experienced researchers, experts in finding a path through the "information fog" that seems to surround us these days.

Not only can reference librarians help you find your way through library catalogs and databases, but they also are knowledgeable about the resources *in the particular library where you will be doing your research.* Some libraries have large collections of books, journals, and electronic resources in which you will be able to find just about everything you need; other libraries have smaller collections in which finding adequate resources may be more of a challenge. One thing all reference librarians do at libraries large and small is help you find what you need. Often, if a particular library does not have something in its collection, the librarian can show you how to obtain that item from another library through interlibrary loan, a service that's almost always free and one of the best bargains you'll find in your college career. So never hesitate to approach reference librarians to ask for help. They expect it; it is what they are paid to do.

The second major resource the library offers to help begin your research is the reference collection. In fact, the reference librarian may begin by directing you to some resource in the reference collection. Obviously, the reference collection is composed of reference books—books that you do not read from cover to cover, such as encyclopedias. (An increasing number of reference sources are becoming available electronically, but the benefits they offer are the same whether in print or electronic format.) For example, a good encyclopedia article can help further your research in a number of ways. To begin, it will provide an overview of a subject, as well as acquaint you with various aspects of that topic, any of which may suggest ways to refine your topic. Perhaps a certain person's writings and thought are of particular importance, or various issues of debate; such information can help refine your topic and focus your research. Furthermore, most encyclopedia articles conclude with a bibliography of books and articles that may provide additional sources for research.

Let's see how this might work in practice. Say that after reading Kari-Shane Davis Zimmerman's chapter on feminist perspectives on environmental issues, you would like to explore this topic further. How would you go about finding an encyclopedia article on that topic?

You can begin by considering the kinds of encyclopedias available. Many students, hearing the word *encyclopedia,* quite naturally think of well-known encyclopedias such as the *Encyclopedia Britannica* or *World Book.* These general-knowledge encyclopedias attempt to cover the broad scope of human knowledge. Most encyclopedias in academic library reference collections, however, are subject-specific. Note the specific subject designations in the titles of the encyclopedias and other reference materials listed below.

Encyclopedia of Ethics

Encyclopedia of Human Behavior

Encyclopedia of Religion

Encyclopedia of Environment and Society

Encyclopedia of World Environmental History

Encyclopedia of Christianity

New Catholic Encyclopedia, 2nd edition

American Contemporary Religion

Encyclopedia of Catholic Social Thought, Social Science, and Social Policy

The New Dictionary of Catholic Social Thought

Handbook of Christian Theology

Encyclopedia of Ethics, 2nd edition

Oxford Companion to Christian Thought

In fact, there is an encyclopedia for almost any subject you can name. Some of these subject-specific encyclopedias are almost as long as *Britannica* or *World Book.* The *Encyclopedia of Religion* listed is thirteen volumes. One way to begin your research is to ask the reference librarian to help you find a subject-specific encyclopedia containing an article on your topic. What kind of encyclopedia might contain an article on feminist perspectives on the environment? The reference librarian can be especially helpful in answering such questions and assisting your search.

One excellent resource you can begin with that is likely to be available in the library of any Catholic institution of higher education is the *New Catholic Encyclopedia* (2nd ed. 2003; some libraries may also have online access to this encyclopedia). The *New Catholic Encyclopedia* is a general-knowledge encyclopedia (in that regard, it is similar to the *Encyclopedia Britannica* or any other general-knowledge encyclopedia), but it is produced for an audience interested in specifically Catholic matters. Therefore, it will often contain articles on religious or theological subjects that you would not expect to find in another general-knowledge encyclopedia. As it happens, an article on "Ecofeminism and Ecofeminist Theology" appears in volume 5, pages 48–50, of the second edition of *New Catholic Encyclopedia.* (No such article is in the first edition of the *New Catholic Encyclopedia* published in 1967. Can you guess why? What does your answer tell you about the importance of knowing when an encyclopedia was published?)

If your library does not own the *New Catholic Encyclopedia*, various theological reference sources have similar articles. For example, perhaps your library owns the *Dictionary of Historical Theology* or the *Dictionary of Feminist Theologies*, both one-volume works that contain an article on "Ecofeminism." (The word *dictionary* in the title of a reference source means the same as *encyclopedia.*) Other reference works may contain relevant articles under different headings. The five-volume *Encyclopedia of Christianity* has no article on *Ecofeminism*, but it does have articles on both "Ecology" and "Feminist Theology." If you have trouble identifying a reference source likely to contain the kind of article you are looking for, just ask the reference librarian for help.

The importance of general-knowledge encyclopedia bibliography sources cannot be underrated. Here is the bibliography found at the end of the article on "Ecofeminism and Ecofeminist Theology" from the *New Catholic Encyclopedia.*

> **Bibliography:** C. J. ADAMS, ed. *Ecofeminism and the Sacred* (New York 1993). C. P. CHRIST, *Rebirth of the Goddess: LendingMeaning in Feminist Spirituality* (Reading, Mass.

1997). A. M. CLIFFORD, "When Being Human Becomes Truly Earthly, an Ecofeminist Proposal for Solidarity," 173–189, in *In the Embrace of God: Feminist Approaches to Christian Anthropology*, ed. A. O'HARAGRAFF (Maryknoll, N.Y. 1995). F. D'EAUBONNE, *Le féminisme ou la mort* (1974), E.T. "Ecofeminism or Death," 64–67, in *New-French Feminisms: An Anthology*, ed. E. MARKS and I. DE COURTIVRON (Amherst, 1980). M. GIMBUTAS, *The Goddesses and Gods of Old Europe* (Berkley 1982). S. MC FAGUE, *The Body of God: An Ecological Theology* (Minneapolis 1993); *Super, Natural Christians: How We Should Love Nature* (Minneapolis 1997). R. RADFORD RUETHER, *Gaia and God: An Ecofeminist Theology of Earth Healing* (San Francisco 1992); *Women Healing Earth: Third World Women on Ecology, Feminism, and Religion* (Maryknoll, N.Y.)

Not only do you now know some additional sources, but also you can use this information to help you find sources that are not even listed in the bibliography. To do this, simply take a title that appears in the bibliography and search in your library catalog to see whether your library owns it. If the book is in your library, you will see a catalog record containing one or more subject headings. Subject headings are terms or phrases that are assigned to a book when it is cataloged to allow you to find books on a particular subject. For example, the first title appearing in the bibliography is *Ecofeminism and the Sacred.* The catalog record for this book shows that the subject heading *Ecofeminism—Religious Aspects* has been assigned to this book. This tells you that you can use *Ecofeminism—Religious Aspects* to search for more books specifically about your subject.

Let's try another one. Here are the subject headings assigned to the book *Gaia and God: An Ecofeminist Theology of Earth Healing.*

Human ecology—Religious aspects—Christianity
Feminism—Religious aspects—Christianity
Creation.

Note that the subject headings are a little different in this case, although still relevant. Often, there is more than one way to search by subject for books on the same subject. In this case, which of the headings above comes closest to designating the kind of book you are looking for, namely, a book about ecofeminism or feminist views of the environment? *Human ecology* and *Creation* certainly cover the environment, but do they include feminism? The subject heading *Feminism* obviously takes care of that but covers a lot more territory than feminism and the environment. In this case, combining two subject headings in a single search (*Human ecology* AND *Creation* or *Feminism* AND *Creation*) would be the appropriate way to use these subject headings to find additional resources. All library catalogs have the capability of combining specific subject searches; ask your librarian to show you how it's done at your library.

At this stage, you have taken a major step forward in your research. Not only have you gotten your feet wet regarding your topic, but you also have identified several possible sources for further research, and you now know how to use your library catalog to find additional sources.

However, there is one additional resource your library offers that you may want to use during research (depending in part on what kinds of resources your instructor expects you to use); namely, journal articles. Almost all academic libraries now offer access to journal articles through electronic databases. One important thing to know about journal databases is that they are just like encyclopedias in a couple of respects. Some journal databases are general-knowledge databases, that is, they provide access to journals covering a wide range of subjects. Other journal databases are subject-specific. In the field of religion and theology, for example, three databases provide coverage. They are the *ATLA Religion Database* (produced by the American Theological Library Association), the *Catholic Periodical and Literature Index* (produced by the Catholic Library Association), and *Religious and Theological Abstracts* (produced by Religious and Theological Abstracts). Any of these three databases may contain articles relevant to the broad subject of theology and the environment. A subject search on *ecofeminism* in the *ATLA Religion Database*, for example, results in 127 bibliographic citations (at the time I am writing this). The details of searching each database will vary somewhat; ask the reference librarian to show you the best way to search for materials if you are unsure. Also, keep in mind that there are databases in other subject fields that may contain relevant material. For example, for subjects such as ecology and the environment, you may want to look for articles in a database of scientific journals or perhaps a database focusing on journals covering public policy issues. Ask your librarian about databases in other subject fields.

Articles on issues related to theology and the environment may be found in many theological journals. There are two important journals publishing articles focusing entirely in this area. (Both are indexed in the *ATLA Religion Database.*)

Environmental Ethics

Journal for the Study of Religion, Nature, and Culture (formerly *Ecotheology*)

A number of other journals focus on environmental issues from other perspectives, whether scientific, political, or economic. Although they may not discuss the religious or ethical aspects of environmental issues, such journals will nevertheless contain much relevant material. Such journals include the following.

American Journal of Environmental Sciences

Conservation

Ecology and Society

Environmental Conservation: An International Journal of Environmental Science

Environmental Hazards

Environment: Science and Policy for Sustainable Development

Frontiers in Ecology and the Environment

Journal of Environmental Health

Local Environment: The International Journal of Justice and Sustainability

Again, ask your librarian if your library subscribes to these or other similar journals.

To summarize, this appendix has tried to get you started with the basics of doing library research as follows:

1. Use the library's reference collection (encyclopedias) to begin research.
2. Use the library's catalog to locate additional sources of information.
3. Use the library's collection of online databases to identify articles in magazines and scholarly journals.

Finally, remember, the reference librarian is always there to help. Using a library can be somewhat intimidating, especially if your library is large. However, using a library can also be very satisfying when you find just what you need. Libraries spend a lot of money to make resources available to you (and you are spending a lot of money to get a college education!). Take advantage of the resources available, both the human ones and the ones on the shelf or online.

GLOSSARY OF TERMS

Editor's note: Not all terms listed as Key Terms at the top of the chapters will be found in the glossary, and not all glossary terms are listed in the chapters as Key Terms. The Key Terms listings have been identified by the authors as particularly significant in the context of their respective chapter. The glossary terms are the choice of the general editor for this book as particularly significant for the book as a whole and a general understanding of environmental theology and ethics.

acquired virtues Virtues that require human effort. These virtues are strengthened when one chooses actions that "exercise" them.

agrarian Related to the land and agriculture.

amana Arabic word meaning "free will." In Islam, free will marks humans (and jinn) as unique, in possessing the free will given by God.

anthropocentrism Being centered around humans.

anthropogenic effects Effects on the natural world that derive from the activities of humans (Greek. *anthropos*), as opposed to processes that occur in the world naturally, without human influence.

Aristotelian Refers to the ancient Greek philosopher Aristotle or the philosophical tradition begun by Aristotle.

aya Arabic word for "sign" (plural: *ayat*).

Babylonian Exile The period in Jewish history after the destruction of Jerusalem and the Temple in which the Babylonians captured the people of the Kingdom of Judah (587–538 BCE).

baptism The sacrament or institution of initiation into the Christian church by a ritual washing with water.

canonical From the Greek *kanon*, "measuring rod." Relating to those books traditionally deemed by the Christian community to be part of the Scriptures.

carbon footprint The amount of greenhouse gas emissions caused by the activities of a person, organization, or place.

cardinal virtues Pivotal virtue that is acquired for its own sake and not for the sake of strengthening another virtue. Cardinal virtues are traditionally recognized as justice, prudence, temperance, and fortitude.

cocreation The belief that a central part of the human vocation is to become cocreators with God, through the capacities of reason and inventiveness, thus bringing all of creation into greater flourishing.

coeval Originating or existing during the same period; lasting through the same era, contemporary.

Columbia River Pastoral Letter A letter issued in 2001 by the Catholic Bishops' Conferences of Oregon and Washington noting the religious significance of the Columbia River for the region and urging protection and preservation of the river for the future.

commodity An economic good, usually a physical product, such as oil or copper, which is sold at an equal price on commodities markets.

common good The set of conditions under which a community and every member of that community may flourish.

conservationism A view of environmental care that emphasizes the careful management of natural resources with a view to long-term sustainability.

discipleship Dedication to living the gospel of Jesus Christ as a follower or student of the master.

diversity of creatures Thomas Aquinas argues that a diversity of creatures with varying inclinations is not only part of God's Eternal Law, but it is also necessary that the universe fulfill its purpose of imitating the divine goodness.

divine providence God's prior knowledge of and sovereign power over events and actions.

domination The use of power without restraint and without regard for the integrity of that over which power is exercised.

dominion Drawing on natural resources for well-being and development, while respecting the integrity of creation as always a good in itself.

Earth Charter An international statement of broad principles in support of environmental sustainability and social justice, released in 2000.

ecocentrism A system of values that is nature-centered rather than human centered. Because all living things share common origins in evolution, they are all interrelated and thus all of the environment is intrinsically valuable, not just human beings.

ecocide Large-scale destruction of the environment through human consumption of natural resources.

ecofeminism A perspective that emphasizes common ground between the feminist and environmentalist movements, based largely on a perceived shared experience of exploitation by women and the natural world.

ecojustice An alternative concept to dominion, posited by ecofeminist thinkers that moves away from top-down ideas toward a view of the relationship between humans and nature that is believed to be more equitable and just.

Eco-Kosher A term coined by Rabbi Zalman Schachter-Shalomi and popularized by Rabbi Arthur Waskow that extends Jewish dietary laws to include environmentally sound living.

ecological anthropology A rethought perspective on the nature and role of humans on Earth in light of the interconnectedness of humans with the natural environment.

ecological economics An economic model promoted by theologian Sallie McFague. Ecological economics is neither concerned with fulfilling the desires of persons (as in neoclassical economics) nor simply with humans. Rather, ecological economics concerns itself with community, justice, and sustainability.

ecological good The good of the environment, which cannot be separated from the good of individuals as integral parts of the environment.

ecological intervention A justification for military action, analogous to humanitarian intervention, with the goal to rescue natural goods from ongoing systematic tyranny or undue exploitation.

ecological literacy A connection with the environment that provides a reminder for humans of where they come from and where they belong (from nature and in nature).

ecological theology A Christian theological position promoted by contemporary Catholic theologian Elizabeth Johnson that emphasizes the presence and action of the creative Spirit of God throughout the natural world.

ecology The study of the relationships between organisms and their environment.

ecumenical Relating to the *oikoumene,* or the inhabited world. In the modern context, it has come to mean the movement for unity among Christian churches, as well as for dialogue among religions.

encyclical A letter, usually concerning an issue of doctrine, which is issued by a pope and addressed to the bishops and people of the Roman Catholic Church. Examples include *Rerum novarum* and *Caritas in veritate.*

end The goal or object of an act.

environmental degradation The deterioration of the natural environment through the depletion of resources, destruction of ecosystems, or both.

Environmental Justice Program (EJP) Begun by the Catholic bishops of the United States in 1993, the EJP seeks to engage and educate Catholics in working for environmental problems and to act in the public sphere for environmental policies that protect the poor and promote sustainable environmental development.

environmental refugees People who are forced by the degradation of their natural habitat to forsake it and often their homes and possessions.

episcopal conferences Regional or national conferences of Catholic bishops (episcopal from *episkopos*, "bishop").

epistemology The philosophical study of the nature of knowledge.

eschatology The part of theology that is concerned with the *eschaton,* or the end times, and the ultimate destiny of humanity and creation.

Eternal Law The immutable law by which God has arranged the universe. Every creature participates in God's Eternal Law, which provides for a variety of inclinations and desires. This is a kind of an inner blueprint for each creature, and every member of every species fulfills its purpose when it properly attains those ends instilled in it by God.

Eucharist From Greek, *eucharistia,* or "thanksgiving." The sacrament of communion, or the Lord's Supper, a central act in the worship of the Christian churches.

exegesis A critical explanation or interpretation of a text, especially a religious text. Exegesis seeks to explore the meaning of the text, which then leads to discovering its significance or relevance.

fitra Arabic word for "disposition" or "nature." In Islam, *fitra* refers to the innate knowledge of God inborn in every human.

fortitude The cardinal virtue that relates to strength, endurance, perseverance, and patience.

framing The notion that humans place things in a framework or context within which they interpret their significance. Framing is the construction and application of an interpretive framework, and it takes place in the midst of particular historical circumstances.

Franciscan A follower of Saint Francis of Assisi; the Catholic order that takes its inspiration and rule from Francis.

Gnosticism Early Christian sects that focused on salvation as a sort of "knowledge" (Greek: *gnosis*). Gnostics believed they alone possessed the secret knowledge that brought salvation and that the material world was fundamentally evil. Some argued that the God of creation was different from the God of redemption.

Hasidism A mystical strain of ultra orthodox Judaism that emerged in eighteenth-century Eastern Europe.

Hellenistic The common classical Greek culture that spread around the Mediterranean after the conquests of Alexander the Great in the fourth century BCE.

hermeneutics The science and art of textual interpretation.

hima Arabic word for "inviolate zone." It refers to an area that is set aside for the conservation of natural resources.

human ecology The relationship between humans and their environments: social, natural, and built.

human impacts Particularly the negative influence of humans on the environment, including a broad range of issues such as global climate change, soil and water depletion and degradation, deforestation, and loss of species and genetic diversity.

immanence Divine presence or closeness in the world.

incarnation The theological event of the divine Son becoming a human in Jesus Christ.

inclusio A literary tool sometimes used by the authors of Scripture in which an important theme is placed at the introduction and then again at the end of a text, encompassing the body of the text like bookends.

infused virtue A type of virtue that is unearned, that becomes part of a person through God's grace. It can be recognized by the actions one performs, both externally and internally.

intrinsic goodness/value The notion that a thing is naturally valuable in itself; in this case, that all creation is intrinsically good because it was created by God and serves God's purposes.

janna Arabic word meaning "garden." The Islamic understanding of paradise.

***jus ad bellum* criteria** Criteria in just war theory that deal with the conditions that must be met for a decision to go to war to be just.

***jus in bello* criteria** Criteria in just war theory that govern the way a war is fought or just conduct once it has begun.

***jus post bellum* criteria** Criteria in just war theory dealing with the restoration of justice after a war.

just cause The first criterion of just war theory, that the cause for which the war is waged must be just.

just war theory A set of moral guidelines for government and military officials when they make decisions about war and for citizens as they morally evaluate the actions of their government and military with respect to those decisions.

kabbalah Literally meaning "tradition," a discipline or school of thought concerned with the mystical aspects of Judaism: questions of the relationship between the eternal Creator God and the created universe.

khalifa An Arabic word meaning "vice regent." In the *Qur'an*, Adam is described as the *khalifa* of God on Earth.

kenosis A word in Greek meaning "emptying," used in Philippians 2:6–7. It refers to Christ's emptying of divine power and glory in becoming a human.

Law of Dependent Co-Origination The Buddhist principle that human actions and the events they encounter are related to their prior choices and other factors in a way that the experiences were unsatisfactory.

liberation theology Originating in the context of twentieth-century Latin America, liberation theology can now function as an umbrella term for various theological approaches concerned with exploring how theology can address various types of oppression and bring about change in the world.

liminal From a Latin word for "threshold"; it refers to an intermediate or transitional phase or condition.

liturgy From the Greek *leitourgia*, "the work of the people." Understood to mean the church's corporate worship.

local food Food grown within a defined region (generally a 100–250-mile radius).

logos The Greek word for "word," "reason," or "logic." This word is used to describe Jesus in the Gospel of John, has roots in Greek philosophy, and describes the fundamental principle of the universe.

National Religious Partnership for the Environment (NRPE) Founded in 1993 by four major environmental advocacy groups, both Jewish and Christian, the NRPE seeks to act as an advocate and voice for faith-based environmental groups.

natural appetites According to Thomas Aquinas, all creatures have natural inclinations, or "appetites," which differ according to the kind of species it is. Aquinas uses a broad understanding of inclination—it applies not only to humans, who can recognize their inmost desires, and not only to animals, who have inclinations whether they can recognize them or not, but also to any species of creature whatsoever.

natural law The universal laws set by nature that have been perceived by human reason and understood as binding principles of justice and morality.

nature-love An understanding of Christian neighbor-love that includes all of creation, nonhuman and human alike.

neighbor-love The command to a horizontal right relationship, to "love your neighbor as yourself." The command is first found in Leviticus 19:18 and is repeated by Jesus in the gospels along with love of God as the "Great Commandment."

noncombatant discrimination The principle that civilians and civilian-related structures cannot be intentionally targeted during war.

ontological Based on the philosophical study (ontology) of being, existence, or reality.

organic food Distinguished from conventional food. For plants, most pesticides, fungicides, and herbicides are not used. Animals raised for meat production are not given antibiotics or growth hormones but are given regular access to pasture. Organic farming methods use less energy than conventional agricultural methods.

orthodox From the Greek *orthodoxos*, meaning, "right opinion or belief." Also used in reference to the Eastern Orthodox Christian churches.

pantheism A belief that there is a strict identity between all that exists (Greek: *pan*) and God (Greek: *theos*). In other words, the universe itself is god.

parable of the Good Samaritan The account recorded in the Gospel of Luke 10:25–37, in which Jesus describes love of neighbor through the story of a man left for dead on a road and finally rescued and cared for by an enemy, a Samaritan.

participation in God Thomas Aquinas's teaching that through its common origin in God, creation participates in God's action and natural law in the universe.

pastoral circle A Christian method of ethical discernment involving the three steps of seeing, judging, and acting.

patriarchal From Greek, *patriarchia,* "rule of fathers." Social systems in which male dominance is central to the organization of society. In the ancient Near East, the patriarchal structure reinforced itself through control of women, land, slaves, and so on.

patron saint A holy person whose life is presented as a particular example of Christian faith and virtue. Patron saints are selected years or centuries after their death to speak to the spiritual aspirations of a contemporary society.

plant dispersal The ability of different plant species to disperse, or move around.

preferential option for the poor The aspect of Catholic social teaching that promotes a priority of economic and spiritual concern for the needs of the poor.

preservationism A view of nature not so much as a source of raw materials to be carefully managed for human consumption, but rather as something to be appreciated in its own right and integrity.

primal narrative For biblical scholar Walter Brueggemann, the basic and fundamental storyline that defines the essence of biblical faith. In the case of the ancient Hebrews, this was the Exodus.

privatization The transfer of ownership or control from the public sphere or a government entity to the private sector.

proportionality The principle that when a legitimate military target is attacked, any unintended civilian deaths or destruction of civilian structures that result must be minimized and be justified by the importance of the target.

protectionism A perspective of environmental care not simply concerned with protecting the environment "out there," but also more broadly with the idea of safeguarding the overall ecological health of a region.

prudence The cardinal virtue related to moral wisdom, enabling someone to size up a situation and to embody other virtues in connection with specific decisions and actions to take.

public sphere The arena of social life in which people freely discuss and identify societal issues and, in turn, influence political action.

Qur'an In Islam, the sacred text of divine revelations given to the Prophet Muhammad.

religious ecological consciousness A religiously inspired awareness of humans' inescapable ecological interdependent relationship with Earth, its elements, and its living organisms.

religious environmentalism The teachings and concerns of a religious tradition being brought to bear on environmental issues.

religious retrieval A broad set of activities taking place across all faiths to select the most appropriate beliefs, human values, and ritual practices to represent its religious identity to the modern world.

Rerum novarum An 1891 encyclical of Pope Leo XIII that was written in response to the issues raised by the economic and social changes of the late nineteenth century. This encyclical is considered the foundation of modern Catholic social teaching.

revelation Divine self-disclosure.

sacraments In Christian churches, these are the divinely instituted "visible signs of invisible grace," such as the Eucharist and baptism. Roman Catholic and Orthodox churches have seven sacraments, while most Protestant churches accept only two.

sanctification Making holy; for Christians, sanctification is the process of growing in holiness, being "made holy" by the Holy Spirit.

Second Vatican Council The twenty-first ecumenical council of the Roman Catholic Church, begun under Pope John XXIII on October 11, 1962, and closed under Pope Paul VI on December 8, 1965. The Council brought many sweeping changes to the Catholic Church, including to its liturgy, to its ecclesiology (*Lumen gentium*), and to its understanding of revelation (*Dei verbum*).

signs of the times A phrase that originally appears in the Gospel of Matthew; it was first used in Catholic social teaching in 1963 by Pope John XXIII in his encyclical *Pacem in terris,* in which each chapter of the document ends with a brief section on the characteristics of the present day, or the signs of the times.

social ecology Term used by Brazilian liberation theologian Leonardo Boff to illuminate the reality that humans are not outside of the ecological web of relationships studied by scientists, but that their history is tied with how they treat one another and Earth.

solidarity The ties in a society that bind people to one another so that they are able to relate to and support people of different backgrounds. In Catholic social teaching, solidarity is the determination to commit oneself to the common good.

stewardship In a Christian understanding, *stewardship* refers to the dominion given by God to humanity in the creation story in Genesis, a dominion in which humans are ultimately responsible to God for their care of creation.

structural sin The social dimension of sin, beyond individual wrongdoing; sin that originates from social systems and for which society shares corporate responsibility.

subordinate ends The four subordinate ends discovered by reason—life, procreation, community, and truth—either from immediate experience or from reflection and inference that are required for persons to become authentic and exemplary friends of God and of neighbor.

subsidiarity A principle in the social teaching of the Catholic Church that matters should be handled by the smallest, lowest, or least centralized competent authority. Political decisions ought to be made at a local level if possible, rather than by a central authority. Subsidiarity was articulated as an attempt to make a middle way between laissez-faire capitalism and communism.

subsidiary virtues Virtues that comprise the cardinal virtues (for example, in the way that patience is part of fortitude) and are more connected to specific actions and decisions. Subsidiary virtues are directed by the cardinal virtues.

sufficiency The Christian concept that people should seek to acquire what they need to live a good, dignified life but should not seek to have more than they legitimately need.

Sukkot Also known as the feast of Tabernacles, this festival was originally celebrated in Israel at the end of the summer harvest and in preparation for the rainy season. It was originally associated with the redemption of the Israelites from Egypt (see Leviticus 23:24), and it involved dwelling in a temporary booth so as to experience the power of God in nature more directly and to be grateful for God's power of deliverance.

Summa Theologiae Thomas Aquinas's monumental work, which attempted to compile arguments for almost all points of Western Christian theology.

superdevelopment An excessive availability of all kinds of material goods.

sustainability The ability of biological systems to remain diverse and productive over time.

tawhid In Islam, the fundamental unity or oneness of God.

temperance Cardinal virtue related to self-control regarding desires. Being "rightly pleased."

theocentrism Being centered on God.

theological anthropology The theological study of humans, their nature, and their relationship to God.

theological virtues The virtues that the Catholic Church recognizes as being particularly connected to God, thus directing the other virtues; faith, hope, and love are the three traditional theological virtues.

Thomistic Refers to the teachings of Thomas Aquinas or the philosophical school that arose from his work.

Torah In Judaism, the written Law in the Hebrew Scriptures, which rabbinic Judaism placed at the center of Jewish life and viewed as the paradigm of the created world.

tradition From the Latin *tradere*, meaning, "to transmit or deliver." This indicates that traditions are not static treasures to be defended but rather living memories, values, and ways of being are shared from one generation to the next.

"two books" of revelation The twofold way by which God has made him known: Scripture and creation.

ultimate end The goal to which all things are inclined by God's imprinted directedness, which is divine goodness itself. All creatures, by nature, are disposed toward the good things that they need for their perfection.

universal purpose of created things Also called the **universal destination of goods.** The Catholic belief that the bounty of Earth's natural resources exists for the purpose of sustaining life on Earth and should be used for the benefit of all.

virtue The right amount of a good characteristic, usually formed by actions that, through repetition, have become good habits.

vocation From the Latin *vocare*, "to call." In the Christian context, it refers to the divine calling to use gifts and talents for specific purposes.

whole food Food that has not been processed or cooked.

SELECT BIBLIOGRAPHY

Al-Damkhi, Ali Mohamed. "Environmental Ethics in Islam: Principles, Violations and Future Perspectives." *The International Journal of Environmental Studies* 65, no. 1, 2008, 11–31.

Allman, Mark J., and Tobias L. Winright. "*Jus Post Bellum*: Extending the Just War Theory." In *Faith and Public Life*, College Theology Society Annual, vol. 53, edited by William J. Collinge, 241–264. Maryknoll, NY: Orbis, 2008.

Armstrong, Regis, OFM Capuchin. *Clare of Assisi—The Lady: Early Documents*. New York: New City Press, 2006.

Artson, Bradley Shavit. "Our Covenant with Stones: A Jewish Ecology of Earth." *Conservative Judaism* 44, 1991–92, 25–35.

Bailey, Kenneth E. *Through Peasant Eyes: More Lucan Parables, Their Culture and Style*. Grand Rapids, MI: Eerdmans, 1980.

Benstein, Jeremy. "One, Walking and Studying . . . : Nature vs. Torah." *Judaism: A Quarterly Journal* 44, 1991–92, 25–35.

———. *The Way into Judaism and the Environment*. Woodstock, VT: Jewish Light, 2006.

Bernstein, Ellen, editor. *Ecology and The Jewish Spirit: Where Nature and the Sacred Meet*. Woodstock, VT: Jewish Light, 2000.

Berry, Thomas. *The Great Work*. New York: Bell Tower, 2000.

———. *Dream of the Earth*. San Francisco: Sierra Club Books, 1988.

Berry, Wendell. *The Art of the Commonplace: The Agrarian Essays of Wendell Berry*. Norman Wirzba, ed. Washington, DC: Shoemaker and Hoard, 2002.

———. *Life Is a Miracle*. Washington DC: Counterpoint, 2000.

Bittman, Mark. *Food Matters: A Conscious Guide to Eating with More than 75 Recipes*. New York: Simon and Schuster, 2008.

Blanchette, Oliva. *The Perfection of the Universe According to Aquinas: A Teleological Cosmology*. University Park, PA: Pennsylvania State University Press, 1992.

Boersma, Jan J. *The Torah and the Stoics; On Humankind and Nature; A Contribution to the Debate on Sustainability and Quality*. Leiden, Boston, Köln: Brill Academic, 2001.

Boff, Leonardo. *Cry of the Earth, Cry of the Poor*. Translated by Phillip Berryman. Maryknoll, NY: Orbis, 1997.

———. *Ecology and Liberation: A New Paradigm*. Translated by John Cumming. Maryknoll, NY: Orbis, 1997.

Boff, Leonardo, and Clodovis Boff. *Introducing Liberation Theology*. Translated by Paul Burns. Maryknoll, NY: Orbis, 1987.

Boff, Leonardo, and Virgil Elizondo. *Ecology and Poverty: Cry of the Earth, Cry of the Poor.* Maryknoll, NY: Orbis, 1995.

Bormann, Bernard T., Richard W. Haynes, and Jon R. Martin. "Adaptive Management of Forest Ecosystems; Did Some Rubber Hit the Road?" *BioScience* 57, no. 2, 2007, 186–191.

Bouma-Prediger, Steven. *For the Beauty of the Earth: A Christian Vision for Creation Care*. 2nd edition. Grand Rapids, MI: Baker Academic, 2010 [1st edition, 2001].

Bria, Ion. "The Liturgy after the Liturgy." In *Baptism and Eucharist: Ecumenical Convergence in Celebration*, edited by Max Thurian and Geoffrey Wainwright. Grand Rapids, MI: Eerdmans, 1983, 213–218.

Brueggemann, Walter. *The Bible Makes Sense*. Winona, MN: Saint Mary's Press, 1977.

Cabin, Robert J. "Science-Driven Restoration: A Square Grid on a Round Earth." *In Restoration Ecology* 15, no. 1, 2007, 1–7.

Carroll, John E. "Catholicism and Deep Ecology." In *Deep Ecology and World Religions: New Essays on Sacred Ground*, edited by David Landis Barnhill and Roger S. Gottlieb. Albany, NY: State University of New York Press, 2001, 169–182.

Carson, Rachel. *The Edge of the Sea*. Boston: Houghton Mifflin, 1955.

———. *Silent Spring*. Boston: Houghton Mifflin, 1962.

Cates, Diana Fritz. "The Virtue of Temperance." In *The Ethics of Aquinas*, edited by Stephen J. Pope. Washington, DC: Georgetown University Press, 2002, 323–324.

Chamberlain, Gary L. *Troubled Waters: Religion, Ethics and the Global Water Crisis*. Lanham, MD: Rowan and Littlefield, 2008.

Chinnici, J., OFM. "Institutional Amnesia and the Challenge of Mobilizing Our Resources for Franciscan Theology." In *The Franciscan Intellectual Tradition*, edited by E. Saggau, OSF. Bonaventure, NY: Franciscan Institute Publications, 2002, 105–150.

Christiansen, Drew. "Ecology and the Common Good: Catholic Social Teaching and Environmental Responsibility." In *And God Saw That It Was Good*, edited by Drew Christiansen and Walter Grazer. Washington, DC: United States Catholic Conference, 1996, 183–196.

Clifford, Anne CSJ. "Foundations for a Catholic Ecological Theology of God." In *"And God Saw that It Was Good": Catholic Theology and the Environment*, edited by Drew Christiansen and Walter Grazer. Washington, DC: United States Catholic Conference, 1996, 19–42.

Clifford, Richard J. "Genesis 1–3: Permission to Exploit Nature?" *The Bible Today* 26, 1988, 133–137.

Comins, Michael. *A Wild Faith: Jewish Ways into Wilderness, Wilderness Ways into Judaism*. Woodstock, VT: Jewish Light, 2007.

Cooley, John K. "The War over Water." In *Conflict after the Cold War: Arguments on Causes of War and Peace*. 3rd edition, edited by Richard K. Betts. New York: Pearson Longman, 2008, 596–606.

Cowdin, Daniel M. "Toward an Environmental Ethic." In *Preserving the Creation: Environmental Theology and Ethics*, edited by Kevin W. Irwin and Edmund D. Pellegrino. Washington, DC: Georgetown University Press, 1994, 112–147.

Crossin, John W. "Some Developing Aspects of Virtue Ethics." *Josephinum Journal of Theology* 7, 2000: 112–125.

David, Bryan. *Cosmos, Chaos and the Kosher Mentality*. Sheffield England: Sheffield Academic Press, 1995.

Davis, Ellen E. *Scripture, Culture and Agriculture: An Agrarian Reading of the Bible*. Cambridge: Cambridge University Press, 2009.

Deane-Drummond, Celia. *Eco-Theology*. Winona, MN: Anselm Academic, 2008.

Delio, Ilia, OSF. *Clare of Assisi: A Heart Full of Love*. Cincinnati, OH: Saint Anthony Messenger Press, 2007.

Delio, Ilia, OSF, Keith Douglas Warner, OFM, and P. Wood. *Care for Creation: A Contemporary Franciscan Spirituality of the Earth*. Cincinnati, OH: Saint Anthony Messenger Press, 2008.

Dettman, Connie L., and Catherine M. Mabry. "Lessons Learned about Research and Management: A Case Study from a Midwest Lowland Savanna, U.S.A." *Restoration Ecology* 16, no. 4, 2008, 532–541.

Dockrat, Hashim Ismail. "Islam, Muslim Society, and Environmental Concerns: A Development Model Based on Islam's Organic Society." In *Islam and Ecology: A Bestowed Trust*, edited by Richard C. Foltz et al. Cambridge, MA: Harvard University Press, 2003, 341–377.

Donahue, John. "Biblical Perspectives on Justice." In *The Faith that Does Justice*, edited by John Haughey, SJ. Mahwah, NJ: Paulist Press, 1977, 68–112.

Drumbl, Mark A. "Waging War against the World: The Need to Move from War Crimes to Environmental Crimes." In *The Environmental Consequences of War: Legal, Economic, and Scientific Perspectives*, edited by Jay E. Austin and Carl E. Bruch. Cambridge: Cambridge University Press, 2000, 220–246.

Egan, Dave. "People Are Wearing Out the Planet." *Ecological Restoration* 23, no. 4, 2005, 229.

Ehrenfeld, David "War and Peace and Conservation Biology." *Conservation Biology* 14, no. 1, 2000, 105–112.

Ehrlich, Paul. "Human Natures, Nature Conservation, and Environmental Ethics." *BioScience* 52, no. 1, 2002, 31–43.

Eisenberg, Evan. *The Ecology of Eden*. New York: Knopf, 1998.

Findlay, Stuart E. G., and Clive G. Jones. "How Can We Improve the Reception of Long-Term Studies in Ecology?" In *Long-Term Studies in Ecology*, edited by Gene E. Likens. New York: Springer-Verlag, 1989, 201–202.

Flinn, Kathryn M., and Mark Vellend. "Recovery of Forest Plant Communities in Post-Agricultural Landscapes." *Frontiers in Ecology and the Environment* 3, no. 5, 2005, 243–250.

Foltz, Richard C., editor. *Worldviews, Religion, and the Environment: A Global Anthology*. Belmont, CA: Wadsworth, 2003.

Freyfogle, Eric T. "Conservation and the Culture War." *Conservation Biology* 17, no. 2, 2003, 354–355.

Fullam, Lisa. "Sex in 3-D: A Telos for a Virtue Ethics of Sexuality." *Journal of the Society of Christian Ethics* 27, 2007, 154–157.

Geaves, Ron. *Aspects of Islam*. Washington, DC: Georgetown University Press, 2005.

Gerstenfeld, Manfred. *Judaism: Environmentalism and the Environment: Mapping and Analysis*. Jerusalem: Rubin Mass, 1998.

Giles, Jim. "We Can Afford to Go Green." *New Scientist* 204, 2009, 8–10.

Gottlieb, Roger S. *A Greener Faith: Religious Environmentalism and Our Planet's Future*. Oxford: Oxford University Press, 2006.

———. "The Beginnings of a Beautiful Friendship: Religion and Environmentalism." *Reflections* 94, no. 1, 2007, 10–13.

Gottwald, Norman. "The Biblical Mandate for Eco-Justice Action." In *For Creation's Sake: Preaching, Ecology, and Justice*, edited by Dieter T. Hessel. Philadelphia: Geneva Press, 1985, 32–44.

Green, Arthur. *Radical Judaism: Rethinking God and Tradition*. New Haven, CT: Yale University Press, 2010.

Gudorf, Christine E., and James E. Huchingson. *Boundaries: A Casebook in Environmental Ethics*. 2nd edition. Washington, DC: Georgetown University Press, 2010.

Gustafson, James. *Ethics from a Theocentric Perspective*. Vol. 2. Chicago: University of Chicago Press, 1984.

———. *A Sense of the Divine: The Natural Environment from a Theocentric Perspective*. Cleveland, OH: Pilgrim, 1994.

Hallman, David G., editor. *Ecotheology: Voices from South and North*. Maryknoll, NY: Orbis, 1994.

Haneef, Sayed Sikandar Shah. "Principles of Environmental Law." *The Arab Law Quarterly* 3, no. 17, 2002, 241–254.

Haq, S. Nomanul. "Islam and Ecology: Toward Retrieval and Reconstruction." In *Islam and Ecology: A Bestowed Trust*, edited by Richard C. Foltz et al. Cambridge, MA: Harvard University Press, 2003, 141–142.

Häring, Bernard, CSSR. *Toward a Christian Moral Theology*. Notre Dame, IN: University of Notre Dame Press, 1966.

Hart, John. *Sacramental Commons: Christian Ecological Ethics*. New York: Rowman & Littlefield, 2006.

———. *What Are They Saying about Environmental Theology?* New York and Mahwah, NJ: Paulist Press, 2004.

Hawken, Paul. *The Ecology of Commerce: A Declaration of Sustainability*. New York: HarperBusiness, 1993.

Hennelly, Alfred, SJ. *Liberation Theologies: The Global Pursuit of Justice*. Mystic, CT: Twenty-Third Publications, 1995.

Hiebert, Theodore. "Rethinking Traditional Approaches to Nature in the Bible." In *Theology for Earth Community: A Field Guide*, edited by Dieter T. Hessel. Maryknoll, NY: Orbis, 1996, 23–30.

———. *The Yahwist's Landscape: Nature and Religion in Early Israel.* New York and Oxford: Oxford University Press, 1996.

Hill, Brennan. *Christian Faith and the Environment: Making Vital Connections.* Maryknoll, NY: Orbis, 1998.

Hillel, Daniel. *The Natural History of the Bible.* New York: Columbia University Press, 2006.

Himes, Kenneth R., OFM. "Environment and National Security: Examining the Connection." In *The Challenge of Global Stewardship: Roman Catholic Responses*, edited by Maura A. Ryan and Todd David Whitmore. Notre Dame, IN: University of Notre Dame Press, 1997, 186–209.

Hinze, Christine Firer. "Catholic Social Teaching and Ecological Ethics." In *And God Saw That It Was Good*, edited by Drew Christiansen and Walter Grazer. Washington, DC: United States Catholic Conference, 1996, 165–182.

Hoge, Dean, Charles Zeck, Patrick McNamara, and Michael J. Donahue. *Money Matters: Personal Giving in American Churches.* Louisville, KY: Westminster, 1996.

Hollenbach, David, SJ. *The Common Good and Christian Ethics.* Cambridge: Cambridge University Press, 2002.

Homer-Dixon, Thomas F. *Environment, Scarcity, and Violence.* Princeton, NJ, and Oxford: Princeton University Press, 1999.

———. "Environmental Changes as Cause of Acute Conflict." In *Conflict after the Cold War: Arguments on Causes of War and Peace.* 3rd edition, edited by Richard K. Betts. New York: Pearson Longman, 2008, 607–622.

Horrell, David, et al. "Appeals to the Bible in Ecotheology and Environmental Ethics: A Typology of Hermeneutical Stances." *Studies in Christian Ethics* 21, 2008, 219–238.

Hulme, Karen. *War Torn Environment: Interpreting the Legal Threshold.* International Humanitarian Law. Vol. 7, edited by Christopher Greenwood and Timothy L. H. McCormack. Leiden and Boston: Nijhoff, 2004.

Hüttermann, Aloys. *The Ecological Message of the Torah: Knowledge, Concepts, and Laws which Made Survival in a Land of "Milk and Honey" Possible.* Atlanta: Scholars Press, 1999.

Irwin, Kevin W. "The Sacramentality of Creation and the Role of Creation in Liturgy and Sacraments." In *Preserving the Creation: Environmental Theology and Ethics*, edited by Kevin W. Irwin and Judith Lee Kissell. Washington, DC: Georgetown University Press, 1994, 67–111.

Jackson, Wes. "Farming in Nature's Image: Natural Systems Agriculture." In *Fatal Harvest*, edited by Andrew Kimbrell. Washington, DC: Island Press, 2003, 41–48.

Jacobs, Mark X. "A Jewish Environmentalism: Past Accomplishments and Future Challenges." In *Judaism and Ecology: Created World and Revealed Word,* edited by Hava Tirosh-Samuelson. Cambridge, MA: Harvard University Press, 2002, 449–477.

Jenkins, Willis. *Ecologies of Grace: Environmental Ethics and Christian Theology*. Oxford: Oxford University Press, 2008.

———. "Biodiversity and Salvation: Thomistic Roots for Environmental Ethics." *Journal of Religion* 83, 2003, 401–420.

Jepson, Paul, and Susan Canney. "Values-Led Conservation, Global Ecology and Biogeography." *Global Ecology and Biogeography* 12, no. 4, 2003, 271–274.

Johnson, Elizabeth A. *Quest for the Living God: Mapping Frontiers in the Theology of God.* New York: Continuum, 2007.

Jones, Ellis. *The Better World Shopping Guide: Every Dollar Makes a Difference.* New York: New Society, 2010.

Jung, L. Shannon. *Sharing Food: Christian Practices for Enjoyment.* Minneapolis: Fortress, 2006.

Katz, Eric. "Nature's Healing Power, the Holocaust, and the Environmental Crisis." *Judaism: A Quarterly Journal* 46, 1997, 79–89.

Kavanagh, Aidan. *On Liturgical Theology*. Collegeville, MN: Liturgical Press, 1992.

Keenan, Marjorie, RSHM. *From Stockholm to Johannesburg: An Historical Overview of the Concern of the Holy See for the Environment 1972–2002.* Vatican City: Pontifical Council for Justice and Peace, 2002.

Kehm, George H. "The New Story: Redemption as Fulfillment of Creation." In *After Nature's Revolt: Eco–Justice and Theology*, edited by Dieter T. Hessel. Minneapolis, MN: Fortress, 1992, 89–109.

Kelly, Kimberley and Thomas Homer-Dixon. "The Case of Gaza." In *Ecoviolence: Links among Environment, Population and Security*, edited by Thomas Homer-Dixon and Jessica Blitt. Lanham, MD: Rowman & Littlefield, 1998, 67–107.

Khalid, Fazlun. "Islam, Ecology, and Modernity: An Islamic Critique of the Root Causes of Environmental Degradation." In *Islam and Ecology: A Bestowed Trust*, edited by Richard C. Foltz, Frederick M. Denny, and

Azizan Baharuddin. Cambridge, MA: Harvard University Press, 2003, 299–322.

Knapp, Henry. "The Messianic Water Which Gives Life to the World." *Horizons in Biblical Theology* 19, 1997, 109–110.

Koenig-Bricker, Woodeene. *Ten Commandments for the Environment: Pope Benedict XVI Speaks Out for Creation and Justice.* Notre Dame, IN: Ave Maria Press, 2009.

Kula, E. "Islam and Environmental Conservation." *Environmental Conservation* 28, no. 1, 2001, 2–9.

Lamoureux, Patricia, and Paul J. Wadell. *The Christian Moral Life: Faithful Discipleship for a Global Society.* Maryknoll, NY: Orbis, 2010.

Lawrence, Peter A. "The Mismeasurement of Science." *Current Biology* 17, no. 15, 2007, 583–585.

Lees, Susan H. *The Political Ecology of the Water Crisis in Israel.* Lanham, MD: University Presses of America, 1998.

Leopold, Aldo. *A Sand County Almanac.* Oxford: Oxford University Press, 1968.

Levy, Ze'ev. "Ethical Issues of Animal Welfare in Jewish Thought." *Judaism: A Quarterly Journal* 45, 1996, 45–57.

Lubchenco, Jane. "Entering the Century of the Environment: A New Social Contract for Science." *Science* 279, 1998, 491–497.

Lysaught, M. Therese. "Love and Liturgy." In *Gathered for the Journey: Moral Theology in Catholic Perspective*, edited by David Matzko McCarthy and M. Therese Lysaught. Grand Rapids, MI: Eerdmans, 2007, 24–42.

Maathai, Wangari. *Unbowed: A Memoir.* New York: Knopf, 2006.

Mabry, Catherine M., and Jennifer M. Fraterrigo. "Species Traits as Generalized Predictors of Forest Community Response to Human Disturbance." *Forest Ecology and Management* 257, 2009, 723–730.

Manahan, Ronald. "Christ as Second Adam." In *The Environment and the Christian: What Does the New Testament Say about the Environment?* edited by Calvin Dewitt. Grand Rapids, MI: Baker House, 1991, 45–56.

Mangunjaya, Fachruddin Majeri. "Developing Environmental Awareness and Conservation through Islamic Teaching." *Journal of Islamic Studies* 22, no. 1, 2011, 36–49.

Martin-Schramm, James B., and Robert L. Stivers. *Christian Environmental Ethics: A Case Method Approach.* Maryknoll, NY: Orbis, 2003.

Massarro, Thomas. *Living Justice: Catholic Social Teaching in Action.* Franklin, WI: Sheed & Ward, 2000.

McAninch, Jay B., and David L. Strayer. "What Are the Tradeoffs between the Immediacy of Management Needs and the Longer Process of Scientific Discovery?" In *Long-Term Studies in Ecology*, edited by Gene E. Likens. New York: Springer-Verlag, 1989, 203–205.

McDonagh, Enda. *The Making of Disciples: Tasks of Moral Theology*. Wilmington, DE: Glazier, 1982.

McFague, Sallie. *Body of God*. Minneapolis: Fortress, 1993.

———. *Life Abundant: Rethinking Theology and Economy for a Planet in Peril*. Minneapolis: Fortress, 2001.

———. *A New Climate for Theology: God, the World, and Global Warming*. Minneapolis: Fortress, 2008.

———. *Super, Natural Christians: How We Should Love Nature*. Minneapolis: Fortress, 1997.

McKibbon, Bill. "Creation Unplugged." *Region and Values in Public Life, The Center for the Study of Values in Public Life at Harvard Divinity School* 4, no. 2/3, 1996, 18–20.

Midgley, Mary. *Beast and Man: The Roots of Human Nature*. Ithaca, NY: Cornell University Press, 1978.

Miller, Richard B. "Just War Criteria and Theocentric Ethics." In *Christian Ethics: Problems and Prospects*, edited by Lisa Sowle Cahill and James F. Childress. Cleveland, OH: Pilgrim, 1996, 334–356.

Moltmann, Jürgen. *Jesus Christ for Today's World*, translated by Margaret Kohl. Minneapolis: Fortress, 1994.

Moo, Douglas J. "Nature in the New Creation: New Testament Eschatology and the Environment." *Journal of the Evangelical Theology Society* 49, no. 3, 2006, 449–488.

Morrow, W. Ross, et al. "Analysis of Policies to Reduce Oil Consumption and Greenhouse Gas Emissions from the U.S. Transportation Sector." *Energy Policy* 38, 2010, 1305–1320.

Muir, John. *Nature Writings*. New York: Penguin Literary Classics, 1997.

Murphy, Charles M. *At Home on Earth: Foundations for a Catholic Ethic of the Environment*. New York: Crossroad, 1989.

Murray, Robert. *The Cosmic Covenant: Biblical Themes of Justice, Peace, and the Integrity of Creation*. Piscataway, NJ: Tigris, 2007.

Nadkarni, Nalani M. "Ecological Outreach to Faith–Based Communities." *Frontiers in Ecology and the Environment* 6, no. 5, 2007, 332–333.

Naess, Arne. "The Shallow and the Deep, Long-Range Ecology Movement: A Summary." *Inquiry* 16, 1973, 95–100.

Nash, James A. *Loving Nature: Ecological Integrity and Christian Responsibility*. Nashville TN: Abingdon, 1991.

Nasr, Seyyed Hossein. *Religion and the Order of Nature*. Oxford: Oxford University Press, 1996.

Nayed, Aref Ali. "Ayatology and Rahmatology: Islam and the Environment." In *Building a Better Bridge: Muslims, Christians and the Common Good*, edited by Michael Ipgrave. Washington, DC: Georgetown University Press, 2008, 161–167.

Nestle, Marion. *Food Politics: How the Food Industry Influences Nutrition and Health*, revised edition. Berkeley, CA: University of California Press, 2007.

Neuhaus, Richard John. *The Naked Public Square: Religion and Democracy in America*. Grand Rapids, MI: Eerdmans, 1984.

Northcott, Michael S. *A Moral Climate: The Ethics of Global Warming*. Maryknoll, NY: Orbis, 2007.

Noss, Reed F. "The Failure of Universities to Produce Conservation Biologists." *Conservation Biology* 11, no. 6, 1997, 1267–1269.

Nothwehr, Dawn, MOSF. *Franciscan Theology of the Environment: An Introductory Reader*. Quincy, IL: Franciscan Press, 2003.

O'Brien, David J., and Thomas A. Shannon. "Introduction to *Gaudium et spes*." In *Catholic Social Thought: The Documentary Heritage*, edited by David J. O'Brien and Thomas A. Shannon. Maryknoll, NY: Orbis, 1992, 164–166.

O'Brien, John J. "Baptismal Waters and the Waters of Life." *Proceedings of the North American Academy of Liturgy*, 2007, 137–160.

O'Brien, Kevin J. *An Ethics of Biodiversity: Christianity, Ecology, and the Variety of Life*. Washington, DC: Georgetown University Press, 2010.

Orr, David. "Four Challenges of Sustainability." *Conservation Biology* 16, no. 6, 2002, 1457–1460.

———. "A Literature of Redemption." *Conservation Biology* 15, no. 2, 2001, 305–307.

Passmore, John. *Man's Responsibility for Nature: Ecological Problems and Western Traditions*. New York: Scribner, 1974.

Patterson, Barbara. "Ethics for Wildlife Conservation: Overcoming the Human-Nature Dualism." *BioScience* 56, no. 2, 2006, 144–150.

Peters, Rebecca Todd. "Supporting Community Farming." In *Justice in a Global Economy: Strategies for Home, Community, and World*, edited by Pamela K. Brubaker, Rebecca Todd Peters, and Laura A. Stivers. Louisville, KY: Westminster, 2006, 17–28.

Pollan, Michael. *The Ominvore's Dilemma: A Natural History of Four Meals.* New York: Penguin, 2007.

Porritt, Jonathon. "Sustainability without Spirituality: A Contradiction in Terms?" *Conservation Biology* 16, no. 6, 2002, 1465–1460.

Pryds, Darlene. *Women of the Streets: Early Franciscan Women and Their Mendicant Vocation*. Saint Bonaventure, NY: Franciscan Institute and the Secretariat for the Franciscan Intellectual Tradition, 2009.

Raboy, Victor. "Jewish Agricultural Law: Ethical First Principles and Environmental Justice." In *Ecology and the Jewish Spirit: Where Nature and the Sacred Meet*, edited by Ellen Bernstein. Woodstock, VT: Jewish Lights, 2000), 190–199.

Riskin, Shlomo. "Shemitta: A Sabbatical for the Land; The Land Will Rest and the People Will Grow." In *Judaism and Ecology*, edited by Aubrey Rose. London. Cassell, 1992, 70–73.

Rogers, Peter. "Facing the Freshwater Crisis." *Scientific American* 299, 2008, 46–53.

Rolston, Holmes, III. "Environmental Virtue Ethics: Half the Truth but Dangerous as a Whole." In *Environmental Virtue Ethics*, edited by Ronald Sandler and Philip Cafaro, 61–78. Lanham, MD: Rowman & Littlefield, 2005.

———. "Does Nature Need to Be Redeemed?" *Horizons in Biblical Theology* 14, no. 2, 1992, 143–172.

Rose, Aubrey. *Judaism and Ecology*. London: Cassell, 1992.

Roughton, Geoffrey. "The Ancient and the Modern: Environmental Law and Governance in Islam." *Columbia Journal of Environmental Law* 32, no. 1, 2007, 99–140.

Rourke, Nancy M. "God, Grace and Creation: Shaping a Catholic Environmental Virtue Ethic." In *God, Grace and Creation*, College Theology Society Annual. Vol. 55, edited by Philip J. Rossi. Maryknoll, NY: Orbis, 2010, 222–235.

Rubio, Julie Hanlon. *Family Ethics: Practices for Christians*. Washington, DC: Georgetown University Press, 2010.

Ruether, Rosemary Radford. "Conclusion: Eco-Justice at the Center of the Church's Mission." In *Christianity and Ecology: Seeking the Well-Being of*

Earth and Humans, edited by Dieter T. Hessel and Rosemary Radford Ruether. Cambridge, MA: Harvard University Press, 2000, 603–614.

———. "Ecofeminism: The Challenge to Theology." In *Christianity and Ecology: Seeking the Well-Being of Earth and Humans*, edited by Dieter T. Hessel and Rosemary Radford Ruether. Cambridge, MA: Harvard University Press, 2000, 97–112.

———. *Gaia and God: An Ecofeminist Theology of Earth Healing*. San Francisco: HarperCollins, 1992.

Ruffo, Susan, and Peter Kaveiva. "Using Science to Assign Value to Nature." *Frontiers in Ecology and the Environment* 7, no. 1, 2009, 3–60.

Sandler, Ronald. "Introduction." In *Environmental Virtue Ethics*, edited by Ronald Sandler and Philip Cafaro. Lanham, MD: Rowman and Littlefied, 2005, 1–15.

Schaefer, Jame. *Theological Foundations for Environmental Ethics: Reconstructing Patristic and Medieval Concepts*. Washington, DC: Georgetown University Press, 2009.

Schaeffer, Francis A. "Pollution and the Death of Man: From Deep Ecology to Radical Environmentalism." *Religion* 31, no. 2, 2001, 175–193.

Scharper, Stephen Bede. *Redeeming the Time: A Political Theology of the Environment*. New York: Continuum, 1997.

Scharper, Stephen Bede, and Hilary Cunningham. *The Green Bible*. Brooklyn, NY: Lantern Books, 2002.

Schindler, Jeanne Heffernan. "Catholic Social Thought and Environmental Ethics in a Global Context." In *Gathered for the Journey: Moral Theology in Catholic Perspective*, edited by David Matzko McCarthy and M. Therese Lysaught. Grand Rapids, MI: Eerdmans, 2007, 329–349.

Schlesinger, William H. "Global Change Ecology." *Trends in Ecology and Evolution* 21, no. 6, 2006, 348–351.

Schmemann, Alexander. *Sacraments and Orthodoxy*. New York: Herder and Herder, 1965.

Schmitt, Michael N. "War and the Environment: Fault Lines in the Prescriptive Landscape." In *The Environmental Consequences of War: Legal, Economic, and Scientific Perspectives*, edited by Jay E. Austin and Carl E. Bruch. Cambridge: Cambridge University Press, 2000, 87–136.

Schumacher, E. F. *Small Is Beautiful: Economics as If People Mattered*. New York: Harper and Row, 1975.

Schwartz, Eilon. "*Bal Tashchit*: A Jewish Environmental Precept." *Environmental Ethics* 19, 1997, 355–374.

Schwarzschild, Steven S. "The Unnatural Jew." *Environmental Ethics* 6, 1984, 347–362.

Segerfeldt, Fredrik. *Water for Sale: How Business and the Market Can Resolve the World's Water Crisis*. Washington, DC: Cato Institute, 2005.

Segundo, Juan Luis. "The Shift within Latin American Theology." *Journal of Theology for Southern Africa* 52, 1985, 17–29.

Shannon, Thomas A. "Commentary on *Rerum novarum*." In *Modern Catholic Social Teaching: Commentaries and Interpretations*, edited by Kenneth R. Himes, et al. Washington, DC: Georgetown, 2004, 128–131.

Shochet, Elijah. *Animal Life in Jewish Tradition: Attitudes and Relationships*. New York: KTAV, 1984.

Short, W. J., OFM. "Recovering Lost Traditions in Spirituality: Franciscans, Camaldolese and the Hermitage." *Spiritus* 3, 2003, 209–218.

Smith, Pamela. *What Are They Saying about Environmental Ethics?* New York and Mahwah, NJ: Paulist Press, 1997.

Sorrell, Roger D. *St. Francis of Assisi and Nature*. New York: Oxford University Press, 1988.

Spohn, William C. *Go and Do Likewise: Jesus and Ethics*. New York: Continuum, 2006.

Stegner, William Richard. "Jesus' Walking on the Water: Mark 6:45–52." In *Gospels and the Scriptures of Israel*, edited by William Richard Stegner and Craig Evans. Sheffield England: Sheffield Academic, 1999, 212–234.

Stern, Frank. *A Rabbi Looks at Jesus' Parables*. New York: Rowman & Littlefield, 2006.

Stone, Christopher D. "The Environment in Wartime: An Overview." In *The Environmental Consequences of War: Legal, Economic, and Scientific Perspectives*, edited by Jay E. Austin and Carl E. Bruch. Cambridge: Cambridge University Press, 2000, 16–35.

Susin, Luiz Carlos. "Sister Dorothy Stang: A Model of Holiness and Martyrdom." In *Eco-Theology*, edited by Elaine Wainwright, Luiz Carlos Susin, and Felix Wilfred. London: SCM Press, 2009, 109–113.

Tal, Alon. "Israel and Environmentalism." In *Encyclopedia of Religion and Nature*, edited by Bron Taylor, 887–891. London: Continuum, 2005.

———. *Pollution in a Promised Land: An Environmental History of Israel*. Berekely, CA, and London: University of California Press, 2002.

Taylor, Bron. "Earth and Nature-Based Spirituality, Part I: From Deep Ecology to Radical Environmentalism." *Religion* 31, no. 2, 2001, 175–193.

———. "Earth and Nature-Based Spirituality, Part II: From Earth First! And Bioregionalism to Scientific Paganism and the New Age." *Religion* 31, no. 3, 2001, 225–245.

Taylor, L. Roy. "Objective and Experiment in Long-Term Research." In *Long-Term Studies in Ecology*, edited by Gene E. Likens. New York: Springer-Verlag, 1989, 20–70.

Taylor, Sarah McFarland. *Green Sisters: A Spiritual Ecology*. Cambridge, MA: Harvard University Press, 2007.

Tirosh-Samuelson, Hava. "Judaism." In *Encyclopedia of Religion and Nature*. vol. 2, edited by Bron Taylor. London: Continuum, 2005, 525–537.

———. "Judaism." In *Oxford Handbook of Religion and Ecology*, edited by Roger S. Gottlieb.Oxford: Oxford University Press, 2006, 25–64.

_____, editor. *Judaism and Ecology: Created World and Revealed Word*. Cambridge, MA: Harvard University Press, 2002.

———. "The Textualization of Nature in Jewish Mysticism." In *Judaism and Ecology: Created World and Revealed Word*, edited by Hava Tirosh-Samuelson. Cambridge, MA: Harvard University Press, 2002, 389–404.

Traer, Robert. *Doing Environmental Ethics*. Boulder, CO: Westview, 2009.

Uhl, Christopher. *Developing Ecological Consciousness: Paths to a Sustainable World*. Lanham, MD: Rowman & Littlefield, 2004.

Vacek, Edward. *Love, Human and Divine*. Washington, DC: Georgetown University Press, 1994.

Van Houten, Kyle S. "Conservation as Virtue: A Scientific and Social Process for Conservation." *Conservation Biology* 20.5, 2006, 1367–1372.

Van Wensveen, Louke. *Dirty Virtues: The Emergence of Ecological Virtue Ethics*. Amherst, NY: Humanity Books, 2000.

———. "The Emergence of Ecological Virtue Language." In *Environmental Virtue Ethics*, edited by Ronald Sandler and Philip Cafaro, 15–30. Lanham, MD: Rowman & Littlefield Publishers, 2005.

Vitousek, Peter, et al. "Human Domination of Earth's Ecosystems." *Science* 277, 1997, 494–499.

Von Rad, Gerhard. "The Theological Problem of the Old Testament Doctrine of Creation." In *Creation in the Old Testament*, edited by Bernhard Anderson. Philadelphia: Fortress, 1984, 53–64.

Wallace, Mark I. *Green Christianity: Five Ways to a Sustainable Future*. Minneapolis: Fortress, 2010.

Warner, Keith Douglass, OFM. "Get Him Out of the Birdbath!" In *Franciscan Theology of the Environment*, edited by Dawn M. Nothwehr. Quincy, IL: Franciscan Press, 2002, 361–376.

———. "The Greening of American Catholicism: Identity, Conversion and Continuity." *Religion and American Culture: A Journal of Interpretation* 18, no. 1, 2008, 113–142.

———. "The Moral Significance of Creation in the Franciscan Theological Tradition: Implications for Contemporary Catholics and Public Policy." *University of Saint Thomas Law Journal* 5, no. 1, 2008, 37–52.

Waskow, Arthur. "From Compassion to Jubilee." *Tikkun Magazine* 5, no. 2, 1990, 78–81.

Weber, Christopher L., and H. Scott Matthews. "Food Miles and the Relative Climate Impacts of Food Choices in the United States." *Environmental Science and Technology* 42, no. 10, 2008, 3508–3513.

Wenz, Peter. "Synergistic Environmental Virtues: Consumerism and Human Flourishing." In *Environmental Virtue Ethics*, edited by Ronald Sandler and Philip Cafaro. Lanham, MD: Rowman & Littlefield, 2005, 200–202.

Westra, Laura. "Virtue Ethics as Foundational for a Global Ethic." In *Environmental Virtue Ethics*, edited by Ronald Sandler and Philip Cafaro. Lanham, MD: Rowman & Littlefield, 2005, 79–92.

White, Lynn Jr. "The Historical Roots of Our Ecologic Crisis." *Science* 155, 1967, 1203–1207.

Whitmore, Todd David. "Catholic Social Teaching: Starting with the Common Good." In *Living the Catholic Social Tradition: Cases and Commentaries*, edited by Kathleen Maas Weigert and Alexia K. Kelly. Lanham, MD: Rowman & Littlefield, 2005, 59–85.

Whitten, Tony, Derek Holmes, and Kathy MacKinnon, "Conservation Biology: A Displacement Behavior for Academia?" *Conservation Biology* 15, no. 1, 2001, 1–3.

Wilcox, William A. Jr., *The Modern Military and the Environment: The Laws of Peace and War*. Lanham, MD: Government Institutes, 2007.

Wyschogrod, Michael. "Judaism and the Sanctification of Nature." *The Melton Journal* 24, Spring 1991, 5–7.

CONTRIBUTORS

Michael Agliardo SJ (PhD, University of California, San Diego; STL, Weston Jesuit School of Theology) is an assistant professor of sociology at Loyola University, Chicago. His doctoral research focused on religion and public life, especially religion and environmental issues. That research also examined religious pluralism, both how particular religious traditions grapple with religious diversity and the way pluralism affects society as a whole. He continues to explore religion, environmental issues, and public life, and how these intersect. He also has an area focus on China.

Mark J. Allman (PhD, Loyola University of Chicago) is an associate professor in religious and theological studies at Merrimack College, where he also serves as a faculty associate in the Center for the Study of Jewish-Christian-Muslim Relations. He is the author of the award winning *Who Would Jesus Kill? War, Peace, and the Christian Tradition* (Anselm Academic, 2008) and coauthor (with Tobias Winright) of *After the Smoke Clears: The Just War Tradition and Post War Justice* (Orbis, 2010). His research and writing interests include war and peace, globalization, economic ethics, and Jewish-Christian-Muslim relations.

Rev. Nicanor Pier Giorgio Austriaco OP (PhD, Massachusetts Institute of Technology; STL, Dominican House of Studies, Washington, DC) is an assistant professor of biology and instructor of theology at Providence College in Providence, Rhode Island. In moral theology, he has published *Beatitude and Biomedicine: An Introduction to Catholic Bioethics* (CUA Press, 2011) and authored numerous journal articles and book chapters in moral theology and bioethics. In biology, Austriaco's NIH-funded laboratory is investigating the genetics of programmed cell death in several eukaryotic model systems. His scientific papers have been published in *Cell*, *PNAS*, and *FEMS Yeast Research*, among others.

Benedict XVI, born Joseph Aloisius Ratzinger, is the 265th pope of the Roman Catholic Church. As a theologian and author of numerous works, he served as a professor at the University of Bonn, the University of Tübingen, and the University of Regensberg.

Thomas Bushlack (PhD, University of Notre Dame) is an assistant professor of moral theology at the University of Saint Thomas in Saint Paul, Minnesota. His dissertation is titled "Justice in the Theology of Thomas Aquinas: Rediscovering Civic Virtue," and his teaching and research interests are in social ethics, Catholic social thought, virtue theory, and natural law.

David Clairmont (PhD, University of Chicago) is an assistant professor of moral theology and comparative religion in the theology department at the University of Notre Dame. His publications include *Moral Struggle and Religious Ethics: On the Person as Classic in Comparative Theological Contexts* (Wiley-Blackwell, 2011) and (coedited with Don Browning) *American Religions and the Family: How Faith Traditions Cope with Modernization and Democracy* (Columbia University Press, 2007). His research and teaching interests include Catholic moral theology, Franciscan spirituality, comparative religious ethics, and the moral thought of Theravada Buddhism.

Kathy Lilla Cox (PhD, Fordham University) is an assistant professor of moral theology at the College of Saint Benedict/Saint John's University and Saint John's School of Theology/Seminary in Collegeville, Minnesota. She has an essay, titled "A Clouded View: How Language Shapes Moral Perception," in a special 2011 issue of *United Seminary Quarterly Review* focused on the environment.

Ronald Crown holds a DPhil in theology (New Testament studies) from the University of Oxford and an MS in library science from the University of Kentucky. He is coeditor of the journal *Theological Librarianship,* published by the American Theological Library Association, and he is the theology reference librarian at Pius XII Memorial Library, Saint Louis University.

June-Ann Greeley (PhD, Fordham University) is an associate professor of theology and religious studies at Sacred Heart University, where she is also director of the graduate program in theology and religious studies and director of the Middle Eastern studies program. Her areas of scholarship include historical theology (medieval and early modern Christianity), mystical theologies of medieval Christianity and Islam, women and religion, and comparative theology (Christianity and Islam).

Cathy Mabry McMullen (MTS, Harvard Divinity School; PhD, Iowa State University) is a faculty member in the Department of Natural Resource Ecology and Management at Iowa State University. She teaches and conducts research in forestry and restoration ecology and has published numerous journal articles on these topics.

Marcus Mescher is pursuing a PhD in theology and education at Boston College, with special interest in the practical dimensions of Catholic social teaching. He plans to focus his dissertation on a "theology of neighbor," using the parable of the Good Samaritan as a paradigm for interpersonal right-relationship through compassion, charity, justice, and preferential option for the poor.

Nancy M. Rourke (PhD, Saint Patrick's College, Maynooth, Ireland) is assistant professor of moral theology in the department of religious studies and theology at Canisius College in Buffalo, New York. Her research areas include virtue ethics, action theory, and the principle of double effect. She teaches courses in fundamental moral theology, bioethics, marriage, just war theory, and environmental ethics.

Julie Hanlon Rubio (PhD, University of Southern California) is associate professor of Christian ethics at Saint Louis University in Saint Louis, Missouri. Her research brings together Catholic social teaching and Christian theology on marriage and family. She is the author of *Family Ethics: Practices for Christians* (Georgetown University Press, 2010) and *A Christian Theology of Marriage and Family* (Paulist Press, 2003). Her current book project is titled *Both Personal and Political: Catholic Reflections on American Social Problems.*

Daniel P. Scheid (PhD, Boston College) is an assistant professor of theology at Duquesne University in Pittsburgh, Pennsylvania. Publications include the article "Common Good" for the *Encyclopedia of Sustainability* (2009); "Vedanta Desika and Thomas Aquinas on the Intrinsic Value of Nature," *Journal of Vaishnava Studies* (2010);

and "Expanding Catholic Ecological Ethics: Ecological Solidarity and Earth Rights," in the *Annual Volume of the College Theology Society* (Orbis, 2011). His research interests are in ecological and comparative theological ethics.

Matthew A. Shadle (PhD, University of Dayton) is an assistant professor of moral theology at Loras College, in Dubuque, Iowa. His book *The Origins of War: A Catholic Perspective* was published by Georgetown University Press in 2011. His research interests include social ethics and fundamental moral theology.

Randall Smith (PhD, University of Notre Dame) is an associate professor of theology at the University of Saint Thomas in Houston, Texas. His dissertation dealt with the relationship between the Mosaic Law and the natural law in the thought of Thomas Aquinas. He has published articles on natural law, the sermons of Thomas Aquinas, church architecture, and the virtues. He is at work on a reader of classic texts in the natural law tradition from Sophocles to John Paul II.

Hava Tirosh-Samuelson (PhD, Hebrew University of Jerusalem) is director of Jewish studies and Irving and Miriam Lowe Professor of Modern Judaism and a professor of history at Arizona State University in Tempe, Arizona. She writes on Jewish intellectual history with a focus on philosophy and mysticism in premodern Judaism, the interaction among Judaism, Christianity, and Islam in the Middle Ages, feminist philosophy, Judaism and ecology, bioethics, and religion and science. Through her interdisciplinary research, she seeks to create bridges among intellectual disciplines, religious traditions, religious and secular outlooks, and gendered perspectives. She is especially committed to understanding the complementary relationship between science and religion from historical perspective.

Christopher P. Vogt (PhD, Boston College) is an associate professor of moral theology at Saint John's University in New York City. He is the author of *Patience, Compassion, Hope, and the Christian Art of Dying Well* (Rowman & Littlefield, 2004); "Fostering a Catholic Commitment to the Common Good: An Approach Rooted in Virtue Ethics," *Theological Studies* (2007); and many other articles that address a variety of topics in theological ethics.

Keith Douglass Warner OFM (PhD, University of California, Santa Cruz; MA, Franciscan School of Theology in Berkeley) is a Franciscan friar and assistant director of education at the Center for Science, Technology, and Society at Santa Clara University in California, where he is also a lecturer. His research focuses on how institutions blend science, policy, and human values for environmental protection initiatives. He has published extensively, including *Agroecology in Action: Extending Alternative Agriculture through Social Networks* (MIT Press, 2007).

Stephen B. Wilson (PhD, University of Notre Dame) is an associate professor of theology at Spring Hill College in Mobile, Alabama. His research interests focus on relationship between liturgy and ethics, as can be seen from two of his publications: "Christ and Cult(ure): Some Preliminary Reflections on Liturgy and Life," *Liturgical Ministry* 12 (2003): 177–187 and "Liturgy and Ethics: Something Old, Something New," *Worship* 81 (2007): 24–45.

Tobias Winright (PhD, University of Notre Dame) is an associate professor of theological ethics at Saint Louis University. He has published (with Mark J. Allman) *After the Smoke Clears: The Just War Tradition and Post War Justice* (Orbis, 2010) and authored numerous journal articles and book chapters on theological ethics and just war, pacifism, policing, capital punishment, the environment, and children. He also is book reviews editor for the international scholarly journal *Political Theology*.

Kari-Shane Davis Zimmerman (PhD, Marquette University) is an assistant professor of theological ethics at the College of Saint Benedict/Saint John's University in Collegeville, Minnesota. She teaches courses and has authored journal articles and book chapters primarily in the areas of sexual ethics, feminist ethics, and Catholic social teaching and economics.

INDEX

Illustrations, footnotes, and sidebars are indicated with i, n, and s, respectively.

A

B

C

N

O

P

S

T

U

V

Y

Z